FIGHTING CORRUPTION IN PUBLIC PROCUREMENT

Anti-corruption measures have firmly taken centre stage in the development agenda of international organisations as well as in developed and developing countries. One area in which corruption manifests itself is in public procurement and, as a result, states have adopted various measures to prevent and curb corruption in public procurement. One such mechanism for dealing with procurement corruption is to debar or disqualify corrupt suppliers from bidding for or otherwise obtaining government contracts.

This book examines the issues and challenges raised by the debarment or disqualification of corrupt suppliers from public contracts. Implementing a disqualification mechanism in public procurement raises serious practical and conceptual difficulties, which are not always considered by legislative provisions on disqualification. Some of the problems that may arise from the use of disqualifications include determining whether a conviction for corruption ought to be a pre-requisite to disqualification, bearing in mind that corruption thrives in secret, resulting in a dearth of convictions. Another issue is determining how to balance the tension between granting adequate procedural safeguards to a supplier in disqualification proceedings and not delaying the procurement process. A further issue is determining the scope of the disqualification in the sense of whether it applies to firms, natural persons, subcontractors, subsidiaries or other persons related to the corrupt firm and whether disqualification will lead to the termination of existing contracts.

The book compares and contrasts the legal, practical and institutional approaches to the implementation of the disqualification mechanism in the European Union, the United Kingdom, the United States, the Republic of South Africa and the World Bank.

Volume 42 in the series Studies in International Law

Studies in International Law

Recent titles in this series

The Democratic Legitimacy of International Law
Steven Wheatley

Reflections on the UN Declaration on the Rights of Indigenous Peoples
Edited by Stephen Allen and Alexandra Xanthaki

Contracting with Sovereignty: State Contracts and International Arbitration
Ivar Alvik

Multi-Sourced Equivalent Norms in International Law
Edited by Yuval Shany and Tomer Broude

The Distinction and Relationship between *Jus ad Bellum* and *Jus in Bello*
Keiichiro Okimoto

International Humanitarian Law and Terrorism
Andrea Bianchi and Yasmin Naqvi

The Militarisation of Peacekeeping in the Twenty-First Century
James Sloan

Accounting for Hunger: The Right to Food in the Era of Globalisation
Edited by Olivier De Schutter and Kaitlin Y Cordes

Promises of States under International Law
Christian Eckart

Multilevel Regulation of Military and Security Contractors: The Interplay between International, European and Domestic Norms
Edited by Christine Bakker and Mirko Sossai

Europe and Extraterritorial Asylum
Maarten den Heijer

The Practice of International and National Courts and the (De)Fragmentation of International Law
Edited by Ole Kristian Fauchald and André Nollkaemper

The Politics of International Criminal Justice: A Spotlight on Germany
Ronen Steinke

For the complete list of titles in this series, see 'Studies in International Law' link at www.hartpub.co.uk/books/series.asp

Fighting Corruption in Public Procurement

A Comparative Analysis of Disqualification or Debarment Measures

Sope Williams-Elegbe

·HART·
PUBLISHING

OXFORD AND PORTLAND, OREGON
2012

Published in the United Kingdom by Hart Publishing Ltd
16C Worcester Place, Oxford, OX1 2JW
Telephone: +44 (0)1865 517530
Fax: +44 (0)1865 510710
E-mail: mail@hartpub.co.uk
Website: http://www.hartpub.co.uk

Published in North America (US and Canada) by
Hart Publishing
c/o International Specialized Book Services
920 NE 58th Avenue, Suite 300
Portland, OR 97213-3786
USA
Tel: +1 503 287 3093 or toll-free: (1) 800 944 6190
Fax: +1 503 280 8832
E-mail: orders@isbs.com
Website: http://www.isbs.com

British Library Cataloguing in Publication Data
Data Available

ISBN: 978-1-84946-020-0

Typeset by Hope Services, Abingdon
Printed and bound in Great Britain by
MPG Books Group Ltd

For my father and mother, Chief F.O Williams CON and
Mrs B.O Williams MON

Preface

The aim of this book is to provide a structured, comprehensive and understandable analysis of the law and practice of contractor disqualifications (also known as debarment) in public procurement. Since the 'corruption eruption' of the mid-1990s when anti-corruption became popular in legal, political and economic discourse, there has been no end of measures suggested and implemented to prevent, reduce and combat corruption in all its forms. Corruption in public procurement has of course also received its fair share of attention, public procurement being one of the areas in which public corruption manifests. Whilst there is information on the typology of corruption in public procurement and the kinds of measures that may be useful in addressing this corruption, there has been little exposition, analysis and critique of the measures that are adopted against procurement corruption.

This book aims to fill that gap by providing a comparative evaluation of contractor disqualifications for corruption as they are currently applied in the European Union, the United Kingdom, the United States, the World Bank and South Africa. Contractor disqualifications have in the last two decades become, in most jurisdictions, a preferred way of combating corruption in public procurement, but there are no studies which examine the sufficiency of legal rules on disqualification, how disqualifications are applied in practice, and whether they are an adequate or useful tool to address procurement corruption.

As a relatively new anti-corruption measure, there is considerable uncertainty over many of the issues that arise in the disqualification context in most jurisdictions, partly as a result of the fact that the legislation in most jurisdictions is unclear and does not contemplate many of the issues that accompany the disqualification mechanism and also because the procuring authorities who take disqualification decisions are not clear on the limits of their discretion in the disqualification context. This book examines the salient issues relating to disqualifications, exposing and analysing the areas in which the legislation is unclear and providing clarity on those areas by reference to the general law or the practice in other jurisdictions. It is hoped that the book will be useful to procurement officials who are required to take disqualification decisions, lawyers advising suppliers facing disqualification and all persons interested in public procurement and corruption more generally.

The work has been a long time in preparation and I am indebted to several persons who have assisted me over the years. In particular, I am grateful for the support of the University of Nottingham, where I worked as a Lecturer between 2003 and 2011, especially the staff at the School of Law. The Head of School, Professor Stephen Bailey, was supportive and considerate throughout the duration of this project and I am most grateful to him. I am also indebted to Professor Sue Arrowsmith, the Director of the Public Procurement Research Group at the University of Nottingham, a friend and a mentor, under whom I honed my research skills and interest in public procurement and who will always be the gold standard for procurement research and teaching. I would also like to thank other colleagues and friends who took time to discuss ideas with me such as Dr Ama Eyo, Dr Annamaria La Chimia, Sangeeta Shah, Dr Aris Georgopoulos, Dr Ping Wang, Professor Geo Quinot, Professor Phoebe Bolton, Professor Craig Rotherham, Dr Peter Trepte, Dr Ezekiel Alawale, Funke Adeyemi, Dr Janelle Byran, Aduke Balogun, Professor Adedokun Adeyemi, Busola Akande, Dapo Akande, Dr Adeline Chong, Bayo Ademiluyi, Dr Abi Jagun, Lola Kogbodoku, Efe Remawa and Muyiwa Amodeni.

I am of course grateful for the love and support of my husband, Dayo Elegbe, my parents, Chief and Mrs Williams and my daughter, Ifeoluwa, who had to endure many months with me ensconced in my study while I worked on this book.

I have endeavoured to state the law as at 31 October 2011.

Sope Williams-Elegbe

Table of Contents

Table of Cases

Australia

Canada

European Court of Human Rights

European Court of Justice

Alphabetical

Chronological

South Africa

United States of America

FAR Case

Table of Legislation

European Union

Action Plans

Communications

Decisions

Directives

Regulations, etc

United Kingdom

Statutory Instruments, etc

United States of America

Regulations, etc

Table of Conventions, Treaties, etc

1

Introduction

CORRUPTION IS A problem of antiquated origin, which has been deplored by the thinkers of every generation.[1] The literature on corruption is extensive, and there is no shortage of material on the history, nature, effects and consequence of corruption. Less prevalent is information on the 'cure' for corruption or on the utility or effectiveness of existing measures against corruption.

Corruption can be defined in several ways, to cover a range of behaviours from 'venality to ideological erosion'.[2] A wide definition of corruption will include the public and private sectors and cover activities consisting of fraud, extortion, embezzlement and abuse of office. This book will focus on public sector corruption, which includes bribery, kickbacks, 'gifts' and illicit payments to government officials in their capacity as public servants, in order that the giving party may achieve a stated purpose. Accordingly, this book will adopt a definition of public sector corruption favoured by social scientists which states that corruption is 'behaviour which deviates from the formal duties of a public role because of private-regarding (personal, close family, private clique) pecuniary or status gains; or violates rules against the exercise of certain types of private-regarding influence'.[3]

Corruption in the public sector has necessitated concerted efforts to fight it by organisations such as the World Bank, the United Nations, the Organisation for Economic Cooperation and Development (OECD), the Council of Europe, and the European Union (EU). The prevalent view is that corruption undermines democratisation, the rule of law, the

[1] E Hamilton and H Cairns (ed), *The Collected Dialogues of Plato,* (New Jersey, Princeton University Press, 1961); R MacMullen, *Corruption and the Decline of Rome* (Yale, Yale University Press, 1990); N Jacoby, P Nehemkis and R Eells, *Bribery and Extortion in World Business: A Study of Corporate Political Payments Abroad* (London, MacMillan Publishing, 1977) 7–43; SH Alatas, *The Sociology of Corruption: The Nature, Function, Causes and Prevention of Corruption* (New York, Times Books, 1980), 9, 77; L Levy Peck, *Court Patronage and Corruption in Early Stuart England* (London, Routledge, 1990); V Byrce and J Bryce, *Modern Democracies* (New York, MacMillan, 1921).

[2] J Nye, 'Corruption and Political Development: A Cost-Benefit Analysis' (1967) 61 *American Political Science Review* 417, 419.

[3] Nye, 'Corruption and Political Development', ibid, 417.

consolidation of market economies,[4] and is a threat to the international economy. To counter this threat, anti-corruption measures have become increasingly global in outlook. For instance, the OECD was the first inter-governmental institution to seek an international framework for combating corruption in 1994.[5] In 2003, the United Nations adopted a Convention against Corruption,[6] obliging states to criminalise a wide range of corrupt activities. Similarly, the EU has in place legislative measures designed to combat corruption within Member States and its institutions.[7]

In addition to international efforts at combating corruption, many national legal systems have mechanisms and legislation aimed at preventing and punishing corruption. One of the 'tools' in the armoury against corruption in national systems is public procurement regulation. Public procurement is the purchasing by a government of the goods and services it requires to function and maximise public welfare. In doing so, a government will often adopt regulations and procedures to ensure that it obtains these goods, services or 'works' (construction contracts) in a transparent, competitive manner and at the best price or the most economically advantageous price.[8] It is believed that transparency in public procurement will assist in ensuring that public procurement procedures foster competition and obtain value for money.[9] Public procurement may also be subject to secondary criteria and a government may use public procurement to achieve non-procurement-related goals such as the development of a region/industrial sector or encouraging environmentally friendly manufacturing, by favouring relevant firms in public contract awards.[10]

[4] S Rose-Ackerman, *Corruption and Government: Causes, Consequences, Reform* (Cambridge, Cambridge University Press, 1999); T Soreide, *Corruption in Public Procurement: Causes, Consequences, Cures* (Bergen, CMI, 2002); P Nichols, 'Outlawing Transnational Bribery through the World Trade Organisation' (1997) *Law and Policy in International Business* 305, 337; P Nichols, 'Regulating Transnational Bribery in times of Globalization and Fragmentation' (1999) 24 *Yale Journal of International Law* 257; J Noonan, *Bribes* (California, University of California Press, 1987).

[5] Recommendations on Bribery in International Business Transactions, 1994.

[6] 43 ILM 37 (2004).

[7] Council Act of 26 July 1995 drawing up a Convention on the Protection of the European Communities Financial Interests [1995] OJ C316/48 and its Protocols [1996] OJ C313/1 and [1997] OJ C151/1; Council Act of 26 May 1997 drawing up on the basis of Art K.3(2)(c) of the Treaty on European Union, the Convention on the Fight Against Corruption Involving Officials of the European Communities or Officials of Member States of the EU [1997] OJ C195/1; Action Plan to Combat Organised crime [1997] OJ C251/1.

[8] S Arrowsmith, *The Law of Public and Utilities Procurement*, 2nd edn (London, Sweet & Maxwell, 2005) ch 3; S Schooner, 'Desiderata: Objectives for a System of Government Contract Law' (2002) 11 *Public Procurement Law Review* 103.

[9] Schooner, 'Desiderata', ibid.

[10] S Arrowsmith and P Kunzlik (eds), *Social and Environmental Policies in EC Procurement Law: New Directives and New Directions* (Cambridge, Cambridge University Press, 2009); R Caranta and M Trybus, *The Law of Green and Social Procurement in Europe* (Copenhagen, DJØF Publishing, 2010); C McCrudden, *Buying Social Justice* (Oxford, Oxford University Press, 2007).

Corruption control can also be included as a goal of procurement regulation. This is consistent with the other goals of procurement regulation – as the elimination of corruption will facilitate the award of contracts to the most competitive firms and not those preferred for ulterior reasons. However, a focus on corruption control can also detract from achieving the competition and efficiency goals of procurement regulation, as anti-corruption measures may be so intricate as to constitute a financial and procedural burden on the procurement process.[11] Anti-corruption measures included in procurement regulation ensure the absence of corruption within the procurement process and ensure that a government contractor is ethical or honest. Whilst criminal and civil sanctions[12] on corrupt firms and corrupt public officials[13] are an obvious way of combating corruption in public procurement, less obvious are the myriad of administrative rules and regulations intended to ensure transparency and openness in the procurement process and deny the conditions under which corruption takes place. Administrative methods for combating corruption may often be more effective than criminal methods, especially as corrupt practices are often clandestine and can make meeting the burden of proof in a criminal trial difficult for prosecutors. As a result, countries are increasingly using non-criminal devices to combat corruption. One such mechanism for dealing with corrupt firms is to disqualify (or debar) them from bidding on government contracts.

A number of questions are raised by the use of procurement regulation to combat corruption. One may begin by asking whether combating corruption through procurement is desirable or necessary. Procurement regulation is designed to ensure that a government obtains the goods and services it needs at the best price, and procurement procedures should reflect the ideals of procurement regulation such as competition, transparency and efficiency. Where corruption control is imposed as an additional objective of the procurement process, by rules requiring the disqualification of corrupt suppliers, this can have serious practical and conceptual implications, which are not always considered by legislative provisions on disqualification. Some of the problems that arise from the use of disqualifications include determining whether it applies to natural persons, subcontractors, subsidiaries or other persons related to the corrupt firm

[11] F Anechiarico and J Jacobs, 'Purging Corruption from Public Contracting: The "Solutions" are Now Part of the Problem' (1995) *New York Law School Law Review* 143.

[12] S White (ed), *Procurement and Organised Crime: An EU Wide Study* (London, Institute of Advanced Legal Studies, 2000); J Jacobs, C Friel and R Radick, *Gotham Unbound: How New York City was Liberated from the Grip of Organised Crime* (New York, New York University Press, 1999); TMC Asser Institute, *Prevention of and Administrative Action Against Organised Crime: A Comparative Law Study of the Registration of Legal persons and Criminal Audits in Eight EU Member States* (The Hague, TMC Asser Press, 1997).

[13] N Kofele-Kale, *The International Law of Responsibility for Economic Crimes: Holding State Officials Individually Liable for Acts of Fraudulent Enrichment*, 2nd edn (Aldershot, Ashgate, Publishing, 2006) ch 6.

and determining whether a conviction for corruption ought to be a pre-requisite to disqualification, bearing in mind that corruption is an activity that thrives in secret, resulting in a dearth of convictions. This leads to the issue of understanding the limits to and efficacy of procurement initiatives in tackling corruption.[14]

Many of these issues, such as determining the limits of disqualification and the issue of convictions, remain unanswered in the few studies on the use of disqualifications in public procurement. In truth, existing work on using government procurement to discourage corruption is limited. Although significant contributions have been made by US authors,[15] there is little literature available on disqualification outside of the US. In relation to the EU, a limited amount of research has been conducted,[16] especially since disqualifications for corruption became mandatory in 2006. There is similarly little research on disqualifications in organisations like the World Bank.[17] Other jurisdictions contain a limited amount of information on procurement disqualifications, but there is not enough information to provide a coherent understanding of all the issues raised by disqualification. In addition, the available literature on disqualifications generally focuses on one jurisdiction, and there is nothing that adopts a multi-jurisdictional approach to understanding the challenges posed by the use of disqualifications in public procurement.

The aim of this book, therefore, is to examine and analyse the legal texts of selected national and multilateral procurement instruments, which provide for the disqualification from public contracts of suppliers who are convicted or otherwise guilty of corruption and provide a legal critique of

[14] Anechiarico and Jacobs, 'Purging Corruption from Public Contracting', above n 11.

[15] F Anechiarico and J Jacobs, *The Pursuit of Absolute Integrity: How Corruption Control makes Government Ineffective* (Chicago, University of Chicago Press, 1996); Jacobs, Friel and Radick, *Gotham Unbound*, above n 12; S Kelman, *Procurement and Public Management: The Fear of Discretion and the Quality of Government Performance* (Washington, AEI Press, 1990).

[16] E Piselli, 'The Scope for Excluding Providers who have Committed Criminal Offences under the EU Procurement Directives' (2000) 6 *Public Procurement Law Review* 267; Arrowsmith, *Public & Utilities Procurement*, above n 8, ch 19; S Arrowsmith, 'Implementation of the New EC Procurement Directives and the Alcatel Ruling in England and Wales and Northern Ireland: A Review of the New Legislation and Guidance' (2006) 3 *Public Procurement Law Review* 86; S Williams, 'The Mandatory Exclusions for Corruption in the New EC Procurement Directives' (2006) 31 *European Law Review* 711; T Medina, 'EU Directives as an Anti-Corruption Measure: Excluding Corruption Convicted Tenderers from Public Procurement Contracts' in KV Thai (ed), *International Handbook of Public Procurement,* (Boca Raton, CRC Press, 2008); S Arrowsmith, 'Application of the EC Treaty and directives to horizontal policies: A critical review' in S Arrowsmith and P Kunzlik (eds), *Social and Environmental Policies in EC Procurement Law: New Directives and New Directions* (Cambridge, Cambridge University Press, 2009).

[17] S Williams, 'The Debarment of Corrupt Contractors from World Bank-Financed Contracts' (2007) 36 *Public Contract Law Journal* 277; T Canni, 'Debarment is no Longer Private World Bank business: An Examination of the Bank's Distinct Debarment Procedures used for Corporate Procurements and Financed Projects' (2010) 40 *Public Contract Law Journal* 147; S Denning, 'Anti-Corruption Policies: Eligibility and Debarment Procedures and the World Bank and Regional Development Banks' (2010) 44 *International Lawyer* 871.

the provisions in these instruments. The book will highlight and analyse the problems that attend the implementation of a disqualification measure, study and compare the approaches of selected jurisdictions to these problems and examine the solutions that the selected jurisdictions have applied or may apply to these problems, to determine the respective advantages and disadvantages of these approaches. The book aims at developing a coherent framework for understanding the rules pertaining to the use of procurement disqualifications as an instrument for sanctioning corruption.

Each chapter of the book will discuss salient issues that arise from the use of procurement disqualifications. Thus, whilst chapter two gives an introduction to the nature of corruption and anti-corruption measures, chapter three will examine public procurement regulation and anti-corruption policy, as well as examine the reasons underpinning the disqualification regime in the selected jurisdictions. Chapter four examines the issue of what kinds of offences may trigger disqualification in the selected jurisdictions and whether suppliers may be disqualified for foreign offences or offences committed in a foreign jurisdiction. In chapter five, the book will highlight the procedural issues relating to disqualification and examine whether the disqualification process in the jurisdictions is fair and transparent In chapter six, the book looks at what kinds of entities are used in the disqualification process and which of these is best placed to make appropriate disqualification decisions. In addition, the chapter will consider the scope of disqualification, or whether a disqualification decision taken by one entity is binding on other procuring entities. In chapter seven, the focus is on the nature and extent of the investigative powers of a disqualifying entity and examines the extent to which such entities are under an obligation to uncover or investigate whether a supplier has committed an offence that may lead to its disqualification.

One of the most contentious issues in the disqualification context is examined in chapter eight – this is the extent to which persons related to a supplier may be disqualified for the offences of the supplier and vice versa. Chapter nine examines another contentious issue, which is whether disqualification will affect on-going contracts. In other words, the issue is whether disqualification will lead to the termination of existing contracts, in light of the disruption that such termination may cause to the delivery of public services. In chapter ten, the book focuses on the extent to which a supplier's rehabilitation may mean it avoids or limits its disqualification, and chapter eleven examines the remedies available to a supplier aggrieved by the disqualification process.

The book will examine these issues through a comparative analysis of the disqualification of corrupt suppliers from public procurement in five 'jurisdictions', namely. the European Union (EU), the United Kingdom (UK), the United States (US), South Africa and the World Bank.

In 2004, the EU adopted a procurement directive, which required the public bodies of Member States to disqualify from public contracts suppliers convicted of corruption, among other offences. This represented a departure from previous EU directives, which permitted, but did not require the disqualification of persons convicted of certain offences. The EU regime was chosen for study because of its significance as the organisation that provides the template for the procurement legislation of 27 nations. However, because European law is better understood within the context of implementation by Member States, the UK has been chosen as the Member State for this study.

The US has had the longest experience in using procurement disqualifications, and its disqualification regime is comprehensive and has been subject to much judicial scrutiny, making the US an ideal candidate for study. South Africa is a developing country with a developed procurement regulation system. Like many developing countries, it has a problem with systemic corruption and has adopted the use of disqualifications in public procurement as an anti-corruption measure. The book will examine the manner in which the disqualifications in South Africa are structured and applied, given the contextual challenges faced by South Africa.

The World Bank was the first development bank to utilise disqualifications where corruption was established within Bank-financed procurement and other development banks have subsequently adopted the Bank's disqualification practice,[18] making the Bank an appropriate system to examine in this book. The practice of disqualification within the Bank provides insight into the challenges that are created by disqualification irrespective of the nature of the legal system or limits of its jurisdiction.

It is worth mentioning that in most of the selected jurisdictions, excepting the US, the use of procurement disqualifications is still very much in its infancy, both in terms of the practical application of the rules on disqualification by procuring authorities and in terms of the interpretation of the rules by the courts. It has thus been necessary in many instances to examine the general law or other areas of procurement regulation to determine how procuring authorities and the courts may address some of the issues arising from the use of procurement disqualifications.

[18] Asian Development Bank Procurement Guidelines (Manila, Asian Development Bank, 2010) para 1.14; African Development Bank Group Rules and Procedure for Procurement of Goods and Works (Procurement and Fiduciary Services Department, 2008) para 1.14.

2

Corruption, Anti-Corruption Measures and Disqualification

2.1 INTRODUCTION

THIS CHAPTER WILL present an overview of the meaning and nature of corruption and examine the measures adopted against corruption. As the book is concerned with the use of contractor disqualifications for corruption, it is important to delineate the meaning of corruption used in the book. The chapter will briefly examine the concept of corruption, including an assessment of the popular definitions and meanings and highlight on-going debates on the nature of corruption. The chapter will also provide a brief synopsis on the effects that corruption may have on the economy, growth and development of a nation and then examine the various measures that are used to combat corruption. These measures will be considered in order to illustrate the various types of mechanisms that may be used against corruption and put the use of procurement-related mechanisms like disqualification into a general context.

2.2 THE MEANING, NATURE AND EFFECTS OF CORRUPTION

Corruption as an economic, social, legal or political concept can be hard to define. First, corruption is steeped in morality[1] and ethics[2] and is imbued with elements of moral approbation, shame and wrongdoing, making it a sensitive subject to address.[3] Secondly, although corruption might offend inherent (and possibly universal) values of morality and ethics, it is also to some extent, culturally specific, with a dichotomy between western and non-western conceptualisations of corruption.[4]

[1] J Wilson, 'Corruption is Not Always Scandalous' in JA Gardiner and DJ Olson (eds), *Theft of the City: Readings on Corruption in Urban America*, 1st edn (Bloomington, Indiana University Press, 1974) 29.

[2] JT Noonan Jnr, *Bribes* (Berkeley, CA, University of California Press, 1987) 702–3.

[3] R Klitgaard, *Controlling Corruption* (Berkeley, University of California Press, 1988) xi.

[4] J Kim and J Kim, 'Cultural Differences in the Crusade against International Bribery: Rice Cake Expenses in Korea and the Foreign Corrupt Practices Act' (1997) 6 *Pacific Rim Law and*

In spite of the recognised definitional difficulties, definitions of corruption are not lacking. As mentioned in Chapter one, one such definition states that corruption is 'behaviour which deviates from the formal duties of a public role because of private-regarding (personal, close family, private clique) pecuniary or status gains; or violates rules against the exercise of certain types of private-regarding influence'.[5] This definition will be adopted as the meaning of corruption in this book, as the focus in the book is on public-sector corruption, or the corruption that occurs between private individuals and public sector agents.

In examining the different definitions of corruption, while it is considered that there is little value in presenting a list of existing definitions, the definitions of corruption may be utilised to determine its the characteristics. An inquiry into some definitions of corruption raises six characteristics of corruption.

(a) corruption is an activity that occurs when the public interest is subjected to private interests.[6]
(b) corruption violates local and universal rules,[7] and duties,[8] but includes an element of cultural specificity.[9]
(c) corruption can be 'trivial or monumental'[10] or as Nye so succinctly puts it, range from 'venality to ideological erosion'.[11]
(d) corruption covers a wide range of activities which may be defined as embezzlement, fraud, bribery or theft.
(e) corruption is present in developed and developing countries, but occurs with varying degrees of severity.[12]

Policy Journal 589; J Hooker, *Working Across Cultures* (Palo Alto, CA, Stanford University Press, 2003) 88, 204 and 317.

[5] J Nye, 'Corruption and Political Development: A Cost-Benefit Analysis' (1967) 61 *American Political Science Review* 417.

[6] Nye, 'Corruption and Political Development', ibid, 417; Klitgaard, *Controlling Corruption*, above n 3, xi.

[7] Noonan, *Bribes*, above n 2, 702–3.

[8] N Kofele-Kale, *The International Law of Responsibility for Economic Crimes: Holding State Officials Individually Liable for Acts of Fraudulent Enrichment*, 2nd edn (Aldershot, Ashgate, Publishing, 2006) 113–64.

[9] S Salbu, 'Are Extra Territorial Restrictions on Bribery a Viable and Desirable International Policy Goal under the Global Conditions of the Late Twentieth Century?' (1999) 24 *Yale Journal of International Law* 223, 232–9; D Tun, 'Bribery among the Korean elite: Putting an End to a Cultural Ritual and Restoring Honour' (1996) 26 *Vanderbilt Journal of Transnational Law* 1071, 1084; M Johnston, 'The Political Consequences of Corruption: A Reassessment' (1986) *Comparative Policy*, 463; S Rose-Ackerman, *Corruption and Government: Causes, Consequences, Reform* (Cambridge, Cambridge University Press, 1999) 2; R Klitgaard, 'Gifts and Bribes' in R Zeckhauser (ed), *Strategy and Choice* (Massachusetts, MIT Press, 1992); Klitgaard, *Controlling Corruption*, above n 3, 62.

[10] Klitgaard, *Controlling Corruption*, above n 3, xi.

[11] Nye, 'Corruption and Political Development', above n 5, 419.

[12] Rose-Ackerman, *Corruption and Government*, above n 9; Klitgaard, *Controlling Corruption*, above n 3, 8–9.

(f) the activity labelled corrupt need not be illegal, it is enough that it is considered unethical or immoral.[13]

Most definitions of corruption characterise corruption from the point of view of the public official. This is not to deny the corruption which takes place in the private sector, but it appears that private-sector corruption poses less of a problem to governments and the international community, since market forces invariably dictate the price that people pay for goods or services. Also, private-sector corruption is less likely to become systemic and cannot be sustained, as the increased costs of doing business will decrease a firm's competitiveness over time, if that firm is not a monopoly. Furthermore, private-sector corruption rarely produces the social costs of public-sector corruption such as the 'contagion of corruption'[14] or the waste and inefficient allocation of public resources.[15]

As stated, this book will focus on public-sector corruption due to its peculiarities such as the tendency for public corruption to be sustainable[16] and its effect on socio-economic development. Also, measures introduced to combat corruption, such as disqualifications are usually, but not exclusively aimed at public-sector corruption.

Whilst there is some agreement on the basic components of a definition of corruption, there is less agreement on the nature and effects of corruption and there is a diversity of opinions as to whether corruption is an economic, social or political phenomenon with each perspective providing models for analysing and understanding corruption.

2.2.1 Economic Theories on Corruption

Within the economic framework,[17] the agency (or incentive) model of corruption is the most dominant.[18] This model assumes that the public servant is the agent of the government and is employed to further the government's (his principal's) interests. In addition to the public interest the agent is supposed to be furthering, the agent also has his own private interests, which may conflict with that of his principal. Corruption occurs when the agent decides to pursue his private ends at the expense of the

[13] F Anechiarico and J Jacobs, *The Pursuit of Absolute Integrity: How Corruption Control makes Government Ineffective* (Chicago, University of Chicago Press, 1996) ch 1.

[14] G Caiden and O Dwivedi, 'Official Ethics and Corruption' in G Caiden (ed), *Where Corruption Lives* (Connecticut, Kumarian Press, 2001) 245.

[15] Rose-Ackerman, *Corruption and Government*, above n 9, 3, 30.

[16] See generally A Doig and R Theobald, *Corruption and Democratisation*, 1st edn (London, Routledge, 2000).

[17] Rose-Ackerman, *Corruption and Government*, above n 9, ch 2.

[18] N Groenendijk, 'A principal-agent model of corruption' (1997) 27 *Crime, Law and Social Change* 207–29; OH Fjeldstad, JC Andvig, I Amundsen, T Sissener and T Soreide, *Corruption: A Review of Comtemporary Research* (Bergen, CMI, 2001).

public interest, or subordinates the public interest to his private goals. The economic model assumes that the agent is a rational (if amoral) being and will weigh up the benefits of being corrupt against the costs, and where the net benefits exceed the net costs, the agent will act corruptly.[19]

The problem with economic models of corruption is that they are clinical and do not take into account any inclinations towards religion, morality or ethics, which may dissuade a public agent from acting corruptly, and ignore normative factors, which can impact on the agent's decision. In assuming that all officials are morally neutral and will act corruptly if it benefits them, the models are unable to explain why some agents are not corrupt, and how the non-economic motivations of non-corrupt officials may be harnessed as an anti-corruption mechanism. The assumption that once it is beneficial and the opportunity presents itself, all public officials will act corruptly is also not based on the evidence in situations where there are few detriments to an agent in acting corruptly because corruption is systemic, tolerated and rarely penalised, and some agents still do not engage in corrupt activities. Whilst economic models of corruption are helpful in understanding the economic drivers behind corruption, they are limited in the nature of solutions that can be proffered, as the solutions are also economically driven, often ignoring the complexity of the subject matter.[20]

2.2.2 Political Theories on Corruption

The political conceptualisation of corruption has similar shortcomings. Here, corruption is perceived as a consequence of a particular system of government (democratic or non-democratic),[21] or a failure of leadership.[22] The arguments are that the non-democratic and non-accountable nature of the political machinery contributes to corruption[23] or that the existing personalities in government are the cause of the problem.[24] However, these theories cannot explain the corruption that takes place in developed democracies and there is conflicting evidence on whether non-democratic

[19] Klitgaard, *Controlling Corruption*, above n 3, 69–74.

[20] G Becker, 'Crime and Punishment: An economic approach' (1968) 76 *Journal of Political Economy* 169–217.

[21] See generally, Doig and Theobald, *Corruption and Democratisation*, above n 16.

[22] KR Hope, 'Corruption and Development in Africa' in KR Hope and BC Chikulu (eds), *Corruption and Development in Africa: Lessons from Country Case Studies* (New York, St Martins Press, 2000) 19.

[23] J Friedrich, 'Corruption Concepts in Historical Perspective' in A Heidenheimer, M Johnston and V LeVine (eds), *Political Corruption: A Handbook*, 2nd edn (New Jersey, Transaction Publishers,1989).

[24] J Coolidge and S Rose-Ackerman, 'Kleptocracy and Reform in African Regimes: Theory and Examples' in KR Hope and BC Chikulu (eds), *Corruption and development in Africa: Lessons from Country Case Studies* (New York, St Martin's Press, 2000) ch 3.

societies are more corrupt that democratic ones.[25] In fact it is claimed that democratic societies may create an atmosphere more conducive to corrupt activity, as

> democratic society encourages wheeling and dealing and give and take. They support negotiation and persuasion. This can mean some persons back into committing technical violations without the intention to commit a crime . . . [f]or elected officials, the line between political contributions and buying favours and extortion can be thin.[26]

Where corruption is blamed on the personalities in government, this removes the responsibility for individual actions from public officials and places it with the leadership. Whilst a corrupt leadership may invariably reproduce itself,[27] even in the most corrupt of regimes, public servants retain the responsibility for their actions in deciding whether to be corrupt.

2.2.3 Social Theories on Corruption

Corruption might be considered to be an anthropological problem[28] or a consequence of the failings inherent in the organisation of society, such as a failure of capitalism.[29] The argument is that corruption comes into play where market forces are unable to efficiently allocate resources, and ensures that opportunities are allocated to the highest bidder.[30] Whilst in an inefficient society, corruption might ensure that opportunities are given to those who desire them the most, the argument fails to recognise that political participation, state resources and opportunities are not private property and should not be for sale. Furthermore, if corruption is used as the means to distribute resources intended for the greater good, the re-distribution of those resources will reflect the increased costs of obtaining them, which will adversely affect society as a whole.[31]

From the above explanations of the causes of corruption, it can be seen that none of the above concepts is sufficient to explain the complex nature

[25] Doig and Theobald, *Corruption and Democratisation*; Fjeldstad, Andvig et al, *Corruption: A Review*, above n 18, ch 4.2 and 6.2; D Treisman, 'The Causes of Corruption: A Cross National Study' (2000) 76 *Journal of Public Economics* 399.

[26] G Marx, 'When the Guards Guard Themselves: Undercover Tactics Turned Inwards' (1992) 2 *Policing and Society* 166.

[27] D Windsor and K Getz, 'Multilateral Cooperation to Combat Corruption: Normative Regimes Despite Mixed Motives and Diverse Values' (2000) 33 *Cornell International Law Journal* 731, 757.

[28] T Sissener, *Anthropological Perspectives on Corruption* (Bergen, CMI, 2001); Fjeldstad, Andvig et al, *Corruption: A Review*, above n 18, ch 5.4.

[29] M Blomstrom and B Hettne, *Development Theory in Transition* (London, Zed Books, 1984).

[30] Rose-Ackerman, *Corruption and Government*, above n 9, ch 2.

[31] W Wittig, 'A Framework for balancing business and accountability within public procurement' (2001) 3 *Public Procurement Law Review* 139.

of corruption. Rather, it is suggested that corruption can only be explained by taking all factors into account, the political, the economic and the social.

As regards the effects of corruption, it is surprising to find that scholars are not in universal agreement on the effects of corruption. One school opines that corruption is intrinsically bad because it undermines the legitimacy of governments and increases public spending without an increase in public welfare.[32] In this school, most writers agree that the end result of corruption where it is systemic is an adverse effect on development, as the state becomes incapable of meeting basic needs or sustaining economic development.[33] The effect of corruption on development has been illustrated by studies showing that corruption or the opportunity to obtain bribes can affect the allocation of public spending and lead to large unnecessary projects given priority over health and education.[34] Corruption can also have very direct effects on public welfare. For instance, if one considers the allocation of a hypothetical water distribution contract to a supplier who was able to bribe public officials to obtain the contract, the provision of water to the end-consumer will either reflect the increased costs to obtain the contract, or will be provided at a sub-standard quality, to recoup these costs. Even if the quality of the water is unaffected, the supplier may not be the most efficient or cost-effective, leading to a waste of public funds.

Other studies into the effects of corruption have revealed that it reduces private investment, foreign direct investment and the rate of economic growth,[35] as it acts as a tax on foreign direct investment thereby reducing real capital flows.[36] Corruption further disrupts democracy and the

[32] P Mauro, 'Corruption and Growth' (1995) 110 *Quarterly Journal of Economics* 681, provides empirical evidence on the link between increased corruption and reduced gross domestic product. P Ward, *Corruption, Development and Inequality: Soft Touch or Hard Graft* (London, Routledge, 1989) 170; Rose-Ackerman, *Corruption and Government*, above n 9, ch 1.

[33] F Khan, 'Top Down or bottom up? The spread of systemic corruption in the Third world' (Dec 2001). Available at www.colbud.hu/honesty-trust/khan/pub01.rtf; Kofele-Kale, *International Law of Responsibility*, above n 8, 105–7; D Frisch, 'The Effects of Corruption on Development' (1996) 158 *The Courier ACP-EU*, 68; C Gray and D Kaufman, 'Corruption and Development' (1998) *Finance and Development* 7; B Heinemann and F Heimann, 'The Long War Against Corruption' (2006) 85 *Foreign Affairs* 75.

[34] P Mauro, 'The Effects of Corruption on Growth, Investment and Government Expenditure: A Cross Country Analysis' in KA Elliot (ed), *Corruption and the Global Economy* (Washington, Institute for International Economics, 1997); V Tanzi, 'Corruption Around the World: Causes, Consequences, Scope and Cures' (1998) 45(4) *IMF Staff Papers* 559; T Soreide, *Corruption in Public Procurement: Causes, Consequences, Cures* (Bergen, CMI, 2002) ch 2.

[35] Mauro, 'Corruption and Growth', above n 32, 700–704.

[36] N Rubin, 'A Convergence of 1996 and 1997 Global Efforts to Curb Corruption and Bribery in International Business Transactions: The Legal Implications of the OECD Recommendations and Convention for the United States, Germany and Switzerland' (1988) 14 *American University International Law Review* 257, 315; SJ Wei, 'How taxing is corruption on international investors?'(1997) *NBER Working Paper* 6030.

citizenry's right to political participation;[37] if one considers that where a public agent alters his decision-making on the receipt of a bribe, he is denying the right of other people to participate in that process, and subverting democracy by flouting formal processes.

In addition, corruption can have fatal and disastrous consequences, especially in the construction context. For instance, in Egypt in 2007, a building collapsed killing several people.[38] Similarly, in India in 2010, 65 people were killed when a building collapsed.[39] These tragedies were blamed on corruption and lax enforcement of building regulations.

On the other hand, some scholars believe that a limited amount of corruption can be beneficial if it succeeds in making markets more efficient and aiding in the allocation of scarce resources.[40] The problem with this reasoning, however, is in defining and imposing the 'limits' of this corruption. In a study into the telecommunications sector in India, Rashid argued that bribes to obtain a telephone line began as price discrimination among customers in an egalitarian system, but quickly degenerated into extortion against customers that impeded service so that officials in charge could obtain larger bribes.[41] Whether or not there is evidence to suggest that corruption can be beneficial for economic development,[42] the majority of scholars affirm the undesirable effects and consequences of corruption.[43] This book is also premised on the view that corruption is inimical to growth and development.

2.3 ANTI-CORRUPTION MEASURES

Anti-corruption measures range from national laws and guidelines to international and multilateral binding instruments. This section will analyse national and major international anti-corruption measures to put procurement disqualifications into context and show that they are only one of the many approaches that may be used against corruption.

[37] Donaldson, *The Ethics of International Business* (Oxford, Oxford University Press, 1989) 89-94.

[38] See: www.msnbc.msn.com/id/22432355/ns/world_news-mideast_n_africa/t/corrupt-work-blamed-egypt-building-collapse/.

[39] www.allvoices.com/contributed-news/7345623-the-worst-disaster-of-building-collapse-in-delhi-killing-60-people.

[40] Nye, 'Corruption and Political Development', above n 5, 419–22; P Huntington, 'Modernization and Development' in MU Ekpo (ed), *Bureaucratic Corruption in Sub-Saharan Africa: Towards a Search for Causes and Consequences* (Maryland, University Press of America, 1979); N Leff, 'Economic Development through Bureaucratic Corruption' in Ekpo (ed), *Bureaucratic Corruption in Sub-Saharan Africa*; T Olsen and G Torsvik, 'Collusion and Renegotiation in Hierarchies: A Case of Beneficial Corruption' (1998) 39 *International Economic Review* 413.

[41] S Rashid, 'Public Utilities in Egalitarian LDC's: The Role of Bribery in Achieving Pareto Efficiency' (1981) 34 *Kyklos International Review for Social Sciences* 448.

[42] Nye, 'Corruption and Political Development', above n 5, 419–22.

[43] Klitgaard, *Controlling Corruption*, above n 3, ix–xv.

2.3.1 Domestic Measures against Corruption.

There are different measures a government may adopt against corruption. These can be classified into administrative, regulatory, and social measures. Administrative measures are measures which may not be specifically required by legislation, but which are permitted under the exercise of executive discretion. Regulatory measures are the obligatory measures which must be imposed where corrupt activity is found to have occurred, including requirements to impose penal and civil sanctions. Social measures encompass the societal ridicule, shame and infamy that attend corrupt activity where it is exposed.

These categories are not exclusive, and administrative and regulatory measures will frequently overlap where legislation authorises the use of an administrative measure against corruption. In addition, social measures may accompany the use of regulatory and administrative measures.

2.3.1.1 Administrative measures

Administrative measures against corruption are measures implemented under the exercise of official discretion. These may include restrictions on obtaining government patronage, licenses, approvals and permits placed upon corrupt persons. An example is a denial of registration as a company, where the proposer has bankruptcies, criminal or fraudulent convictions against him.[44] Administrative tools also include measures that deny corrupt suppliers access to government contracts, which is the subject matter of this book. Such measures may also include measures which deny potential suppliers registration on qualification lists for public contracts.[45]

Other administrative measures are increased levels of public sector financial management, viz, accounting and audit requirements. These requirements are on the rise, as financial controls become an important part of public sector reform and consequently, an important part of corruption control.[46] Public sector financial management seeks accountability in terms of results, and not just in terms of the process.[47] Specifically, the purpose of such audits is to ensure that imbalances or areas of leakage in public finances are identified and properly addressed.[48]

[44] TMC Asser, *Prevention of and Administrative Action Against organised Crime: A Comparative Law Study of the Registration of Legal persons and Criminal Audits in Eight EU Member States* (The Hague, TMC Asser Press, 1997).

[45] H Xanthaki, 'First Pillar Analysis' in S White (ed), *Procurement and Organised Crime* (London, Institute of Advanced Legal Studies, 2000).

[46] M Power, 'Evaluating the Audit Explosion' (2003) 25 *Law & Policy* 185; Anechiarico and Jacobs, *The Pursuit of Absolute Integrity*, above n 13, ch 9.

[47] C Hood, 'The New Public Management in the 1980s: Variations on a Theme' (1995) 20 *Accounting, Organisations and Society* 93.

[48] C Walsh, 'Creating a Competitive Culture in the Public Service: The Role of Audits and other Reviews' (1995) 54 *Australian Journal of Public Administration* 325.

The increased supervision of public officials is another anti-corruption tool. This can be implemented through series of approvals necessary before major decisions can be taken and implemented. Supervision of public officials is closely tied to restricting the levels of discretion available to public agents, which some jurisdictions consider a necessary component of corruption control.[49]

2.3.1.2 *Regulatory Measures*

Regulatory measures include the laws or regulations that a government may adopt against corruption. This includes legal prohibitions against corruption and criminal and civil penalties and forfeitures directed both at the public and private sectors. For instance, a corrupt public official in addition to a fine or custodial sentence that may be imposed following a criminal trial may invariably also lose his employment and in some jurisdictions, forfeit his pension and related benefits.[50]

2.3.1.3 *Social measures*

Social measures against corruption are those elements of disapprobation, such as the shame, ridicule and disgrace that follow the exposition of corrupt activity. Social measures against corruption are rarely used as primary instruments against corruption, since they are informal and unorganised mechanisms. Nevertheless, they might follow the use of regulatory measures, where the press sensationalises corruption scandals and exposes the parties involved in a criminal trial. However, social measures may be effective in the absence of criminal convictions. For instance, the UK Parliamentary expenses scandal which dominated the UK media in 2009 led to public outrage and the resignation of some Members of Parliament. Similarly, in the Philippines in the early 1970s, government officials who were found to be corrupt had their details published in national media. This amounted to a disgrace that was considered so serious, some officials committed suicide.[51]

Social measures may also accompany the use of administrative measures where for instance, it becomes publicly known that a firm has been excluded from government contracts as a result of corruption and this affects its ability to obtain business from other sectors, or its share price.[52]

[49] S Kelman, *Procurement and Public Management: The Fear of Discretion and the Quality of Government Performance* (Washington, AEI Press, 1990) ch 1; C Gray, *Anti-Corruption in Transition 2: Corruption in Enterprise-State Interactions in Europe and Central Asia 1999–2002* (Washington, World Bank, 2004) 11.

[50] G Becker and G Stigler, 'Law Enforcement, Malfeasance and Compensation of Enforcers' (1974) 3 *Journal of Legal Studies* 1.

[51] Klitgaard, *Controlling Corruption*, above n 3, ch 3.

[52] *Gonzalez v Freeman*, 334 F2d 570, 574 (DC Cir 1964).

2.3.2 International Measures against Corruption.

International measures against corruption have gained prominence in the last two decades. These measures can be divided into binding international instruments such as treaties and conventions and soft law instruments such as OECD recommendations,[53] United Nations and General Assembly resolutions and declarations,[54] and non-binding instruments from the EU.[55] Technical assistance programmes[56] (mainly directed at developing and transition economies) and 'naming and shaming' corrupt nations[57] may also be used against corruption. For depth of analysis, this chapter will focus on the international/multilateral binding instruments against corruption, which are regarded as the most important in terms of their geographical significance and number of ratifications/accessions.

The starting point for any discussion of international or multilateral attempts at combating corruption is usually the US Foreign Corrupt Practices Act of 1977 (FCPA).[58] Whilst this is a piece of domestic legislation, it is accepted as the genesis of extraterritorial attempts at controlling corruption and it provided the impetus for multilateral measures to criminalise overseas bribery.[59]

[53] OECD Recommendation of the Council on Bribery in International Business Transactions, 33 ILM 1389 (1994); OECD Recommendation of the Council on the Tax Deductibility of Bribes to Foreign Public Officials, 35 ILM 1311 (1996); OECD Revised Recommendation of the Council on combating Bribery in International Business Transactions, 36 ILM 1016 (1997); OECD Recommendation of the Council on Guidelines for Managing Conflict of Interest in the Public Service (June 2003); OECD Recommendation of the Council on Enhancing Integrity in Public Procurement [C (2008) 105].

[54] UN General Assembly Resolution 51/59 on Action Against Corruption and the International Code of Conduct for Public Officials, A/RES/51/59; UN Declaration against Corruption and Bribery in International Commercial Transactions, A/RES/51/191; General Assembly Resolution 55/61 on An Effective International Legal Instrument Against Corruption, A/RES/55/61.

[55] Communication from the Commission to the Council and European Parliament on a Union Policy Against Corruption, COM (97) 192; Communication from the Commission to the Council and European Parliament on a Comprehensive EU Policy Against Corruption, COM (2003) 317; Action Plan to Combat Organised Crime [1997] OJ C251/1; Resolution on the Communication from the Commission to the Council and the European Parliament on a Union Policy Against Corruption [1998] OJ C328/46; Communication from the Commission to the European Parliament, the Council and the European Economic and Social Council on Fighting Corruption in the EU, COM (2011) 308.

[56] Technical assistance is provided by the EU (through SIGMA, PHARE), the OECD, the United Nations and the World Bank.

[57] The Corruption Perceptions Index, the Bribe Payers index and the Global Corruption Barometer are compiled by Transparency International. See www.transparency.org .

[58] Pub L No 95-213, 91 Stat 1494.

[59] A Posadas, 'Combating Corruption under International Law' (2000) 10 *Duke Journal of Comparative and International Law* 345; D Tarullo, 'The Limits of Institutional Design: Implementing the OECD Anti-Bribery Convention' (2004) 44 *Virginia Journal of International Law* 665; Windsor and Getz, 'Multilateral Cooperation to Combat Corruption', above n 27, 731.

2.3.2.1 *The OECD Anti-Bribery Convention*

The OECD Convention on Combating Bribery of Foreign Public Officials[60] had an interesting legislative history.[61] After the enactment of the FCPA, it became apparent to the US government that without international cooperation it could not solve the problem of international corruption. Instead, the FCPA was criticised for harming US interests by making it difficult for US firms to obtain foreign business, as non-US firms who were willing to pay bribes now had an advantage over their US competitors.[62] To mitigate this, the government put pressure on its peers at the OECD[63] and was able to convince them that bribery hindered international trade – leading to the adoption of an OECD Recommendation criminalising overseas bribery in 1994.[64]

This Recommendation was followed by the Convention, which entered into force in 1999. The Convention obliges states to prevent their citizens from bribing foreign officials, but does not address the *taking* of bribes by those foreign officials. There are three major obligations imposed by the Convention: first, Article 1 obliges signatories to:

> take such measures as may be necessary to establish that it is a criminal offence under its law for any person intentionally to offer, promise or give any undue pecuniary or other advantage . . . to a foreign public official for that official or for a third party, in order that the official act or refrain from acting in relation to the performance of official duties, in order to obtain or retain business or other improper advantage in the conduct of international business.

This obligation is supported by subsequent articles providing for appropriate criminal and civil sanctions against firms guilty of foreign bribery.[65] The second obligation imposed by the Convention is aimed at preventing accounting and financial recording mechanisms that disguise foreign

[60] 37 ILM 1 (1998).

[61] B George, K Lacey and J Birmele, 'The 1998 OECD Convention: An Impetus for Worldwide Changes in Attitudes Toward Corruption in Business Transactions' (2000) 37 *American Business Law Journal* 485; Rubin, 'A Convergence of 1996 and 1997 Global Efforts to Curb Corruption', above n 36, 257; J Nesbitt, 'Transnational Bribery of Foreign Officials: A New Threat to the Future of Democracy' (1998) 31 *Vanderbilt Journal of Transnational Law* 1273; P Nichols, 'The Myth of Anti-Bribery Law as Transnational Intrusion' (2000) 33 *Cornell Journal of International Law* 627; C Hudson and P Pierros, 'The Hard Graft of Tackling Corruption in International Business Transactions: Progress in International Cooperation and the OECD Convention' (1998) 32(2) *Journal of World Trade* 77; S Salbu, 'A Delicate Balance: Legislation, Institutional Change and Transnational Bribery' (2000) 33 *Cornell International Law Journal* 657; P Jennings, 'Public Corruption: A Comparative Analysis of International Corruption Conventions and United States Law', (2001) 18 *Arizona Journal of International and Comparative Law* 793.

[62] Tarullo, 'The Limits of Institutional Design', above n 59; Windsor and Getz, 'Multilateral Cooperation to Combat Corruption', above n 27, 748.

[63] Posadas, 'Combating Corruption under International Law', above n 59, 377–9.

[64] 33 ILM 1389 (1994).

[65] OECD Convention, art 3(1).

bribes. Member States are obliged to punish such accounting malpractices by effective, proportionate and dissuasive penalties.[66] The third obligation is for State parties to provide mutual legal assistance to each other, in investigating relevant cases,[67] including the possibility of extradition where necessary.[68]

The OECD monitors compliance with the Convention through a process of peer-review of anti-corruption legislation adopted by State parties. The process also includes a formal evaluation procedure by the OECD and an examination into the enforcement mechanism of State parties, to assess the effectiveness of State parties' anti-corruption legislation.[69]

The OECD has focused on ensuring that the administrative and legislative mechanisms necessary to implement the Convention are in place in signatory States. While many commentators view the Convention as a positive step, most are of the view that the Convention has not been as successful in combating international bribery, as it was hoped for.[70] This is due in part to the major loopholes in the Convention, which are that it excludes passive bribery (bribe-taking) and 'small facilitation payments' from its ambit[71] as well as similar lacunae in the implementing legislation of State parties.[72] Also, because the Convention is not a model for legislation, but a set of guidelines mandating a broad outcome, it does not 'require uniformity or changes in the fundamental principles of a Party's legal system'.[73] As a result, State parties are not required to do much more than criminalise foreign bribery in order to have complied with the Convention.[74] Coupled with a weak implementation mechanism, the Convention's success may be found in the harmonisation of a set of norms on foreign bribery and not

[66] OECD Convention, art 8.

[67] OECD Convention, art 9(1).

[68] OECD Convention, art 10.

[69] C Corr and J Lawler, 'Damned If You Do, Damned If You Don't? The OECD Convention and the Globalisation of Anti-Bribery Measures' (1999) 32 *Vanderbilt Journal of Transnational Law* 1249, 1319–24.

[70] L Miller, 'No More This for That? The Effect of the OECD Convention on Combating Bribery of Foreign Public Officials in International Business Transactions' (2000) 8 *Cardozo Journal of International and Comparative Law* 139; C Calberg, 'A Truly Level Playing Field for International Business: Improving the OECD Convention on Combating Bribery using Clear Standards' (2003) 26 *Boston College International and Comparative Law Review* 95; Tarullo, 'The Limits of Institutional Design', above n 59; P Carrington, 'Enforcing International Corrupt Practices Law' (2010) 32 *Michigan Journal of International Law* 129.

[71] OECD, Commentaries on the Convention on Combating Bribery of Officials in International Business Transactions, OECD Negotiating Conference, 1. Available at: www.oecd.org .

[72] Miller, 'No more this for that', above n 70, 150–58; D Heifetz, 'Japan's Implementation of the OECD Anti-Bribery Convention: Weaker and Less Effective that the US Foreign Corrupt Practices Act' (2002) 11 *Pacific Rim Law and Policy Journal* 209.

[73] OECD, Commentaries, above n 71, 2.

[74] P Ala'I, 'The Legacy of Geographical Morality and Colonialism: A Historical Assessment of the Current Crusade Against Corruption' (2000) 33 *Vanderbilt Journal of Transnational Law* 877, 923–4.

much more.[75] The shortcomings of the Convention led to the adoption in 2009 of a Recommendation for Further Combating Bribery of Foreign Public Officials in International Business Transactions, which suggests further measures to combat international bribery.[76] Some of these measures include the adoption of best practices to make companies liable for foreign bribery, the review of State policy on facilitation payments and improvements in effective reporting and whistle-blower protections.

2.3.2.2 *The Organisation of American States Corruption Convention*

The Organisation of American States (OAS) is a regional organisation of western hemisphere states. The path to a multilateral anti-corruption Convention began in 1994 at the Miami Summit, where the adopted Declaration of Principles and Plan of Action[77] made the link between effective democracy and the eradication of corruption. As a result of the commitments in the Plan of Action, OAS Member States adopted the Inter-American Convention against Corruption,[78] which took effect in 1997.

The Convention follows the same pattern of the criminalisation of overseas bribery as the OECD Convention.[79] However, the Inter-American Convention is broader in scope than the OECD Convention in that it addresses the demand and the supply side of corruption, and applies where a corrupt act was committed in a State party and where the act has *effects* in a State party.[80] Presumably, an effect may include where a firm from a State party was denied a contract because the firm refused to give a bribe. However, it is not clear how this might be addressed by the Convention.

The Convention also contains measures necessary to prevent corruption,[81] and provides for the implementation in national systems of measures to prevent corruption in government activities, including, but not limited to the tax system, the procurement system[82] and the civil service. It also provides for the creation of mechanisms that will support good accounting practices within firms as a means of detecting corrupt acts where they occur.[83]

75 Ala'I, 'The Legacy of Geographical Morality', above n 74, 928.

76 Recommendation for Further Combating Bribery of Foreign Public Officials (December 2009). See also OECD Recommendation on Tax Measures for Further Combating Bribery of Foreign Public Officials in International Business Transactions, 2009.

77 Summit of the Americas: Declaration of Principles and Plan of Action 34 ILM 808 (1995).

78 35 ILM 724 (1996).

79 L Low, A Bjorklund and K Atkinson, 'The Inter-American Convention Against Corruption: A Comparison with the United States FCPA' (1998) 38 *Virginia Journal of International Law* 243.

80 OAS Corruption Convention, art IV.

81 OAS Corruption Convention, art III.

82 OAS Corruption Convention, arts III (5) and (6).

83 OAS Corruption Convention, art III (8).

The Convention contains a series of mandatory multilateral obligations. These include a commitment to extradite persons found to have committed acts of corruption,[84] affording mutual assistance in preventive, investigative and enforcement efforts,[85] including assistance in the seizure and forfeiture of assets.[86]

Unlike the OECD Convention, there is no monitoring or compliance mechanism, leaving implementation to the discretion of State parties. Another feature of the Inter-American Convention, which does not have parallels in the OECD Convention is that some of the offences in the Inter-American Convention are subject to the Constitution and fundamental principles of the State party. Thus a State party may refrain from criminalising those offences in question if it feels they are incompatible with its legal system.[87]

2.3.2.3 The European Conventions

The anti-corruption instruments in Europe differ in rationale from the other regional conventions against corruption. Thus, while the Inter-American and the African Convention locate corruption as a barrier to democracy, economic growth and development, the European Conventions endeavour to protect Union finances, and seek, in conformity with the purpose behind the Union, the closer integration of the internal market.

The major European Conventions against corruption are those which were adopted by the European Union, viz, the Convention on the Protection of the European Communities Financial Interests and its Protocols and Convention on the Fight against Corruption Involving Officials of the European Communities or Officials of Member States of the EU, and the conventions adopted by the Council of Europe against corruption, viz, one mandating criminal penalties for corruption and the other specifying civil remedies for the victims of corruption.

(a) The Convention on the Protection of the European Communities' financial interests (PFI Convention) and its Protocols

The PFI Convention[88] was passed to thwart the misappropriation of Union finances and criminalise through domestic law, actions which adversely affect European revenue. The Convention is designed to criminalise any act which leads to the misapplication or wrongful retention of Union funds and it ensures that business leaders can be made liable for the

[84] OAS Corruption Convention, art XIII.
[85] OAS Corruption Convention, art XIV.
[86] OAS Corruption Convention, art XV.
[87] OAS Corruption Convention, art VIII.
[88] [1995] OJ C316/48.

actions of their subordinates where the action constitutes a fraud affecting the EU's financial interests.

The Protocols to the Convention elaborate the scope of the Convention. The First Protocol[89] defines the terms 'official' and 'active' and 'passive' corruption for the purposes of the Convention and the Second Protocol[90] provides for the liability of legal persons, confiscation of corruptly derived proceeds and cooperation between EU Member States and the Commission for the purpose of protecting the Union's financial interests.

(b) The Convention on the fight against Corruption involving officials of the European Communities or officials of Member States of the EU

This Convention[91] is intended to criminalise 'active' and 'passive' corruption by public officials of Member States or officials of EU institutions. Similar to the PFI Convention, it provides for the criminal liability of business heads, in so far as a person under their authority committed the corrupt act and the person was acting on behalf of the business.

(c) The Council of Europe Criminal Law Convention on Corruption

The Council of Europe has adopted two anti-corruption Conventions – one requiring State parties to criminalise acts of corruption within their borders and the other specifying for the provision of civil remedies to the victims of corruption.

The Criminal Law Convention on Corruption[92] entered into force in 2002. The Convention has a broader sphere of application than the EU-driven instruments, having been ratified by several states outside the EU.[93] The Convention is more comprehensive than the OECD and the Inter-American Conventions, obliging State parties to criminalise a wide range of offences, including, but not limited to the active and passive corruption of national, foreign and international officials,[94] active and passive corruption of national, foreign and supranational parliaments and courts, trading in influence and laundering of the proceeds of corruption.[95] The Convention also addresses private-sector bribery[96] and obliges State parties to cooperate with each other in the areas of extradition,[97] investigation and enforcement.[98]

89 [1996] OJ C313/1.
90 [1997] OJ C221/11.
91 [1997] OJ C195/1.
92 38 ILM 505 (1999).
93 conventions.coe.int/treaty/Commun/ChercheSig.asp?NT=173&CM=&DF=&CL=ENG
94 Council of Europe Criminal Law Convention on Corruption, chapter II.
95 Council of Europe Criminal Law Convention on Corruption, chapter II.
96 Council of Europe Criminal Law Convention on Corruption, arts 7 and 8.
97 Council of Europe Criminal Law Convention on Corruption, art 27.
98 Council of Europe Criminal Law Convention on Corruption, arts 21 and 26.

Ratification of the Convention implies automatic submission to the Group of States against Corruption (GRECO),[99] which monitors the compliance of State parties to the Council of Europe's Corruption Conventions by means of a system of mutual evaluation and peer pressure.[100]

(d) The Council of Europe Civil Law Convention on Corruption

The Civil Law Convention on Corruption[101] entered into force in 2003 and has also been ratified by non-members of the EU.[102] The Convention is aimed at providing civil remedies for citizens of State parties who have suffered damage as a result of corruption and obtain compensation where appropriate.[103] State parties are obliged to provide a private right of action for full compensation against persons who have committed or authorised acts of corruption or failed to prevent them from occurring.[104] It also provides for State liability for acts of corruption committed by public officials.[105] As with the Criminal Law Convention, the Civil Law Convention obliges State parties to cooperate with each other in the fight against corruption[106] and compliance is also monitored by GRECO.[107]

2.3.2.4 *The African Convention on Corruption*

The African Union Convention on Preventing and Combating Corruption[108] entered into force in 2006. The Convention aims to promote and strengthen measures to prevent and combat corruption in Africa. This includes cooperation in respect of anti-corruption measures and the harmonisation of anti-corruption policies and legislation among State parties.[109]

The Convention is similar to the Inter-American Convention in its thrust, as it is believed that corruption undermines political stability and socio-economic development in Africa.[110] The objectives of the Convention include promoting socio-economic development by removing obstacles to

[99] Council of Europe Criminal Law Convention on Corruption, art 24.
[100] See: www.greco.coe.int .
[101] ETS No 174.
[102] See: conventions.coe.int/Treaty/Commun/ChercheSig.asp?NT=174&CM=&DF=&CL=ENG .
[103] Council of Europe Civil Law Convention on Corruption, arts 1 and 3.
[104] Council of Europe Civil Law Convention on Corruption, arts 3 and 4.
[105] Council of Europe Civil Law Convention on Corruption, art 5.
[106] Council of Europe Civil Law Convention on Corruption, art 13.
[107] Council of Europe Civil Law Convention on Corruption, art 14.
[108] 43 ILM 5 (2004); N Udombana, 'Fighting Corruption Seriously? Africa's Anti-Corruption Convention' (2003) 7 *Singapore Journal of International and Comparative Law* 447.
[109] African Convention on Corruption, art 2.
[110] Y Osinbajo, 'Human Rights, Economic Development and the Corruption Factor' in P Zeleza and P McConnaughay (eds), *Human Rights, the Rule of Law and Development in Africa* (Philadelphia, University of Pennsylvania Press, 2004).

the enjoyment of economic, social, cultural, civil and political rights.[111] It thus has a slightly different objective than the OECD Convention, which is designed to eradicate bribery in international business, or the EU's PFI Convention, which is aimed at protecting EU revenue.

The African Convention applies to the giving or receiving of a bribe or other benefit and the diversion of public funds or state property.[112] The Convention also applies to private sector corruption.[113] State parties are also enjoined to criminalise conspiracy, the concealment of fraudulently obtained proceeds,[114] the laundering of corruptly obtained property[115] and illicit enrichment,[116] while seeking to protect whistle-blowers.[117]

The Convention includes a commitment that State parties will require public officials to declare their assets at the inception and conclusion of their period in public service and requires State parties to ensure transparency in public procurement. Like the other Conventions, there are provisions relating to international cooperation, mutual assistance and extradition.[118] The Convention also provides for the establishment of a monitoring mechanism, through the Advisory Board on Corruption within the African Union, which promotes the adoption of anti-corruption legislation in State parties, and reports to the Executive Council of the African Union on progress made to comply with the Convention.[119]

2.3.2.5 *The United Nations Convention against Corruption*

The United Nations Convention against Corruption[120] is the only truly international instrument against corruption, being open to all members of the United Nations.[121] The Convention came into force in 2005. It is very ambitious in its scope[122] and covers four main issues: the prevention of corruption;[123] the criminalisation of corruption;[124] international cooperation[125] and asset recovery.[126]

[111] African Convention on Corruption, art 2.
[112] African Convention on Corruption, art 4.
[113] African Convention on Corruption, arts 4(1)(e) and (f) and art 11.
[114] African Convention on Corruption, art 4(1)(h).
[115] African Convention on Corruption, art 6.
[116] African Convention on Corruption, art 8.
[117] African Convention on Corruption, art 5.
[118] African Convention on Corruption, arts 15–19.
[119] African Convention on Corruption, art 22.
[120] 43 ILM 37 (2004).
[121] It is also the most widely adopted. See I Carr, 'The United Nations Convention on Corruption: Making a Real Difference to the Quality of Life of Millions?' (2006) 3 *Manchester Journal of International Economic Law* 3
[122] I Carr, 'Fighting Corruption Through the United Nations Convention on Corruption 2003: A global Solution to a Global Problem' (2005) 11 *International Trade Law Review* 24.
[123] UN Corruption Convention, chapter II.
[124] UN Corruption Convention, chapter III.
[125] UN Corruption Convention, chapter IV.
[126] UN Corruption Convention, chapter V.

The Convention's methods for preventing corruption include the development of anti-corruption policies and the establishment of an anti-corruption agency. The Convention imposes a commitment on State parties to maintain an educated and well-trained civil service, and touches on measures necessary to establish transparent and competitive procurement systems as well as measures necessary to secure the integrity of the judiciary. In providing for the criminalisation of corruption, the Convention casts its net wide to include public sector corruption, the bribery of foreign public officials and officials of international organisations, private sector corruption, diversion of public funds, or *anything of value* entrusted to a public official. The Convention also criminalises trading in influence and private sector embezzlement.

In relation to international cooperation on corruption matters, the Convention calls for the mutual extradition of offenders, and extends the requirement of cooperation to include the transfer of sentenced persons or criminal proceedings from the territory of one State party to another, as well as the 'widest measure' of mutual legal assistance.

Under the asset recovery provisions of the Convention, State parties are enjoined to afford each other the widest measure of cooperation and assistance in detecting the existence of corruptly obtained proceeds and permitting each other to directly recover assets by means of civil action.

Unfortunately, the Convention's monitoring and compliance provisions are sadly lacking.[127] The Convention provides for a Conference of the State parties to the Convention,[128] which is aimed at improving 'the capacity of and cooperation between State Parties' to achieve the objectives of the Convention and review its implementation.

2.4 PUBLIC PROCUREMENT AND CORRUPTION

This section will discuss the susceptibility of public procurement to corruption, the kind of corrupt activity that occurs in public procurement and the particular measures that procurement regulation utilises in order to combat corruption to give an indication of how procurement-related anti-corruption measures overlap and impact each other.

2.4.1 The Incidence of Corruption in Public Procurement

From the above, it can be seen that most international anti-corruption conventions require the maintenance of transparent, competitive and efficient

[127] P Webb, 'The United Nations Convention Against Corruption: Global Achievement or Missed Opportunity?' (2005) 8 *Journal of International Economic Law* 191, 218.

[128] UN Corruption Convention, art 63.

procurement systems as part of the measures to address corruption. This is because public procurement as a sphere of government activity is one of the areas in which bureaucratic corruption manifests. Public procurement is susceptible to corruption[129] due partly to the large sums involved, the (usually) non-commercial nature of procuring entities, the nature of the relationship between the decision-maker and the public body,[130] the measures of unsupervised discretion, bureaucratic rules and budgets that may not be tied to specified goals as well as non-performance-related pay and low pay. Public procurement also presents the opportunity for corruption because of the asymmetry of information between the public official and his principal – ie the government. As the public official holds more information about the procurement process and the procurement market, the official is able to use this knowledge to his advantage by manipulating the procurement process, should he choose to do so.

The incidence of corruption within government procurement is well documented in Europe[131] and in economies where there is little regulation and non-transparency.[132]

2.4.2 The Common Types of Corrupt Activity in Public Procurement

Corruption is usually characterised from the standpoint of the public or the private sector. Similarly, procurement corruption can take the form of public or private corruption.[133] Public corruption is that which involves public officials and is generally that which moves from a private individual (the supplier) to the public official responsible for taking procurement decisions. This corruption will frequently take the form of bribes or other inducements granted to the public official to influence the exercise of his discretion. In public procurement, the public official may improperly

[129] Soreide, *Corruption in Public Procurement*, above n 34; Kelman, *Procurement and Public Management*, above n 49, ch 2; Anechiarico and Jacobs, *The Pursuit of Absolute Integrity*, above n 13, ch 8.

[130] European Parliament Directorate General for Research Working Paper, Measures to Prevent Corruption in EU Member States, Legal Affairs Series JURI 101 EN 03-1998, (Annex: Combating Corruption in Public Procurement Contracts).

[131] E Pontarollo, 'Regulatory Aspects and the Problem of Corruption in Public Procurement in Italy' (1995) 5 *Public Procurement Law Review* 201; I Hors, 'Shedding Light on Corrupt Practices in Public Procurement' (2003) 5 *Public Procurement Law Review* NA101.

[132] P Nichols, G Siedel and M Kasdin, 'Corruption as a Pan-Cultural Phenomenon: An Empirical Study in Countries at Opposite Ends of the Former Soviet Empire' (2004) 39 *Texas International Law Journal* 215; B Earle, 'Bribery and Corruption in Eastern Europe, the Baltic States and the Commonwealth of Independent States: What is to be done?' (2000) 33 *Cornell International Law Journal* 483; T Jingbin, 'Public Procurement in China: The way Forward' (2001) 4 *Public Procurement Law Review* 207; O Oko, 'Subverting the Scourge of Corruption in Nigeria: A Reform Prospectus' (2002) 34 *New York University Journal of Law and Politics* 397.

[133] V Key, 'Techniques of Political Graft' in A Heidenheimer, M Johnston and V LeVine (eds), *Political Corruption: A Handbook* (New Jersey, Transaction Publishers, 1989) 46–8.

exercise his discretion in deciding which firms to invite for tender, by emphasising or designing evaluation criteria that favours a preferred company[134] or by simply awarding the contract to a preferred company, in breach or in spite of rules on competitive procurement procedures. Improper exercises of discretion may also occur where a procurement official decides to split a large contract into several small contracts that fall below legislative thresholds for complying with certain procedural requirements,[135] so as to circumvent the requirement for publication of the tender in the required medium[136] in order to favour a preferred supplier. Other benefits that a supplier may seek include the avoidance of a government-imposed cost or requirement such as fees, taxes, or production of various documents.[137]

Another way in which public corruption manifests in public procurement is through auto-corruption. This type of public corruption may not always involve another individual and occurs when a public official wrongly secures for himself or an associate, the privileges which rightly belong to the public,[138] by bypassing or manipulating the formal procedures necessary for the award of these privileges.[139] This type of corruption might manifest where conflicts of interest[140] cause an official to corruptly favour the company in which he is interested,[141] or where an official uses a dummy corporation to hide awards involving personal interest. Public corruption is arguably the most pervasive type of corruption that occurs in public procurement[142] and is one reason behind the

[134] Rose-Ackerman, *Corruption and Government*, above n 9, 64; Soreide, *Corruption in Public Procurement*, above n 34, ch 3.

[135] Directive 2004/18/EC on the coordination of procedures for the award of public works contracts, public supply contracts and public service contracts [2004] OJ L134/114, arts 7 and 8 [hereafter PSD] and Directive 2004/17/EC coordinating the procurement procedures of entities operating in the water, energy, transport and postal services sectors 2004] OJ L134/1, arts 16 and 17 [hereafter UD].

[136] JP Bueb and N Ehlermann-Cache, 'Inventory of Mechanisms to Disguise Corruption in the Bidding Process and Some Tools for Prevention and Detection' in OECD (ed), *Fighting Corruption and Promoting Integrity in Public Procurement* (Paris, OECD, 2005).

[137] V Tanzi, 'Corruption Around the World: Causes, Consequences, Scope and Cures' (1998) 45(4) *IMF Staff Papers* 559.

[138] Key, 'Techniques of Political Graft', above n 133, 46–8. An example given by Tanzi, above is where a public official has a facility such as an airport built in his small hometown.

[139] From a broad definitional perspective, auto-corruption will include embezzlement.

[140] OECD, *Managing Conflicts of Interest in the Public Sector: A Toolkit* (Paris, OECD, 2001) 2; S Arrowsmith, J Linarelli and D Wallace, *Regulating Public Procurement: National and International Perspectives* (The Hague, Kluwer Law, 2000) 39–40.

[141] HJ Priess, 'Distortions of Competition in Tender Proceedings: How to deal with Conflicts of Interest (Family Ties, Business Links and Cross-Representation of Contracting Authority Officials and Bidders) and the Involvement of Project Consultants' (2002) 11 *Public Procurement Law Review* 153, 154–5.

[142] Measures to Prevent Corruption in EU Member States: Combating corruption in Public Procurement Contracts (European Parliament Directorate General for Research Legal Affairs Series Juri 101 EN 03-1998); Soreide, *Corruption in Public Procurement*, above n 34, ch 2.

criminalisation of the bribery of foreign public officials in the major anti-corruption instruments.

The second type of corruption that occurs in public procurement is private corruption, which manifests as collusion, price-fixing, maintenance of cartels or other uncompetitive practices committed by suppliers, which prevent the government from obtaining value for money.[143] While this kind of corruption falls outside the scope of this book, it is important to mention that they form a part of the activities that could be targeted under national or international procurement regulation.

2.4.3 Measures Used in Procurement Regulation to Fight Corruption

Most procurement regulation contains measures directed at preventing corruption in public procurement. These measures can again be divided into administrative, regulatory and social measures. The measures included in procurement legislation against corruption might not be explicitly directed at corruption, such as requirements for transparency,[144] open competition and increased accountability in government contracts,[145] but others might be directly concerned with ensuring that an environment exits where corruption cannot thrive. As was mentioned above, administrative measures are measures, which are permitted under the exercise of executive discretion; regulatory measures are obligatory measures, which must be imposed where corruption occurs and social measures encompass the societal ridicule, shame and infamy that may follow public revelations of corrupt activity. Again, the above categorizations are not exclusive and will frequently overlap.

2.4.3.1 Administrative measures

As mentioned above, administrative tools against corruption encompass discretionary measures implemented by a public official. In public procurement, these may include denying corrupt persons access to government contracts. Such denials may be temporary or permanent. Similar measures, which have the effect of denying access to government contracts, are those, which deny corrupt persons registration on qualifying lists for government contracts.[146]

Other administrative/ regulatory measures directed towards suppliers include the use of 'integrity pacts' or the extraction of a commitment from

[143] Klitgaard, *Controlling Corruption*, above n 3, ch 6.

[144] S Arrowsmith, *The Law of Public and Utilities Procurement*, 2nd edn (London, Sweet & Maxwell, 2005) ch 7.12.

[145] J Hansen, 'Limits of Competition: Accountability in Government Contracting' (2003) 112 *Yale Law Journal* 2465.

[146] Xanthaki, 'First Pillar Analysis', above n 45.

a supplier not to engage in corrupt activities, which is obtained during the procurement process. These might extend beyond a commitment not to bribe, and include commitments not to collude with competitors. Similar undertakings include those, which are currently utilised by the World Bank under which a bidder for a Bank-financed contract undertakes to comply with the Borrower country's anti-corruption legislation.[147]

In relation to public officials, administrative measures aimed at protecting the government against conflicts of interest are procedures, which provide for the rotation of officials to prevent the formation of corrupt relationships. Other administrative/regulatory measures include those requiring officials to declare their assets at the inception and termination of public office, and those requiring the disclosure of public officials business interests in order to ensure neutrality and impartiality.[148]

As mentioned above, other administrative measures against corruption include the creation of various approval mechanisms within a government agency. In public procurement, these may include requirements for various levels of approval before a public contract is awarded. Another administrative measure is the reliance on a division that ensures that prices paid by the government are fair and reflect market rates.

2.4.3.2 *Regulatory measures*

Regulatory measures against corruption in procurement regulation are those, which are mandatorily imposed through legislation. In public procurement, the most obvious of these are criminal sanctions for bribes. Although the prohibitions against bribery may not be situated within the procurement legislation, it is usually a criminal offence for a public official to accept bribes or other inducements in the exercise of his public function. The prohibition against bribery is frequently accompanied by severe punishments including custodial sentences.

As mentioned above, conflicts of interest may frequently be targeted through administrative procedures, but it is not uncommon for legislative intervention to exist to prevent such conflicts.[149] Such legislation may require the official with an interest in the contract to disclose such an interest as soon as possible and take no part in the contract award procedure.[150]

[147] Guidelines: Procurement for Goods, Works and non-consulting services under IBRD Loans and IDA Credits and Grants by World Bank Borrowers (Jan. 2011), para 1.17 [hereafter BPG].

[148] Priess, 'Distortions of Competition in Tender Proceedings', above n 141, 156; *Fairclough Building Ltd. v Borough Council of Port Talbot* (1992) 62 BLR 86.

[149] Priess, 'Distortions of Competition in Tender Proceedings', above n 141; Arrowsmith, Linarelli and Wallace, *Regulating Public Procurement*, above n 140, ch 2.

[150] Local Government Act 1972 (UK), s 49(1); 18 USC 203 (US); Anechiarico and Jacobs, *The Pursuit of Absolute Integrity*, 50–53.

In relation to suppliers, mandatory legislative provisions which blacklist or disqualify from public contracts, suppliers who are seen as unethical or corrupt[151] and conversely, provisions which 'white-list' or grant access to public contracts to firms who can prove they meet minimum ethical requirements and have sound internal management practices are some of the measures which could be integrated into procurement legislation.

It was stated above that there are other regulatory measures, which are not solely directed towards corruption in procurement but serve to create an environment where corruption cannot thrive. These include the requirements for procurement transparency, open competition and best value. Transparency in public procurement is often touted as one of the goals of a procurement system,[152] and is usually a mandatory requirement in regulated procurement systems.[153] Transparency suggests that the procurement procedure is conducted in an open and impartial manner and that the parties to the process are aware of information on specific procurements[154] and that all participants in the process are subject to the rules applicable to the process. According to Arrowsmith, transparency also includes the presence of rules-based decision making that limits discretion which may prevent concealed discrimination.[155] As unjustified or illegal discrimination is at the heart of corruption in public procurement, it is clear that a transparent procurement system can prevent corruption where the rules that define the procurement process and the opportunities for contracting are publicly available and applied, making it difficult to conceal improper practices.[156]

The requirement for open competition[157] is also one of the pillars of a developed procurement system.[158] Open competition supports anti-corruption efforts by ensuring that all qualified suppliers have access to available contracts and limits the scope for corruption-induced favouritism. Open competition removes the restriction to participation created against non-corrupt suppliers and is supported by a transparent regime.

Best value is the third regulatory obligation, which may support anti-corruption measures. Best value, also termed 'value for money' is a policy

[151] PSD, art 45.

[152] Case C-324/98 *Telaustria Verlags GmbH and Telefonadress GmbH v Telekom Austria* [2000] ECR I-10745, paras 60 and 61, as well as being an express obligation on contracting authorities. PSD, art 2. See also S Schooner, 'Desiderata: Objectives for a System of Government Contract Law' (2002) 11 *Public Procurement Law Review* 103, 105; M Kinsey, 'Transparency in Government Procurement: An International Consensus' (2004) 34 *Public Contract Law Journal* 155.

[153] PSD, art 2.

[154] S Arrowsmith, 'Towards a Multilateral Agreement on Transparency in Government Procurement' (1998) *International and Comparative Law Quarterly* 793, 796.

[155] Arrowsmith, *Public and Utilities Procurement*, above n 144, ch 3.9.

[156] Arrowsmith, *Public and Utilities Procurement*, above n 144, ch 3 and ch 7.12.

[157] See US Competition in Contracting Act, 1984 Pub L No 98-369; Recital 2, PSD; Arrowsmith, *Public and Utilities Procurement*, above n 144, ch 3.10.

[158] Schooner, 'Desiderata', above n 152, 105.

goal to obtain the best bargain with the public's money.[159] Best value is not synonymous with lowest price as quality or life-cycle considerations may mean the cheapest products do not necessarily provide the best value. Best value can be achieved through the other regulatory provisions discussed above. For instance, the requirement for competition supports best value as a competitive environment ensures that the government has a 'pool' of suppliers to choose from and will pay a competitive price and avoid monopolistic prices.[160] Transparency also supports best value by promoting open competition and making it clear when the government has not obtained value for money. The relationship between best value and anti-corruption provisions is that where contracts are awarded as a result of corrupt activity, this will have adverse implications for best value, since corruption stifles competition and the costs of corruption may be passed onto the government. However, it should be noted that in some cases, there could be conflict between the requirements for best value and anti-corruption measures. This may occur where anti-corruption mechanisms are expensive to implement and cause transactional inefficiencies in the procurement process.[161]

2.4.3.3 *Social measures*

As discussed above, social measures are rarely used as the primary tools against corruption. In public procurement regulation, social tools may attend the use of administrative and regulatory measures. For instance, where a supplier has been convicted of, or otherwise involved in corruption, the infamy that results from such a conviction where it is published in the media will frequently lead to a loss of business and may in some cases signal the end for that company. Likewise, where a firm is disqualified from public contracts as a result of corruption, such a firm may find that its tarnished reputation makes it difficult for it to obtain business elsewhere.[162]

[159] Schooner, 'Desiderata', above n 152, 108.

[160] A Beviglia- Zampetti, 'The UNCITRAL Model Law on Procurement of Goods, Construction, Services' in B Hoekman and P Mavrodis (eds), *Law and Policy in Public Purchasing: The WTO Agreement on Government Procurement* (Michigan, University of Michigan Press, 1997) ch 15.

[161] Anechiarico and Jacobs, 'Purging Corruption from Public Contracting', 143; Schooner, 'Desiderata', above n 152, 108; Arrowsmith, Linarelli and Wallace, *Regulating Public Procurement*, above n 140, 28–31.

[162] T Canni, 'Shoot First, Ask Questions Later: An Examination and Critique of Suspension and Debarment Provisions under the FAR, Including a Discussion of the Mandatory Disclosure Rule, the IBM Suspension and other Noteworthy Developments' (2009) 38 *Public Contract Law Journal* 547, 603; *Gonzalez v Freeman*, above n 52.

2.5 THE USE OF DISQUALIFICATIONS IN PUBLIC PROCUREMENT

Government suppliers may be denied access to public contracts for committing various infringements or offences. Such measures are variously referred to as disqualification, debarment, exclusion, suspension, rejection or blacklisting. These terms may be used interchangeably, with their meanings dependent on the jurisdiction in which they are being used.[163] Such measures are defined by Schooner as administrative remedies available to a government that prevent suppliers from obtaining new government contracts, or acquiring extensions to existing contracts, for alleged breaches of law or ethics.[164]

This book will use the jurisdiction-neutral term 'disqualification' to refer to the measures discussed in this book. First, the term will refer to measures, which deny a supplier access to public contracts for a set period of time. Disqualifications which apply for a set period of time are used in most jurisdictions and may apply to a wide range of offences or behaviour, which may not be related to a particular procurement, such as corruption, organised crime, drug offences, money laundering, fraud and tax offences. Because such disqualifications affect a supplier for a specified period of time, they are also described as being general or not being contract-specific, since the effect of the measure is not limited to one contract.

Second, the term 'disqualification' will be used to refer to the one-off exclusion of a supplier from a particular procurement process, without any implications beyond that particular procurement process. This kind of disqualification is contract specific, in the sense that the measure is directed at one particular contract. In the jurisdictions under study, this kind of disqualification is normally, but not exclusively used to deny a supplier access to a contract for offences committed in relation to the particular procurement process. However such disqualifications may also apply to offences or issues that are not related to the particular procurement. This may include where the supplier is unable to meet financial or technical criteria or where the supplier's past professional integrity is in question, which may point to its being unable to satisfactorily perform the contract.

In some cases, a supplier may be disqualified from a particular contract as the procuring authority implements a general disqualification decision taken against the supplier by another entity. This is the case in jurisdictions such as the US, the World Bank and South Africa where lists of

[163] For instance, the US and the World Bank refer to disqualifications as 'debarments' or 'suspension' depending on the length of the disqualification. In the EU, the terminology is 'exclusion' or 'blacklisting'.

[164] S Schooner, 'The Paper Tiger Stirs: Rethinking Exclusion and Debarment' (2004) 5 *Public Procurement Law Review* 211, 212–13.

suppliers disqualified for a period of time are available for perusal by procuring authorities to ensure contracts are not awarded to such disqualified suppliers. It is also possible for the legislation to require the disqualification of certain persons and procuring authorities implement this requirement in particular contracts as is the case in the EU/UK.

The term disqualification is used to refer to both kinds of measures in this book as they only differ in relation to their consequences and time limits.

Disqualification may be mandatory or discretionary. A mandatory measure is one in which the legislation or policy *requires* the disqualification of a supplier once the supplier has committed a specified offence. Here, the disqualifying entity does not have a discretion not to impose the measure, but may still retain a discretion in relation to some aspects in implementing the measure such as determining whether the offence was committed (where the measure is not based on a conviction), the length of the disqualification and which persons should be disqualified.

A discretionary measure is a measure where there is a general rule that suppliers who have committed certain offences may be disqualified, but the disqualifying entity retains the discretion in deciding whether the measure is appropriate in any case and retains discretion to decide all aspects in relation to implementing the measure. The distinction between a mandatory and a discretionary measure lies in the nature of and the limits to the discretion of the disqualifying entity.

There are different ways in which a measure may fall to be described as mandatory or discretionary. First, a measure may be mandatory because the law requires that all suppliers who have committed the offence must be disqualified for a stated period of time or a general disqualification measure imposed by a central authority must be implemented by individual procuring authorities. This is the approach under the South African regulations and in the World Bank. It should be noted that a measure may be referred to as being mandatory, but is in reality discretionary in its operation because although the legislation *requires* the disqualification of suppliers from public contracts for certain offences, individual procuring authorities may exercise a measure of discretion in deciding whether to utilise 'public interest' exceptions to award a contract to a convicted/guilty supplier. This is the situation in the EU/UK, where the provisions are referred to in the literature and in this book as being mandatory, although the provisions allow procuring authorities the discretion to utilise limited public interest derogations to circumvent the disqualification provisions.

Second, a measure may be discretionary because the law provides that suppliers who have committed certain offences may be denied access to contracts for a stated period of time. Third, a measure will also be regarded as discretionary where the legislation gives a central entity the discretion to disqualify a supplier for an offence, and once this is done, individual contracting authorities also have discretion to disqualify that supplier from particular procurements. This approach is found within the EU/UK and the US.

Whether a measure is regarded as mandatory or discretionary will depend on legislative provisions and the degree of discretion left to the disqualifying entity.

Disqualification measures may be triggered by three situations. First, they may be implemented for past violations of law, ethics or anti-corruption norms that may be unrelated to public procurement.[165] This is the approach adopted by the US, the EU, the UK and the World Bank. Thus, as will be seen in chapters 3 and 4, in the US, a supplier could be disqualified from contracts if he has obtained a conviction or a civil judgment for embezzlement, theft, forgery, bribery, falsification of records, tax evasion and receiving stolen property.[166] Likewise, the EU and the UK require contracting authorities to disqualify from public contracts, suppliers who have been convicted of corruption, participating in a criminal organisation, fraud or money laundering.[167]

Secondly, disqualification could be used to deny a supplier access to a particular procurement for a breach of the rules of that process. This type of disqualification is permitted in South Africa and under World Bank guidelines, wherein if a supplier acted corruptly during a procurement process, he is excluded from further participating in the process.[168]

Thirdly, a supplier could be disqualified from future contracts for past procurement violations. This type of disqualification is utilised by the US, the World Bank and South Africa.

There are several rationales behind the use of disqualifications in public procurement. First, disqualifications which target general (or non-procurement) violations such as corruption may support the anti-corruption policies of government and can be viewed as a political statement[169] that indicates a government's lack of tolerance for corruption.[170] However, anti-corruption policies are not the only policies that disqualification may support, and disqualification may support a government's tax, competition, social security and environmental policies.[171] This rationale will be referred to as the policy rationale.

[165] The use of procurement regulations to disqualify suppliers for non-procurement related improprieties has been criticized. See C Yukins, 'Suspension and Debarment: Rethinking the Process' (2004) 5 *Public Procurement Law Review* 255, 256.

[166] Federal Acquisition Regulations 9.406-2 [hereafter FAR].

[167] PSD, art 45.

[168] BPG, para 1.16(b).

[169] S Schooner, 'Suspensions are Just a Sideshow' (1 May 2002) available at www.govexec.com .

[170] Schooner, 'The Paper Tiger Stirs', above n 164, 216.

[171] S Arrowsmith, HJ Priess and P Friton, 'Self-Cleaning – An Emerging Concept in EC Procurement Law?' in H Punder, HJ Priess and S Arrowsmith, *Self-Cleaning in Public Procurement Law* (Koln, Carl Heymanns Verlag, 2009).

Secondly, disqualification could be punitive,[172] and may act as a deterrent against breaches of anti-corruption legislation by increasing the economic costs of corruption, because in addition to the immediate detrimental financial effect on the disqualified supplier, the disqualification can damage the reputation of the firm, affecting its ability to obtain business from other sectors.[173] This is one of the attractions of disqualification as an anti-corruption tool – the attendant infamy entails a more severe and lasting impact, especially where the disqualification is published. Disqualification may be regarded as punitive if it is tied to the objectives of deterrence or retribution, and is imposed as a result of the suppliers past conduct, without regard to his present integrity.[174] This will be referred to as the punitive and deterrent rationale.

Thirdly, disqualification could be directed towards maintaining the integrity of the procurement process and protect the government by ensuring it only transacts with responsible suppliers, thereby safeguarding public funds as contracting authorities are prevented from entering into business with an unreliable supplier, evidenced by that supplier's lack of business integrity. This will be referred to as the protective rationale.

There are two issues related to the rationale for disqualification in a jurisdiction that are not addressed by the legislation requiring disqualification in any of the jurisdictions. The first is whether and to what extent disqualification offends the rule against double jeopardy, especially where disqualification follows the receipt of a conviction for an offence and the second is whether disqualification is ever disproportionate to the purpose behind the disqualification regime.

In relation to the rule against double jeopardy, all the selected jurisdictions have similar prohibitions against multiple punishments for the same offence. In the EU, this rule (*ne bis in idem*) is a fundamental aspect of EU law[175] and where there is

> the threefold condition of identity of the facts, unity of offender and unity of the legal interest protected . . . the same person cannot be sanctioned more than once for a single unlawful course of conduct designed to protect the same legal asset.[176]

[172] Arrowsmith, Priess and Frtiton, 'Self-Cleaning', ibid. See also R Kramer, 'Awarding Contracts to Suspended and Debarred Firms: Are Stricter Rules Necessary?' (2005) 34 *Public Contract Law Journal* 539, 543.

[173] A Schutz, 'Too Little Too Late: An Analysis of the General Service Administration's Proposed Debarment of WorldCom' (2004) 56 *Administrative Law Review* 1263.

[174] E Tomko and K Weinberg, 'After the Fall: Conviction, Debarment and Double Jeopardy' (1992) 21 *Public Contract Law Journal* 355, 363–5.

[175] Case R-18/65 *Gutmann v Commission of the European Atomic Energy Community* [1966] ECR 135; Convention for the Protection of Human Rights and Fundamental Freedoms (European Convention on Human Rights) 231 UNTS 222, Protocol 7, art 4.

[176] Case C-204/00P *Aalborg Portland A/S v Commission* [2004] ECR I-123 para 338.

Thus, it is possible to argue that a disqualification following a conviction may amount to more than one sanction for the same offence. However, in *Tokai Carbon*[177] the claimant challenged its prosecution in the EU on the basis that it had already been prosecuted in the US and Canada for the same price-fixing offence and this would offend the double jeopardy rule. The Court of First Instance held that the *ne bis in idem* principle did not apply in the circumstances, as

> the procedures conducted and penalties imposed by the Commission on the one hand and the United States and Canadian authorities on the other clearly did not pursue the same ends. The aim of the first was to preserve undistorted competition within the European Union or the EEA, whereas the aim of the second was to protect the United States or the Canadian market . . . The application of the principle *ne bis in idem* is subject not only to the infringements and the persons sanctioned being the same, but also to the unity of the legal right being protected.[178]

By way of analogy, it may be the case that disqualification may not offend the rule against double jeopardy in the EU, because, as is discussed in chapter three, the policy and protective purpose behind disqualification in the EU differ from the retributive/deterrent purpose behind criminal convictions.

The UK also adopts a common law[179] prohibition against being tried or punished for the same offence more than once, subject to the Criminal Justice Act 2003, which relaxes the rule in relation to specified serious crimes. In *Borders (UK) v Commissioner of Police of the Metropolis*,[180] it was held that where punitive damages had been awarded against the respondent in addition to a confiscation order, this did not offend the double jeopardy rule as 'there was no duplication of penalty'.[181] Although the decision in this case has been criticised,[182] it suggests, similar to the EU approach, that where multiple penalties for the same offence do not have the same purpose, there may be no breach of the double jeopardy rule. Thus, it is again possible to argue that a mandatory disqualification following a conviction may not strictly offend the double jeopardy rule since the policy rationale for disqualification in the UK differs from the rationales for criminal penalties.[183]

177 Case T-236/01 *Tokai Carbon Co Ltd v Commission* [2004] ECR II-1181.

178 *Tokai Carbon*, ibid, para 134.

179 W Blackstone, *Commentaries on the Laws of England* Book IV (1800) ch 26, 355–56; Law Commission: *Double Jeopardy- A summary* (Consultation Paper 156, 2001).

180 *Borders (UK) v Commissioner of Police of the Metropolis* [2005] EWCA Civ 197.

181 *Borders (UK)*, para17.

182 R Cunnington, 'The border between Compensation, Restitution and Punishment' (2006) *Law Quarterly Review* 382.

183 L Zaibert, *Punishment and Retribution* (Aldershot, Ashgate, 2006) chs 1–3; D Golash, *Case Against Punishment: Retribution, Crime Prevention and the Law* (New York, New York University Press, 2005) chs 1, 2 and 7; S Easton and C Piper, *Sentencing and Punishment: The Quest for Justice*, 2nd edn (Oxford, Oxford University Press, 2008).

A similar approach is adopted by the US[184] and the scope of the rule against double jeopardy extends to a prohibition against multiple punishments for the same offence.[185] Thus, where a supplier has been convicted and disqualified it is possible to argue that in reality, the supplier is faced with multiple punishments for the same offence – even if the disqualification is not intended to be punitive.[186] The court in *US v Halper* held that

> a defendant who had already been punished in a criminal prosecution may not be subjected to an additional civil sanction to the extent that the second sanction may not be fairly characterised as remedial, but only as a deterrent or retribution.[187]

Thus, since the purpose of disqualification in the US is protective and not remedial, it may be the case that disqualification offends the rule against double jeopardy. On the other hand, the courts have also held that if an action (such as disqualification) which appears to be punitive is related to a legitimate non-punitive goal,[188] such as the protection of public finances or maintaining the integrity of the procurement process,[189] then the action will not be regarded as punitive so as to offend the double jeopardy rule.

Similar to the other jurisdictions, South African law also recognises a rule against double jeopardy in the criminal and civil contexts. In the employment context, it has been held that an employee may not be dismissed or further sanctioned for an offence for which the employee has already been punished or acquitted.[190] If this approach is carried into the procurement context, it is arguable that a supplier ought not to be further sanctioned by disqualification under South African procurement law if the supplier has already been convicted for corruption. However, in South Africa, the judicial disqualifications under the Corruption Act may not offend the rule against double jeopardy because the double jeopardy rule does not 'limit legislative authority to define punishment'.[191] As such, a disqualification order imposed alongside other criminal penalties by a court may not amount to a multiple punishment so as to offend the rule against double jeopardy, as the rule cannot be used to limit the sentences in a single trial.[192]

[184] G Thomas, *Double Jeopardy: The History, The Law* (New York, New York University Press, 1998) chs 1 and 2.

[185] *United States v Halper* 490 US 435 (1989). See however, A Bowen Poulin, 'Double Jeopardy and Multiple Punishment: Cutting the Gordian Knot' (2006) 77 *University of Colorado Law Review* 595.

[186] In *Halper*, ibid at 448, it was held that civil sanctions may constitute a punishment for the purposes of the double jeopardy rule.

[187] *Halper*, ibid.

[188] *Bell v Wolfish*, 441 US 520, 539 (1979).

[189] *Brown Constr Trades v US* 23 Cl Ct 214 (1991).

[190] *BMW (SA) (Pty) Ltd v Van Der Walt* (2000) 21 ILJ 113 (LAC); *SA Transport and Allied Workers Union on behalf of Finca v Old Mutual Life Assurance Co (SA) Ltd & Another* (2006) 27 ILJ 1204 (LC).

[191] Bowen Poulin, 'Double Jeopardy', above n 185, 597.

[192] Bowen Poulin, ibid, 598.

Whether a jurisdiction is under an obligation to consider the disproportionate effect of disqualification on a supplier is also tied to the rationales for disqualification in that jurisdiction. However, none of the selected jurisdictions address this issue, as will be discussed further in chapter nine in the context of the termination of existing contracts for disqualification. In the context of the EU, it was held in *Michaniki* that in accordance with the principle of proportionality, a disqualification regime must not go beyond what is necessary to achieve its objectives.[193]

It is thus suggested that even where disqualification is held not to offend the double jeopardy rule, the disproportionate effect of disqualification on a supplier should mean that disqualification should only be utilised where it is absolutely necessary to fulfil policy objectives that were not met by the conviction, where relevant.

The use of disqualification as an anti-corruption tool in public procurement raises several practical and conceptual difficulties, many of which will be examined in this book. In spite of the difficulties attending the use of disqualifications, however, there appears to be no sign that it will be rejected as an anti-corruption tool, partly because it is attractive to governments as the costs of the action are hidden within the procurement process, and the decision to include anti-corruption measures such as disqualification within procurement criteria may sometimes be made without domestic legislative approval.[194] Further, the use of disqualification as an anti-corruption device in public procurement is on the increase and disqualification is now a part of some international instruments. For example, the revised WTO GPA text recommends the disqualification of suppliers who have committed serious offences or show a lack of commercial integrity[195] and the OECD Revised Recommendation on Combating Bribery in International Business Transactions[196] recommends that OECD Members should disqualify firms that have bribed a foreign public official from participating in domestic public contracts.[197]

[193] Case C-213/07 *Michaniki AE v Ethniko Simvoulio Radiotileorasis* [2008] ECR I-9999, paras 47–49; *Michaniki AE* [2008] ECR I-9999, Opinion of AG Maduro, para 34; Case C-21/03 and C-34/03 *Fabricom South Africa v Etat Belge* [2005] ECR I-1559, para 34.

[194] Arrowsmith, *Public and Utilities Procurement*, above n 144, ch 19.3.

[195] Government Procurement Agreement, art VIII(3).

[196] 36 ILM 1016 (1997).

[197] OECD Revised Recommendation on Combating Bribery in International Business Transactions, art VI(ii).

3

An Overview of Procurement Regulation, Anti-Corruption and Disqualification Policy in the Jurisdictions

3.1 INTRODUCTION

THIS CHAPTER WILL give a brief introduction to public procurement regulation in the jurisdictions under study, examine their anti-corruption policies and outline the approaches to and the purpose behind disqualification in those jurisdictions.

3.2 THE EUROPEAN UNION

3.2.1 Public Procurement Regulation in the EU

The EU is a complex organisation that 'houses' what was previously referred to as the European Communities. These Communities were the European Coal and Steel Community (ECSC), which was created by a 1951 treaty that expired in 2002; the European Atomic Energy Community (EURATOM) and the European Economic Community (EEC), which was renamed the European Community (EC) in 1993, both of which entered into existence in 1958.[1] The initial goal of the EC was to establish a common market and an economic and monetary union amongst Member States. The EU was created by the Treaty of Maastricht[2] in 1992 to bring about closer integration amongst Member States. It added new fields of activity to the existing Communities but did not replace them. In 2007, however, the Treaty of Lisbon was passed in which the EU replaced and became the successor to the EC and together with EURATOM constitutes

[1] See generally, P Craig and G de Burca, *EU Law: Text, Cases and Materials*, 4th edn (Oxford, Oxford University Press, 2007).

[2] [1993] OJ L293/61.

the 'first pillar' of the EU's organisational structure under the umbrella of the EU.[3] The Treaty of Lisbon entered into force in December 2009.[4]

The EU has regulated public procurement in Member States since 1964.[5] In 1971 and 1977, two directives were passed to coordinate the public procurement of public works and public supplies.[6] Member States were required to implement the directives into national law and in doing so, prevent discrimination in public procurement.[7] However, the lack of proper implementation meant the directives were not achieving their purpose,[8] and the Commission proposed to extend and amend the directives. The existing directives were initially amended[9] and later, new directives were adopted to consolidate the existing legislation[10] and incorporate the utility sector into the procurement regime,[11] as well as to provide enforcement legislation for the breach of the procurement directives.[12] Increasingly, the obligations in the directives have become stricter, diminishing Member States'

[3] S Arrowsmith (ed), *EU Public Procurement Law: An Introduction* (Asia Link Text, 2010) ch 1.

[4] Treaty of Lisbon, amending the Treaty on European Union and the Treaty establishing the European Community [2007] OJ C306/1 [hereafter Treaty on the Functioning of the European Union (TFEU)].

[5] Council Directive 64/427/EEC of 7 July 1964 [1964] OJ 117/1863; Council Directive 64/428/EEC of 7 July 1964 [1964] OJ 117/1871 and Council Directive 64/429/EEC of 7 July 1964 [1964] OJ 117/1880; P Trepte, *Public Procurement in the EU: A Practitioner's Guide*, 2nd edn (Oxford, Oxford University Press, 2007) ch 1; F Weiss, *Public Procurement in the European Community* (London, Athlone Press, 1993) ch 1; F Martin, *The EC Procurement Rules: A Critical Analysis* (Oxford, Clarendon Press, 1996) ch 1.

[6] Council Directive 71/305/EEC concerning the coordination of procedures for the award of public works contracts [1971] OJ L185/5; Council Directive 77/62/EEC coordinating the procedures for the award of public supply contracts [1977] OJ L13/1.

[7] Directive 71/305, recital 2; Case C-31/87 *Beentjes* [1988] ECR 4635, 4657. See M Trybus, 'Improving the Efficiency of Public Procurement Systems in the Context of the European Union Enlargement Process' (2006) 35 *Public Contract Law Journal* 409–15.

[8] White Paper on Completing the Internal Market COM (1985) 310 final; WS Atkins Consultants, 'The Cost of Non-Europe in public sector procurement' in *The cost of non-Europe, Basic findings*, vol 5, (1988).

[9] Council Directive 89/440/EEC amending Directive 71/305/EEC concerning the coordination of procedures for the award of public works contracts [1989] OJ L210/1 and Directive 88/295/EEC amending Directive 77/62/EEC relating to the coordination of procedures on the award of public supply contracts [1988] OJ L127/1.

[10] Council Directive 93/36/EEC coordinating procedures for the award of public supply contracts [1993] OJ L199/1; Council Directive 93/37/EEC concerning the coordination of procedures for the award of public works contracts [1993] OJ L199/54; Council Directive 92/50/EEC relating to the coordination of procedures relating to the award of public service contracts [1992] OJ L209/1.

[11] Directive 90/531 on the procurement procedures of entities operating in the water, energy, transport and telecommunications sectors [1990] OJ L297/1 as amended by Council Directive 93/38/EEC coordinating the procurement procedures of entities operating in the water, energy, transport and telecommunications sectors [1993] OJ L199/84.

[12] Council Directive 89/665/EEC on the coordination of laws, regulations and administrative provisions relating to the application of review procedures to the award of public supply and public works contracts [1989] OJ L395/33, Council Directive 92/13/EEC coordinating the laws, regulations and administrative provisions relating to the application of Community rules on the procurement procedures of entities operating in the water, energy, transport and telecommunications sectors [1992] OJ L76/14.

discretion in relation to domestic procurement procedures and policy.[13] The main aim of EU procurement regulation is to create an internal market by prohibiting discrimination between Member States in awarding government contracts, removing restrictions on access to those markets, and providing for transparency in contract award procedures to ensure that discriminatory practices cannot be concealed.[14] EU regulation of public procurement thus aims to secure the non-discrimination provisions of the Treaty.[15]

In 2004, the EU adopted two new procurement directives, namely Directive 2004/18/EC on the coordination of procedures for the award of public works contracts, public supply contracts and public service contracts[16] and Directive 2004/17/EC coordinating the procurement procedures of entities operating in the water, energy, transport and postal services sectors.[17] These are the directives currently in force, which will be examined in this book.

The aims of the directives were to modernise the legislation in response to recent procurement developments[18] and simplify the regime by consolidating the rules on the public sector (previously contained in three separate directives) into a single instrument, which Member States had to implement by 31 January 2006.[19] Member States had to amend existing legislation or pass new legislation to comply with the directives. The major changes introduced by the directives include a general exemption from the rules applicable to utilities for entities which operate in competitive markets, reflecting the liberalisation of that sector[20] and the introduction of new award procedures,[21] providing greater flexibility in relation to complex contracts and electronic procurement.

Further changes to the EU's procurement directives are likely in the near future as in January 2011, the European Commission issued a Green Paper calling for consultations on various aspects of EU procurement

[13] Arrowsmith, *The Law of Public and Utilities Procurement*, 2nd edn (London, Sweet & Maxwell, 2005) 133; S Arrowsmith, 'The Past and Future Evolution of EC Procurement Law: From framework to Common Code?' (2006) 35 *Public Contract Law Journal* 337, 352–3.

[14] Arrowsmith, 'The Past and Future Evolution of EC Procurement Law', above n 13, 337.

[15] Arts 18, 28, 34, 49 TFEU.

[16] [2004] OJ L134/114.

[17] [2004] OJ L 134/1; Arrowsmith, *Public and Utilities Procurement*, above n 13, chs 15 and 16.

[18] S Arrowsmith, 'An Assessment of the New Legislative Package on Public Procurement' (2004) 41 *Common Market Law Review* 1277, 1278.

[19] Public Sector Directive, art 80; Utilities Directive, art 71. M Trybus and T Medina, 'Unfinished Business: The State of Implementation of the new EC Public Procurement Directives in the Member States on February 1, 2007' (2007) 16 *Public Procurement Law Review* NA89.

[20] UD, art 30(1).

[21] Competitive dialogue in PSD, art 29; framework contracts in PSD, art 32 and UD, art 14; electronic auctions in PSD, art 54 and UD, art 56; dynamic purchasing systems in PDS, art 33 and UD, art 15.

policy.[22] The main thrust of the Green Paper is to support the Europe 2020 Strategy and in the light of global financial constraints, seek the more efficient use of public funds. The Green Paper seeks to do this by making and seeking recommendations to update and simplify EU procurement legislation and further permit procurement to be used in support of other policies.

As is usually the case with procurement reform, the Green Paper is not without an anti-corruption element. The Green Paper proposes measures to prohibit conflicts of interest – an area that had not previously been addressed by the procurement directives – and measures increasing transparency to prevent corruption in the procurement process and providing reporting/whistleblower mechanisms. In relation to disqualification measures, the Green Paper also contemplates clarifying and expanding the grounds for disqualification as well as providing uniform rules on the rehabilitation of corrupt suppliers (also referred to as 'self-cleaning' measures).

It is expected that the consultations on the Green Paper will lead to legislative proposals in 2012.

3.2.2 The EU's Policy Against Corruption

The EU's anti-corruption programme gained momentum in the last two decades, in parallel with increasingly firm international action against corruption. EU policy on corruption has three interrelated but distinct objectives. Initially, the policy was directed at protecting Union finances,[23] in partial response to the corruption that appeared to characterise EU institutions.[24] However, corruption control has expanded in scope and is now an integral part of EU internal and external trade policies, and countries which obtain aid or trade concessions from the EU must undertake domestic anti-corruption reform.[25]

[22] European Commission, Green Paper on the Modernisation of EU Public Procurement Policy: Towards a more efficient EU procurement market, 27 January 2011 COM(2011) 15 final.

[23] TFEU, art 325; Convention drawn up on the basis of Art K.3 of the Treaty of the European Union on the Protection of the European Communities' Financial Interests [1995] OJ C316/48 and Protocols; Council Regulation (EC, Euratom) 2988/95 of 18 December 1995 on the Protection of the Communities' Financial Interests [1995] OJ L312/1.

[24] Committee of Independent Experts, First Report regarding allegations of fraud, mismanagement and nepotism in the European Commission, (15 March 1999).

[25] Cotonou Partnership Agreement 2000/483/EC [2000] OJ L317/3; Opinion of the Economic and Social committee on Development aid, good governance and the role of socio-economic interest groups [1997] OJ C287/4. See generally, P Szarek-Mason, 'The European Union Policy against Corruption in the Light of International Developments' in C Eckes and T Konstadinides (eds), *Crime within the Area of Freedom, Security and Justice: A European Public Order* (Cambridge, Cambridge University Press, 2011). See also P McAuslan, 'Good Governance and Aid in Africa' (1996) 40 *Journal of African Law* 168.

The second objective of EU anti-corruption policy is to provide EU citizens with a high level of safety in an area of freedom, security and justice, devoid of criminal activity, corruption, fraud, terrorism etc. The power to act against corruption is derived from Article 4 of the TFEU, under which the EU and Member States share competence over matters relating to freedom, security and justice. In addition, Article 67 of the TFEU places an obligation on the EU to ensure a high level of security through measures to combat crime and Article 83 of the TFEU gives the EU the power to establish minimum rules and sanctions in areas of serious crime with cross-border implications such as corruption. There has been a lot of legislative and non-legislative activity in the area of corruption and more recently, there is an initiative to monitor and evaluate anti-corruption efforts within the EU with the establishment of an EU Anti-Corruption Report, which will from 2013 monitor and report on Member States efforts to tackle corruption.[26]

The third rationale for EU anti-corruption measures relates to the liberalisation of the internal market,[27] and although there is no explicit Treaty provision linking the elimination of corruption to market integration, corruption is at variance with the principles of non-discrimination and free competition advocated by the single market.[28] The elimination of corruption facilitates competition by ensuring that corrupt practices do not interfere with the transparent and open conduct of trade.[29] In a free market, corruption might have cross-border implications,[30] leading to the 'contagion of corruption'[31] where Member States which would not normally condone corruption, do so, in order to compete for business with countries that ignore such practices. Corruption also increases the costs of economic activity thereby reducing the optimal use of resources in the EU.[32]

[26] Communication from the Commission to the Council, the European Parliament and the European Economic and Social Committee on a comprehensive EU policy against corruption COM (2003) 317 final; Commission Decision of 6.6.2011 establishing an EU anti-corruption reporting mechanism for periodic assessment COM(2011) 3673 final.

[27] Resolution on the Communication from the Commission to the Council and the European Parliament on a Union Policy against Corruption. [1998] OJ C328/46; Communication from the Commission to the European Parliament, the Council and the European Economic and Social Council on Fighting Corruption in the EU COM(2011) 308 final, para 4.

[28] L Ferola, 'Anti-Bribery Measures in the European Union: A Comparison with the Italian Legal Order' (2000) 28 *International Journal of Legal Information* 512; Joint Action 98/742/JHA of 22 December 1998 adopted by the Council on the basis of Article K.3 TEU on Corruption in the Private Sector [1998] OJ L358/2; Council Framework Decision 2003/568/JHA of 22 July 2003 on Combating Corruption in the private sector [2003] OJ L192/54.

[29] Ferola, 'Anti-Bribery Measures', above n 28, 515.

[30] Art 83 TFEU.

[31] G Caiden and O Dwivedi, 'Official Ethics and Corruption' in G Caiden (ed), *Where Corruption Lives* (Connecticut, Kumarian Press, 2001) 245.

[32] A Ades and R di Tella, 'Rents, Competition and Corruption' (1999) 89(4) *American Economic Review* 982; European Parliament, Committee on Civil Liberties and Internal Affairs, Economic and Political Corruption in Europe, Report on Combating Corruption in Europe Doc A4-0314/95.

The link between procurement regulation and EU anti-corruption goals takes the following form: first, the EU finances several large projects within and outside Europe and must protect its investments by ensuring the absence of corruption therein. Secondly, protecting EU finances and providing EU citizens with an area of freedom, security and justice necessitates a comprehensive policy targeting corruption in the sphere of public finance, including public procurement.[33] Thirdly, the adoption of measures to address corruption may be justified by the adverse impact that corruption may have on the internal market, as described above. In addition, because open public procurement may lead to increased opportunities for corruption, as corrupt elements may have access to the public procurement markets in other Member States[34] where they may not be known to be corrupt, the EU has an interest in ensuring that procurement regulation reduces the scope for corruption that may arise from opening up markets across borders.

3.2.3 Disqualification in the EU

The disqualification of suppliers from public contracts in the EU is not a new concept. EU procurement directives have historically contained provisions allowing Member States to exclude suppliers from public contracts for reasons ranging from legal violations to professional infringements.[35] The previous directives contained provisions giving Member States a measure of discretion in deciding whether or not to utilise disqualifications in public procurement in support of their own policies,[36] and also permitted Member States to disqualify a supplier who: was bankrupt or being wound up; had not fulfilled obligations in relation to social security and tax payments; was guilty of serious misrepresentation in the procurement context; or was convicted of an offence regarding his professional conduct.[37] This provided the possibility to disqualify a supplier for offences which might

[33] See Communication from the Commission to the Council, the European Parliament and the European Economic and Social Committee on a comprehensive EU policy against corruption COM (2003) 317 final, See generally Action Plan to Combat Organised Crime, Part II. [1997] OJ C251/1.

[34] C Stefanou, 'Databases as a Means of Combating Organised Crime within the EU' (2010) 17 *Journal of Financial Crime* 100.

[35] Council Directive 77/62/EEC coordinating the procedures for the award of public supply contracts [1977] OJ L13/1, art 20.

[36] Council Directive 93/36/EEC coordinating procedures for the award of public supply contracts [1993] OJ L199/1, art 20(1). The relevant provisions in the three previous public sector procurement directives are identical. See Council Directive 93/38/EEC coordinating the procurement procedures of entities operating in the water, energy, transport and telecommunications sectors [1993] OJ L199/84, art 31; E Piselli, 'The Scope for Excluding Providers who have Committed Criminal Offences under the EU Procurement Directives' (2000) 6 *Public Procurement Law Review* 267.

[37] Directive 93/36/EEC, art 20(1)(d).

have been related to his profession,[38] which may have included corruption offences, but could also have included breaches of offences relating to tax and social security liability, breaches of employment and immigration requirements and breaches of environmental legislation. The previous directives also permitted the disqualification of a supplier guilty of grave professional misconduct,[39] possibly permitting disqualification for corruption and other offences in the absence of a conviction,[40] and also permitting disqualification for breaches of professional norms. It should be noted that these provisions permit procuring authorities to disqualify suppliers both for past offences and possibly present offences or offences committed within the specific procurement process.

These provisions remain in essentially the same form in the current directives, which provide in Article 45(2) PSD that:

> Any economic operator may be excluded from participation in a contract where that economic operator:
>
> . . .
>
> (c) has been convicted by a judgment which has the force of res judicata in accordance with the legal provisions of the country of any offence concerning his professional conduct;
> (d) has been guilty of grave professional misconduct proven by any means which the contracting authorities can demonstrate . . .

The current directives took a novel approach to disqualification. Apart from retaining the options for Member States to disqualify suppliers at their discretion, discussed above,[41] the directives introduced a new element into the disqualification regime by making it *mandatory* for procuring authorities in the EU to disqualify from public contracts, firms convicted of various offences. Thus, the directives provide in Article 45(1) that:

> Any candidate or tenderer who has been the subject of a conviction by final judgment of which the contracting authority is aware for one or more of the reasons listed below shall be excluded from participation in a public contract:
>
> (a) participation in a criminal organisation as defined in Article 2(1) of Council Joint Action 98/733/JHA;
> (b) corruption, as defined in Article 3 of the Council Act of 26 May 1997 and Article 3 of Council Joint Action 98/742/JHA[42] respectively;

[38] Piselli, 'The Scope for Excluding Providers', above n 36, 272.

[39] Directive 93/36/EEC, art 20(1)(d).

[40] Case C-71/92 *Commission v Spain* [1993] ECR I-5923; HJ Priess and C Pitschas, 'Secondary Policy Criteria and their Compatibility with EC and WTO Procurement Law: The case of the German Scientology Declaration' (2000) 4 *Public Procurement Law Review* 171, 175.

[41] PSD, art 45(2) and UD, art 54(4).

[42] Council Joint Action 98/742/JHA has been repealed and replaced by Council Framework Decision 2003/568/JHA [2003] OJ L192/54.

(c) fraud within the meaning of Article 1 of the Convention relating to the protection of the financial interests of the European Communities;
(d) money laundering as defined in Article 1 of Council Directive 91/308/EEC of 10 June 1991 on prevention of the use of the financial system for the purpose of money laundering.[43]

Member states shall specify, in accordance with their national laws and having regard for Community law, the implementing conditions for this paragraph. They may provide for a derogation from the requirement referred to in the first subparagraph for overriding requirements in the general interest.

The provisions on disqualification fall into two categories – the discretionary disqualifications wherein procuring authorities are permitted to disqualify suppliers who are convicted or guilty of various professional infringements and the mandatory disqualifications where procuring authorities are *required* to disqualify suppliers who have been convicted of committing the listed offences. As was discussed in chapter two, although the disqualification provisions for serious criminal offences in the EU are referred to as being mandatory, the provisions give procuring authorities the discretion to utilise limited public interest exceptions in deciding not to apply the mandatory disqualifications.

The mandatory disqualifications for serious criminal offences are intended to support the EU's policy against crime. This policy is aimed at protecting the internal market from criminal activity and blocking the legal loopholes arising from the incongruities between the criminal justice systems of Member States, which are exploited by criminals.[44] Other aims of the policy are harmonisation and coherence in tackling criminal activity with a European dimension. This is especially relevant in the public procurement arena where the reduction of trade barriers may allow criminal elements access to the procurement systems of Member States.

The mandatory disqualification for corruption, and to an extent, the disqualifications for fraud, money laundering and organised crime support the EU's policy against corruption by strengthening the Union's 'arsenal of means' against corruption;[45] by protecting Union finances from corruption; preventing the adverse effect that corruption can have on the

[43] Council Directive 91/308/EEC on the prevention of the use of the financial system for the purpose of money laundering [1991] OJ L166/77, which is mentioned in Art 45(1)(d) PSD has been repealed and replaced by Council Directive 2005/60/EC on the Prevention of the use of the financial system for the purpose of money laundering and terrorist financing [2005] OJ L309/15.

[44] L Ferola, 'The Fight Against Organised Crime in Europe: Building an Area of Freedom, Security and Justice in the EU' (2002) 30 *International Journal of Legal Information* 53, 54; Communication from the Commission to the Council and the European Parliament, The prevention of crime in the European Union: Reflection on common guidelines and proposals for Community financial support COM(2000) 786 Final.

[45] Proposal for a Directive of the European Parliament and of the Council on the coordination of the procedures for the award of public supply contracts, public service contracts and public works contracts COM(2000) 275 final/2. Explanatory Memorandum, 33.

internal market and public procurement[46] – since corruption necessarily entails discrimination on unlawful grounds; preventing the cross-border corruption that can occur in liberalised markets; and protecting EU projects in Member States from corruption.[47]

From the above, it may be inferred that the rationales for disqualification in the EU appear to fall within both the policy and the protective rationales as discussed in chapter two, since these disqualifications support EU policy against serious crimes and protect the EU budget from being lost through corruption. As is discussed in the context of South Africa below, although disqualification in some jurisdictions is intended to be punitive, it has been argued by Arrowsmith et al that the disqualifications in the EU are not intended to have a punitive purpose.[48]

It should be noted that in the EU, the discretionary and the mandatory disqualifications are not tied to the ability of the contractor to perform,[49] and there are specific provisions which assess reliability by assessing the contractors financial standing,[50] technical or professional ability[51] and past contract performance.[52] In relation to criteria assessing reliability and capability, the EU directives provide that such criteria are relevant in so far as they relate to the contract.[53] Thus a procuring authority may not specify either qualification or award criteria that are unconnected with the contract[54] or are unconnected with the objectives sought to be achieved by the procuring authority.[55]

In relation to the discretionary and possibly the mandatory disqualifications, opinion is divided as to whether the disqualifications also serve the purpose of assessing the reliability of the supplier. In *La Cascina*, Advocate-General Maduro opined that discretionary exclusions in Italian law which excluded firms that had not complied with tax and social security obligations were intended to ensure the reliability and solvency of suppliers as well ensuring that a level playing field was maintained

[46] P Trepte, *Public Procurement in the EU: A Practitioner's Guide*, 2nd edn (Oxford, Oxford University Press, 2007) 338.

[47] S Williams, 'The Mandatory Exclusions for Corruption in the new EC Procurement Directives' (2006) 31 *European Law Review* 711.

[48] S Arrowsmith, HJ Priess and P Friton, 'Self-Cleaning- An Emerging Concept in EC Procurement Law?' in H Punder, HJ Priess and S Arrowsmith (eds), *Self-Cleaning in Public Procurement Law* (Koln, Carl Heymanns Verlag, 2009).

[49] S Arrowsmith, 'Application of the EC Treaty and Directives to Horizontal Policies: A Critical Review' in S Arrowsmith and P Kunzlik (eds), *Social and Environmental Policies in EC Procurement Law: New Directives and New Directions* (Cambridge, Cambridge University Press, 2009); HJ Priess, *European Public Procurement Law* (London, Informa, 2000) 44–5.

[50] PSD, art 47.

[51] PSD, art 48.

[52] PSD, art 48(2)(a)(i).

[53] PSD, art 44(2).

[54] Case C-513/99 *Concordia Bus Finland v Helsinki* [2002] ECR I-7213.

[55] Case C-448/01 *EVN and Wienstrom v Austria* [2003] ECR I-14527.

between suppliers.[56] This argument may also be made in relation to the mandatory disqualifications, as a supplier who has been convicted of corruption, fraud or money laundering may not be reliable.

It appears however, that the EU directives consider the disqualifications for the serious criminal offences as conceptually distinct from the other selection criteria, as Article 44(1) PSD provides for the checking of the performance (financial etc) criteria of those *who have not been excluded under the mandatory exclusions*.[57] Trepte also suggests that the disqualifications relate to 'eligibility' and not 'capability',[58] as conditions of eligibility do not depend on the ability of the contractor to perform the contract, since they determine whether or not the contractor may be permitted to bid for the contract regardless of his abilities.[59] His view is shared by Piselli, who asserts that exclusions for criminal convictions are not limited to the ability of the contractor to perform the contract, as if this were the case, the grounds for exclusion would have been incorporated into the provisions concerning financial and technical standing.[60]

If indeed the disqualifications for serious criminal offences represent a separate and independent category of qualification criteria, they do not need to be tied to the contractor's ability to perform and may legitimately be directed at achieving other objectives, such as protecting the EU from the cross-border effects of serious crime.

Finally, it should be mentioned that the offences for which the discretionary and the mandatory disqualifications may be imposed in the EU relate to general and procurement-related offences. A similar position obtains in the UK, the US and the World Bank, whilst South Africa disqualifies suppliers solely for procurement-related offences.

3.3 THE UNITED KINGDOM

3.3.1 Public Procurement Regulation in the UK

It is trite to say that EU Member States are under an obligation to implement EU legislation. As a result of this obligation, the UK's public procurement system has undergone several changes in response to the changing nature of EU regulation of public procurement. Traditionally, UK procurement was not regulated through a strict legal regime[61] and

[56] Case C-226/04 *La Cascina* [2006] ECR I-1347, Opinion of AG Maduro, para 24.

[57] Arrowsmith, *Public and Utilities Procurement*, above n 13, 748.

[58] P Trepte, *Regulating Procurement: Understanding the Ends and Means of Public Procurement Regulation* (Oxford, Oxford University Press 2004) 195, 317.

[59] Trepte, *Public Procurement in the EU*, above n 46, 321.

[60] Piselli, 'The Scope for Excluding Providers' above n 36, 273.

[61] C Turpin and P Brown, *Government Procurement and Contracts* (London, Longman, 1989) chs 1–4; P Vincent-Jones, *The New Public Contracting: Regulation. Responsiveness, Relationality*

informal direction on UK public procurement policy was the responsibility of the Treasury;[62] procurement being regulated mainly through administrative instruments.[63] However, since 1991, the UK has adopted a more formal approach to procurement regulation in response to increasingly stringent EU regulation on public procurement.[64]

Before the unification of procurement regulation brought about by the adoption and application of EU procurement instruments, procurement regulation in the UK occurred at the local and central government levels[65] and although there were differences in the regulation of procurement at these levels, the underlying principles remained similar.[66]

The formal regulation of public procurement at the local government level can be traced to the attempts by the Conservative Government of the time[67] to reduce the size of the public sector and introduce greater competition and efficiency into local government procurement.[68] This was done through an initiative known as Compulsory Competitive Tendering (CCT),[69] which was designed to ensure that local authorities would directly provide certain services only if they could do so competitively. Where this was not possible, local authorities were required to contract-out the provision of these services.[70] The CCT regime and implementing legislation[71] was repealed by the Labour Government, as it was found to be problematic, inflexible and created tension between suppliers and local authorities.[72] CCT was replaced with the Best Value initiative,[73] under which local author-

(Oxford, Oxford University Press, 2006) 13–16; Arrowsmith, *Public and Utilities Procurement*, above n 13, ch 2.

[62] Turpin and Brown, *Government Procurement*, above n 61, 61.

[63] S Arrowsmith, 'Implementation of the New EC Procurement Directives and the Alcatel Ruling in England and Wales and Northern Ireland: A Review of the New Legislation and Guidance' (2006) 3 *Public Procurement Law Review* 86, 89.

[64] See generally, M Trybus and P Craig, 'Public Contracts: England and Wales' in R Nogouellou and U Stelkens (eds), *Comparative Law on Public Contracts Treatise* (Brussels, Bruylant, 2010) 339.

[65] P Badcoe, 'Best Value–A New Approach in the UK' in S Arrowsmith and M Trybus (eds), *Public Procurement: The Continuing Revolution* (The Hague, Kluwer Law, 2003).

[66] Arrowsmith, *Public and Utilities Procurement*, above n 13, ch 2; P Badcoe, 'The National Procurement Strategy for Local Government' (2004) 6 *Public Procurement Law Review* NA181.

[67] 1979–97.

[68] Badoce, 'Best Value: A New Approach', above n 65, NA182.

[69] P Gosling, The effects of Compulsory Competitive Tendering and European Law on Local Authorities (The Hague, Kluwer Law, 2001) chs 1–3.

[70] P Badcoe, 'Best Value: An Overview of the United Kingdom Government's Policy for the Provision and Procurement of Local Authority Services' (2001) 2 *Public Procurement Law Review* 63.

[71] Local Government Planning and Land Act 1980, Local Government Act 1988.

[72] Badcoe, 'Best Value: An Overview', above n 70, 63–8; Arrowsmith, *Public and Utilities Procurement*, above n 13, ch 2; T Entwistle and S Martin, 'From Competition to Collaboration in Public Service Delivery: A New Agenda for Research' (2005) 83 *Public Administration* 233.

[73] Modernising Local Government- Improving Local Services through Best Value (March 1998). See S Martin, 'Implementing Best Value: Local Public Services in Transition' (2000) 78 *Public Administration* 209.

ities are required to 'secure continuous improvement in the way in which its functions are exercised, having regard to a combination of economy, efficiency and effectiveness'.[74] Although the Best Value initiative is important to local government procurement, it has implications that extend beyond procurement and seeks to provide improved performance and value for money in the delivery of all local government services.[75]

Whilst the Best Value initiative was directed at local government, central government procurement also underwent reform.[76] At central level, a policy of increasing competition in central government procurement was supported by the Deregulation and Contracting Out Act 1994, which permitted the contracting out of both local and central government functions, although central government decisions to contract out are to be determined on a case-by-case basis.[77]

In 1995, the publication of a government White Paper on procurement[78] led to changes in central government procurement. Following the White Paper, a government study was commissioned, which sought increased efficiency in central procurement,[79] through the increased use of electronic procurement, electronic payment of invoices, increased collaboration between departments, the increased use of central procurement agencies and the development of a professional procurement workforce in central government. The White Paper led to a review of central government civil procurement, in light of the government's efficiency objectives.[80] This review recommended the harmonisation of procurement strategy, procedures and standards and the creation of a central organisation responsible for coordinating procurement policy and promoting best practice in public procurement. This organisation, the Office of Government Commerce (OGC), was up until 2011, responsible for issuing policy advice and direction on public procurement, as well as information and training on EU procurement regulation.[81]

Since the global financial crises, the UK government has further tried to increase efficiency and transparency in public procurement as a means of obtaining better value.[82] The government commissioned a review of

[74] Local Government Act 1999, s 3 (1).

[75] Arrowsmith, *Public and Utilities Procurement*, above n 13, ch 2.8.

[76] Arrowsmith, *Public and Utilities Procurement*, above n 13, ch 2.13.

[77] 12 Guiding principles in using market testing and contracting out issued by the Chancellor (1997).

[78] Setting New Standards: The Government's procurement strategy (Cm 2840 May 1995).

[79] HM Treasury, Efficiency in Civil Government Procurement (July 1998).

[80] Peter Gershon, Review of Civil Procurement in central government (April 1999).

[81] www.ogc.gov.uk. Arrowsmith, 'Implementation of the New EC Procurement Directives', 86; S Norris, 'The Gershon Review: A Driver for Reform at the Heart of Central Government Procurement' (1999) 6 *Public Procurement Law Review* CS177.

[82] S Smith, 'The UK Government's Operational Efficiency Programme: Collaborative Procurement Report' (2010) 1 *Public Procurement Law Review* NA22; P Henty and C Manning, 'The Public Sector Transparency Agenda' (2011) 2 *Public Procurement Law Review* NA45.

central government procurement in 2010,[83] and as a result of the findings of this review, introduced substantive changes in the nature of procurement organisation in central government. Thus in 2011, the government disbanded the OGC, transferred its functions to the Cabinet Office and appointed for the first time in UK public procurement history, a Chief Procurement Officer who is the head of procurement at the Cabinet Office.[84] The agency that was formerly responsible for bulk purchasing – Buying Solutions – has been renamed the Government Procurement Service, and will among other things, deliver centralised procurement and savings to central government departments and the public sector. The objective of these reforms is to consolidate procurement by central government departments and ensure that as much as possible the government leverages its buying power and acts more as a 'single customer'. For common goods used by many government departments, Crown Representatives have been appointed to manage the relationship between key suppliers and central government departments.

Apart from domestic policies and legislation on procurement, the largest influence on UK procurement is EU procurement regulation. Some of the implications of the EU procurement directives for UK procurement occur in the context of procedures, the requirements of publication of contracts, transparency and the increase in the range of bodies whose procurement is subject to regulation.[85] The EU directives prescribe the framework of procedures for the award of public contracts but do not give policy direction on public procurement to Member States. However, in prescribing the procedures for contract awards and through the judicial interpretation of the directives by the Court of Justice of the EU (CJEU),[86] EU policies on public procurement are implemented in Member States. It has been suggested that there is often tension between the goals of EU procurement regulation and the goals of Member States,[87] and this tension may at times be irreconcilable leading to an unwillingness by Member States to fully implement EU procurement legislation.[88]

The previous UK procurement regulations[89] were repealed when the current set were adopted in 2006. The UK's approach to the implementa-

[83] Philip Green, Efficiency Review: Key Findings and Recommendations (11 October 2010).

[84] Public Procurement (Miscellaneous Amendments) Regulations 2011, SI 2011/2053, reg 16.

[85] S Arrowsmith, 'The Entity Coverage of the EC Procurement Directives and UK Regulations: A Review' (2004) 2 *Public Procurement Law Review* 59.

[86] Arrowsmith, *Public and Utilities Procurement*, above n 13, ch 3.50–3.55.

[87] Arrowsmith, *Public and Utilities Procurement*, above n 13, ch 2.10, ch 3.10–3.11, 3 50–3.55; S Arrowsmith, 'The EC Procurement Directives, National Procurement Policies and Better Governance: The Case for a New Approach' (2002) 27 *European Law Review* 3.

[88] P Braun, 'Strict Compliance versus Commercial Reality: The Practical Application of EC Public Procurement Law to the UK's Private Finance Initiative' (2003) 9 *European Law Journal* 575.

[89] Public Works Contracts Regulations 1991, SI 1991/2680; Public Services Contracts Regulations 1993, SI 1993/3228; Public Supply Contracts Regulations 1995, SI 1995/201.

tion of the directives is through detailed legislative implementation,[90] wherein the content of the directives is reproduced in binding regulations, albeit in a slightly re-worded and restructured form.[91] As a result, the UK procurement regulations are very similar to the EU directives, although there are a few areas where the UK clarified the provisions in the directives.[92] The benefits of the UK's approach to implementation, apart from the clarification provided by a detailed text, is that the procurement regulations avoid errors in transposition[93] and avoid any 'super-equivalence which risks being at odds with the meaning of the Directive'.[94] However, the disadvantages of the UK's approach are that the UK regulations fail to translate the implied obligations in the directives and retain the ambiguities that exist in the directives.[95]

3.3.2 The UK's Policy Against Corruption

The UK's anti-corruption policy can be said to have three strands. First, the policy is concerned with domestic corruption, although the government's policy against domestic corruption is subsumed within a broader policy against crime. Prior to 2010, legislative prohibitions against corruption existed in three statutes: the Public Bodies Corrupt Practices Act 1889, the Prevention of Corruption Act 1906 and the Prevention of Corruption Act 1916.[96] Together, these three statutes criminalised bribery in the public and private sectors. However, in 2010, the Bribery Act was passed which repealed these statutes and consolidated the prohibitions against public and private corruption and foreign bribery.[97] The Bribery Act criminalises the giving or receiving of a bribe as an inducement for a person to do or refrain from doing anything in the exercise of his public functions, in connection with a business or in the course of his employment.[98]

Apart from the statutory offences, there exists the common law offence of bribery, which applies to public bribery[99] and is defined as the 'receiving or offering any undue reward by or to any person whatsoever, in a

[90] S Arrowsmith, 'Legal Techniques for Implementing Directives: A Case Study of Public Procurement' in P Craig and C Harlow (eds), *Lawmaking in the European Union* (The Hague, Kluwer Law, 1998) 497.

[91] Arrowsmith 'Legal Techniques', above n 90.

[92] Arrowsmith, *Public and Utilities Procurement*, above n 13, ch 3.42.

[93] Arrowsmith, 'Implementation of the New EC Procurement Directives', above n 63, 90.

[94] OGC, *Regulatory Impact Assessment- Public Contracts Regulations 2006*. Available at www.ogc.gov.uk

[95] Arrowsmith, *Public and Utilities Procurement*, above n 13, ch 3.42.

[96] Collectively cited as the Prevention of Corruption Acts 1889–1916.

[97] The Act came into force in July 2011. See F Warin, C Falconer and M Diamant, 'The British are Coming!: Britain Changes its Law on Foreign Bribery and joins the International Fight against Corruption' (2010) 46 *Texas International Law Journal* 1.

[98] Bribery Act 2010, ss 1 to 4.

[99] *R v Whitaker* [1914] 3 KB 1283, 1296.

public office, in order to influence his behaviour in office, and incline him to act contrary to the known rules of honesty and integrity'.[100]

In addition to the criminal prohibitions against corruption, public officials are also subject to codes of conduct[101] and regulations prohibiting conflicts of interest, which are designed to maintain certain ethical standards amongst employees.

The second strand of the UK's anti-corruption policy is directed at corruption in developing countries. The thrust of this policy is to ensure corruption does not lead to a waste of financial aid and that probity and transparency are apparent in countries that receive UK aid.[102] In addition, the UK government is keen to ensure that corruption does not undermine development efforts in these countries, as it is believed that corruption can have an adverse effect on the functioning of governments and economies.[103] Another driver behind the government's interest in corruption in developing countries is a 2006 report that revealed the UK's complicity in the corruption that occurs in Africa.[104] In response to this report, the UK government reiterated its commitment to tackle international corruption through various measures including the introduction of new anti-corruption legislation (the Bribery Act 2010), the establishment of an international taskforce to investigate international corruption, including money laundering by corrupt politicians from developing countries, and the appointment of a ministerial anti-corruption champion.[105]

The third strand of the UK's anti-corruption policy is related to the anti-corruption policy in developing countries and is aimed at reducing corruption in international business, especially where this involves UK firms engaging in corruption to obtain public contracts in developing countries. Corruption in international business was initially criminalised through the Anti-Terrorism, Crime and Security Act 2001 (ATCSA), which gave effect to the UK's obligations under the OECD Convention on Combating Bribery of Foreign Public Officials.[106] The corruption provisions of the ATCSA were however repealed by the Bribery Act 2010, which criminalises the bribery of foreign officials and officials of international

[100] CJ Turrner (ed), *Russell on Crime* (Stevens, 1964) 381.

[101] General Medical Council, Good Medical Practice (2006); Civil Service Code (June 2006); Ministerial Code (July 2007); Local Authorities (Model Code of Conduct) (England) Order 2007, SI 2007/1159; Code of Conduct for Members of Parliament (2005) HC 251; House of Lords Code of Conduct (March 2002); Code of Conduct for NHS managers (October 2002).

[102] L Elliott, 'Brown tells African leaders: Make corruption history or lose confidence of Western donors', *The Guardian*, 23 May 2006.

[103] Joint Committee on the Draft Corruption Bill, 'Draft Corruption Bill: Report and Evidence' (HL (2002–03) Paper 157, HC (2002–03) 705) 81–2.

[104] All Africa Parliamentary Group, 'The Other Side of the Coin: The UK and Corruption in Africa' (March 2006).

[105] Prime Minister announces crackdown on international corruption, as part of Gleneagles implementation plan. Available at www.dfid.gov.uk/news/files/pressreleases/anticorruption-champion.asp.

[106] 37 ILM 1 (1998).

organisations.[107] The Bribery Act also deliberately targets corporations engaging in corruption in international business by creating a new offence, which penalises the failure of a commercial organisation to prevent bribery.[108]

3.3.3 Disqualification in the UK

Disqualification is not an unknown concept in UK public procurement, and was historically used in limited contexts to secure compliance with various government policies.[109] In implementing the previous edition of the EU procurement directives, discretionary disqualifications for breaches of various norms were permitted under the previous UK procurement regulations. Under these regulations, suppliers could have been disqualified from public contracts for a conviction for a criminal offence relating to the contractors professional conduct, or because the contractor had committed an act of grave professional misconduct.[110]

The previous regulations reproduced almost verbatim the corresponding provisions in the previous edition of the EU procurement directives. However, there is little empirical information available on the extent to which these disqualifications were utilised under the previous procurement regime,[111] and whether indeed these discretionary disqualifications were ever used against contractors convicted or guilty of corruption. These discretionary disqualifications have been retained in the current version of the UK procurement regulations[112] in the same form as under the previous regulations. Thus, the current regulations provide that a procuring authority may treat as ineligible or decide not to select a supplier on the grounds that the supplier has been convicted of a criminal offence relating to the conduct of his business or profession or has committed an act of grave misconduct in the course of his business or profession.[113] As was discussed above in the context of the EU, these discretionary provisions may be relied on to disqualify a supplier from a procurement process where that supplier commits an act of corruption within that procurement process.

[107] Bribery Act 2010, s 6.

[108] Bribery Act 2010, s 7.

[109] See generally, B Bercusson, *Fair Wages Resolutions* (London, Mansell, 1978); J Carr, *New Roads to Equality: Contract Compliance for the United Kingdom* (London, Fabian Society, 1987); C McCrudden, *Buying Social Justice* (Oxford Oxford University Press, 2007).

[110] Public Works Contracts Regulations 1991, SI 1991/2680, reg 14; Public Supply Contracts Regulations 1995, SI 1995/201, reg 14; Public Services Contracts Regulations 1993, SI 1993/3228, reg 14.

[111] Piselli, 'The Scope for Excluding Providers', above n 36.

[112] Public Contract Regulations 2006, SI 2006/5 as amended by the Public Contracts (Amendment) Regulations, 2009, SI 2009/2992, reg 23(4) [hereafter PCR].

[113] PCR reg 23(4)(d) and (e).

Apart from the discretionary disqualifications, the current UK procurement regulations contain, like the EU directives, mandatory disqualifications for serious criminal offences,[114] which are intended to implement the provisions in the EU procurement directives. However, the UK regulations re-worded the offences to fit within the existing scheme of the relevant criminal offences in the UK and also take into account EU definitions of the various offences.

Regulation 23(1) of the Public Contracts Regulations (PCR) provides:

> Subject to paragraph (2), a contracting authority shall treat as ineligible and shall not select an economic operator in accordance with these Regulations if the contracting authority has actual knowledge that the economic operator or its directors or any other person who has powers of representation, decision or control of the economic operator has been convicted of any of the following offences –
>
> (a) conspiracy within the meaning of section 1 or 1A of the Criminal Law Act 1977 . . . where that conspiracy relates to participation in a criminal organisation as defined in Article 2 of Council Framework Decision 2008/841/JHA . . .;
> (b) corruption within the meaning of section 1 of the Public Bodies Corrupt Practices Act 1889 or section 1 of the Prevention of Corruption Act 1906, where the offence relates to active corruption;
> (c) the offence of bribery, where the offence relates to active corruption;
> (ca) bribery within the meaning of section 1 or 6 of the Bribery Act 2010;
> (d) fraud, where the offence relates to fraud affecting the financial interests of the European Communities as defined by Article 1 of the Convention relating to the protection of the financial interests of the European Union, within the meaning of –
>
> (i) the offence of cheating the Revenue;
> (ii) the offence of conspiracy to defraud;
> (iii) fraud or theft within the meaning of the Theft Act 1968 . . . and the Theft Act 1978 . . .;
> (iv) fraudulent trading within the meaning of section 458 of the Companies Act 1985 . . . or section 993 of the Companies Act 2006;
> (v) fraudulent evasion within the meaning of section 170 of the Customs and Excise Management Act 1979 or section 72 of the Value Added Tax Act 1994;
> (vi) an offence in connection with taxation in the European Community within the meaning of section 71 of the Criminal Justice Act 1993;
> (vii) destroying, defacing or concealing of documents or procuring the extension of a valuable security within the meaning of section 20 of the Theft Act 1968 . . .;
> (viii) fraud within the meaning of section 2, 3 or 4 of the Fraud Act 2006, or

[114] PCR reg 23(1) as amended by the Public Procurement (Miscellaneous Amendments) Regulations, 2011, SI 2011/2053; S Williams, 'The Mandatory Contractor Exclusions for Serious Criminal Offences in UK Public Procurement' (2009) 15 *European Public Law* 429.

(ix) making, adapting, supplying or offering to supply articles for use in frauds within the meaning of section of the Fraud Act 2006

(e) money laundering within the meaning of section 340(11) of the Proceeds of Crime Act 2002;
(ea) an offence in connection with the proceeds of criminal conduct within the meaning of section 93A, 93B or 93C of the Criminal Justice Act 1988 . . .
(eb) an offence in connection with the proceeds of drug trafficking within the meaning of section 49, 50 or 51 of the Drug Trafficking Act 1994;
(f) any other offence within the meaning of Article 45(1) of the Public Sector Directive as defined by the national law of any relevant State.

(1A) In paragraph (1), 'active corruption' means corruption as defined in Article 3 of the Council Act of 26 May 1997 or Article 3(1) of Council Joint Action 98/742/JHA.

The mandatory disqualifications for serious criminal offences were included in the UK regulations in compliance with the EU procurement directives. Thus, the rationales for the use of disqualifications in the UK are similar to the rationales behind their inclusion in the EU directives.[115] These rationales were identified above as supporting the EU's policy against serious crime, strengthening the EU's 'arsenal of means' against these offences; preventing the adverse effect that fraud and corruption can have on the internal market and public procurement;[116] and protecting EU projects in Member States from fraud and corruption, while denying organised criminal syndicates access to these projects and preventing such projects from being used for money laundering purposes.[117] Thus, the rationales for disqualification in the UK are policy related, in that the disqualification provisions are aimed at giving effect to the EU directives, and in doing so, the UK disqualifications also meet the protective rationale of protecting the EU budget from crime as discussed in the context of the EU disqualifications. In addition, because the disqualifications apply to UK domestic offences, they also support domestic anti-corruption policy.

In relation to whether the disqualifications in the UK relate to the capability or eligibility of the supplier to perform, the UK regulations take both into account and in relation to the discretionary disqualifications for offences committed in the conduct of the supplier's business, the disqualifications may be directed at the capability of the supplier to perform. However, in relation to the mandatory disqualifications for serious criminal offences, the UK regulations suggest that the disqualification relates to eligibility and not capability, as the opening paragraph of Regulation 23 provides that a contractor convicted of the relevant offences shall be 'ineligible' to obtain a public contract.

[115] S Williams, 'The Mandatory Contractor Exclusions in the UK', ibid.
[116] Trepte, *Public Procurement in the EU*, above n 46, 338.
[117] S Williams, 'The Mandatory Exclusions for Corruption in the new EC Procurement Directives' (2006) 31 *European Law Review* 711.

3.4 THE UNITED STATES

3.4.1 Public Procurement Regulation in the United States

In contrast with the UK, but similar to the position in South Africa, the US adopts a highly formal approach to procurement regulation, which relies on legally binding rules in order to achieve procurement objectives.[118] US procurement is decentralised and occurs at three levels, the federal, State and local level, but this book will concentrate on federal procurement regulation. Procurement regulation at the federal level is governed by the Federal Acquisition Regulations (FAR) and for some strategic federal agencies; there are agency-specific procurement regulations, which are modelled on the FAR. Procurement regulation at the State level is governed by State-specific legislation.

The regulation of public procurement was historically driven by the needs of military procurement, with the first formal procurement regulations issued by Congress in 1777. These regulations were aimed at organising the purchasing and issue of military supplies and preventing fraud by requiring procurement officials to record information on all purchases and issues, appraise themselves of market prices and give a bond to Congress for the 'faithful performance of their duties'.[119]

The genesis of the modern US procurement system is traceable to the passage of two Acts intended to standardise and streamline public procurement procedures.[120] Streamlining procurement was accompanied by an anti-fraud element and the Truth in Negotiations Act 1962[121] required contractors to submit certifiable cost and pricing data to the government. Procurement reform[122] coincided with judicial pronouncements giving procurement regulations the force of law,[123] which meant that aggrieved contractors had the right to pursue litigation where procuring officials breached the regulations.

In 1969, the US government established the Commission on Government Contracting, which scrutinised federal procurement and recommended a

[118] J Cibinic and R Nash, *Formation of Government Contracts*, 3rd edn (Alphen aan den Rijn, Wolters Kluwer, 1998) 1; KV Thai and D Drabkin, 'US Federal Government Procurement: Structure, Process and Current Issues' in L Knight, C Harland, J Telgen, et al (eds), *Public Procurement: International Cases and Commentary* (Abingdon, Routledge, 2007) 89.

[119] J Nagle, *A History of Government Contracting* (Washington, George Washington University Press, 1999) 33–4.

[120] Armed Services Procurement Act 1947 10 USC § 2301; Federal Property and Administrative Services Act 1949 41 USC § 251.

[121] Pub L 87-653; 10 USC 2306a.

[122] Nagle, *History of Government Contracting*, above n 119, ch 22; D Koffsky, 'Coming to Terms with Bureaucratic Ethics' (1995) 11 *Journal of Law and Politics* 235.

[123] *Paul v United States* 371 US 245 (1963); *GL Christian & Assocs v United States* 312 F2d 418 (Ct Cl 1963).

uniform system of procurement regulations under the auspices of the Office of Federal Procurement Policy (OFPP).[124] In 1983, the OFPP drafted the FAR, which was intended to be a uniform set of regulations for government procurement,[125] although supplementary regulations could be issued by federal agencies. This led to a similar problem that the FAR was designed to solve, namely, an over-burdening of the system with multiple regulations.[126] This was not the only problem with procurement and in 1983 a scandal erupted over government contract prices, which were much higher than market prices. This scandal led to the Competition in Contracting Act 1984,[127] designed to ensure that the government obtained the best value in its procurements.[128] Another scandal over defence procurement[129] in 1988 led to the Procurement Integrity Act 1988,[130] which increased the range of punitive measures against the improper disclosure of contract information.[131] This was closely followed by the Ethics Reform Act 1990.[132]

In 1993, President Clinton committed himself to a programme of procurement reform[133] as part of his campaign to reinvent government. The FAR was remodelled[134] to grant procurement officials more discretion,[135] include past performance in evaluation criteria and make procurement more flexible and innovative.[136] The passage of two new statutes – the Federal Acquisition Streamlining Act of 1994[137] and the Federal Acquisition Reform Act 1996[138] – sought to streamline the federal procurement

[124] Nagle, *History of Government Contracting*, 488; Office of Federal Procurement Policy Act Pub L No 93-400, § 3(b), 88 Stat 796 (1974).

[125] W Keyes, *Government Contracts in a Nutshell*, 4th edn (West, 2004) 2–3.

[126] Keyes, *Government Contracts*, ibid, 3; J Schwartz, 'Regulation and Deregulation in Public Procurement Law Reform in the United States' in G Piga and KV Thai (eds), *Advancing Public Procurement: Practices, Innovation and Knowledge-Sharing* (Boca Raton, PrAcademic Press, 2006) 177, 179.

[127] 10 USC § 2306; S Kelman, Procurement and Public Management: The Fear of Discretion and the Quality of Government Performance (Washington, AEI Press, 1990) 14.

[128] Nagle, *History of Government Contracting*, ch 23.

[129] J Greenspun, '1988 Amendments to the Federal Procurement Policy Act: Did the "Ill Wind" bring an Impractical Overreaction that may run Afoul of the Constitution?' (1990) 19 *Public Contract Law Journal* 393; E Dietrich, 'The Potential for Criminal Liability in Government Contracting: A Closer Look at the Procurement Integrity Act' (2005) 34 *Public Contract Law Journal* 521.

[130] 41 USC § 423.

[131] S Donaldson, 'Section 6 of the Office of Federal Policy and Procurement Act 1988: A New Ethical Standard in Government Conduct?' (1990) 20 *Cumberland Law Review* 421; R Wallick, P Wellington and J Howe, 'Procurement Integrity: Pondering some Imponderables' (1990) 19 *Public Contract Law Journal* 349.

[132] Pub L No 101-280, 104 Stat 149.

[133] S Kelman, *Unleashing Change: A Study of Organizational Renewal in Government* (Washington, Brookings Institution Press, 2006) 18–21.

[134] 59 Fed Reg 26,772 (1994).

[135] Schwartz, 'Regulation and Deregulation in Public Procurement', above n 126, 178.

[136] Nagle, History of Government Contracting, 513.

[137] Pub L No 103-355, 108 Stat 3243.

[138] Pub L No 104-106, 110 Stat 186, 642.

system.[139] In the new millennium, the government's goals have been to increase efficiency,[140] avoid fraud,[141] increase decision-making based on 'best-value', foster better relationships between the government and the private sector[142] and (since the global financial crisis) to use procurement as a means of stimulating the economy,[143] whilst still reducing waste in public procurement by increasing competition.[144]

3.4.2 The United States' Policy Against Corruption

The US adopts a multi-level policy against corruption. First the US is concerned about corruption in the conduct of international business.[145] This is evidenced by the existence of the renowned Foreign Corrupt Practices Act 1977, which was the first piece of domestic legislation to criminalise the bribery of foreign public officials,[146] and gave the impetus to the passage

[139] J Pegnato, 'Assessing Federal Procurement Reform: Has the Pendulum Stopped Swinging?' (2003) 3 *Journal of Public Procurement* 145.

[140] W Lucyshyn, 'Market Based Government: Lessons Learnt from Five Cases' in G Piga and KV Thai (eds), *Advancing Public Procurement: Practices, Innovation and Knowledge-Sharing* (Boca Raton, PrAcademic Press, 2006), 117; R Berrios, 'Government Contracts and Contractor Behaviour' (2006) 63 *Journal of Business Ethics* 119, 121; R Utt, 'Competitive Contracting: An Avenue for Improvement' (2004) *Foreign Service Journal* 41; S Schooner, 'Fear of Oversight: The Fundamental Failure of Business-Like Government' (2001) 50 *American University Law Review* 627, 674; S Schooner, 'Model Behaviour? Anecdotal Evidence between Evolving Commercial Public Procurement Practices and Trade Policy' (2003) 9(1) *International Trade Law and Regulation* 4.

[141] M Stanek, 'Gotta Have Faith: Why the New Contractor Ethics Rules Miss the Mark' (2009) 38 *Public Contracts Law Journal* 427; C McCue, K Buffington and A Howel, 'The Fraud / Red Tape Dilemma in Public Procurement: A Study of US State and Local Governments' in L Knight, C Harland, J Telgen, et al (eds), *Public Procurement: International Cases and Commentary* (Abingdon, Routledge, 2007) 247.

[142] S Kelman, 'Remaking Federal Procurement' (2002) 31 *Public Contract Law Journal* 581, 602–10.

[143] D Conway, 'Emerging Trends in International, Federal and State and Local Government Procurement in an Era of Global Economic Stimulus Funding' (2010) 32 *University of Hawaii Law Review* 29.

[144] Conway, 'Emerging Trends', ibid, 34–5.

[145] George W Bush, Message to the Senate of the United States, 27 October 2005. Available at www.whitehouse.gov; I Bantekas, 'Corruption as an International Crime and Crime Against Humanity' (2006) 4 *Journal of International Criminal Justice* 466.

[146] M Koehler, 'The Foreign Corrupt Practices Act in the Ultimate Year of the Decade of its Resurgence' (2010) 43 *Indiana Law Review* 389; M Bixby, 'The Lion Awakes: The Foreign Corrupt Practices Act 1977–2010' (2010) 12 *San Diego International Law Journal* 89; A Goldbarg, 'The Foreign Corrupt Practices Act and Structural Corruption' (2000) 18 *Boston University International Law Journal* 273; J Nesbitt, 'Transnational Bribery of Foreign Officials: A New Threat to the Future of Democracy' (1998) 31 *Vanderbilt Journal of Transnational Law* 1273; P Nicholls, 'The Myth of Anti-Bribery Law as Transnational Intrusion' (2000) 33 *Cornell Journal of International Law* 627; C Hudson and P Pieros, 'The Hard Graft of Tackling Corruption in International Business Transactions: Progress in International Cooperation and the OECD Convention' (1998) 32 *Journal of World Trade* 77; S Salbu, 'A Delicate Balance: Legislation, Institutional Change and Transnational Bribery' (2000) 33 *Cornell International Law Journal* 657; P Jennings, 'Public Corruption: A Comparative Analysis of International

of the OECD Convention on Combating Bribery of Foreign Public Officials.[147] The US government believes that such corruption hurts businesses by raising transaction costs and the risks of doing business and is keen to ensure that US firms are not adversely affected by corruption in international business – one of the reasons behind the United States' championing of instruments like the OECD Convention and the UN Corruption Convention.[148] In furtherance of this strand of its anti-corruption policy, in 2010, the G20 adopted the proposal of President Obama to adopt a comprehensive anti-corruption plan, aimed at strengthening G20 members' anti-corruption efforts, supporting integrity in international business and promoting a clean business environment.[149]

Secondly, and similar to the UK, the US is committed to the fight against corruption in developing nations. To combat corruption in developing nations, the US passed the International Anti-Corruption and Good Governance Act 2000, designed to ensure that United States assistance programmes promote good governance by assisting other countries to combat corruption throughout society and to improve transparency and accountability at all levels of government and throughout the private sector.[150] The drivers behind US policy are the desire to foster and encourage growth and development in developing countries, as it is accepted that corruption stifles this growth,[151] and a desire that foreign aid is used for its intended purpose. As such, aid monies are increasingly tied to the improved responsibility of developing countries.[152] The US is also keen to ensure that corruption does not have a destabilising effect on new or transition economies and democracies, especially as there is evidence to suggest that corruption fosters the growth of organised criminal organisations.[153]

The Bush administration was particularly vocal in the fight against corruption, backing its rhetoric with legislative intervention and US dollars. For instance, in 2002, the Millennium Challenge Account was created to provide development assistance to countries meeting anti-corruption and

Corruption Conventions and United States Law' (2001) 18 *Arizona Journal of International and Comparative Law* 793.

[147] 37 ILM 1 (1998).

[148] C Hall, 'The Foreign Corrupt Practices Act: A Competitive Disadvantage, But for How Long?' (1994) 2 *Tulane Journal of International and Comparative Law* 289; Nesbitt, 'Transnational Bribery', above n 146; Nicholls, 'The Myth of Anti-Bribery Law'n.139 Hudson and Pieros, 'The Hard Graft', above n 146; Salbu, 'A Delicate Balanace' above n 146; Jennings, 'Public Corruption' above n 146.

[149] G20 Seoul Summit Final Declaration, Annex 3, Anti-Corruption Action Plan, November 2010.

[150] Preamble, International Anti-Corruption and Good Governance Act, Public Law 106-309.

[151] P Mauro, 'Corruption and Growth' (1995) 110 *Quarterly Journal of Economics* 681.

[152] Statement of President Bush, International Conference on Financing for Development, Monterrey, 2002.

[153] UN Office of Drugs and Crime, Results of a Pilot Survey of Forty selected organized criminal groups in sixteen countries (United Nations, 2002).

other governance criteria.[154] Another legislative initiative is the Foreign Operations, Export Financing and Related Programs Appropriations Act 2001,[155] which entitles the Treasury to withhold 10 per cent of its funding to international financial institutions if the Secretary of the Treasury is not satisfied that the institution is taking steps 'to establish an independent fraud and corruption investigative organisation or office'.

Thirdly, the US is concerned about corruption on the domestic plane.[156] The legislative arena is replete with instruments designed to protect the public purse from corruption, fraud and mismanagement.[157] However, since September 11, 2001 the threat of terrorism also drives the government's efforts to tackle domestic corruption, as it is believed that corruption and money laundering may be used by terrorist groups for the furtherance of their aims, and anti-corruption efforts have taken on a new 'sense of urgency' as a result.[158]

3.4.3 Disqualification in the US

The United States has used disqualification in some form since 1928[159] and utilises two kinds of disqualification measures against corrupt suppliers in public procurement. These are referred to in the FAR as debarment and suspension. Debarment is disqualification from participation in public contracts for a specified period of time, usually no more than three years,[160] while a suspension is a temporary measure,[161] lasting no longer than 12 months (or 18 months if an Assistant Attorney-General requests an extension).[162] Both measures will be referred to in this book as 'disqualification' and will be examined together since they operate in the same way, except in relation to length and certain procedural requirements.

In the US, disqualification may occur for the breaches of various norms. Similar to what obtains in the EU and the UK, disqualification in the US is generally directed at past violations of law or ethics that may be unrelated

[154] S Radelet, 'Will the Millennium Challenge Account be Different?' (2003) 26 *The Washington Quarterly* 171.

[155] Public Law 106-429 § 588.

[156] M Warren, 'What Does Corruption Mean in a Democracy?' (2004) 48 *American Journal of Political Science* 328.

[157] For a compilation of these statutes go to: www.usoge.gov/laws_regs/pdf/comp_fed_ethics_laws.pdf.

[158] J Brandolino, Director for Anticorruption and Governance Initiatives, Bureau of International Narcotics and Law Enforcement Affairs, 'The United States and International Anti-Corruption Efforts' *Federal Ethics Report* (January 2003).

[159] P Gantt and I Panzer, 'The Government Blacklist: Debarment and Suspension of Bidders on Government Contracts' (1957) 25 *George Washington Law Review* 175, 185.

[160] FAR 9.406-4.

[161] FAR 9.407-4.

[162] FAR 9.407-1.

to public procurement,[163] but a supplier could also be disqualified for past procurement-related violations[164] or violations committed in the specific procurement process.

The rationale behind disqualification in the US is primarily protective. This rationale finds support in the jurisprudence[165] and the legislation.[166] The federal procurement statutes provide that public contracts may only be awarded to 'responsible' contractors.[167] This requirement is incorporated into the FAR,[168] which requires a procuring officer to make an affirmative determination of the responsibility of the contractor before awarding a contract.[169] Responsibility covers factors such as financial, technical and integrity criteria as well as past contract performance.[170] Where a determination of responsibility cannot be made, the procuring officer must make a determination of non-responsibility,[171] which precludes the contractor from obtaining a contract in the specific instance. Contracting with a responsible contractor ensures that government resources are used to obtain contractually described goods and services,[172] as a responsible contractor may be more likely to comply with the procurement agreement. The relationship between a determination of non-responsibility and disqualification is that the determination may often be the genesis of disqualification proceedings against a supplier.

A second rationale behind the use of disqualification is policy related, similar to the position in the EU and the UK, and disqualifications in the US may indicate the government's lack of tolerance for corruption and fraud,[173] and thereby maintain public trust in the procurement system.[174] A number of corruption scandals in US procurement led to various measures against procurement corruption. Disqualification further reinforces the government policy against corruption.

[163] See FAR 9.406-2 and C Yukins, 'Suspension and Debarment: Rethinking the Process' (2004) *Public Contract Law Journal* 255, 256.

[164] Schooner, 'The Paper Tiger Stirs', below n 172, 214.

[165] *Roemer v Hoffman* 419 F Supp 130 (DDC 1976).

[166] FAR 9.402; R Kramer, 'Awarding Contracts to Suspended and Debarred Firms: Are Stricter Rules Necessary?' (2005) 34 *Public Contract Law Journal* 539.

[167] 10 USC § 2305(c) and 41 USC § 253(b).

[168] FAR 9.103(a).

[169] FAR 9.103(b). This book will not examine the law and practice relating to responsibility.

[170] FAR 9.104-1.

[171] FAR 9.103(b).

[172] S Schooner, 'The Paper Tiger Stirs: Rethinking Exclusion and Debarment' (2004) 5 *Public Procurement Law Review* 211, 212–13.

[173] M Madsen, 'The Government's Debarment Process: Out of Step with Current Ethical Standards' (2004) 5 *Public Procurement Law Review* 252, 253; J McCollough, 'Government Contract Suspension and Debarment: What Every Contractor Needs to Know' (2004) 5 *Public Procurement Law Review* 240, 241–2, Yukins, 'Suspension and Debarment', above n 163, 255.

[174] Schooner, 'The Paper Tiger Stirs', above n 172, 216–17; J Gansler, 'A Vision of the Government as a World Class Buyer: Major Procurement Issues for the Coming Decade' in M Abramson and R Harris III (eds), *The Procurement Revolution* (Rowman & Littlefield, 2003) 15.

Thirdly, although the courts and the FAR indicate that disqualification is not intended to be punitive,[175] and is designed to protect the government from the risk of dealing with non-responsible contractors,[176] the effects of a disqualification[177] may have such far-reaching consequences for a contractor that it amounts to a 'corporate death penalty'[178] and may thus be sufficient to act as a deterrent against the breaches of the norms that call for disqualification.

As will be seen in later chapters, the non-punitive nature of the US disqualification policy informs its implementation, as disqualification is discretionary and is imposed for limited periods where the evidence suggests that the government will be at risk from contracting with a supplier. Unlike the EU, the UK and South Africa, there are no provisions for mandatory disqualifications in the federal procurement context.

The provisions relating to disqualification in US procurement are found in sub-part 9.4 of the FAR. Disqualification may be imposed for several offences and the FAR provides in 9.406-2 that a procuring authority official may disqualify:

(a) A contractor for a conviction of or a civil judgment for –
  (1) Commission of fraud or a criminal offense in connection with –
    (i) Obtaining;
    (ii) Attempting to obtain; or
    (iii) Performing a public contract or subcontract.
  (2) Violation of Federal or State antitrust statutes relating to the submission of offers;
  (3) Commission of embezzlement, theft, forgery, bribery, falsification or destruction of records, making false statements, tax evasion, violating Federal criminal tax laws or receiving stolen property;
  (4) Intentionally affixing a label bearing a 'Made in America' inscription (or any inscription having the same meaning) to a product sold in or shipped to the United States or its outlying areas, when the product was not made in the United States or its outlying areas (see Section 202 of the Defense Production Act (Pub. L. 102-558));
  (5) Commission of any other offense indicating a lack of business integrity or business honesty that seriously and directly affects the present responsibility of a Government contractor or subcontractor.

[175] *Bae v Shalala*, 44 F3d 489 (7th Cir 1995), *United States v Bizzell*, 921 F2d 263 (10th Cir 1990).

[176] Kramer, 'Awarding Contracts to Suspended and Debarred Firms', above n 166, 543.

[177] In *Gonzalez v Freeman*, 334 F2d 570, 574 (DC Cir 1964), the impact of disqualification was stated to be a loss of bank credit, adverse impact on price of shares, 'loss of face' in the business community and the loss of profits from the business denied as a result of the disqualification. See also *Fischer v RTC*, 59 F3d 1344 (DC Cir 1995).

[178] Schooner, 'The Paper Tiger Stirs', above n 172, 214; McCollough. 'Government Contract Suspension and Debarment', above n 173, 240–44.

(b)

(1) A contractor, based upon a preponderance of the evidence, for any of the following –

(i) Violation of the terms of a Government contract or subcontract so serious as to justify debarment, such as –

(A) Wilful failure to perform in accordance with the terms of one or more contracts; or

(B) A history of failure to perform, or of unsatisfactory performance of, one or more contracts.

(ii) Violations of the Drug-Free Workplace Act of 1988 (Pub. L. 100-690), as indicated by –

(A) Failure to comply with the requirements of the clause at 52.223-6, Drug-Free Workplace; or

(B) Such a number of contractor employees convicted of violations of criminal drug statutes occurring in the workplace as to indicate that the contractor has failed to make a good faith effort to provide a drug-free workplace (see 23.504).

(iii) Intentionally affixing a label bearing a 'Made in America' inscription (or any inscription having the same meaning) to a product sold in or shipped to the United States or its outlying areas, when the product was not made in the United States or its outlying areas (see Section 202 of the Defense Production Act (Pub. L. 102-558)).

(iv) Commission of an unfair trade practice as defined in 9.403 (see Section 201 of the Defense Production Act (Pub. L. 102-558)).

(v) Delinquent Federal taxes in an amount that exceeds $3,000 . . .

(vi) Knowing failure by a principal, until 3 years after final payment on any Government contract awarded to the contractor, to timely disclose to the Government, in connection with the award, performance, or closeout of the contract or a subcontract thereunder, credible evidence of –

(A) Violation of Federal criminal law involving fraud, conflict of interest, bribery, or gratuity violations found in Title 18 of the United States Code;

(B) Violation of the civil False Claims Act (31 U.S.C. 3729–3733); or

(C) Significant overpayment(s) on the contract, other than overpayments resulting from contract financing payments as defined in 32.001.

(2) A contractor, based on a determination by the Secretary of Homeland Security or the Attorney General of the United States, that the contractor is not in compliance with Immigration and Nationality Act employment provisions (see Executive Order 12989, as amended by Executive Order 13286). Such determination is not reviewable in the debarment proceedings.

(c) A contractor or subcontractor based on any other cause of so serious or compelling a nature that it affects the present responsibility of the contractor or subcontractor.

The offences that may lead to a temporary disqualification (suspension) are almost identical, except that such a disqualification may be imposed 'upon adequate evidence' of the commission of the offences. In addition, such a disqualification may not be imposed for a breach of the Immigration and Nationality Act.

The US disqualifications are tied both to the eligibility and the capability of the contractor. As discussed, disqualification may follow a determination of non-responsibility, which indicates that the contractor's ability to perform the contract will be adversely affected by its inability to meet the standards for responsibility. However, because other procuring authorities are required not to contract with a supplier who has been disqualified, disqualification also affects a supplier's eligibility for future contracts.

3.5 THE WORLD BANK

3.5.1 Procurement Regulation in the World Bank

The World Bank funds capital-intensive projects in developing countries, which are implemented through procurements in these countries. By its Articles of Agreement,[179] the Bank is required to ensure that loan proceeds are used for their intended purpose, with due regard to considerations of economy and efficiency.[180] The Articles also prohibit the Bank from taking political or non-economic considerations into account[181] or interfering in the political affairs of its members.[182] This raised a quandary for the Bank in deciding how to ensure that the disbursement of loan proceeds through project procurements is conducted in an open, transparent and competitive manner in countries that might have weak public administration systems, or lax public procurement regulation, without interfering with the Borrower's internal administration. To circumvent this problem, the Bank made it a condition of its finance that project procurement is done according to Bank procurement guidelines.[183] Although the procurement process is subject to Bank rules, the process is managed by the Borrower, with the Bank merely taking a supervisory role to ensure that the process is properly conducted.[184]

179 International Bank for Reconstruction and Development Articles of Agreement 2 UNTS 134, as amended by 606 UNTS 294 [hereafter IBRD Articles of Agreement].

180 IBRD Articles of Agreement, art III s 5(b).

181 ibid.

182 IBRD Articles of Agreement, art IV s 10.

183 BPG, para 1.1.

184 S Arrowsmith, J Linarelli and D Wallace, *Regulating Public Procurement: National and International Perspectives* (The Hague, Kluwer Law, 2000) 137.

The first formal direction on Bank procurement was issued in 1964, which contained the procedures to be used by Bank staff in conducting international competitive bidding (ICB).[185] These initial documents have undergone significant revision over the years, 'to reflect the Bank's changing membership, changes in the field of procurement and in the Bank's own lending procedures'.[186] In relation to corruption control, the most significant review of Bank procurement procedures occurred in 1996 when the Bank introduced a new paragraph dealing with fraud and corruption in Bank-funded procurements.[187] This paragraph established the Bank's intention to disqualify corrupt firms from Bank-financed contracts and also contained a clause permitting Borrowers to include a 'no-bribery' pledge in bid documentation. The paragraph on corruption was revised in 2004 to include collusion and coercive practices in the list of prohibited activities[188] and to grant the Bank contractual access to bid and contract documentation[189] and the power to audit the accounts of suppliers.[190] Again in 2006, the procurement guidelines were revised to include 'obstructive practices' as part of the definition of fraud and corruption and to extend Bank sanctions to offences committed outside the procurement context, but still within Bank projects.[191] The most recent revision to the procurement guidelines occurred in 2011 when the Bank introduced a provision prohibiting conflicts of interest in Bank projects.[192]

The Bank's procurement guidelines are quite detailed, providing procedural requirements relating to bidding procedures, splitting of contracts, advertising, and the qualification of bidders. They also provide information on the nature of tender documentation, bid evaluation, payment methods and contract award procedures. The emphasis in the guidelines is on the need for economy and efficiency in the procurement process, and on promoting competition, transparency and encouraging local industry.[193] The guidelines require the use of ICB within certain parameters[194] and thresholds as defined in the Loan Agreement between the Bank and the Borrower. ICB means that procurements are advertised internationally and are open to persons beyond the Borrower country.

[185] R Hunja, 'Recent Revisions to the World Bank's Procurement and Consultant Selection Guidelines' (1996) 6 *Public Procurement Law Review* 217, 218.

[186] ibid.

[187] BPG, para 1.16.

[188] BPG, para 1.16.

[189] F Bentchikou, 'The World Bank Sanctions Process' in OECD (ed), *Fighting Corruption and Promoting Integrity in Public Procurement* (Paris, OECD, 2005) 241.

[190] BPG, para 1.16.

[191] S Williams, 'World Bank Introduces New Measures to Reduce Fraud and Corruption in Bank-Financed Projects and the Administration of Bank Loans' (2007) 16 *Public Procurement Law Review* NA152.

[192] BPG, paras 1.6 and 1.7.

[193] BPG, para 1.2.

[194] BPG, para 1.2.

It was previously thought that in future, the Bank's procurement guidelines might have become less important to Bank-funded procurements as the Bank between 2008 and 2011 conducted a pilot to examine the possibility of increasing its reliance on country procurement systems for Bank-funded contracts.[195] Country procurement systems would have been required to meet a test of 'equivalence' with the guidelines and the guidelines would still be used where a country system was not sufficiently developed to be used for Bank-funded projects.[196] However, the pilot was not very successful and very few Bank Borrowers were able to meet the stringent requirements of the Bank in the pilot.

3.5.2 The World Bank's Anti-corruption Policy

The Bank's concern with corruption as a developmental issue emerged with the assumption of James Wolfensohn to the Presidency of the Bank in 1995.[197] Before then, the Bank was resolute in not taking measures against corruption,[198] especially beyond the projects it financed. However, it was always clear that growth and development were directly correlated with corruption,[199] and the Bank was criticised for its attitude towards corruption in Borrower countries. According to a former Bank Legal Counsel,

> as the world's major development finance institution and the coordinator of foreign aid to many of its members, the Bank cannot realistically ignore issues which significantly influence the effective flow and appropriate use of external resources in its borrowing countries.[200]

The growing prominence of corruption in economic, political and developmental discourse[201] as a development inhibitor led the Bank to eventually adopt a comprehensive, multi-pronged policy against corruption.

[195] BPG, para 3.20; World Bank, Detailed Methodology for Procurement Country Systems Piloting Program. Available at: siteresources.worldbank.org/INTPROCUREMENT/Resources/CS-ConsultationsDocument.doc .

[196] C Palas and J Wood, 'The World Bank's Use of Country Systems in Procurement: A Good Idea Gone Bad?' (2009) 27 *Development Policy Review* 215.

[197] I Shihata, 'Corruption: A General Review with an Emphasis on the Role of the World Bank' (1997) 15 *Dickinson Journal of International Law* 451, 475; N Wallace-Bruce, 'Corruption and Competitiveness in Global Business: The Dawn of a New Era' (2000) 24 *Melbourne University Law Review* 349, 362.

[198] J Wolfensohn, 'Corruption Impedes Development–and Hurts the Poor' (1998) 25 *International Journal of Government Auditing* 1.

[199] P Mauro, 'The Effects of Corruption on Growth, Investment and Government Expenditure: A Cross Country Analysis' in KA Elliott (ed), *Corruption and the Global Economy* (Washington, Institute for International Economics, 1997)

[200] Shihata, 'Corruption: A General Review', above n 197, 476.

[201] Termed the 'corruption eruption'. The term was first used by Moisés Naím, 'The Corruption Eruption' (1995) 2 *Brown Journal of World Affairs* 245; Hudson and Pieros, 'The Hard Graft of Tackling Corruption in International Business Transactions', above n 146, 79; D Hess and T Dunfee, 'Fighting Corruption, A Principled Approach–The C2 Principles' (2000) 33

For the purpose of its anti-corruption policy, the Bank adopted a definition of corruption which is now widely used in anti-corruption discourse.[202] The Bank defines corruption as the 'abuse of public office for private gain'.[203] This definition is broad enough to cover acts like bribery, theft of state assets, fraud, nepotism, the misallocation of government benefits and other forms of bureaucratic corruption.[204]

The Bank has since inception disbursed billions of dollars as development finance[205] and is thus 'exposed to significant operational risk for fraud and corruption'.[206] Within the Bank's Articles of Association, there is no express provision requiring the Bank to take measures against corruption in Bank-financed projects. For many years, this, and the provisions prohibiting the Bank from interfering in, or being influenced by the internal affairs of a Borrower country were cited as reasons why the Bank did not take action against corruption in Borrower countries and within Bank projects.[207] The Articles, however, also provide that the Bank shall ensure that the proceeds of any loan are used only for the purposes for which the loan is granted.[208] When the Bank eventually decided to face the problem of corruption, this provision was interpreted as being broad enough to grant legitimacy to the Bank's anti-corruption efforts.[209]

The Bank's anti-corruption policy stems from a desire to ensure that Bank funds are utilised for the purposes for which they were granted, as required by the Articles of Agreement and also from the realisation that ineffective lending harms development and has severe consequences for

Cornell International Law Journal 593; S Rose-Ackerman, *Corruption and Government: Causes, Consequences, Reform* (Cambridge, Cambridge University Press, 1999); P Nichols, 'Regulating Transnational Bribery in Times of Globalization and Fragmentation' (1999) 24 *Yale Journal of International Law* 257; J Williams and M Beare, 'The Business of Bribery: Globalisation, Economic Liberalisation and the Problem of Corruption' (1999) 32 *Crime Law and Social Change* 115.

[202] D Kaufman, 'Corruption: The Facts' (1997) 107 *Foreign Policy* 114; M Johnston, 'The Search for Definitions: The Vitality of Politics and the Issue of Corruption' (1996) 48 *International Social Science Journal* 321; Warren, 'What Does Corruption Mean in a Democracy', above n 156.

[203] World Bank, Helping Countries Combat Corruption: The Role of the World Bank (Washington, World Bank, 1997) [hereafter Helping Countries, 1997] 8.

[204] Helping Countries, ibid, 9–10.

[205] See World Bank, Annual Report 2011.

[206] P Chanda, 'The Effectiveness of the World Bank's Anti-Corruption Efforts: Current Legal and Structural Obstacles and Uncertainties' (2004) 32 *Denver Journal of International Law and Policy* 315, 316.

[207] Helping Countries 1997; R Thornburgh, P Gainer, C Walker, Report to Shengman Zhang, Managing Director and Chairman of the Oversight Committee on Fraud and Corruption, The World Bank Concerning Mechanisms to Address Problems of Fraud and Corruption (Washington, World Bank, 2000) 8–9 [hereafter, Thornburgh Report]; Shihata, 'Corruption: A general Review', above n 197, 474.

[208] IBRD Articles of Agreement, art III s 5.

[209] Chanda, 'The Effectiveness of the World Bank's Anti-Corruption Efforts', above n 206, 349.

citizens in Borrower countries.[210] In desiring the proper expenditure of Bank funds, the Bank was responding to widespread criticism against its complicit role in corruption in Borrower countries such as Russia,[211] Indonesia,[212] Kenya[213] and Bangladesh.[214] To ensure that Bank loans were not lost to corruption, the Bank took steps to ensure transparency in its procurement procedures and revised its procurement guidelines to make corruption a ground for excluding a tender, disqualifying a contractor or cancelling a loan to a Borrower country. Other measures introduced to curb corruption included capacity building assistance to Borrower countries[215] and the suspension of further loans in countries where corruption is found to be endemic.[216]

An examination of the Bank's policy against corruption in its projects reveals four main strategies. The first is to ensure that the procurement process contains preventive and punitive elements against corruption. The Bank's policy of disqualifying corrupt contractors assists in executing both these elements. Secondly, the Bank ensures that the pre-approval stage of loans and projects is rigorous and contains input from all interested parties.[217] Thirdly, measures are taken to ensure that institutionally, the Bank is corruption free.[218] Finally, the Bank has improved auditing and supervision requirements in its projects.[219]

A few comments may be made about the success of the Bank's anti-corruption measures. It was estimated by Bank staff that about 30 per cent of Bank funds has been lost to corruption since the Bank began lending.[220]

[210] J Winters, 'Criminal Debt' in J Pincus and J Winters (eds), *Reinventing the World Bank* (Ithaca, Cornell University Press, 2002), 120; Mauro, 'The Effects of Corruption on Growth, Investment and Government Expenditure', above n 190; C Gray and D Kaufman, 'Corruption & Development' (1998) *Finance and Development* 7.

[211] J Stiglitz, *Globalisation and its Discontents* (WW Norton, 2002) ch 5.

[212] J Levinson, 'Living Dangerously: Indonesia and the Reality of the Global Economic System' (1998) 7 *Journal of International Law and Practice* 425; J Winters, *Power in Motion: Capital Mobility in the Indonesian State* (Ithaca, Cornell University Press, 1996).

[213] K Kibwana and S Wanjala, *The Anatomy of Corruption in Kenya: Legal, Political, and Socio-economic Perspectives* (Nairobi, Clairpress Ltd, 1996).

[214] T Tucker, 'A Critical Analysis of the Procurement Procedures of the World Bank' in S Arrowsmith and A Davies (eds), *Public Procurement: Global Revolution* (London, Kluwer Law, 1998) 153, 155.

[215] Rose-Ackerman, *Corruption and Government*, above n 201, 112; OECD DAC Network on Governance, Synthesis of Lessons Learned of Donor Practices in fighting Corruption (Paris, OECD, 2003).

[216] The Bank has in the past suspended loans on projects in Indonesia (September 1999), Kenya (January 2006), Chad (January 2006), Uzbekistan (March 2006), Cambodia (June 2006). See www.brettonwoodsproject.org .

[217] World Bank Operational Directive (OD) 14.70. See S Schlemmer-Schulte, 'The impact of Civil Society on the World Bank, the International Monetary Fund and the World Trade Organisation: The Case of the World Bank' (2001) 2 *ILSA Journal of International and Comparative Law* 399.

[218] World Bank Staff Manual, Principle 3.

[219] World Bank Operational Manual, OP/BP 10.02.

[220] Winters, 'Criminal Debt', above n 210, 102 and 111.

However, subsequent evidence suggests that many Bank-financed projects are still subject to corruption and that approximately 10–15 per cent of contract value goes into bribery.[221] If these figures can be taken as an indication of the effect that Bank's anti-corruption efforts have had, it may be assumed that Bank efforts have only had a limited impact in reducing corruption in its projects.

The limited success of past Bank anti-corruption initiatives led to further strategies for tackling corruption[222] and the Bank introduced a system to minimise the risk of corruption in its projects through the use of anti-corruption teams who work to protect the projects from corruption, develop anti-corruption strategies and strengthen procurement systems.[223] These reforms were designed to provide a more holistic approach to corruption control, by the Bank taking a more integrated and proactive approach to the institutional reform of Borrower country procurement systems, as well as controlling the risks of corruption in Bank-funded projects, by targeting the demand and supply side of corruption in these projects.

3.5.3 Disqualification in the World Bank

The Bank uses two kinds of disqualification measures against corrupt suppliers. These are termed 'rejection' and 'debarment'. Rejection is the exclusion of a contractor's bid from a particular procurement process, while debarment is the disqualification of a contractor from Bank contracts for a specified period of time. For the purposes of this book, the term 'disqualification' will refer to both measures since the only differences between them are the long-term consequences and procedural differences.

The Bank's procurement guidelines provide in paragraph 1.16 that:

> It is the Bank's policy to require that Borrowers (including beneficiaries of Bank loans), bidders, suppliers, contractors and their agents (whether declared or not), sub-contractors, sub-consultants, service providers or suppliers and any personnel thereof observe the highest standards of ethics during the procurement and execution of Bank-financed contracts. In pursuance of this policy, the Bank:
>
> (a) defines for the purposes of this provision, the terms set forth below as follows:
>
> (i) 'corrupt practice' is the offering, giving, receiving or soliciting, directly or indirectly, of anything of value to influence improperly the actions of another party.

221 N Hobbs, 'Corruption in World Bank Financed Projects: Why Bribery is a Tolerated Anathema' (DESTIN Working Papers, 2005) 24–9. Available at: www.lse.ac.uk.

222 World Bank, *Strengthening Bank Group Engagement on Governance and Anti-Corruption* (Washington, World Bank, 2006). Available at: www.worldbank.org .

223 ibid.

(ii) 'fraudulent practice' is any act or omission, including a misrepresentation, that knowingly or recklessly misleads, or attempts to mislead, a party to obtain a financial or other benefit or to avoid an obligation.
(iii) 'collusive practice' is an arrangement between two or more parties designed to achieve an improper purpose, including to influence improperly the actions of another party.
(iv) 'coercive practice' is impairing or harming, or threatening to impair or harm, directly or indirectly, any party or the property of the party to influence improperly the actions of a party.
(v) an 'obstructive practice' is –

(aa) deliberately destroying, falsifying, altering or concealing of evidence material to the investigation or making false statements to investigators in order to materially impede a Bank investigation into allegations of a corrupt, fraudulent, coercive or collusive practice; and/or threatening, harassing or intimidating any party to prevent it from disclosing its knowledge of matters relevant to the investigation or from pursuing the investigation, or
(bb) acts intended to materially impede the exercise of the Bank's contractual rights of audit or access to information . . .
(b) will reject a proposal for award if it determines that the bidder recommended for award or any of its personnel or agents or its sub-consultants or sub-contractors, service providers, suppliers and/or their employees has, directly or indirectly, engaged in corrupt, fraudulent, collusive, coercive or obstructive practices in competing for the contract in question;
. . .
(d) will sanction a firm or individual, at any time in accordance with the Bank's prevailing sanctions procedures including by publicly declaring such firm or individual ineligible, either indefinitely or for a stated period of time:

(i) to be awarded a Bank-financed contract and
(ii) to be nominated a sub-contractor, consultant, supplier or service provider of an otherwise eligible firm being awarded a Bank-financed contract . . .

The Bank's disqualification policy is directed at persons who commit breaches of the Bank's anti-corruption provisions in Bank-funded projects, irrespective of whether the offences were committed in the procurement context. Disqualifying contractors for non-procurement related offences is also the approach of the EU, the UK and the US.

The rationale behind the Bank's disqualification policy is three-fold. The first rationale is protective, similar to what obtains in the US and the EU. Thus, disqualification is intended to protect the Bank's funds in accordance with the prescripts of its Articles of Agreement by ensuring that its funds are not lost to fraud and corruption.[224] Secondly, disquali-

[224] D Thornburgh, R Gainer and C Walker, *Report Concerning the Debarment Processes of the World Bank* (Washington, World Bank, 2002) 33, 61 [hereafter Thornburgh, *Report Concerning Debarment Process*].

fication has a policy rationale as it is intended to support the Bank's anti-corruption policy by indicating its willingness to punish corruption.[225] Thirdly, disqualification is intended to have a deterrent rationale,[226] because disqualification from Bank contracts increases the economic costs of corruption as the disqualified supplier loses the potential to compete for future Bank-financed contracts, and also because where the disqualification is published, as is current Bank practice, this can damage the reputation of the firm, affecting its ability to obtain business from other sectors.

The Bank's disqualification policy is tied to the eligibility and not the capability of the supplier, as Bank contracts cannot be awarded to a supplier that has been disqualified, irrespective of the supplier's capabilities.[227]

3.6 SOUTH AFRICA

3.6.1 Public Procurement Regulation in South Africa

Similar to the position in the US, South Africa also adopts a highly regulated and formal approach to public procurement, which utilises Constitutional provisions as well as binding legislation and regulations to achieve procurement objectives. Similar to the US, also, procurement regulation occurs at the federal level and the provincial (state) and local levels.[228]

The regulation of procurement in South Africa has an interesting socio-political history. During the apartheid regime, public procurement was used to protect the interests of the minority of large white-owned enterprises[229] and discriminated against small, medium and black-owned businesses. In particular, 'tender procedures were complicated and favoured large firms to the detriment of small emerging firms'.[230] At the federal level, procurement was regulated by the State Tender Board Act 1968[231] and the regulations made there under, which required all federal procurement to be conducted through the State Tender Board. The centralisation of procurement was important in protecting the interests of white-owned

[225] Thornburgh, *Report Concerning Debarment Process*, 61; World Bank Sanctions Procedures 2010, art 1 s 1.01 [hereafter WBSP].

[226] World Bank Sanctioning Guidelines. Available at: siteresources.worldbank.org/EXTOFFEVASUS/Resources/WorldBankSanctioningGuidelines.pdf.

[227] BPG para 1.10.

[228] P Bolton, *The Law of Government Procurement in South Africa* (Durban, LexisNexis Butterworth, 2007) ch 3.

[229] C Rogerson, 'Pro-Poor Local Economic Development in South Africa: The Application of Public Procurement' (2004) 15 *Urban Forum* 180, 181.

[230] World Bank, 'Public and Private Sector Procurement Programmes and their Contribution to Emerging Enterprises in South Africa' (Report prepared for the Workshop on Small, Medium and Micro Enterprise Development and Financing, 3 Nov 1994); D Sharp, P Mashingo, P Burton, *Assessment of Public Sector Procurement to Small, Medium and Micro-Enterprises* (Ntisika Enterprise Promotion Agency, 1999).

[231] Act 86 of 1968.

businesses. This legislation has now been repealed to require procurement to be conducted through the accounting officers of government departments.[232]

At the demise of apartheid, it was determined that public procurement would be utilised to democratise the economy and provide employment and business opportunities for marginalised and disadvantaged individuals and communities, commonly referred to as 'target groups'.[233] Significant reform was required for this and the government initially implemented interim measures within the existing legislative framework,[234] and issued a Green Paper[235] setting out the required legislative and policy changes.

The major proposals of the Green Paper on using public procurement to democratise the economy and create access to opportunities to persons previously disadvantaged by the system have been implemented through legislation. However, there is conflicting evidence on whether the procurement system has been successful in meeting the Green Paper's objectives especially in relation to granting access to the target groups, de-racialising patterns of business ownership and stimulating economic growth by creating employment opportunities.[236]

The importance of procurement to democratic government in South Africa can be seen in the fact that the basic principles on which the procurement system was to be based were given constitutional status. Thus, Section 217 (1) of the Constitution provides that:

> When an organ of state in the national, provincial or local sphere of government, or any other institution identified in national legislation, contracts for goods or services, it must do so in accordance with a system which is fair, equitable, transparent, competitive and cost-effective.[237]

The requirement for a system that is 'fair and equitable' can be interpreted, in the context of South Africa's political history,[238] as requiring the

[232] Amended State Tender Board Regulations (Government Gazette 7836, 5 December 2003).

[233] TE Manchidi and I Harmond, 'Targeted Procurement in the Republic of South Africa: An Independent Assessment' (Report for the Dept of Public Works, the Development Bank of Southern Africa and the International Labour Organisation, 2002).

[234] Public Sector Procurement Reform in South Africa: Interim Strategies–A 10 point plan (29 November, 1995).

[235] Green Paper on Public Sector Procurement Reform (Government Gazette 17928, 14 April 1997). [hereafter Green Paper].

[236] Some of the problems that have arisen within the procurement system are 'fronting' or the use of fictitious black persons so that a white-owned company qualifies for targeted procurement; the rise of 'fly by night' tenderer's who submit unsustainable bids; and the lack of access to credit for emerging contractors. See *Viking Pony Africa Pumps (Pty) Ltd t/a Tricom Africa v Hidro-Tech Systems (Pty) Ltd and City of Cape Town* [2010] ZACC 21; Bolton, *Law of Government Procurement*, above n 228, 293; C Rogerson, 'The Impact of the South African Governments SMME programmes – A Ten Year Review 1994–2004' (2004) 21 *Development South Africa* 765.

[237] Constitution of the Republic of South Africa Act 108 of 1996.

[238] I Currie and J de Waal, *The Bill of Rights Handbook*, 5th edn (Cape Town, Juta, 2005) 156.

adoption of a system without discrimination and unjustifiable preferences.[239] The Constitution also requires the procurement system to be 'transparent'. Transparency has been interpreted as requiring publicised contracts; disclosure of the rules governing procurement in general and governing specific procurements; rule-based decision-making and opportunities for verification and enforcement.[240] It has been suggested that constitutional provisions on transparency are a response to the culture of secrecy in the apartheid regime, which was used to restrict the access of black South Africans to economic opportunities.[241]

The principles of competition and cost-effectiveness in the Constitution complement each other. Competition suggests that a sufficient number of suppliers should be invited to tender for available contracts, ensuring the government does not pay uncompetitive prices. Competition supports anti-corruption efforts, in that if qualified suppliers have access to available contracts, this will limit the scope for corruption-induced awards and remove the restrictions to participation created against non-corrupt suppliers. Cost-effectiveness can be interpreted as the obligation to obtain value for money.[242] It means that procuring entities should at all times seek to obtain the best bargain and the most advantageous contractual terms,[243] and procurement procedures should be transactionally efficient.[244]

Section 217(2) of the South African Constitution provides that government bodies may use preferential procurement policies to protect or advance disadvantaged groups, giving constitutional legitimacy to using the procurement system to empower the groups disadvantaged under apartheid.[245]

Apart from constitutional provisions, there are several statutes concerned with procurement regulation. First, the Public Finance Management

[239] Bolton, *Law of Government Procurement*, ch 3; Government of the Republic of South Africa: General Procurement Guidelines. Available at: www.treasury.gov.za .

[240] Arrowsmith, *Public and Utilities Procurement*, above n 13, ch 7.12; S Arrowsmith, 'Towards a Multilateral Agreement on Transparency in Government Procurement' (1998) 47 *International and Comparative Law Quarterly* 793, 796; S Evenett and B Hoekman, 'Transparency in Procurement Regimes: What Can We Expect from International Trade Agreements' in S Arrowsmith and M Trybus (eds), *Public Procurement: The Continuing Revolution* (The Hague, Kluwer Law, 2003).

[241] R Watermeyer, 'Transparency Within the South African Public Procurement System' in B Hoekman (ed), *Unpacking Transparency in Government Procurement* (CUTS, 2004) 173.

[242] S Schooner, 'Desiderata: Objectives For a System of Government Contract Law' (2002) *Public Procurement Law Review* 105.

[243] A Beviglia-Zampetti, 'The UNCITRAL Model Law on Procurement of Goods, Construction, Services' in B Hoekman and P Mavroidis (eds), *Law and Policy in Public Purchasing: The WTO Agreement on Government Procurement* (Michigan, University of Michigan Press, 1997) ch 15.

[244] Arrowsmith, Linarelli and Wallace, *Regulating Public Procurement*, above n 184, 31–2.

[245] P Bolton, 'The Use of Government Procurement as an Instrument of Policy' (2004) 121 *South African Law Journal* 619; P Bolton, 'Government Procurement as a Policy Tool in South Africa' (2006) 6 *Journal of Public Procurement* 193; P Bolton, 'An Analysis of the Preferential Procurement Legislation in South Africa' (2007) 3 *Public Procurement Law Review* 36.

Act (PFMA) and the Regulations thereto aim to regulate public financial management, ensure that government revenue, expenditure, assets and liabilities are properly managed and secure transparency and accountability in government departments.[246] The PFMA is important to the functioning of public procuring entities, as it lays the ground-rules for public financial transactions and obliges public bodies to maintain appropriate procurement systems.[247] The regulations to the PFMA provide detailed instructions on the implementation of the PFMA, by providing for competitive procurement methods and advertising requirements.[248]

Secondly, the Preferential Procurement Policy Framework Act 2000 (PPPFA) and the Regulations[249] thereto provides for the use of a preferential procurement policy[250] and prescribes the points system government agencies must use to determine whether bids meet contract criteria.[251]

Finally, the Broad Based Black Economic Empowerment Act 2003 (BBBEEA)[252] provides the general legislative framework for the economic empowerment of black South Africans.[253] In public procurement, the Act provides the basis for the preferential treatment of black South Africans. The Act is implemented through Codes of Good Practice on Black Economic Empowerment, which describe how public bodies may effect black economic empowerment in their activities. Where a code has been issued, every organ of state and public entity must take it into account in developing and implementing a preferential procurement policy.[254]

3.6.2 South Africa's Anti-corruption Policy

South Africa's anti-corruption policy is part of a broader policy against crime.[255] Unlike those of the UK and the US, South African anti-corruption policy is mainly concerned with domestic corruption, and not with corruption in other countries or in international business. In South Africa, it is considered that public sector corruption and economic crimes con-

[246] Public Finance Management Act 1 of 1999 (Government Gazette 19814, 2 March 1999), s 2 [hereafter PFMA]; Public Finance Management Act Regulations (Government Gazette 22219, 9 April, 2001, as amended by Government Gazette 23463, 25 May, 2002); [hereafter PFMA regulations].

[247] PFMA, s 38(1).

[248] PFMA Regulations, reg 16.A6.3.

[249] The Preferential Procurement Policy Framework Act 5 of 2000 (Government Gazette 20854, 3 February 2000) [hereafter PPPFA]; Preferential Procurement Policy Framework Act Regulations (Government Gazette 34350, 8 June 2011) [hereafter PPPFA regulations].

[250] See articles cited at n 245.

[251] PPPFA, s 2.

[252] Act 53 of 2003 (Government Gazette 25899, 9 January 2004) [BBBEEA].

[253] BBBEEA s 1.

[254] BBBEEA s 10(b).

[255] National Crime Prevention Strategy (Department of Safety and Security, 22 May 1996).

tribute to organised crime and promote 'a sense of lawlessness'[256] in society. Thus the policy is aimed at eradicating corruption in the public and private spheres and particularly within public procurement.

Within the broader anti-crime strategy, measures against corruption include the establishment of codes of conduct for businesses and government in relation to white-collar crime and corruption[257] and the implementation of legislation to restrict money laundering.[258] The anti-corruption policy adopts a multi-pronged approach to the eradication of corruption, with corruption control viewed as the joint responsibility of the government and civil society.[259] To this end, civil society, business and government created, as a joint initiative, the National Anti-Corruption Forum, which seeks to develop a national consensus on anti-corruption, advise the government on anti-corruption measures and share information and best practice on sectoral anti-corruption initiatives.[260]

A number of measures have been adopted to implement South Africa's anti-corruption policy. In respect of public sector corruption, the government issued the Public Service Anti-Corruption Strategy.[261] The Strategy is the primary policy document on public sector corruption and provides a coherent and integrated approach to combating public sector corruption, through prevention, investigation, prosecution and public participation initiatives.

Pursuant to the Strategy, the government consolidated the legislative framework on corruption through the Prevention and Combating of Corrupt Activities Act (Corruption Act).[262] In accordance with the Strategy, the Corruption Act disqualifies corrupt firms from obtaining government contracts. Further, and in line with the Strategy, the PFMA requires the maintenance of a procurement system that includes sufficient controls to eliminate the risk of corruption. Other initiatives include the creation in 2010 of an anti-corruption unit within the Department of Public Service and Administration, which was established to

> investigate officials doing business with government without disclosing their business interests, officials performing remunerative work outside the public

[256] Pillar 2.4, National Crime Prevention Strategy.

[257] Code of Conduct for the Public Service (Government Gazette 5947, 10 June, 1997), Code of Conduct for all parties engaged in Construction procurement (Government Gazette 25656, 31 October, 2003).

[258] Pillar 2.4 National Crime Prevention Strategy.

[259] Ch.8 National Crime Prevention Strategy and South African Civil Society Workshop – Civil Society Taking Corruption Seriously (21 March, 2005, Pretoria).

[260] National Anti-Corruption Forum, South Africa, Memorandum of Understanding. Available at www.nacf.org.za/about-nacf/index.html .

[261] Public Service Anti-Corruption Strategy (Department of Public Service and Administration, January 2002).

[262] Act 12 of 2004 (Government Gazette 26311, 28 April 2004), [Corruption Act]; O Sibanda, 'The South African Corruption Law and Bribery of Foreign Public Officials in International Business Transactions: A Comparative Analysis' (2005) 1 *South Africa Criminal Justice* 1.

service without permission and officials who solicit bribes in return for performing or not performing official duties as well as those receiving grants or benefits unlawfully.[263]

Whilst the anti-corruption policy is for the greater part concerned with the elimination of public corruption, it is also concerned with fighting private sector corruption, although the eradication of private sector corruption has not received the same attention as public sector corruption.[264]

3.6.3 Disqualification in South Africa

Disqualification in South Africa is in part a legislative response to the Public Service Anti-Corruption Strategy. Like the EU and UK, South Africa utilises both mandatory and discretionary measures against corrupt suppliers. The provisions on disqualification are found in three legislative instruments. The Corruption Act and the PPPFA regulations provide for discretionary disqualifications and the PFMA regulations provide for both discretionary and mandatory disqualifications.

As has already been mentioned, South Africa differs from the EU, the UK and the US in that disqualification is triggered by the commission of procurement-related offences whilst in the other jurisdictions, disqualification may be imposed for general as well as procurement-related corruption offences.

In South Africa, there is a lack of clarity on the rationales for disqualification. As stated in chapter two, disqualification may be regarded as punitive if it is tied to the objectives of deterrence or retribution, and is imposed as a result of the contractor's past conduct.[265] Whilst there has been no clear statement as to the purpose of disqualifications it is suggested that the South African disqualifications are intended to be punitive.[266] Three reasons tend towards this conclusion. First, under the Corruption Act, disqualification is imposed at the same time as criminal sanctions, which are punitive in nature. Secondly, none of the disqualification provisions under the Corruption Act, the PFMA regulations and the PPPFA regulations permit the possibility of derogating from the disqualification once it is imposed. Thirdly, disqualifications are not tied to the capability of the supplier and do not depend on the supplier's ability to perform the contract.

The relevant provisions on disqualification are found in sections 12, 13 and 28 of the Corruption Act, regulation 16 of the PFMA Regulations and regulation 13 of the PPPFA regulations.

[263] New anti-corruption unit launched. Available at www.sagoodnews.co.za.

[264] South African Civil Society Workshop, above n 247.

[265] E Tomko and K Weinberg, 'After the Fall: Conviction, Debarment and Double Jeopardy' (1992) 21 *Public Contract Law Journal* 363, 365.

[266] S Williams, 'The Use of Exclusions for Corruption in Developing Country Procurement: The Case of South Africa' (2007) 51 *Journal of African Law* 1, 12.

Section 12 of the Corruption Act provides:

(1) Any person who, directly or indirectly –

(a) accepts or agrees or offers to accept any gratification from any other person, whether for the benefit of himself or herself or for the benefit of that other person or of another person; or

(b) gives or agrees or offers to give to any other person any gratification, whether for the benefit of that other person or for the benefit of another person,

(i) in order to improperly influence, in any way –

(aa) the promotion, execution or procurement of any contract with a public body, private organisation, corporate body or any other organisation or institution; or

(bb) the fixing of the price, consideration or other moneys stipulated or otherwise provided for in any such contract; or

(ii) as a reward for acting as contemplated in paragraph *(a)*,

is guilty of the offence of corrupt activities relating to contracts.

Section 13 of the Corruption Act provides:

(1) Any person who, directly or indirectly, accepts or agrees or offers to accept any gratification from any other person, whether for the benefit of himself or herself or for the benefit of another person, as –

(a) an inducement to, personally or by influencing any other person so to act –

(i) award a tender, in relation to a contract for performing any work, providing any service, supplying any article, material or substance or performing any other act, to a particular person; or

(ii) upon an invitation to tender for such contract, make a tender for that contract which has as its aim to cause the tenderee to accept a particular tender; or

(iii) withdraw a tender made by him or her for such contract; or

(b) a reward for acting as contemplated in paragraph *(a)*(i) (ii) or (iii),

is guilty of the offence of corrupt activities relating to procuring and withdrawal of tenders.

(2) Any person who, directly or indirectly –

(a) gives or agrees or offers to give any gratification to any other person, whether for the benefit of that other person or the benefit of another person, as –

(i) an inducement to, personally or by influencing any other person so to act, award a tender, in relation to a contract for performing any work, providing any service, supplying any article, material or substance or performing any other act, to a particular person; or

(ii) a reward for acting as contemplated in subparagraph (i); or *(b)* with the intent to obtain a tender in relation to a contract for performing any work, providing any service, supplying any article, material or substance or performing any other act, gives or agrees or offers to give any gratification to any person who has made a tender in relation to that contract, whether for the benefit of that tenderer or for the benefit of any other person, as –

(i) an inducement to withdraw the tender; or
(ii) a reward for withdrawing or having withdrawn the tender,

is guilty of the offence of corrupt activities relating to procuring and withdrawal of tenders.

Section 28 of the Corruption Act provides:

(1) *(a)* A court convicting a person of an offence contemplated in section 12 or 13, may, in addition to imposing any sentence contemplated in section 26, issue an order that –

(i) the particulars of the convicted person;
(ii) the conviction and sentence; and
(iii) any other order of the court consequent thereupon,

be endorsed on the Register.

(b) If the person so convicted is an enterprise, the court may also issue an order that –

(i) the particulars of that enterprise;
(ii) the particulars of any partner, manager, director or other person, who wholly or partly exercises or may exercise control over that enterprise and who was involved in the offence concerned or who knows or ought reasonably to have known or suspected that the enterprise committed the offence concerned; and
(iii) the conviction, sentence and any other order of the court consequent thereupon,

be endorsed on the Register.

(c) The court may also issue an order contemplated in paragraph *(a)* in respect of –

(i) any other enterprise owned or controlled by the person so convicted; or
(ii) the particulars of any partner, manager, director or other person, who wholly or partly exercises or may exercise control over such other enterprise,

and which –

(aa) enterprise, partner, manager, director or other person was involved in the offence concerned; or
(bb) partner, manager, director or other person knew or ought reasonably to have known or suspected that such other enterprise was involved in the offence concerned.

(d) Whenever the Register is endorsed as contemplated in paragraph *(a)*, *(b)* or *(c)*, the endorsement applies, unless the court directs otherwise, to

every enterprise to be established in the future, and which enterprise will be wholly or partly controlled or owned by the person or enterprise so convicted or endorsed, and the Registrar must, in respect of every such enterprise, endorse the Register accordingly.

(2) Where a court has issued an order under subsection (1), the registrar or clerk of such court must forthwith forward the court order to the Registrar and the Registrar must forthwith endorse the Register accordingly.

(3) *(a)* Where the Register has been endorsed in terms of subsection (2), in addition to any other legal action, the following restrictions may or must, as the case may be, be imposed;

(i) The National Treasury may terminate any agreement with the person or enterprise referred to in subsection (1)*(a)* or *(b)*: Provided that –

(aa) in considering the termination of an agreement, the National Treasury must take into account, among others, the following factors, namely –

(aaa) the extent and duration of the agreement concerned;
(bbb) whether it is likely to conclude a similar agreement with another person or enterprise within a specific time frame;
(ccc) the extent to which the agreement has been executed;
(ddd) the urgency of the services to be delivered or supplied in terms of the agreement;
(eee) whether extreme costs will follow such termination; and
(fff) any other factor which, in the opinion of the National Treasury, may impact on the termination of the agreement; and

(bb) if that agreement involves any purchasing authority or Government Department, such restriction may only be imposed after consultation with the purchasing authority or Government Department concerned;

(ii) the National Treasury must determine the period (which period may not be less than five years or more than 10 years) for which the particulars of the convicted person or the enterprise referred to in subsection (1)*(a)*, *(b)*, *(c)* or *(d)* must remain in the Register and during such period no offer in respect of any agreement from a person or enterprise referred to in that subsection may be considered by the National Treasury; or

(iii) during the period determined in subparagraph (ii), the National Treasury, the purchasing authority or any Government Department must –

(aa) ignore any offer tendered by a person or enterprise referred to in subsection *(1)(a)*, *(b)*, *(c)* or *(d)*; or

(bb) disqualify any person or enterprise referred to subsection (1)*(a)*, *(b)*, *(c)* or *(d)*, from making any offer or obtaining any agreement relating to the procurement of a specific supply or service.

(b) A restriction imposed under paragraph *(a)* only comes into effect after any appeal against the conviction or sentence or both has been finalised by the court: Provided that if the appeal court sets aside, varies or amends the order referred to in subsection (1), the National Treasury must, if necessary, amend the restrictions imposed under paragraph *(a)* accordingly.

(c) Where the National Treasury has terminated an agreement in terms of paragraph *(a)*(i), it may, in addition to any other legal remedy, recover from the person or enterprise any damages –

(i) incurred or sustained by the State as a result of the tender process or the conclusion of the agreement; or

(ii) which the State may suffer by having to make less favourable arrangements thereafter.

(4) The National Treasury –

(a) may at any time vary or rescind any restriction imposed under subsection (3)*(a)*(i) or (ii); and

(b) must, when the period determined in terms of subsection (3)*(a)*(ii) expires, remove the particulars of the person or enterprise concerned, from the Register.

(5) When the National Treasury imposes a restriction under subsection *(3)(a)*(i) or (ii), or amends or rescinds such a restriction, it must within 14 days in writing notify –

(a) the person whose particulars have been so endorsed;

(b) any purchasing authority on which it may decide; and

(c) all Government departments, of any resolution or decision relative to such restriction or the amendment or rescinding thereof, and request such authorities and departments to take similar steps.

(6) *(a)* Any person whose particulars, conviction and sentence have been endorsed on the Register as contemplated in this section and who has been notified as contemplated in subsection *(5)(a)*, must in any subsequent agreement or tender process involving the State, disclose such endorsement, conviction and sentence.

(b) Any person who fails to comply with paragraph *(a)*, is guilty of an offence.

Regulation 16A9.1 of the PFMA regulations provides:

The accounting officer or accounting authority must –

. . .

(e) reject a proposal for the award of a contract if the recommended bidder has committed a corrupt or fraudulent act in competing for the particular contract.

Regulation 16A9.2 (a) provides

The accounting officer or accounting authority –

(a) may disregard the bid of any bidder if that bidder, or any of its directors –

(i) have abused the institution's supply chain management system
(ii) have committed fraud or any other improper conduct in relation to such system; or
(iii) have failed to perform on any previous contract . . .

Regulation 13 of the PPPFA regulations provides:

(1) An organ of state must, upon detecting that

(a) the B-BBEE status level of contribution has been claimed or obtained on a fraudulent basis; or
(b) any of the terms of the contract have not been filled

act against the person awarded the contract.

(2) An organ of state may, in addition to any other remedy it may have against the person contemplated in sub-regulations (1) –

(a) disqualify the person from the tendering process

. . .

(d) restrict the tenderer or contractor, its shareholders and directors or only the shareholders and directors who acted on a fraudulent basis from obtaining business from any organ of state for a period not exceeding 10 years, after the *audi alteram partem* (hear the other side) rule has been applied.

4

The Offences and the Requirement of a Conviction for Disqualification

4.1 INTRODUCTION

THIS CHAPTER WILL examine the offences which may lead to disqualification in the selected jurisdictions and examine whether criminal convictions for corruption are required for disqualification. Where disqualification is made on the basis of a conviction, the disqualification may be imposed by the court as a part of any sentence imposed following the conviction, as occurs in South Africa, but more commonly, the decision is made by the procuring authority on the receipt of evidence of the conviction as is the case in the US, the EU and the UK.

Also discussed in this chapter is whether a supplier will be disqualified where he has received a foreign conviction for corruption. This issue will become more important as countries open up their procurement markets to suppliers from other countries through agreements like the WTO Government Procurement Agreement.[1]

4.2 THE EUROPEAN UNION

4.2.1 Offences for Disqualification

As discussed, the EU adopts discretionary and mandatory disqualifications against suppliers guilty of certain offences. In relation to the discretionary measures, a supplier may be disqualified where he has been convicted of 'any offence concerning his professional conduct' or where he is 'guilty of grave professional misconduct'. Offences of professional misconduct cover a broad category of offences, which relate to the manner in which the provider carries out his profession or business.[2] Although corruption is not specifically mentioned here, professional misconduct

[1] See Arrowsmith, *The Law of Public and Utilities Procurement*, 2nd edn (London, Sweet & Maxwell, 2005) ch 20.

[2] E Piselli, 'The Scope for Excluding Providers Who Have Committed Criminal Offences under the EU Procurement Directives' (2000) 6 *Public Procurement Law Review* 267, 272.

offences will include breaches of anti-corruption norms or legislation, where these breaches occurred in the context of the business or profession. These can relate to past offences or offences committed within an on-going procurement process. Also a supplier involved in breaches of environmental legislation,[3] non-compliance with legislative provisions on the equal treatment of workers,[4] tax evasion, insider trading, or who acts in an anti-competitive manner[5] may be guilty of professional misconduct and liable to disqualification on those grounds. Professional misconduct would also include breaches of professional codes of conduct, where these exist. Whilst there cannot be an exhaustive definition of professional misconduct, as this would depend on the type and nature of the profession concerned, it has been suggested that the discretionary disqualifications offer the possibility to disqualify suppliers for corruption offences.[6]

In relation to the mandatory disqualifications, the corruption offence requiring disqualification is specified in Article 45 of the PSD as:

> (b) corruption, as defined in Article 3 of the Council Act of 26 May 1997 . . . and Article 3 of Council Joint Action 98/742/JHA . . . respectively . . .

The definitions of corruption incorporated into Article 45 are:

(i) Article 3 of Council Act of 26 May 1997 – the Convention on the fight against corruption involving officials of the European Communities or officials of Member states of the EU[7] defines active corruption as

> the deliberate action of whosoever promises or gives, directly or through an intermediary, an advantage of any kind whatsoever to an official for himself or for a third party for him to act or refrain from acting in accordance with his duty or in the exercise of his functions in breach of his official duties . . .

(ii) Article 3(1) of Council Joint Action adopted by the Council on the basis of Article K.3 of the Treaty on European Union on corruption in the private sector[8] provides

> the deliberate action of whosoever promises, offers or gives, directly or through an intermediary, an undue advantage of any kind whatsoever to a person, for himself or for a third party, in the course of the business activities of that person in order that the person should perform or refrain from performing an act, in breach of his duties, shall constitute active corruption in the private sector.

These corruption offences cover both private and public sector corruption. However, as stated, for all the selected jurisdictions, this book will focus on public sector corruption.

[3] PSD, recital 43.
[4] ibid.
[5] Piselli, 'The Scope for Excluding Providers', above n 2, 272.
[6] Piselli, 'The Scope for Excluding Providers', ibid, 274.
[7] [1997] OJ C195/1.
[8] [1998] OJ L358/2.

The definition of public sector corruption in the Convention against corruption involving officials of the EU or officials of Member States appears to be limited to corruption that involves public officials from the EU and Member States. This is because 'official' is defined in Article 1 of that Convention as 'any Community or national official, including any national official of another Member State'. This may mean that the mandatory disqualification provisions may be very narrow in their application, as the provisions may be interpreted as meaning that where a supplier has been convicted of corruption involving officials of non-EU countries, such a supplier ought not to be disqualified under the procurement directives. However, it should be noted that the definition of corruption adopted by Member States in their legislation implementing the EU procurement directives may include corruption involving officials outside the EU. Thus, as will be seen below in the context of the UK, the offence of corruption for which a supplier may be disqualified under the UK procurement regulations includes corruption involving foreign (ie non-EU) officials.

4.2.2 Disqualifying on the Basis of Convictions

In the EU, a discretionary disqualification from public contracts may be imposed under Article 45(2)(c) PSD where the supplier has been convicted by a 'judgment which has the force of res judicata'. Res judicata is not defined by the directives and the issue is further complicated by the fact that the provisions on the mandatory disqualifications for corruption provide that disqualification is required where the supplier 'has been the subject of a conviction by final judgment'[9] for a relevant offence.

It is not clear what is meant by 'final judgment' and it may be the case that Member States have the flexibility to determine what amounts to a 'final judgment' for the purposes of the disqualification provisions. However, this may lead to differences in the treatment of convicted suppliers in the Member States, dependent on whether the conviction is considered under national law to have been ordered in a final judgment.[10] The recitals to the public sector directives indicate that a final judgment is one that has the force of res judicata.[11] This does not, however, provide any more clarity on the meaning of 'final judgment' as there are differ-

[9] PSD, art 45(1).

[10] Presidency Working Document (Working Party on Public Procurement) Proposal for a Directive of the European Parliament and of the Council on the coordination of procedures for the award of public works contracts, public supply contracts and public service contracts. DG C II, Brussels 18 October 2001, SN 3663/01 (MAP). Reproduced in JM Hebly (ed), *European Public Procurement: Legislative History of the 'Classic' Directive* (Alphen aan de Rijn, Kluwer Law International, 2007) 1130.

[11] PSD, recital 43.

ences in the meaning of 'res judicata' in different Member States. For instance, in the UK, a 'res judicata' is a decision pronounced by a court or tribunal with jurisdiction over the parties, which disposes of the issues litigated, so that those issues may no longer be re-litigated between the same parties, even though the judgment may still be subject to an appeal.[12] However, some Member States interpret a 'final judgment' as one that can no longer be subject to an appeal.[13]

The preparatory documents to the directives initially provided for disqualification where there was a conviction by way of 'definitive judgment' for the relevant offences.[14] However, this was changed in subsequent revisions to the proposals. A definitive judgment may be understood as one excluding interlocutory or interim orders. However, the proposals for the procurement directives and the other preparatory documents are not clear as to what substantive changes, if any, were intended to be reflected by the change in the nomenclature from 'definitive judgment' to 'final judgment'.

There are two benefits which arise from requiring convictions for disqualification. First, the conviction provides the disqualified firm with a measure of procedural safeguards, since the firm's guilt would have been established beyond a reasonable doubt at the criminal trial. Secondly, the requirement for a conviction reduces (but does not eliminate)[15] the investigative burden on a procuring authority, since the convicting court will have dealt with all matters of evidence and proof. However, the requirement for a conviction may limit the effectiveness of disqualification in the Member States. This is because convictions for corruption are notably rare, especially the conviction of legal persons[16] and where disqualifications are dependent on such convictions, there may be few disqualifications from public contracts for corruption.

In relation to the discretionary disqualifications for grave professional misconduct under Article 45(2)(d) PSD, a conviction is not required and a supplier may be disqualified once the procuring authority can prove the misconduct by any means, which the procuring authority 'can demonstrate'.

Presumably, the procuring authority will be able to prove and demonstrate the misconduct where a professional body has determined that the misconduct occurred. Whether evidence short of this, such as a charge laid by a public prosecutor or media reports, may be used to prove professional misconduct remains to be seen. The EU may in future adopt a position

[12] *Halsbury's Laws of England*, vol 11, para 1168 (5th edn, 2009).

[13] Piselli, 'The Scope for Excluding Providers', above n 2, 271.

[14] Proposal for a Directive of the European Parliament and of the Council on the co-ordination of procedures for the award of public supply contracts, public service contracts and public works contracts [2001] OJ C/029E, art 46.

[15] See ch 7 below.

[16] C Nicholls, T Daniel, M Polaine and J Hatchard, *Corruption and Misuse of Public Office*, 1st edn (Oxford, Oxford University Press, 2006) 40–43.

similar to the US, where temporary disqualifications may be imposed where a supplier has committed a relevant offence, and this is evidenced by the commencement of investigations or litigation against the supplier, but he has not received a conviction or a civil judgment, because investigations into the alleged offence or litigation are still pending.

4.2.3 The Status of Foreign Convictions

The EU directives are silent as to whether disqualification is required under the mandatory provisions where a conviction has been obtained outside the EU. Foreign convictions may be relevant in two circumstances. First, an EU supplier may have obtained a conviction in a non-EU Member State. For instance, a multinational German firm – Lahmeyer International GmbH – was convicted of bribery in Lesotho in 2003.[17] Another EU firm – ABB Vetco Gray (UK) Ltd – was convicted in 2004 of offering bribes to Nigerian public officials in a Houston court.[18] The issue is whether such firms convicted of corruption outside the EU are eligible to tender for a contract governed by the EU procurement directives.

As was discussed above, the definition of public sector corruption imported into the EU directives relates to corruption involving EU officials, or officials of Member States. It is likely that in most cases, corruption involving EU or Member State officials will be prosecuted within the EU. However, it is also possible that a conviction for the corruption of an EU/Member State official is obtained outside the EU, where for instance it is prosecuted in the US under the Foreign Corrupt Practices Act. In such cases, suppliers involved in the corruption of EU/Member State official may be disqualified under the directives. However, where a EU supplier is convicted for corruption outside the EU for corruption involving foreign (ie non-EU) officials, it appears to be the case that such suppliers may not be disqualified under the EU procurement directives.

If this is the right interpretation of the EU provisions, limiting disqualification to convictions for the corruption of EU/Member State officials may not aid the EU in fully meeting the objectives of the disqualification regime as discussed in chapter three, since corrupt EU suppliers who have been convicted of corruption involving non-EU officials may not face disqualification. Although the corruption offences imported into the

[17] J McCormick and N Paterson, 'The Threat Posed by Transnational Political Corruption To Global Commercial and Development Banking' (2006) *Journal of Financial Crime* 183, 185–6; Transparency International, *Global Corruption Report* (2005) ch 2; S Williams, 'World Bank Introduces New Measures to Fight Corruption in Bank-Financed Contracts and the Administration of Bank Loans' (2007) 16 *Public Procurement Law Review* NA152.

[18] *United States v ABB Vetco Gray, Inc and ABB Vetco Gray UK, Ltd* (Case No 04-CR-279-01) (SD Tex July 2004). See ABB Vetco Gray and ABB Vetco Gray (UK) plead guilty to foreign bribery charges. Available at www.usdoj.gov/opa/pr/2004/July/04_crm_465.htm.

EU directives may give rise to this conclusion, as will be seen in the context of the UK below, whether a supplier is disqualified for foreign corruption will ultimately depend on the definitions of corruption in a Member State's procurement legislation.

Secondly, foreign convictions may be relevant where a third country supplier that has access to EU contracts has received a conviction in its own country.[19] In such cases the EU procurement directives are unclear as to whether such a conviction will lead to the disqualification of the third country supplier from EU contracts, given the narrow definition of corruption in the EU directives discussed above. It is submitted, however, that where a third country supplier is granted access to EU procurement, through the World Trade Organization Government Procurement Agreement (WTO GPA) for instance, then in relation to such suppliers, Member States are required to treat that supplier no less favourably than they treat suppliers from other Member States.[20] In doing so, such a supplier must take the benefit as well as the burden of EU procurement legislation and will be required to submit to the same eligibility criteria as EU suppliers.[21] Consequently, where it is revealed that the supplier has been convicted of a relevant offence, the supplier ought to be disqualified as it would be inappropriate for a convicted supplier from a third country to be permitted to tender for a contract, in circumstances where an EU supplier would not be permitted. As stated, the obligations under trade agreements granting access to EU procurement markets such as the GPA are to treat third country nationals no less favourably, but not better than EU nationals.[22]

One issue that arises in relation to foreign convictions is whether a procuring authority in a Member State has the discretion to disregard a foreign conviction where there is evidence that the trial lacked basic procedural fairness.[23] This may become a real issue as the EU expands to admit countries where the rule of law may still be in its infancy.[24]

In relation to the discretionary provisions, the EU directives are similarly silent on the issue of foreign convictions. However, as most aspects

[19] M Dischendorfer, 'Third Country Access to Public Procurement in the Community: The Case of Companies and Nationals from Central and Eastern European Countries' (2003) 12 *Public Procurement Law Review* 256; A Davies, 'Government Procurement' in S Lester and B Mercurio (eds), *Bilateral and Regional Trade Agreements: Commentary & Analysis* (Cambridge, Cambridge University Press, 2009).

[20] PSD, recital 7; PSD, art 5; WTO GPA, art III.

[21] WTO GPA, art VIII.

[22] WTO GPA, art III(1).

[23] English courts do not recognise judgments obtained in a manner contrary to natural justice or contrary to public policy or obtained by fraud – C Clarkson and J Hill, *The Conflict of Laws*, 3rd edn (Oxford, Oxford University Press, 2006) 151–3. Procuring authorities may have to do the same.

[24] N Simidjiyska, 'From Milosevic's Reign to the European Union: Serbia and Montenegro's Stabilization and Association Agreement' (2007) 21 *Temple International and Comparative Law Journal* 147; G de Búrca, 'Beyond the Charter: How Enlargement has Enlarged the Human Rights Policy of the European Union' (2004) 27 *Fordham International Law Journal* 679.

of these provisions are discretionary, it is possible to argue that it is left to the disqualifying entity to determine whether foreign convictions will be taken into account.

4.3. THE UNITED KINGDOM

4.3.1 Offences for Disqualification

The offences that would lead to disqualification from UK public contracts are based on the provisions of the EU procurement directives, but the offences were expanded to fit the scheme of relevant offences in the UK. As is the case under the EU directives, the offences for disqualification in the UK are similarly divided into offences for which disqualification is discretionary and offences that will lead to a mandatory disqualification.

As mentioned, this book will focus on the offence of public sector corruption. In relation to the mandatory disqualifications, the corruption offences for which disqualification is required are listed in Regulation 23(1) of the Public Contracts Regulations (PCR) as:

(b) corruption within the meaning of section 1 of the Public Bodies Corrupt Practices Act 1889 or section 1 of the Prevention of Corruption Act 1906, where the offence relates to active corruption;
(c) the offence of bribery where the offence relates to active corruption;
(ca) bribery within the meaning of section 1 or 6 of the Bribery Act 2010
...
(f) any other offence within the meaning of Article 45 (1) of the Public Sector Directive as defined by the national law of any relevant State ...

(1A) In paragraph (1), 'active corruption' means corruption as defined in Article 3 of the Council Act of 26 May 1997 or Article 3(1) of Council Joint Action 98/742/JHA.

The Bribery Act 2010 repealed the Public Bodies Corrupt Practices Act and the Prevention of Corruption Act. The UK regulations were thus amended to incorporate the definition of corruption in the Bribery Act by the Bribery Act (Consequential Amendments) Order 2011. The Bribery Act, 2010 provides in sections 1 and 6:

1. (1) A person (P) is guilty of an offence ...
(2) ... where –
  (a) P offers, promises or gives a financial or other advantage to another person, and
  (b) P intends the advantage
    (i) to induce a person to perform improperly a relevant function or activity, or
    (ii) to reward a person for the improper performance of such a function or activity.

> 6 (1) A person ('P') who bribes a foreign public official ('F') is guilty of an offence if P's intention is to influence F in F's capacity as a foreign public official.
> (2) P must also intend to obtain or retain
>
> (a) a business
> (b) an advantage in the conduct of a business . . .[25]

Although the Bribery Act contains a wide range of offences and prohibits active and passive bribery in the public and private sector, the offences that will lead to disqualification as incorporated into the regulations are limited to active bribery, ie bribe-giving and the bribery of foreign public officials.

The offence of bribery mentioned in Regulation 23(1)(c) incorporates the EU definitions of bribery into the PCR. As discussed above, these definitions criminalise the bribery of officials of the EU or officials of Member States[26] and bribery in the private sector.[27]

Regulation 23(1)(f) brings within the disqualifications, convictions for comparable offences in other relevant states even though the precise definitions will naturally differ. This provision suggests that suppliers will be disqualified for the relevant offences even if they were convicted outside the UK. A relevant state has been defined in the regulations as a Member State, but includes the non-Member States of Iceland, Liechtenstein and Norway.[28]

As can be seen, the corruption offences in the UK regulations are broader than the offences within the EU directives, as corruption is not limited to corruption involving officials of EU institutions or other Member States. The offences in the UK procurement regulations cover corruption involving foreign public officials, as defined in the Bribery Act, as well as corruption offences committed in 'relevant states'.

In relation to the discretionary disqualifications, the UK regulations provide in Regulation 23(4) PCR that:

> a contracting authority may treat an economic operator as ineligible or decide not to select an economic operator . . . on one or more of the following grounds, namely that the economic operator –
>
> . . .
>
> (d) has been convicted of a criminal offence relating to the conduct of his business or profession;

[25] See Ministry of Justice, The Bribery Act 2010: Guidance (2011).

[26] Council Act of 26 May 1997, Convention on the fight against corruption involving officials of the European Communities or officials of Member States of the EU [1997] OJ C195/1, art 3.

[27] Council Joint Action adopted by the Council on the basis of Article K.3 of the Treaty on European Union on corruption in the private sector [1998] OJ L358/2, art 3(1). Note that Council Joint Action 98/742/JHA has been repealed and replaced by Council Framework Decision 2003/568/JHA [2003] OJ L192/54

[28] PCR, reg 4(4).

(e) has committed an act of grave misconduct in the course of his business or profession.

As discussed in the context of the EU directives, offences in relation to the conduct of a business or a profession may include breaches of regulatory legislation governing the conduct of business and breaches of professional norms including integrity norms. Thus discretionary disqualification in the UK may be imposed for corruption committed in the course of a business and professional misconduct involving corruption.[29]

4.3.2 Disqualifying on the Basis of Convictions

Like the EU procurement directives, a discretionary disqualification in the UK may be imposed for a conviction for an offence committed in the conduct of a business or profession. In relation to the mandatory disqualifications, a supplier will be disqualified for a conviction for statutory corruption or the common law offence of bribery. Unlike the EU directives, however, the UK procurement regulations do not refer to a final judgment, since, under English law all judgments given by a court which disposes of the issues litigated is regarded as a final judgment, whether or not the judgment may still be made the subject of an appeal.[30]

As was discussed in the context of the EU, although the requirement for a conviction provides the disqualified firm with procedural safeguards, the rarity of corruption convictions, especially in relation to legal persons, may limit the effectiveness of disqualification measures based on convictions in the UK.

Two cases illustrate the difficulties of prosecuting and convicting for corruption in general and legal persons in particular. In 2004, the Serious Fraud Office (responsible for the investigation of serious fraud and corruption allegations) commenced an investigation into the activities of BAE Systems.[31] BAE was investigated for bribing Saudi public officials in order to secure defence contracts in Saudi Arabia. In spite of the evidence surrounding BAE's complicity in the corruption allegations, including admissions by former BAE staff, the investigations were terminated in 2006. Thus, BAE was never tried and consequently never convicted of corruption in the UK.

In 2008, the managing director of a security firm was convicted of giving bribes to Ugandan officials to secure lucrative public contracts.[32] The

[29] R Novak, P Henty and C Tullis, 'The Bribery Act and its Interaction with the Public Procurement Rules in the UK' (2011) 5 *Public Procurement Law Review* NA230.

[30] *Halsbury's Laws of England*, vol 11 para 1156 (5th edn, 2009).

[31] S Williams, 'The BAE/Saudi Al-Yamamah Contracts: Implications in Law and Public Procurement' (2008) 57 *International and Comparative Law Quarterly* 200.

[32] *R v Tumukunde & Tobiasen* (unreported 2008); Lewis and Evans, 'Ugandan is jailed in UK bribery crackdown', *The Guardian* (23 September 2008). Available at: www.guardian.co.uk/uk/2008/sep/23/ukcrime.law .

charge was laid against the managing director of the company, and not the company itself, and this was justified by the head of the prosecuting authority on the basis that '[c]ompanies themselves are not fraudulent it is individuals within organisations who are committing the crime'.[33] This case illustrates that prosecutors may find it easier to prosecute and obtain convictions against individuals even if the corruption was committed in order to facilitate the firm obtaining government contracts.

In relation to the commission of an act of grave misconduct, the UK procurement regulations do not require the supplier to have been convicted and do not require the procuring authority to be able to prove this misconduct, as is required by the EU directives. Thus, as will be discussed further in chapter seven, the kinds of evidence that will suffice for this disqualification may depend on the circumstances and the information available to a procuring authority. It may be the case as discussed in the context of the EU directives that a determination of misconduct made by a relevant professional body may be relied on by a procuring authority to disqualify a supplier.

4.3.3 The Status of Foreign Convictions

Similar to the EU directives, the UK procurement regulations are not explicit on whether a mandatory disqualification is required for relevant foreign convictions. As discussed in the context of the EU above, foreign convictions may have been omitted from the EU directives but it is not clear whether EU Member States will adopt a similar approach.

Foreign convictions may be relevant in the UK in three ways. First, an EU based firm may have obtained a corruption conviction from within the EU. In such cases however, a UK procuring authority will disqualify such firms based on Regulation 23(1)(f) PCR, which provides for disqualification for 'any other offence within the meaning of Article 45(1) of the Public Sector Directive as defined by the national law of any relevant State'. Such firms may also be disqualified on the basis of Regulation 23(1)(c), which imports the EU procurement directives definitions of corruption into the PCR thereby providing for the disqualification of firms convicted of corruption involving EU and Member States officials.

Secondly, an EU-based firm may have obtained a conviction outside the EU, such as that obtained by Lahmeyer (a German firm) from a Lesotho court in 2003 or a UK firm, or a UK subsidiary of a multinational corporation, may have received a corruption conviction outside the EU, as happened in the case of ABB Vetco Gray (UK) convicted in the US as discussed

[33] C Cowan, Head of the Overseas Anti-Corruption Unit, within the Metropolitan Police Force. See business.timesonline.co.uk/tol/business/law/article4832416.ece .

above. Thirdly, a supplier from a third country wishing to participate in a UK public contract may have received a conviction outside the EU.

The lack of clarity on this issue in the EU procurement directives and the differences in the definition of corruption between the EU and the UK means that in analysing the status of foreign convictions for the purposes of the mandatory disqualifications, recourse may be had to UK law. Under the common law, the UK does not generally enforce foreign criminal judgments. This rule was expressed in *Huntingdon v Attrill*,[34] where the court found that:

> [t]he rule has its foundation in the well-recognised principle that crimes, including in that term all breaches of public law punishable by pecuniary mulct or otherwise, at the instance of the State Government, or of some one representing the public, are local in this sense, that they are only cognizable and punishable in the country where they were committed. Accordingly no proceeding, even in the shape of a civil suit, which has for its object the enforcement by the State, whether directly or indirectly, of punishment imposed for such breaches by the *lex fori*, ought to be admitted in the Courts of any other country.

This rule was further applied in *United States v Inkley*,[35] where the US government was not allowed to enforce a default criminal judgment against the defendant in a UK court.

Although these cases refer to the enforcement of foreign penal sanctions in the UK, it is not clear whether similar reasoning will apply to the recognition of foreign convictions for disqualification purposes. In some cases, UK courts take foreign convictions into account as evidence of the character of an accused where it is relevant to the matters before the court.[36] This information may be used in sentencing an offender who has committed a crime in the UK. Apart from this, foreign convictions may also be relevant for purposes such as immigration, for disqualification from obtaining a driver's licence or becoming a director of a company.[37] Thus, it is arguable by way of analogy that foreign convictions may also be relevant for the purpose of disqualification from UK public contracts.

Some support for this interpretation may be found in the OGC Guidance on the mandatory disqualifications.[38] Although the UK regulations do not mention foreign convictions, the OGC Guidance provides that a procuring authority should disqualify a supplier that has received a relevant conviction, whether that supplier is from an EU Member State, a country which is a signatory to the GPA or a third country.[39] Although this does not answer

[34] *Huntingdon v Atrill* [1893] AC 150.

[35] *United States v Inkley* [1989] QB 255.

[36] Criminal Justice Act 2003, s 101(1)(d); *R v Kordasinski (Leszek)* [2007] 1 Cr App R 17.

[37] Company Directors Disqualification Act 1986.

[38] Office of Government Commerce, *Guidance on the Mandatory Exclusion of Economic Operators in the 2006 Procurement Regulations* (March 2009) [hereafter OGC Guidance].

[39] OGC Guidance, para 3.

the question whether the convictions received by these suppliers were obtained from outside the EU, it appears that a reliance on foreign convictions (ie convictions obtained outside the EU) is implied by the OGC Guidance. This is because requiring UK procuring authorities to disqualify suppliers from third countries must be interpreted as a possibility that that these suppliers may have received the conviction in those countries.

The discretionary disqualification provisions are also silent as to whether foreign convictions may be taken into account and, as was discussed in the context of the EU, this may be an indication that this issue has been left to the discretion of the disqualifying entity.

4.4 THE UNITED STATES

4.4.1 Offences for Disqualification

Disqualification in the US is discretionary and a supplier may be disqualified from government contracts for various procurement and non-procurement related offences[40] and the commission of any offence indicating a lack of business integrity or business honesty affecting the present responsibility of the contractor.[41]

As stated in the context of the other jurisdictions, this book will focus on those offences that may broadly be defined as public sector corruption. Accordingly, the relevant US offences are:

(i) Offences committed in obtaining, attempting to obtain, or performing a public contract or subcontract.[42] For a supplier to be disqualified for these offences, the supplier has to have received a conviction or a civil judgment, but may be temporarily disqualified from public contracts where there is evidence that this offence was committed, without the necessity for a conviction. This head of offences may be used to disqualify a supplier for a corruption offence committed in obtaining, attempting to obtain or performing a public contract.

(ii) The offence of bribery,[43] whether the offence was committed in the procurement context or not. For a longer lasting disqualification, the supplier needs to have been convicted or incurred a civil judgment for the offence, but may be temporarily disqualified in the absence of a conviction.[44]

(iii) Any offence indicating a lack of business integrity or honesty that seriously and directly affects the present responsibility of such

[40] FAR 9.407-2(a)(1)–(7).
[41] FAR 9.407-2(a)(7).
[42] FAR 406-2(a)(1).
[43] FAR 9.406-2(a)(3).
[44] *TS Generalbau GmbH*, Comp Gen Dec B-246034, 92-1 CPD ¶ 189.

contractor.[45] For longer lasting disqualifications, a conviction or a civil judgment needs to have been incurred but a supplier may be temporarily disqualified for these offences without a conviction.

(iv) Any other cause of a serious and compelling nature that it affects the present responsibility of the contractor.[46] Under this offence, a conviction is not required for either the temporary or longer lasting disqualification. There is no indication of the kinds of conduct that will fall under this provision and it has been argued that it can relate to both contractual performance and integrity issues.[47] It has also been suggested that this catch-all-phrase may be used as the basis of disqualification for conduct that is neither criminal nor related to government contracting.[48]

4.4.2 Disqualifying on the Basis of a Conviction

As can be seen, a supplier may be disqualified where it has obtained a criminal conviction or a civil judgment for a relevant offence. A conviction is defined by the regulations as a judgment or conviction for a criminal offence by any court of competent jurisdiction, whether entered upon a verdict or a plea, and includes a conviction entered upon a plea of *nolo contendere*.[49] A civil judgment is defined as a judgment or a finding of a civil offence by a court of competent jurisdiction.[50]

As discussed in the context of the EU, the requirement for a conviction reduces the investigative burden on the disqualifying official and ensures that the disqualifying official can be assured that the evidence of the facts giving rise to the offence has been thoroughly tested in a competent court. In the US, where an uncontested plea (*nolo contendere*) may give rise to a conviction, procuring authorities in some cases require independent evidence to establish the facts of the alleged criminal offence.[51]

In the US, unlike the position in the EU and the UK, disqualification is not an automatic consequence of the receipt of a conviction for corruption.[52] Disqualification is at the discretion of the procurement official and it is not regarded as appropriate to disqualify where the offence was

45 FAR 9.406-2(a)(5).

46 FAR 9.406-2(c).

47 J Cibinic and R Nash, *Formation of Government Contracts* (Alphen aan den Rijn, Wolters Kluwer, 1998) 464.

48 S Shaw, 'Access to Information: The Key Challenge to a Credible Suspension and Debarment Programme' (2004) 5 *Public Procurement Law Review* 230, 232.

49 FAR 2.4.1. A plea of *nolo contendere* is a plea entered by a defendant that does not explicitly admit guilt, but subjects the defendant to punishment, while allowing denial of the alleged facts in other proceedings.

50 FAR 9.403.

51 Cibinic and Nash, *Formation*, above n 47, 462.

52 Cibinic and Nash, *Formation*, ibid, 457.

not serious or where there are strong mitigating factors in favour of the supplier.[53]

Apart from disqualifying on the basis of convictions, a supplier may be temporarily disqualified (suspended) where it has committed a relevant offence but has not received a conviction or a civil judgment, either because investigations into the alleged offence or litigation is still pending against the contractor. The US thus incorporates an element of proportionality into the disqualification system by requiring a conviction or a civil judgment for longer lasting disqualifications and not requiring them for temporary disqualifications. In both cases, however, the disqualification may only be imposed where it is necessary to protect the government.[54]

4.4.3 The Status of Foreign Convictions

Like the EU, UK and South Africa, the US regulations are silent as to the status of foreign convictions and it is unclear whether a conviction obtained outside the US may lead to disqualification from US public contracts, although it appears that US jurisprudence is against such an interpretation.

In *Small v US*[55] the Supreme Court held that the phrase 'convicted in any court' – contained in a statute[56] prohibiting a person who had been convicted in *any court* of a crime punishable by imprisonment exceeding one year from possessing firearms – related to domestic and not foreign convictions. The Court argued that it is appropriate to assume that US Congress has domestic, not foreign concerns in mind when it writes statutes, since foreign convictions can involve conduct that is not criminal under US law. The Supreme Court also opined that the statute's context and language did not suggest any reach beyond domestic convictions.

Although *Small* related to a breach of a criminal statute, the Supreme Court did not expressly limit its decision to criminal statutes. Further, the disqualification from possessing firearms in *Small* may be compared to disqualification from government contracts for a criminal conviction, except that unlike the disqualification that *Small* was subject to, procurement disqualifications are not mandatory in the US. It is thus arguable that a similar interpretation may apply to foreign corruption convictions for the purpose of disqualification. In the first place, this will obviate the need for disqualifying officials in the US to compare whether the foreign conviction is for a relevant offence as defined by the FAR.[57] Secondly, a

[53] FAR 9.406-1(a).
[54] FAR 9.407-1(b)(1).
[55] *Small v US* 544 US 385 (2005).
[56] 18 USC § 922(g)(1).
[57] *Small*, above n 55, 385–87.

disqualifying official would not have to consider the issue of whether the foreign conviction included the necessary protections and procedural safeguards for the offender. Thirdly, as argued by the Court in *Small,* the language and the context of the FAR do not suggest any reach beyond domestic convictions.

As will be seen below, the practice in the US is in any event that procuring officials do not always disqualify persons convicted or guilty of relevant offences committed overseas.

4.5 THE WORLD BANK

4.5.1 Offences for Disqualification

The World Bank adopts an approach similar to the US and disqualification is discretionary and may be imposed at the option of the Bank. The Bank's procurement guidelines list the offences that may lead to disqualification, which includes offences committed in Bank-projects in the non-procurement context.[58] The corruption offence that may lead to disqualification is defined as follows:

> (i) 'corrupt practice' is the offering, giving, receiving or soliciting, directly or indirectly, of anything of value to influence improperly the actions of another party.[59]

'Corrupt practice' comprises active and passive bribery. Bribery in international transactions[60] and particularly in the execution of infrastructure projects[61] is a serious problem for the Bank, and is regarded as the most pernicious kind of corruption that exists in international development projects.[62] It is thus not surprising that the procurement guidelines attach sanctions to bribery in the first place.

The Bank's definition of corrupt practice has its parallels with the definition of corruption stated in chapter 1. In the definition of the offence by

[58] Williams, 'World Bank Introduces New Measures', above n 17.

[59] BPG, para 1.16.

[60] S Salbu, 'Transnational Bribery: The Big Questions' (2001) 21 *Journal of International Law and Business* 435; S Salbu, 'A Delicate Balance: Legislation, Institutional Change, and Transnational Bribery' (2000) 33 *Cornell International Law Journal* 657; S Salbu, 'Are Extraterritorial Restrictions on Bribery a Viable and Desirable International Policy Goal Under the Global Conditions of the Late Twentieth Century?' (1999) 24 *Yale Journal of International Law* 223.

[61] M Weihen, *Transparency and Corruption on Building Large Dams* (Transparency International, 1999), 14. Available at www.dams.org.; World Bank, *Infrastructure: Lessons from the Last Two Decades of Bank Engagement* Discussion Paper (Washington, World Bank, 2006) 41–2. Available at: www.worldbank.org.

[62] N Hobbs, 'Corruption in World Bank Financed Projects: Why Bribery is a Tolerated Anathema' (DESTIN Working Papers, 2005) 23. Available at: www.lse.ac.uk.

in the Bank, the motive of the offender is important, and the actions must be directed at securing a particular outcome. By focusing on motive, the offences are able to cross cultural boundaries and circumvent arguments relating to the cultural specificity of the nature of corruption.[63]

4.5.2 Disqualifying on the Basis of Convictions

The Bank conducts its own investigations into allegations of corruption and does not rely on domestic prosecutions or take corruption convictions into account for the purposes of its disqualification procedures. Unlike some domestic jurisdictions, the Bank does not require suppliers to supply information on the existence of previous convictions during the procurement process.

Although the Bank does not generally use corruption convictions as the basis of disqualification, a corruption conviction in relation to a Bank-financed project may be the basis for an investigation. On one occasion, a firm that had been through the Bank's disqualification process and emerged with a determination that there was insufficient evidence to disqualify it was later convicted in a domestic court of corruption in relation to a Bank-financed project.[64] The Bank then re-opened its investigation, and with the evidence that emerged at trial, disqualified the firm.[65] This case illustrates that some of the limitations the Bank faces in investigating accused firms, such as not being able to compel the production of relevant documents or witnesses,[66] may lead to an approach that increasingly utilises relevant corruption convictions in the disqualification process.

[63] D Treisman, 'The Causes of Corruption: A Cross-National Study' (2000) *Journal of Public Economics* 401; B Harms, 'Holding Public Officials Accountable in the International Realm: A New Multi-Layered Strategy to Combat Corruption' (2000) 33 *Cornell International Law Journal* 159; D Smith, 'Kinship and Corruption in Contemporary Nigeria' (2001) 66 *Ethnos* 344. Cf D Kaufman, 'Anti-Corruption Within a Broader Developmental and Governance Perspective–Some Lessons from Empirics and Experience' Statement to the High Level Political Signing Conference for the United Nations Convention against Corruption in Mexico, 9–11 December 2003. Available at: www.worldbank.org; D Kennedy, 'The International Anti-Corruption Campaign' (1999) 14 *Connecticut Journal of International Law* 465; KA Elliott, 'Corruption as an International Policy Problem: Overview and Recommendations' in Elliott (ed), *Corruption and the Global Economy* (Washington Institute for International Economics, 1997) 175, 177.

[64] Williams, 'World Bank Introduces New Measures', above n 17.

[65] Williams, 'World Bank Introduces New Measures', ibid; Press Release, World Bank, World Bank Sanctions Acres International Ltd (23 July 2004).

[66] D Thornburgh, R Gainer and C Walker, *Report Concerning the Debarment Processes of the World Bank* (Washington, World Bank, 2002) 17 [hereafter Thornburgh, *Report Concerning Debarment Process*].

4.5.3 The Status of Foreign Convictions

As the Bank is an institution without a legal system of its own, it is incorrect to talk about foreign convictions, as all convictions that the Bank may rely on in disqualification proceedings will be foreign in the sense of being outside the Bank's internal investigative process.

As discussed above, the Bank is able to rely on domestic corruption convictions to establish the grounds for disqualification from Bank-financed contracts. Another issue that may lead to increased relevance of domestic corruption convictions is the 2010 agreement between international financial institutions to cooperate and enforce each other's disqualification measures.[67] This cooperation may lead to a greater use by the Bank of external investigations, disqualification decisions, penalties and possibly convictions in the Bank's disqualification process.[68]

4.6 SOUTH AFRICA

4.6.1 Offences for Disqualification

There are three South African statutes which provide for the disqualification of corrupt contractors.

4.6.1.1 Prevention and Combating of Corrupt Activities Act 2004

The Corruption Act contains the most detailed provisions on disqualification from public contracts for corruption offences. The relevant provisions are in section 28(1), which provides that where a court is convicting a person of the relevant offences it may also issue an order that the particulars of the convicted person, the conviction and the sentence be endorsed on the Register for Tender Defaulters.[69] This Register contains information on firms disqualified from government contracts, is managed by the National Treasury and is available electronically.

Under the Act, disqualification is a sanction solely against procurement-related offences and there are two offences that could lead to disqualification. The first is 'corrupt activities in relation to contracts'. This covers

[67] E Nwogwugwu, 'Towards the Harmonisation of International Procurement Policies and Practices' (2005) 3 *Public Procurement Law Review* 131; International Financial Institutions Anti-Corruption Task Force: *Uniform Framework for Preventing and Combating Fraud and Corruption* (September 2006); World Bank, *Mutual Enforcement of Debarment Decisions among Multilateral Development Banks* (March 2010).

[68] World Bank, *Mutual Enforcement of Debarment Decisions among Multilateral Development Banks*, ibid, para 30.

[69] Corruption Act 2004, ss 28(1)(a) and 29.

situations where a person accepts or agrees to accept, offers or agrees to offer any gratification in order to influence in any way, the promotion, execution or procurement of a contract with a public entity,[70] and covers bribery in public contracting. The second offence is 'corrupt activities in the procuring and withdrawal of tenders'. This offence relates to situations where a person offers, agrees to offer or accepts or agrees to accept any gratification as an inducement to, or in order to influence another person to award a tender, make a tender or withdraw a tender for a contract,[71] and may cover bribery and collusion in public contracts.

The offences for which a supplier may be disqualified under the Corruption Act are concerned with violations of the procurement system and disqualifications do not operate against general or non-procurement-related corruption. This might result in the disqualifications not being wholly effective in combating public corruption, as they will only affect persons who have been convicted of procurement-related corruption and who are government suppliers but where a government supplier is convicted of non-procurement corruption, that person will not be disqualified from government contracts. The South African approach thus unwittingly elevates procurement corruption above other forms of public corruption.

Some of the offences requiring disqualification under the Corruption Act correspond to the offence of public sector corruption, where this corruption occurs in the procurement context.

4.6.1.2 Preferential Procurement Policy Framework Act Regulations

The PPPFA regulations provide for the disqualification of fraudulent or corrupt suppliers from government contracts, where the fraud/corruption relates to the PPPFA. Under the regulations, where an 'organ of state' detects that a preference under the PPPFA, ie the Broad-Based Black Economic Empowerment (B-BBEE) status level of a supplier, has been fraudulently claimed or obtained, it must restrict the contractor, its shareholders and directors from obtaining business from any organ of state for a period not exceeding 10 years.[72] An organ of state may also for the same offence, disqualify the fraudulent supplier from the instant tendering process, without any implications beyond that process.[73]

There are two offences, which may lead to disqualification under the PPPFA regulations. The first is the use of a fraudulently obtained B-BBEE preference in bidding for a public contract. The use of fraudulent means to obtain the preferences that may bolster a tender has been documented

[70] Corruption Act 2004, s 12.
[71] Corruption Act 2004, s 13.
[72] PPPFA reg 13(2)(d).
[73] PPPFA reg 13(2)(a).

elsewhere.[74] The most pervasive method of fraudulently obtaining such preferences is 'fronting' or the use of fictitious or tokenistic persons from the groups previously discriminated against (target groups) in bidding for a public contract. This may occur, for instance where black people (who are subject to preferences in South African procurement) are signed up as fictitious shareholders in a 'white'-owned company.[75]

The second offence that may lead to disqualification is past contractual failure. Thus under the PPPFA regulations, where the terms of the contract have not been filled, the procuring authority (or organ of state) may disqualify the supplier from the instant procurement procedure.[76] It is likely that this provision will be used to disqualify persons who have not filled the requirements of the PPPFA for local production/content and subcontracting.

4.6.1.3 Public Finance Management Act Regulations

The PFMA regulations provide for two offences that will lead to disqualification. The first offence, which will lead to a mandatory disqualification, is where '. . . the recommended bidder has committed a corrupt or fraudulent act in competing for the *particular* contract'.[77] Here, the accounting officer of a government department must disqualify the supplier by rejecting the proposal for the award of a contract. Such acts will include bribery, 'fronting', collusion and misrepresentation in the submission of tenders[78] and may overlap in some cases with the offences leading to disqualification under the Corruption Act and the PPPFA regulations.

The second offence that may lead to a discretionary disqualification is where 'the bidder or any of its directors have committed fraud or other improper conduct in relation to the procuring entity's supply chain management system'.[79] This covers a broader set of offences than the Corruption Act or the PPPFA regulations, being a prohibited activity in the *entire* supply chain management system and extends to prohibited conduct in procurement planning, contract implementation and execution. Thus, a supplier who provides false qualification documentation; mismanages a contract; fraudulently provides substandard/non-compliant goods to save costs; engages in collusion or other anti-competitive conduct; or submits a tender that is below costs in order to increase the contract price once he has

[74] Bolton, *Law of Government Procurement*, ch 10.
[75] Bolton, *Law of Government Procurement*, 294.
[76] PPPFA reg 13(2)(a).
[77] PFMA reg 16A9.1(e).
[78] P Bolton, 'The Exclusion of Contractors from Government Contract Awards' (2006) 10 *Law, Development, Democracy* 25.
[79] PFMA reg 16A9.2(a)(ii).

obtained the contract,[80] might be guilty of an offence in relation to the procuring entity's supply chain management system.

Where these offences occur, the accounting officer of a public entity may at his discretion, disqualify the supplier from a particular contract by disregarding his bid.

4.6.2 Disqualifying on the Basis of Convictions

As may be seen from the above, in South Africa, a criminal conviction for corruption is only required where disqualification is imposed under the Corruption Act.

The PPPFA regulations do not indicate whether a conviction is necessary for disqualification, but a textual interpretation of the regulations does not support the requirement for a conviction. The Regulations provide that the procuring entity may disqualify a supplier where a B-BBEE status level is fraudulently obtained or claimed. Although a procuring entity may detect the fraud through the existence of a conviction, it is likely to be the case that where there is any doubt or suspicion as to the existence of the preferences claimed by the supplier, this will trigger the requirement to disqualify the supplier.

If a conviction is not necessary under the PPPFA regulations, then the issues that arise include determining what procedure will be used in making the decision to disqualify; ensuring that the procuring entity guarantees procedural fairness in making the decision; and the adoption of a standardised approach to avoid the adoption of different criteria for disqualification by various procuring authorities. The PPPFA regulations give a broad framework for these procedural issues by requiring procuring entities to give a supplier a fair hearing, in accordance with the *audi alteram partem* rule. These issues will be discussed in chapter five.

Similar to the PPPFA regulations, the PFMA regulations do not require a conviction as a condition precedent to disqualification. Under the mandatory disqualification provisions, the disqualification is triggered by fraud or corruption in competing for a particular contract, and is directed at impropriety in the specific procurement procedure, and not past procurement violations. In relation to the discretionary disqualifications, although the offences are not limited to the particular procurement procedure, it appears as though there is no requirement for convictions, as a public official may disqualify a supplier who has engaged in fraud or other 'improper conduct'. Whilst fraud could be proven through the

[80] Cibinic and Nash, *Formation*, above n 47, chs 7 and 8; S Arrowsmith, J Linarelli and D Wallace, *Regulating Public Procurement: National and International Perspectives* (The Hague, Kluwer Law, 2000) 699–701.

existence of a conviction, improper conduct may not, as such an offence does not exist in South African law. What will thus be required to establish proof of this conduct, and indeed what will amount to this improper conduct has been left by the regulations to the discretion of the public official. It should be noted that this offence gives procuring authorities a lot of discretion as the offence is very broad in scope and may be abused.

4.6.3 The Status of Foreign Convictions

Similar to the disqualification provisions in the EU, the UK, and the US, none of the South African provisions mention the status of foreign convictions. It appears that foreign convictions are not relevant in South Africa, as under the Corruption Act, disqualification is imposed by the courts as part of the punishment imposed for an offence committed under the Act, as decided by the South African High Court. Further, foreign convictions are not relevant under the PPPFA and the PFMA regulations, as they do not require any convictions, foreign or otherwise before a disqualification is imposed.

4.7 SUMMARY AND ANALYSIS OF MAIN ISSUES

From the above discussion, it can be seen that there are a number of divergent approaches to the requirement that a conviction should precede disqualification and to the use of foreign convictions as a basis for disqualification. This section will examine the issues raised by these divergent approaches and examine which approach might be more appropriate.

4.7.1 Requirement for Convictions

As stated, there are different approaches to the issue of whether convictions are required for disqualification. In the EU and in the context of the UK regulations implementing the EU directives, convictions are required for the mandatory disqualifications for corruption and the other serious criminal offences and the discretionary disqualification for an offence relating to the conduct of a business or a profession. The US generally requires convictions for longer lasting disqualifications, but does not require convictions for temporary disqualifications. The World Bank does not require convictions at all, but has on occasion utilised a conviction as the basis of disqualification proceedings against a contractor. In South Africa, convictions are only relevant where the disqualification relates to offences under the Corruption Act.

Where convictions are required for corruption, the supplier would invariably have had the advantage of all the procedural safeguards of a criminal prosecution, in the sense that he would have had an opportunity to be heard and to examine and defend the allegations made against him. A conviction further implies that the offender's guilt is not in doubt. This is the main benefit of requiring convictions for disqualification.

On the other hand, corruption allegations are notoriously difficult to prosecute, leading to a dearth of such convictions, especially in relation to legal persons. As a result, where disqualification is based on a conviction, the lack of convictions may make the disqualification measure ineffective in practice. A comparison may be made between the World Bank and the US which do not require convictions for disqualification (temporary disqualifications in the US) and South Africa (under the Corruption Act) which disqualifies on the basis of convictions.

In the World Bank and the US, disqualifications are fairly commonplace and follow investigations once there has been the receipt of incriminating information. Under the South African Corruption Act, which requires convictions for disqualification, there have been only two disqualifications since 2004 when the Act came into force.[81] Although South Africa has had a much shorter experience of disqualification legislation than either the US or the World Bank, this may still allude to the absence of relevant corruption convictions.

Whilst there are merits to requiring convictions as a condition precedent to disqualification, it is submitted that this requirement will reduce the effectiveness of disqualification as an anti-corruption tool. Therefore, it might be preferable for an approach that relies on indictments and compelling evidence, as is the case in the US and the World Bank. However, where convictions are not required, adequate safeguards must be required to ensure that disqualification is justified and the disqualification measure is not abused. Thus, as is discussed further in chapter five, the evidence relied on must be compelling, the supplier ought to be made aware of the existence of the evidence and should also be given an opportunity to respond to the allegations that will form the basis of the disqualification.

For instance, in the World Bank where convictions are not required, the Bank gives suppliers the opportunity to respond to the allegations of corruption for which the supplier may be disqualified. Similarly, in the US, where a conviction is not required, the disqualification is normally made on the basis of an indictment and the supplier is given an opportunity to respond to the allegations against him.

[81] As at 30 October 2011.

4.7.2 The Issue of Foreign Convictions

It was shown that none of the selected jurisdictions, except the UK, in the form of the OGC Guidance document, made explicit references to the position of foreign convictions, with the jurisprudence of the US being against an interpretation that favours reliance on foreign convictions for disqualification.

However, recognising foreign corruption convictions for disqualification would increase the effectiveness and possibly the deterrent effect of disqualification. The harmonisation of corruption offences as achieved through the major corruption conventions means that some of the barriers against the recognition of foreign convictions highlighted by the US Supreme Court in *Small*, such as different definitions of offences and the criminalisation of different kinds of conduct, are not as relevant in relation to corruption offences. As discussed in chapter two, the major conventions against corruption criminalise the bribery of foreign public officials, the domestic public officials, and employees of international organisations and have adopted similar definitions of the offence of corruption. Thus, there will be few disparities in the definitions of offences or in the kinds of conduct criminalised by countries that have ratified these instruments.

Although most jurisdictions are against the enforcement of the penal laws of other states as discussed above, it is submitted that states ought to recognise foreign corruption convictions for the purpose of disqualification. There are several rationales for this. First, recognising foreign corruption convictions for the purpose of disqualification would not amount to an enforcement of the foreign country's penal laws unless that country *requires* and imposes disqualification at the time of conviction as one of the penalties imposed for a corruption conviction. There are already instances, as discussed above where countries rely on foreign convictions for various other kinds of disqualifications, and disqualification from public contracts will simply operate in addition to those instances.

Secondly, a refusal to recognise foreign corruption convictions for disqualification purposes may be criticised on public policy grounds. This is because disqualifying domestic suppliers from public contracts in circumstances where a supplier with a foreign corruption conviction would not be disqualified sends a message that foreign corruption is more tolerable than domestic corruption and will lead to differences in the treatment of domestic and (possibly) foreign suppliers. This issue has already arisen in the context of a responsibility determination in the US, where a procuring authority held a supplier to be responsible despite the supplier's contravention of Japanese bid-rigging regulations, on the basis that bid-rigging is common in Japan and therefore not regarded as serious. In an action for judicial review, the court held that the authority's determination was 'arbitrary and capricious'.[82] Thirdly, recognising foreign convictions may increase the effectiveness of the disqualification measure, as it may be the case that the threat of disqualification in another country may be more serious for a multinational corporation than disqualification at home.

As will be discussed further in chapter six, a major issue that arises with the recognition of foreign convictions for disqualification purposes is how a procuring authority in one country may discover the existence of such convictions. Where information on convictions is publicly available, it may be possible for procuring authorities to obtain this information, but such information is generally not publicly available, and it may be difficult for a procuring authority to obtain this information, in the absence of cooperation from the authorities of the country where the conviction was obtained. In 2008, the UK government highlighted this difficulty when it revealed that it was unable to check the foreign criminal records of employed airport 'airside' workers.[83] In the US case discussed above, the contractor was not initially required to reveal details of its foreign violations, although the procuring official still declared the supplier responsible after he had obtained information on the bid-rigging offences.[84]

A related issue is whether procuring authorities are in any event under a duty to discover the existence of any convictions, whether foreign or domestic, where convictions are required for disqualification. This issue is dealt with in chapter seven, and it will be seen that none of the selected jurisdictions impose a requirement on procuring authorities to conduct investigations to discover the existence of convictions.

[82] *Watts-Healy Tibbits A JV v United States* 82 Fed Cl 614 (2008).

[83] Lords Hansard Text 15 May 2008, available at: www.parliament.the-stationery-office.co.uk/pa/ld200708/ldhansrd/text/80515-0002.htm; Hope and Millward, 'Foreign criminals work at airports unchecked', *The Telegraph* (8 May 2008).

[84] *Watts-Healy*, above n 82.

5

Procedural Issues Affecting Disqualification

5.1 INTRODUCTION

THE AIM OF this chapter is to examine and compare in detail the procedural issues that arise from the use of disqualification, the approaches the jurisdictions have adopted to these issues, and whether these approaches are appropriate.

First, the chapter will examine the procedure for disqualifying suppliers in the jurisdictions. The focus is on the procedural requirements for disqualifying, including: notice of the disqualification to a supplier; opportunity to make representations; notice of the factors that are relevant to the disqualifying entity's decision; whether the supplier is given reasons for its disqualification as well as whether the procedures are fair and transparent and are thus able to give rise to disqualification decisions that are fair, reasonable, transparent, non-discriminatory and justified by the available evidence.

In many jurisdictions, the legislation is silent as to whether procedural safeguards must accompany the disqualification process and in such cases, the disqualification process may be conducted according to the requirements of administrative law. Where this is the case, administrative law will be examined to determine how the issue of procedure may be approached. The chapter will examine whether the procedures for disqualification in the jurisdictions are in alignment with the transparency objectives of public procurement regulation and are sufficient to ensure that the disqualification system fulfils its purpose in each jurisdiction. The chapter will also suggest what improvements may be made in relation to procedural issues in a jurisdiction where there are perceived shortcomings. The issue of procedure is important, as it determines what rights a supplier may have to challenge the decision to disqualify it.

The second issue discussed in this chapter is the time limits for disqualification. Time limits are relevant to the fairness of the measures and may be tied to the rationales behind disqualification in the jurisdictions. Time limits are important in different ways depending on the nature of the measure in question: they may be relevant to determining when an offence or conviction ceases to be relevant for the purposes of disqualification and to the length of a disqualification.

5.2 PROCEDURE FOR DISQUALIFYING

This section focuses on the procedural requirements for the disqualification decision, to ensure that the decision is substantively fair. The procedural requirements are examined by reference to the different stages of the disqualification decision. The chapter will split the decision to disqualify into several procedural stages and examine the procedural requirements governing each stage of the disqualification process. In some of the jurisdictions, the legislation is silent on the procedural requirements for disqualification and the procedures are at the discretion of the disqualifying entity. Where the legislation is silent, the courts or the general law on administrative decision-making may provide disqualifying entities with a framework for the procedural requirements. In other jurisdictions, the legislation has provided detailed procedural requirements for each stage of the disqualification process.

The section will also examine whether the procedures for disqualification in the jurisdictions may be regarded as fair and transparent.

5.2.1 The Stages of the Disqualification Process and Accompanying Procedural Requirements

The decision to disqualify a supplier may be split into several procedural stages and each separate stage of the decision to disqualify may be made by one entity or may be split between different entities. The stages of disqualification decision-making adopted in this chapter are not comprehensive, but the stages are chosen because they are general to most disqualification systems and the proposed sequence of the stages is adopted for convenience, as in practice some of the stages may overlap.

The first stage of a disqualification determination is deciding whether a relevant offence has been committed. The procedures relevant at this stage depend on whether the disqualification is linked to a conviction. At the second stage, the disqualifying entity may need to decide whether to inform the supplier of its proposed disqualification and invite the supplier to make representations to the entity. Procedural requirements relevant at this stage will include the timing and the sufficiency of the notice, and the opportunity to and extent to which the supplier may make representations.

At the third stage of a disqualification decision and depending on the discretion available to the entity, the entity may need to consider whether disqualification is justifiable on the basis of the available evidence, or whether there are other factors such as 'rehabilitation measures' that mean that the supplier ought not to be disqualified despite the existence of a conviction/offence. Rehabilitation measures are discussed in chapter ten. The relevant procedures here include whether the supplier is given notice of the factors that the entity takes into account in deciding to disqualify and how the disqualifying entity determines whether disqualification should be waived.

Fourthly, an entity may decide whether to give a supplier notice of the disqualification decision, including the reasons on which the decision is based. The procedural requirements here may include rules on the sufficiency and adequacy of the notice informing the supplier that it has been disqualified (including information on which aspects of the supplier's business are affected and how long the disqualification will last) as well rules on the existence of a duty to give reasons.

5.2.1.1 Has a relevant offence been committed?

In deciding whether an offence warranting disqualification has been committed, the disqualifying entity has to decide whether there are reasonable grounds to believe that the supplier committed the offence. As stated, this stage of the disqualification decision is tied to whether a conviction is required for disqualification. Where a conviction is required for disqualification, deciding that an offence was committed may be simple where the disqualifying entity is able to obtain conclusive information from police or judicial databases. In such cases, the disqualifying entity may have two options – to either itself obtain the information on the conviction from national databases of criminal records or to require proposed suppliers to provide certification on previous convictions. Where disqualification is tied to an offence of professional misconduct, it may be possible for the disqualifying entity to obtain information on the supplier's past conduct from the relevant professional organisations. Where disqualification is for an offence committed in an on-going procurement procedure, the disqualifying entity may obtain evidence of the offence from the relevant participants in the procurement process.

The procedural requirements for this stage of the disqualification decision include the process for obtaining information on offences, such as the procedure used to approach relevant organisations which maintain databases of criminal records or information on professional offences. These procedures are not concerned with the investigative powers of a disqualifying entity, which is covered in chapter seven, but rather deal with whether an entity has procedures in place to access the information on relevant offences. Despite the importance of this information to the disqualification determination, not all jurisdictions are explicit on the procedure for a disqualifying entity obtaining this information.

In relation to the mandatory and the discretionary disqualifications, the EU procurement directives suggest that disqualifying entities may obtain information on convictions or offences from suppliers and where they have further doubts they may apply to competent authorities, such as judicial or administrative authorities to obtain information on the supplier.[1] The EU has also provided a list of the authorities that are competent to provide this information in Member States.[2] Where the disqualification is tied to a conviction, the information obtained from national databases on criminal convictions ought to be determinative of whether an offence has been committed.[3] The EU procurement directives do not provide disqualifying entities with any special procedure or format for approaching these competent authorities and the procedure is left to the discretion of the disqualifying entity or the requirements of the competent authority.

In implementing the EU directives, the UK regulations did not go further than the directives and also suggest that in relation to the mandatory disqualifications, a procuring authority may ask suppliers to provide the necessary information and may further apply to a competent authority to obtain details of convictions.[4] Although the regulations are silent on the procedure for obtaining this information, the OGC Guidance suggests that a procuring authority should ask suppliers, in a pre-qualification questionnaire or an invitation to tender, to state whether they have been convicted of a relevant offence.[5] The OGC Guidance also suggests the wording that UK procuring authorities may use in requesting this information from suppliers.[6] Where the procuring authority is not satisfied with the information provided by a supplier, the disqualifying entity also has the option of obtaining information on convictions from the Criminal Records Bureau or Disclosure (Scotland).[7] Whilst the OGC Guidance is not legally binding, in the absence of other direction, it is likely to be relied upon by procuring authorities.

A similar approach is adopted in relation to the discretionary disqualifications and the UK regulations suggest that the procuring authority may ask a supplier to provide documentation proving he has not committed any of the relevant offences and further list the kinds of documentation

[1] Directive 2004/18/EC of 31 March 2004 on the coordination of procedures for the award of puc works contracts, public supply contracts and public service contracts (Public Sector Directive), art 45(1).

[2] See: ec.europa.eu/internal_market/publicprocurement/2004_18/index_en.htm .

[3] T Medina, 'EU Directives as an Anti-Corruption Measure: Excluding Corruption-Convicted Tenderers from Public Procurement Contracts' in KV Thai (ed), *International Handbook of Public Procurement* (Boca Raton, CRC Press, 2009).

[4] Public Contracts Regulations 2006 SI 2006/5, reg 23(3) [hereafter PCR].

[5] OGC Guidance, para 3.

[6] OGC Guidance, para 3.3.

[7] OGC Guidance, para 5; S Williams, 'The Mandatory Contractor Exclusions for Serious Criminal Offences in UK Public Procurement' (2009) 15 *European Public Law* 440.

that are conclusive evidence in relation to some of the offences.[8] This approach may be useful in obtaining information on past offences and offences committed in the specific procedure. Whilst there is no mentioned procedure for this, it is likely that the procedure used to obtain information on convictions will be adopted by procuring authorities in obtaining information on offences.

In obtaining information on convictions, the US adopts a similar approach to the EU and the UK. The FAR provides that information on convictions or offences may be requested from suppliers or be voluntarily submitted by suppliers.[9] In the US, the procedure for obtaining this information is subsumed within the process of obtaining information on the supplier's capability to perform the contract and its responsibility.[10] Where a US procuring authority is disqualifying a supplier on the basis of a disqualification previously imposed by another entity, the procuring authority is required to examine the Excluded Parties List System (EPLS),[11] which is a database of disqualified suppliers,[12] and to reject the bid of any supplier that has been listed.[13]

Where disqualification is not based on a conviction and the disqualifying entity has a discretion in deciding whether an offence was committed, sufficient procedures for obtaining this information may be required to ensure that a supplier is not disqualified on the basis of insufficient evidence or 'mere suspicion, unfounded allegation or error'.[14] Thus, apart from obtaining information from suppliers and the FAPIIS (Federal Awardee Performance and Integrity Information System) database, suppliers are also required to submit certifications that they have not committed any acts that impact on their responsibility and could lead to disqualification. This is similar to the EU/UK approach, which requires suppliers to provide a declaration stating that they have not committed any of the relevant offences that may lead to a discretionary disqualification not based on a conviction.[15]

In the US, where there is a dispute over the facts in cases where the disqualification is not based on a conviction, a disqualifying official may refer the matter to another official for findings of fact and the disqualifying official is required to prepare written findings of fact in such cases.[16]

8 PCR, reg 23(5).

9 Federal Acquisition Regulation 9.105-1; FAR 9.103(c); Cibinic and Nash, *Formation*, 441.

10 FAR 9.104-6. Procuring authorities are required to consult the Federal Awardee Performance and Integrity Information System (FAPIIS), which contains comprehensive information on suppliers. Cibinic and Nash, *Formantion*, 441; Anechiarico and Jacobs, *The Pursuit of Absolute Integrity*, ch 8.

11 FAR 9.404 and 9.405.

12 See www.epls.gov/ .

13 FAR 9.405 (d).

14 *Transco Security v Freeman* 454 US 820 (1981).

15 PSD, art 45(3); PCR, reg 23(5)(c).

16 FAR 9.406-3(d).

No other jurisdiction requires the disqualifying entity to prepare a written record as part of the process to determine if an offence was committed.

In the World Bank, the process of determining if an offence has been committed is within the discretion of the official that conducts the disqualification process – the Evaluations Officer (EO). Allegations of fraud and corruption in Bank-funded projects are first referred to the Bank's Department of Institutional Integrity (INT), which investigates whether an offence that may lead to disqualification has occurred. Once the INT completes its investigation it refers the evidence to the EO,[17] who examines this evidence and decides if it supports a finding that the supplier engaged in corruption.

In relation to the Bank's one-off disqualification, determining whether an offence was committed is the function of the Bank's Task Manager, who approves the Borrower's decision to award the contract to a particular supplier through a 'no-objection notice'.[18] Where the Task Manager is aware of corrupt activity in competing for the contract, and the Borrower proposes to award the contract to the corrupt bidder, the Bank may refuse to assent to the award of the contract to this bidder and thus disqualify the bidder. However, there is no process by which the Task Manager decides that an offence was committed and he has sole discretion in managing the process. The procedures for disqualification in such cases are subsumed within the Bank's procedures for the prior review of contracts.[19]

South Africa provides different means for storing and retrieving information on disqualification depending on the nature of the disqualification. Thus in relation to the administrative measures that deny suppliers access to contracts for a specified period of time, such as those under the Preferential Procurement Policy Framework Act (PPPFA) regulations, a procuring authority may obtain this information by consulting the internet-based Database of Restricted Suppliers.[20] Similarly, where a court imposes disqualification under the Corruption Act, procuring authorities are required to examine the internet-based Register of Tender Defaulters.[21] Both databases are simplified versions of the US EPLS and are publicly available on the website of the National Treasury.

In relation to measures that deny a supplier access to a particular contract, neither the PPPFA nor the Public Finance Management Act (PFMA) regulations give any indication as to how a procuring authority might obtain the information that a relevant offence was committed.

[17] World Bank Sanctions Procedures art II.

[18] BPG, appendix 1, para 2.

[19] BPG, appendix 1, para 2; S Williams, 'The Debarment of Corrupt Contractors from World Bank-Financed Contracts' (2007) 36 *Public Contract Law Journal* 277, 290–91.

[20] www.treasury.gov.za/publications/other/Database%20of%20Restricted%20Suppliers.pdf.

[21] www.treasury.gov.za/publications/other/Register%20for%20Tender%20Defaulters.pdf.

5.2.1.2 Giving the supplier notice of a proposed disqualification and an opportunity to make representations

Informing a supplier about the proposed disqualification and giving the supplier the opportunity to be heard or make representations is a fundamental aspect of the notion of procedural fairness.[22] As is discussed further below on the content of procedural fairness, adequate notice to the supplier about the proposed disqualification should enable the supplier to answer the allegations against it. Such notice should contain information that disqualification is being contemplated against the supplier and the basis for the disqualification. A supplier should also be informed at this stage whether and in what form it may make representations to the disqualifying entity.

Permitting a supplier to make representations to the disqualifying entity will improve the quality of the disqualification decision[23] but the nature and extent of such representations would vary depending on the discretion available to the disqualifying entity and the kind of disqualification measure.[24] Thus, where disqualification is mandatory, is based on a conviction, and there are no factual questions to be answered, although notice and an opportunity to make representations may be ideal, they may not be required in practice as a relevant conviction may serve as sufficient notice to the supplier that it will be denied public contracts. In such cases, representations will only be valuable to assist the disqualifying entity to determine if there are factors necessitating a waiver, where the entity possesses discretion to waive the requirement to disqualify. Where the disqualifying entity possesses a larger measure of discretion on the continuum of disqualification, notice and representations should form an integral part of the disqualification decision. However, the kind of hearing afforded the supplier may be limited by whether the disqualification measure is a one-off measure designed to affect one contract or a general decision that will affect the supplier's access to contracts for a period of time.[25]

In jurisdictions such as the US, the World Bank and South Africa under the PPPFA regulations, notice and the opportunity to be heard is an express requirement in the regulations. This may in part be due to the fact that convictions are not necessarily required for disqualification. However, in the EU, UK and South Africa under the PFMA regulations, the disqualifying entity has discretion in these matters – although in these jurisdic-

[22] D Galligan, *Due Process and Fair Procedures: A Study of Administrative Procedures* (Oxford, Clarendon Press, 1997) chs 5 and 6.

[23] S Arrowsmith, *Government Procurement and Judicial Review* (Toronto, Carswell, 1988) 164.

[24] *Lloyd v McMahon* [1987] AC 625 *per* Lord Bridge, 702; Arrowsmith, *Procurement and Judicial Review*, above n 23, 166.

[25] Arrowsmith, *Procurement and Judicial Review*, above n 23, ch 8.

tions, the discretion of the disqualifying entity is likely to be constrained by administrative law rules on decision-making by public bodies.

In the EU, the procurement directives are silent on whether notice of a proposed disqualification is required and whether a supplier will be given an opportunity to be heard. This was intended to give Member States the discretion to adopt procedures that conform to national models of administrative decision-making, and the EU expected Member States to fill the lacunae in the directives by adopting relevant procedures,[26] which would meet certain procedural and substantive standards[27] and comply with EU principles of equal treatment,[28] non-discrimination[29] and transparency.[30] It is also possible that national procedures would be expected to comply with the EU principle that a person whose interests will be adversely affected by the decision of a public authority has a right to be heard.[31]

Where a Member State has not adopted procedures that provide for notice and the opportunity to make representations, this does not mean that disqualifying entities in such states are free from this obligation. In *La Cascina,* which dealt with the discretionary disqualifications, the CJEU held that the principles of transparency and equal treatment, which govern the procedures for the award of public contracts, require that the substantive and procedural conditions concerning participation in a contract be clearly defined in advance.[32] One way of ensuring that suppliers are aware of the conditions for their participation in (or disqualification from) a contract is to give a supplier notice of an intention to disqualify it from a contract and the basis for its disqualification.

In implementing the EU directives, the UK procurement regulations are also silent on the issue of notice and representations. However, apart from the fact that UK public bodies must comply with EU principles as discussed above, UK administrative law also requires procedural fairness as a general rule in administrative decision-making,[33] which may include advance notice of the case against a person and the right to be heard.[34] In disqualification cases, the form of the notice and the formality of the hearing should be sufficient for a proper determination of the case,[35] with due

[26] S Williams, 'The Mandatory Exclusions for Corruption in the New EC Procurement Directives' (2006) *European Law Review* 711, 732; Case C-226/04 *La Cascina* [2006] ECR I-1347.

[27] P Craig, *EU Administrative Law* (Oxford, Oxford University Press, 2006) 270.

[28] Case C-243/89 *Commission v Denmark (Storebaelt case)* [1993] ECR I-3353; Case C-87/94 *Commission v Belgium (Walloonia Buses)* [1996] ECR I-2043.

[29] Case C-16/98 *Commission v France* [2000] ECR I-8315.

[30] Case T-203/96 *Embassy Limousines v European Parliament* [1998] ECR II-4239; Case C-324/98 *Telaustria* [2000] ECR I-10745.

[31] Case C-17/74 *Transocean Marine Paint v Commission* [1974] ECR 1063, para 15; Case T-450/93 *Lisrestal v Commission* [1994] ECR II-1177; Case C-32/95 *Commission v Lisrestal* [1996] ECR II-3773 para 59.

[32] Case C-226/04 *La Cascina,* above n 26, para 32.

[33] *Council of the Civil Service Unions v Minister for the Civil Service* [1985] AC 374.

[34] *Kanda v Government of Malaya* [1962] AC 322 *per* Lord Denning.

[35] *Haoucher v Minister of State for Immigration* (1990) 93 ALR 51.

regard to considerations of economy and efficiency in the procurement process.[36]

Where disqualification is discretionary and is not based on a conviction, a right to be heard is a necessary component of the proper exercise of the disqualifying entity's discretion, as this will ensure that the disqualifying official considers relevant information which may not be known to the official[37] and that the official does not abuse his discretion by failing to take relevant considerations into account.[38] Thus, whilst administrative law suggests that a hearing may be appropriate in these cases, the form of that hearing is left to the discretion of the procuring authority.[39]

In the UK, the cases that have dealt with the removal of suppliers from an approved list of tenderers under statutory provisions may give an indication as to how the issue of notice and hearing in disqualification decisions may be approached, bearing in mind that these cases concerned a general exclusion from contracts similar to the mandatory disqualification provisions. In cases of general exclusion, a more involved hearing may be appropriate compared to one-off disqualification situations. Thus, in *R v Enfield London Borough Council ex parte Unwin*,[40] a supplier was removed from the local authority's approved list of suppliers without being given notice of this action or a chance to answer the allegations levelled against it. It was held that the local authority was required to give the supplier notice of the allegations and a chance to respond and the authority had acted unfairly in not doing so.[41] In other contexts, administrators have also been required to give notice of adverse decisions to affected persons. Thus, in *Abbey Mine Ltd v The Coal Authority*,[42] which dealt with the denial of a coal-mine licence, it was held that fairness required that 'an applicant be told the substance of the decision-maker's concerns about his own case'.

Although the procurement regulations do not indicate whether a notice of a proposed disqualification is required, it seems likely that by analogy with the courts' approach in similar situations, UK procuring authorities may be required to give a supplier notice of the proposed disqualification and rights of representation depending on the context of the disqualification where the measure is not based on a conviction.

As mentioned above, in the US, the giving of notice to a supplier proposed for disqualification is elaborated within the legislation,[43] although

[36] Arrowsmith, *Procurement and Judicial Review*, above n 23, 165–6.

[37] Galligan, *Due Process and Fair Procedures*, above n 22, 266.

[38] *Prescott v Birmingham Corporation* [1955] Ch 210.

[39] Galligan, *Due Process and Fair Procedures*, above n 22, 136; *Board of Education v Rice* [1911] AC 179 *per* Lord Loreburn.

[40] *R v Enfield London Borough Council ex parte Unwin* [1989] COD 466.

[41] *Enfield* ibid, *per* Lord Glidewell.

[42] *Abbey Mine Ltd v The Coal Authority* [2008] EWCA Civ 353.

[43] FAR 9.406-3.

there are differences in approach depending on the length of the disqualification, and the notice requirement is tailored to reflect the seriousness of the measure. For longer disqualifications, procuring authorities are required to send a supplier and named related persons a notice of proposed disqualification including the reasons for the disqualification, and the sections of the FAR on which the proposed disqualification is based.[44] This notice should also inform the supplier of the effect of a disqualification – which is that the supplier will be listed in the EPLS, the database of disqualified firms – as well as information regarding the procuring authority's disqualification procedures. This notice gives the supplier 30 days within which to respond and guarantees the supplier the right to submit representations in writing.[45] The US courts have also affirmed that disqualification must be accompanied by notice to the contractor and an opportunity to be heard[46] and notices should be sufficient to enable the supplier adequately to rebut the allegations.[47]

In relation to the shorter disqualifications in the US, where the disqualification is based on an indictment, notice from the procuring authority is not required as the indictment is deemed to constitute sufficient notice of the disqualification to the supplier.[48] Where the disqualification is not based on an indictment, procuring authorities have a duty to provide a supplier with notice of the fact that the supplier has been suspended and an opportunity to make representations by appearing with counsel.[49] However, a hearing will be denied where the US Department of Justice decides that a hearing will prejudice contemplated or pending legal proceedings.[50]

The differing notice and hearing requirements in the US may be because the shorter disqualifications may have less of an adverse effect on suppliers,[51] since they generally last for no longer than 12 months and also because where a shorter disqualification is based on allegations of wrongdoing, the government may need to protect the secrecy of an investigation.[52] In addition, the shorter disqualifications give the procuring authority the ability to quickly disqualify people with which it does not wish to deal.[53]

44 FAR 9.406-3(c).

45 FAR 9.406-3(b).

46 *Gonzalez v Freeman* 334 F2d 570 (DC Cir 1964).

47 *Transco Security v Freeman*, above n 14, 323; *Mullane v Central Hanover Bank & Trust Co*, 339 US 306, 314 (1949); *Memphis Light, Gas & Water Division v Craft*, 436 US 1 (1978).

48 *SDA Inc*, Comp Gen Dec B-253355, 93-2 CPD ¶ 132.

49 FAR 9.407-3(b)(2).

50 FAR 9.407-3(c).

51 *Horne Bros Inc v Laird*, 463 F2d 1268, 1270 (DC Cir 1972).

52 *Transco Security*, above n 14, 324 and *Horne Bros Inc*, ibid; S Gordon, 'Suspension and Debarment from Federal Programs' (1994) 23 *Public Contract Law Journal* 573, 591.

53 T Canni, 'Shoot First, Ask Questions Later: An Examination and Critique of Suspension and Debarment Provisions under the FAR, including a Discussion of the Mandatory Disclosure Rule, the IBM Suspension and Other Noteworthy Developments' (2009) 38 *Public Contracts Law Journal* 547.

The World Bank adopts a similar approach to notifying suppliers as the US. As mentioned earlier, once the Evaluations Officer is convinced that the supplier engaged in corruption, he issues a notice of disqualification proceedings to the firm, giving it 30 days to explain in writing why it should not be temporarily disqualified from future Bank contracts pending the final outcome of the proceedings.[54] In relation to the one-off disqualification, a supplier is not entitled to a hearing on the Bank's decision to disqualify it. However, if a supplier complains about the Bank's refusal to issue a 'no-objection' notice, the Bank's Regional Procurement Adviser may suspend the award of the contract until the complaints are dealt with,[55] and this may give a disqualified bidder an opportunity to be heard.

In relation to the South African system, for the non-judicial disqualifications, the PPPFA regulations provide for some kind of notice and a hearing, by requiring disqualifying entities to comply with the *audi alteram partem* rule. The nature of the hearing in such disqualification proceedings was clarified by the National Treasury by virtue of a practice note issued to procuring entities in 2006.[56] Under the terms of the practice note, procuring entities must inform a supplier of the proposed disqualification, the reasons for the disqualification and the proposed length of the disqualification, giving the supplier 14 days to respond with reasons why it should not be disqualified. It should be noted that the requirements for notice and a hearing only apply to the disqualifications which apply for a period of time and there isn't a similar requirement for the disqualifications under the PPPFA and the PFMA regulations that only affect a particular contract. In relation to the one-off disqualifications, procuring authorities will be required to comply with the requirements of the Promotion of Administrative Justice Act discussed below.

As stated, the PFMA regulations are silent on the issue of notice and a hearing, and the practice note only applies to disqualification under the PPPFA regulations. However, public authorities are required in carrying out their public functions to comply with the Promotion of Administrative Justice Act (PAJA)[57] and the regulations[58] made thereunder, which guarantee a minimum level of procedural fairness to persons affected by administrative decisions. As South African jurisprudence has determined that all aspects of the procurement process amount to 'administrative action'

[54] Art II, S 2.02 WBSP.

[55] Appendix 3, para 13 BPG; Williams, 'The Debarment of Corrupt Contractors', above n 19, 294.

[56] National Treasury Supply Chain Management Office Practice Note Number SCM 5 of 2006, Restriction of Suppliers, 9 October 2006, para 2.2.

[57] Act 3 of 2000 (Government Gazette 20853, 3 February 2000) [hereafter PAJA].

[58] Promotion of Administrative Justice Act Regulations on Administrative Procedures 2002 (Government Gazette 23674, 31 July 2002) [hereafter PAJA Regulations].

within section 1 of PAJA,[59] the decision to disqualify a supplier must accord with the procedural standards under PAJA. Section 3(2) of PAJA specifically provides that a person affected by administrative action is entitled to notice of the proposed administrative action and an opportunity to be heard. The PAJA regulations elaborate the limits of such notice and hearing by providing that a person materially and adversely affected by administrative action is entitled to be informed about the action. This notice must contain information on a right to reasons for the action and a right to a review of the action, where applicable.[60]

In the disqualification context, the South African courts have interpreted the provisions of PAJA as requiring a disqualifying entity to give the supplier adequate written notice of the nature and purpose of the disqualification and a reasonable opportunity to make representations.[61] Where this is not done, the courts have shown a willingness to nullify disqualification decisions. In *Supersonic Tours*,[62] the State Tender Board disqualified the applicant and its directors from public contracts for 10 years, without allowing the applicant to make any representations on the allegations against it. The High Court held that the PAJA had not been complied with and ordered that the decision to disqualify the applicant be set aside.

5.2.1.3 *Deciding if disqualification is justifiable on the available evidence*

Deciding whether disqualification is justifiable on the available evidence is the core of the disqualification decision, and the justification determines whether the decision to disqualify is fair. A fundamental aspect of the exercise of public power is that it must not be exercised in a manner that is arbitrary or irrational.[63] This section considers whether the decision to disqualify is justifiable in relation to the reasons given for the disqualification. In other words, is there a logical connection between the disqualification and the reasons adduced for the disqualification? Justifying a decision is described as a process of showing the facts and the standards to be applied and then demonstrating the reasoning process by which the standards were applied to the facts.[64] This is a substantive as well as a procedural issue, since the justifiability (or validity) of the disqualification depends on the substantive reasons on which the disqualification is based.

59 *ABBM Printing and Publishing (Pty) Ltd v Transnet Ltd* 1998 (2) SA 109 (W) 117G–H; *Nextcom (Pty) Ltd v Funde NO and Others* 2000 (4) SA 491 (T) 504G–J; *Grinaker LTA Ltd and another v Tender Board (Mpumalanga) and others* (2002) 3 All SA 336 (T) para 32; *Logbro Properties CC v Bedderson NO and Others* 2003 (2) SA 460 (SCA) para 5.

60 PAJA Regulations, reg 23.

61 *Supersonic Tours (Pty) Ltd v State Tender Board* [2007] JOL 19891 (T) affd, *Chairman State Tender Board v Supersonic Tours (Pty) Ltd* 2008 (6) SA 220 (SCA).

62 *Supersonic Tours*, ibid.

63 Arrowsmith, *Procurement and Judicial Review*, above n 23, 194.

64 Galligan, *Due Process and Fair Procedures*, above n 22, 430.

The procedural issues that arise at this stage include whether the supplier is furnished with the factors (the standards) that the disqualifying entity will take into account in deciding to disqualify and the procedures that the entity uses to decide whether it will waive the disqualification.

Deciding if disqualification is justifiable is closely linked to the trigger for disqualification (a conviction or otherwise) and the discretion available to the disqualifying entity. If the disqualification is mandatory and based on a conviction, the procuring authority's discretion is limited and procedures will be limited to deciding if the disqualification will be waived, where the entity has the discretion to do so. However, where the disqualification gives the entity discretion in deciding whether an offence was committed and whether it will waive the disqualification, the entity may need to apply procedures ensuring that its decision to disqualify is justifiable on the basis of the available evidence and that the supplier is aware of the factors (or standards) that will be applied to its case.

Where a disqualifying entity is permitted to waive disqualification or take rehabilitation measures into account, procedures may be necessary to decide whether a waiver is appropriate or rehabilitation measures are sufficient for the supplier to avoid a disqualification. For instance, how will the disqualifying entity request evidence of the rehabilitation measures from the supplier? The procedures here will be affected by the level of discretion that the disqualifying entity possesses in taking rehabilitation measures into account.

It should be noted that this stage of the disqualification decision may in practice overlap with the previous stage on notice and representations, since most jurisdictions contemplate that notice of the proposed disqualification should give the supplier information on the factors to be taken into account in disqualifying the supplier, if the supplier is going to be able to make tenable representations. It is also likely that this stage may overlap in practice with the last stage of the disqualification decision discussed below – giving the supplier reasons for the decision to disqualify it. However, because of the importance of this stage of the disqualification decision, it will be treated as a distinct stage of the disqualification process.

There are two factors that are relevant to this stage of disqualification. The first is the weight of evidence and/or the factors that are relevant for a supplier to be disqualified or to avoid disqualification and the second is whether the supplier knows these factors.

Where disqualification is triggered by a conviction, as is the case in the EU, UK, the US and South Africa, the issue of the weight of the evidence required for disqualification and, to an extent, the factors to be taken into account are met by the conviction. However, where disqualification is not based on a conviction, the weight of evidence required to disqualify is of great importance and the supplier needs to be aware of the factors relevant to the disqualifying entity's decision-making.

In relation to the discretionary disqualifications in the EU, the weight of evidence required for disqualification is either a conviction for an offence relating to professional misconduct or being 'guilty' of professional misconduct.[65] Where a conviction is not required, the directives are silent on the factors that are to be taken into account in deciding to disqualify and the weight of evidence required for disqualification. As discussed above, the EU expected Member States to adopt procedures for disqualification, which would comply with EU administrative law principles that the decisions of public bodies ought to be justifiable.[66] In *HI*,[67] Advocate-General Tizzano suggested that the procedures under the EU procurement directives must always be interpreted in a manner that guarantees transparency and thus cannot be interpreted as having limits which leave stages or phases of the procedures uncovered. The case of *La Cascina* is also relevant to the obligation on EU procuring authorities to give suppliers information on the factors to be taken into account and to ensure that the decision to disqualify is justifiable. In this case it was held that the procedural and substantive factors relevant to disqualification ought to 'be determined with absolute certainty and made public in order that the persons concerned may know exactly the procedural requirements . . .'.[68]

Thus case law from the CJEU suggests that procuring authorities may be required to give suppliers information on the factors to be taken into account in deciding to disqualify and further, that the decision to disqualify ought to be justifiable, in keeping with the principle of transparency.

The UK regulations followed a similar approach as the EU in not specifying whether a procuring authority is required to give suppliers information on the factors relevant to a disqualification decision (where the disqualification is not based on a conviction) or whether the decision to disqualify must be justifiable. Apart from the fact that UK procuring authorities will be required to abide by EU law as discussed above, UK jurisprudence also provides information on the approach that entities are expected to adopt. By law, the decisions of public bodies must not be unreasonable,[69] arbitrary or reached without sufficient evidence.[70] In *R v Bristol City Council ex parte DL Barrett*,[71] where the supplier was removed from an approved list of tenderers, the court held that the procuring authority's decision was not justifiable, as the decision did not 'stand up to critical scrutiny'.[72] Thus, the exercise of the entity's discretion must be

[65] PSD, art 45(2)(c) and (d).

[66] Case C-97/91 *Borelli v Commission* [1992] ECR I-6313, para 14; Case C-1/99 *Kofisa Italia* [2001] ECR I-207, para 46; Case C-226/99 *Siples* [2001] ECR I-277, para 17.

[67] Case C-92/00 *HI* [2002] ECR I-5553, Opinion of AG Tizzano, para 21.

[68] Case C-236/04 *La Cascina*, above n 26, para 32.

[69] *Associated Provincial Picture Houses v Wednesbury Corp* [1948] KB 223.

[70] *Gavaghan v Secretary of State for the Environment* (1989) 60 P & CR 515.

[71] *R v Bristol City Council ex parte DL Barrett* [2001] 3 LGLR 11.

[72] *R v Bristol City Council ex parte DL Barrett*, *per* Jackson J, para 66.

based on justifiable evidence and where this is not the case, as is discussed in chapter eleven on remedies, the decision to disqualify may be litigated in the High Court,[73] and may be subject to judicial review[74] in certain circumstances.[75]

In the US, where disqualification is not made on the basis of a conviction, the legislation is clear on the weight to be given to the evidence and the factors to be taken into account in disqualifying a supplier for the decision to be regarded as justifiable. In such cases, disqualification may only be made on the basis of an indictment against the supplier or on the basis of 'adequate evidence',[76] which is defined as information sufficient to support the belief that a particular act or omission has occurred.[77] US jurisprudence has also described 'adequate evidence' as a 'minimal standard of proof'[78] and has likened it to the probable cause necessary for an arrest, a search warrant or a preliminary hearing, which must be more than uncorroborated suspicion or accusation.[79]

The FAR suggests that in assessing the adequacy of the evidence, agencies should consider factors such as the availability and credibility of the information, whether important allegations are corroborated and what inferences may reasonably be drawn.[80] This assessment should include an examination of basic documents such as contracts, inspection reports, and correspondence.

In the World Bank, where the Evaluations Officer issues a letter of disqualification to a supplier and the supplier does not contest the allegations, the EO imposes an appropriate sanction. If the supplier contests the allegations, the matter proceeds to the Sanctions Board, which has to decide whether it is 'more likely than not' that the respondent committed the alleged offences.[81] This standard is interpreted as a preponderance of evidence that the supplier committed the offence.[82] The factors to be taken into account in disqualifying suppliers will have been included in the

[73] PCR, reg 47.

[74] S Bailey, 'Judicial Review and Contracting Decisions' (2007) 3 *Public Law* 444; S Bailey, 'Judicial Review and the Public Procurement Regulations' (2005) 6 *Public Procurement Law Review* 29; *R (on the application of Cookson & Clegg) v Ministry of Defence* [2005] EWCA Civ 811; C Lewis, *Judicial Remedies in Public Law*, 4th edn (London, Sweet and Maxwell, 2009) ch 4.

[75] Judicial review will be available where there has been fraud, corruption, or bad faith in decision-making. See *R (on the application of Menai Collect Ltd & North West Commercial Services Ltd) v Dept of Constitutional Affairs* [2006] EWHC Admin 724; *Mercury Energy Ltd v Electricity Corporation of New Zealand* [1994] 1 WLR 521, *R v Lord Chancellors Department ex parte Hibbit & Saunders* [1993] COD 326, *R v Legal Aid Board ex parte Donn & Co* [1994] 3 All ER 1; Bailey, 'Judicial Review and Contracting Decisions', above n 71, 446.

[76] FAR 9.407-2(b) and (c).

[77] FAR 2.101.

[78] *In the matter of Frank Lagrua* HUDBCA No 95-G-141-D25.

[79] *Transco Security v Freeman*, above n 14.

[80] FAR 9.407-1(b).

[81] WBSP, art VIII, s 8.01.

[82] WBSP, art VIII, s 8.02.

notice of disqualification and it is where these are contested that the supplier is given a right to appear before the Sanctions Board.[83] In relation to the Bank's one-off disqualification process, there is no indication as to what factors will be taken into account, or whether the disqualification has to be justifiable.

In South Africa, although neither the PPPFA nor the PFMA regulations address the issue of whether a disqualification decision has to be justifiable, in relation to the disqualification under the PPPFA regulations, it seems likely that they are expected to be justifiable, as the practice note issued by the National Treasury on disqualification procedures under the PPPFA regulations provides that the supplier has a right to challenge its disqualification in court proceedings and the accounting officer of the procuring authority will be accountable for the disqualification decision.[84] This can be interpreted as meaning that the accounting officer will bear the responsibility of showing that a disqualification decision was justifiable.

Generally, the PAJA gives the courts the power to examine the legality, reasonableness and fairness of administrative decisions.[85] A decision that is lawful, reasonable and fair is one that will be regarded as justifiable. In *National & Overseas Modular Construction v Tender Board*[86] the court held that the decision of the Tender Board to reject a tender was not justifiable on the basis of the reasons given. Similarly, in *Kawari Wholesalers v MEC: Dept of Health*,[87] where a procuring authority based its decision not to award a contract on factors that were not brought to the applicant's notice, the court held that the decision was not justifiable on the basis of the reasons given for the decision.[88]

Thus, the courts have shown that at least in relation to the consideration of tenders, procuring authorities must give suppliers the factors to be taken into account in deciding to reject a tender and must also ensure that the decision to reject a tender can be justified on the basis of the reasons given for the rejection. Where this is not the case, the courts may set aside the decision. It is likely that similar considerations may apply in the disqualification context, since all aspects of the procurement process are subject to similar procedural requirements.

In relation to whether a procedure exists for a disqualifying entity to take into account rehabilitation measures or other factors that will mean that the supplier will avoid disqualification, not all the jurisdictions are clear on whether disqualifying entities have a discretion to waive disqualification.[89]

[83] WBSP, art VI.

[84] National Treasury Supply Chain Management Office Practice Note Number SCM 5 of 2006, Restriction of Suppliers, 9 October 2006, para 2.5.

[85] PAJA s 6(2).

[86] *National & Overseas Modular Construction v Tender Board*, 1999 (1) SA 701.

[87] *Kawari Wholesalers v MEC: Dept of Health* [2008] ZANWHC 12.

[88] *Grinaker LTA v Tender Board (Mpumalanga)* (2002) 3 All SA 336.

[89] Waivers are dealt with in chapter 10 of this volume.

Where the legislation gives a disqualifying entity the discretion to waive disqualification, the legislation is silent on the procedures for implementing such waivers. This is the case where such waivers are based on the existence of facts that make disqualification inappropriate, such as rehabilitation measures implemented by a supplier, and where such waivers are based on a policy rationale such as national security.

In relation to the EU and the UK, future interpretation by the CJEU as illustrated by the courts approach in *La Cascina* may mean that EU procuring authorities will be required to adopt suitable procedures in relation to waivers. The US adopts a similar approach to the EU and UK. Whilst the US regulations state some of the factors to be taken into account in waiving disqualification, there is no established procedure for doing so.[90] The discretion of procuring authorities in waiving disqualification in the US is however constrained by the fact that the decision may only be made by the head of the procuring authority and this power cannot be delegated.[91] In the World Bank there is no possibility for a Borrower's agency to waive a disqualification imposed by the Bank.[92] Although the South African legislation is silent on whether procuring authorities may waive disqualification, and there are no established procedures for doing this, the National Treasury practice note discussed above provides that a procuring authority may lift or amend a disqualification where there are grounds to do so,[93] thus possibly giving procuring authorities the power to take rehabilitation measures into account in the disqualification process.

5.2.1.4 *Giving reasons for the decision to disqualify*

The giving of reasons for a decision is defined as explaining the basis on which a decision is made and justifying that basis by reference to a set of standards.[94] In the disqualification context, the detail of the reasons may vary depending on whether the measure is imposed on the basis of a conviction or other evidence. Where disqualification is not based on a conviction, the reasons for the decision should be spelt out with sufficient clarity so the supplier understands the basis for the decision and can appeal the decision where possible. The giving of reasons has two purposes: it ensures the decision was properly made and provides a basis upon which the decision may be evaluated or challenged. The giving of reasons may improve the decision-making process by concentrating the decision-maker's mind on the right questions; by proving to the applicant that this

[90] R Bednar (ed), *The Practitioner's Guide to Suspension & Debarment*, 3rd edn (American Bar Association, 2002) ch IV.

[91] FAR 23.506(e).

[92] BPG, appendix 1, para 8.

[93] National Treasury Supply Chain Management Office Practice Note Number SCM 5 of 2006, Restriction of Suppliers, 9 October 2006, para 2.4.

[94] Galligan, *Due Process and Fair Procedures*, above n 22, 429.

was the case; by showing that the issues have been conscientiously addressed and how the result has been reached; or alternatively alerting the applicant to a justiciable flaw in the process.[95]

As discussed, the giving of reasons is closely tied to the requirement that the decision should be justifiable and some writers define the giving of reasons to include the validity of those reasons.[96] In truth, these two stages of the disqualification process are intricately linked, as a reason that is unjustifiable or does not provide any indication as to why a decision was taken may not amount to a 'reason' in law.[97] This section will use reasons to mean the satisfactory rationalisation for a disqualification by reference to a previously determined standard. What is satisfactory will depend on the administrative culture, the procedural requirements in a given jurisdiction and the particular context and nature of the disqualification.

There are two approaches adopted by the jurisdictions in relation to the requirement to give reasons. The first approach is for the legislation to require a disqualifying entity to furnish the supplier with a notice containing information on the disqualification including the reasons on which the disqualification is based. The second approach is for the legislation to be silent on this aspect of the procedure, but in such jurisdictions a duty to furnish reasons may be required by administrative law rules that require reasons where a public body takes a decision that affects a private interest.[98]

In the jurisdictions under study, the UK, US, World Bank and South Africa (PPPFA regulations) adopt the first approach. In the UK, the procurement regulations go further than the EU directives and require procuring authorities to notify suppliers of their disqualification from public contracts.[99] Although the regulations do not explicitly mention reasons, this may implied as there would be little merit to a requirement to notify suppliers without including a corresponding obligation to provide a statement of reasons. Under the common law, where reasons are required in administrative decision-making based on a statutory scheme,[100] the obligation is to give appropriate and reasonable reasons having regard to the circumstances of the case.[101] In cases analogous to disqualification (where there was a statutory duty to give reasons) the courts have required that

[95] *R v Higher Education Funding Council, ex parte Institute of Dental Surgery* [1994] 1 All ER 651, 665, *per* Sedley J. Failure to give reasons may make judicial review impossible – *R v The Mayor and Commonalty and Citizens of the City of London ex parte Matson* [1996] COD 161.

[96] Galligan, *Due Process and Fair Procedures*, above n 22, 430.

[97] *R (on the application of Asha Foundation) v Millennium Commission* [2003] EWCA Civ 88, para 24.

[98] Galligan, *Due Process and Fair Procedures*, above n 22, 431.

[99] PCR, reg 29A.

[100] *R (on* the *application of Hasan) v Secretary of State for Trade and Industry* [2008] EWCA Civ 1312; *R v Secretary of State for the Home Department ex parte Doody* [1994] 1 AC 531; *R v Civil Service Appeal Board ex parte Cunningham* [1992] ICR 816; *R v Higher Education Funding Council ex parte Institute of Dental Surgery* [1994] 1 WLR 242, 255.

[101] *Millennium Commission,* above n 97, para 24.

the reasons be valid and sufficient.[102] Similar to the UK, the US Federal Acquisition Regulation (FAR) requires a disqualifying entity to give a supplier notice of its disqualification including reasons for the disqualification[103] and where administrative action has been challenged, US courts have held that discretionary decisions by administrators should be supported by reasoned opinions.[104]

In the World Bank, a requirement of giving reasons for disqualification is implied in the Bank's disqualification process. As mentioned above, once the Evaluations Officer examines the evidence obtained by the INT and decides that the offence was committed, the EO sends a notice to the supplier giving it 30 days to explain why it should not be temporarily disqualified from Bank contracts on the basis of the available evidence. This notice gives the supplier the evidence on which it is to be disqualified, which are the reasons for the proposed disqualification. In relation to the one-off disqualifications, a supplier is entitled to an explanation from the Borrower in writing or at a debriefing meeting.[105] However, where the supplier is not satisfied with the reasons or the explanation from the Borrower, in cases where it is disqualified for corruption, the supplier may request a meeting with the Bank's Regional Procurement Adviser.[106]

In South Africa, the PPPFA regulations provide for the application of the *audi alteram partem* rule and the National Treasury has expressed this to include a requirement for a procuring authority to give a supplier reasons for the decision to disqualify it.[107]

The EU and South Africa (PFMA regulations and PPPFA regulations in relation to one-off disqualifications) adopt the second approach to furnishing reasons and the legislation is silent as to whether such a requirement exists. As discussed earlier, in the EU, this silence can be understood from the perspective that specifying a requirement to give notice and furnish reasons may have been unduly prescriptive, and Member States were expected to fill the lacunae in the directives by adopting relevant procedures for disqualification.[108] EU administrative law imposes a duty on public authorities to give reasons for their decisions as a precursor to effective judicial review,[109] where the measure affects the exercise of a fun-

[102] *R v Bristol City Council ex parte DL Barrett*, above n 71.

[103] FAR 9.406-3(e); 9.407-3(c).

[104] *Environmental Defense Fund v Ruckelshaus* 439 F2d 584 (DC Cir 1971).

[105] BPG, para 2.65.

[106] BPG, appendix 3, para 15.

[107] National Treasury Supply Chain Management Office Practice Note Number SCM 5 of 2006, Restriction of Suppliers, 9 October 2006, para 2.2.

[108] S Williams, 'The Mandatory Exclusions for Corruption in the new EC Procurement Directives' (2006) *European Law Review* 711, 732; Case C-226/04 *La Cascina*, above n 26.

[109] Case C-222/86 *UNECTEF v Heylens* [1987] ECR 4097; Case C-70/95 *Sodemare SA v Regione Lombardia* [1997] ECR I-3395 Opinion of AG Fennelly, para 17; G Anthony, *UK Public Law and European Law* (Oxford, Hart Publishing, 2002) 125–30.

damental right conferred by the Treaty.[110] The EU procurement directives also impose an obligation on procuring authorities, where requested to quickly inform unsuccessful tenderers on the reasons for which they were unsuccessful in relation to a public contract.[111] Although this obligation does not specifically refer to the disqualification context, it is broad enough to be interpreted as extending to any situation in which a supplier has been unsuccessful in the context of a public contract. Coupled with the EU legal duty to give reasons, it is arguable that Member States will be expected to furnish suppliers with reasons in the disqualification context.

Although the South African PFMA and PPPFA regulations on the one-off disqualifications are silent on the issue of reasons, as discussed above, the PAJA and the regulations made thereunder give all persons the right to receive written reasons where a person's rights are adversely affected by administrative action.[112] Where reasons for an administrative decision have not been given in the disqualification context, the courts have been willing overturn the decision.[113]

5.2.2 Are Disqualification Procedures Fair and Transparent?

5.2.2.1 Are disqualification procedures fair?

By whichever name it is known – whether 'procedural fairness', 'natural justice' or 'due process',[114] it is generally accepted that procedural fairness imposes two obligations on decision-makers: the obligation to give a fair hearing and the obligation not to be biased in decision-making. This section will examine what is necessary in the disqualification context to ensure that disqualification procedures meet the fair hearing aspect of procedural fairness. As a starting point, one may agree with the UK Supreme Court that fairness will often require that a person who may be adversely affected by the decision will have an opportunity to make representations either before the decision is taken with a view to producing a favourable result; or after it is taken, with a view to procuring its modification; or both.[115] The US courts have also stated that 'basic fairness' requires an opportunity to be heard in the disqualification context.[116] Ensuring procedural fairness is important as it is regarded as a precursor to substantive fairness, since procedures define the conditions within which substantive rules may be properly and fairly applied.[117]

110 Case C-70/95 *Sodemare*, above n 109, para 19.
111 PSD, art 41.
112 PAJA s 5; PAJA Regulations regs 23 to 27.
113 *Supersonic Tours*, above n 61.
114 Galligan, *Due Process and Fair Procedures*, chs 5 and 6.
115 *per* Lord Mustill in *Doody*, above n 100.
116 *Gonzalez v Freeman*, above n 46.
117 Galligan, *Due Process and Fair Procedures*, above n 22, 54–6 and 316.

Several arguments can be advanced on what the fair hearing aspect of fairness requires in the context of disqualification measures. At one extreme, one may advocate that fairness requires an adversarial type hearing – giving the supplier the opportunity to submit evidence and appear with counsel. At the other end, the need to prevent disruption and delay to a procurement process (where a procuring authority is the disqualifying entity) may mean that no hearing should be provided to the supplier in disqualification cases. A middle ground is suggested by Arrowsmith, who asserts that the requirement of fairness should be tailored to suit the kind of disqualification decision.

The first kind of disqualification decision identified by Arrowsmith is the decision to generally deny a supplier access to public contracts – such as the kind of disqualification under the mandatory provisions in the EU/UK and the disqualifications in the US, World Bank and the South African Corruption Act and PPPFA regulations. The second kind of decision is one to deny a supplier access to a particular contract without implications beyond that contract – such as a decision to deny a particular contract for breaches of the particular procurement process. Although a general disqualification decision will affect subsequent individual contract awards, Arrowsmith suggests that a hearing should *always* be provided in the making of general disqualification decisions, but the nature or extent of the hearing should depend on the consequences of the disqualification for the supplier. In relation to disqualifications limited to individual contract awards, a hearing may be available, depending on whether the hearing will cause delays to the procurement process and the consequences of the disqualification for the supplier.[118] Support for this view is found in the work of Galligan, who suggests that the procedural requirements for administrative decision-making should depend on the interests at stake.[119]

It is suggested that one more factor may be added to determine the availability and nature of a hearing in disqualification cases. Thus, the nature of a hearing – whether oral or written should depend not only on the kind of disqualification measure, the consequences of the disqualification or the interests at stake, but also on the discretion that is available to the disqualifying entity.[120] Thus, the nature and availability of a hearing should be defined by the nature of the decision-making power and the consequences for the affected person. This will mean that there will be very limited rights to a hearing where the disqualification does not entail the exercise of discretion by the disqualifying entity[121] and the disqualification is limited to a specific contract.

[118] Arrowsmith, *Procurement and Judicial Review*, above n 23, 166–70.

[119] Galligan, *Due Process and Fair Procedures*, above n 22, 234.

[120] *Council of the Civil Service Unions*, above n 33; S Arrowsmith, 'Judicial Review and the Contractual Powers of Public Authorities' (1990) 106 *Law Quarterly Review* 277, 283.

[121] Cf S Arrowsmith, 'Judicial Review of Public Procurement: The Recent Decisions in the National Lottery Case and R v Bristol City Council ex p. DL Barrett (2001) 10 *Public Procurement Law Review* NA41.

For instance where disqualification is mandatory and is based on a conviction, the only discretion exercised by the disqualifying entity may be in relation to derogations from the disqualification requirement, where permitted. In the EU and UK, the mandatory disqualifications permit derogations in limited public interest circumstances. Except in the case of rehabilitation measures, these circumstances are generally considered from the viewpoint of the procuring authority and as such, a supplier may not always be able to provide relevant information on whether it meets the public interest exceptions with reference to the needs of the procuring authority. As Arrowsmith suggested, the case for a hearing is stronger where the supplier is in a good position to supply relevant information, and this may not always be the case in relation to the waivers.

Where the disqualification decision entails more discretion on the part of the disqualifying entity, fairness should require that a hearing is required and here Arrowsmith's suggestions that the extent of the hearing should depend on the consequences of the decision becomes pertinent. The approach of Arrowsmith is already used in jurisdictions like the US and the World Bank where longer disqualifications come with a statutory requirement for a full adversarial hearing and the shorter/one-off disqualifications do not.[122]

If this approach is applied to the discretionary disqualifications in the EU, UK and South Africa, suppliers proposed for disqualification ought to be given a right to present information rebutting the allegations against them. This may take the form of written submissions within specified time limits to avoid delays to the procurement process, or a fuller and possibly oral hearing where the decision to disqualify is made outside the procurement process.

5.2.2.2 Are disqualification procedures transparent?

Transparency is a goal of public procurement[123] and a goal of administrative process more generally.[124] As an aspect of disqualification procedures, transparency is tied to non-discriminatory procedures and the giving of reasons for disqualification decisions.

Transparency in public procurement has been classified into four distinct but interrelated aspects.[125] Three of these aspects are particularly relevant to the disqualification process: publicity for the rules governing

[122] *ATL Inc v United States* 736 F2d 677 (Fed Cir 1984).

[123] S Arrowsmith, *The Law of Public and Utilities Procurement*, 2nd edn (London, Sweet & Maxwell, 2005) 127–8 and ch 7; S Arrowsmith, J Linarelli and D Wallace, *Regulating Public Procurement: National and International Perspectives* (The Hague, Kluwer Law, 2000) ch 2; S Arrowsmith, 'Towards a Multilateral Agreement on Transparency in Public Procurement' (1998) 47 *International and Comparative Law Quarterly* 793.

[124] Lord Mustill in *Doody*, above n 100.

[125] Arrowsmith, *Public and Utilities Procurement*, above n 123, 127–8.

the disqualification process; rule-based decision-making that limits discretion; and opportunities for verification and enforcement through the giving of reasons for the disqualification.[126] To ensure transparency in the disqualification process and transparent disqualification decisions it is necessary to ensure that the factors for disqualification are clearly specified and known to suppliers and that the disqualification is justified by reference to these factors and that suppliers are given reasons for the disqualification decision.

In the jurisdictions, the absence of clearly defined procedures for disqualification, especially in the context of the EU, the UK and South Africa, means that the disqualification procedures fall short of the requirements of transparency. In the EU, this issue has been partly clarified by the cases of *La Cascina* and *HI* but there is still no clarity on how much detail on procedures Member States are required to provide in their legislation implementing the disqualifications. Further clarification from the CJEU on the structure and the limits of Member States' discretion in managing the disqualification process is required and such clarification will invariably lead to better disqualification decisions. In addition, the lack of transparency within the EU disqualification system may mean that procuring authorities in Member States may not come to consistent disqualification decisions, leading to the discriminatory treatment of suppliers.

In Member States like the UK, the absence of clearly-defined, transparent procedures may be counter to the EU transparency principle[127] and the procurement directives,[128] but also to the express provisions of the disqualification rule requiring Member States to specify the conditions for disqualification.[129] As stated, the CJEU in *La Cascina* has demonstrated a requirement for transparent procedures in the disqualification context, and a Member State that has not included clearly defined and transparent procedures for disqualification in its implementing legislation may be regarded in future by the CJEU to be in breach of its transparency obligations.

Similar comments may be made about the South African system for the disqualifications under the PFMA regulations and the one-off disqualifications under the PPPFA regulations. Whilst the PAJA provides a framework within which administrative procedures should be established, the

[126] ibid.

[127] Case C-470/99 *Universale-Bau & Others v Entsorgungsbetriebe Simmering* [2002] ECR I-11617; A Tomkins, 'Transparency and the Emergence of a European Administrative Law' (2000) 19 *Yearbook of European Law* 217; S Peers, 'From Maastricht to Laeken: The Political Agenda of Openness and Transparency in the EU' in V Deckmyn (ed), *Increasing Transparency in the European Union* (Maastricht, EIPA, 2002); P Braun, 'A Matter of Principle(s) – the Treatment of Contracts falling outside the Scope of the Public Procurement Directives' (2000) 9 *Public Procurement Law Review* 39; A Brown, 'Seeing Through Transparency: the European Court's Case Law on the requirement to Advertise Public Contracts and Concessions under the EC Treaty' (2007) 16 *Public Procurement Law Review* 1.

[128] PSD, art 2.

[129] PSD, art 45.

omission in the legislation to establish clear and transparent conditions for disqualifications may mean that procuring authorities may not adopt transparent procedures for disqualification.[130] In South Africa, transparency in public procurement has been given constitutional status and procuring authorities are thus under a constitutional obligation to ensure transparency in disqualification procedures.[131]

In addition, in jurisdictions where procuring authorities use defined procedures for other aspects of the procurement process, it is possible that this may create a (procedural) legitimate expectation[132] on the part of suppliers that clear procedures for disqualification will be followed and there would be no arbitrary disqualification of suppliers.[133]

The US, the World Bank and South Africa under the PPPFA regulations are the only jurisdictions where the procedures for disqualification are fairly transparent, at least in relation to general disqualification measures. In relation to the World Bank one-off disqualifications, the procedures, being subsumed within the process for prior review of contracts, are not clearly defined and a supplier would be required to understand the procedure for prior review for it to understand the disqualification process.

It is suggested that the other jurisdictions may wish to adopt an approach where transparent disqualification procedures in the sense of the availability and publicity of the rules governing the disqualification process are provided to suppliers. However, as discussed in the context of fairness, whilst procedures for disqualification should always be available, the *extent*[134] and the detail of these requirements may vary[135] depending on the nature of the measure; the trigger for the measure (whether based on a conviction); the nature of the disqualifying entity (whether a procuring authority or otherwise); and the stage of the procurement process during which the measure is being considered.[136] Thus, the procedural rules for measures that are triggered by a conviction and are

[130] *Supersonic Tours*, above n 61.

[131] South African Constitution s 217(1); Bolton, *Law of Government Procurement*, ch 3.

[132] *Council of the Civil Service Unions*, above n 32, *per* Lord Fraser; C Knight, 'Expectations in Transition: Recent Developments in Legitimate Expectations' [2009] *Public Law* 15; P Sales and K Steyn, 'Legitimate Expectations in English Public Law: An Analysis' [2004] *Public Law* 564, 566; S Arrowsmith, 'Legitimate Expectations and Judicial Review in Contract Award Procedures: A Note on R v The Lord Chancellor ex p. Hibbit v Sanders' (1993) 4 *Public Procurement Law Review* CS104; T Allan, *Constitutional Justice: A Liberal Theory of the Rule of Law* (Oxford, Oxford University Press, 2001) 130; Bolton, *Law of Government Procurement*, chs 2 and 6.

[133] *Hutfield v Board of the Fort Saskatchewan General Hospital District No 98* (1986) ALR 256; D Jones, 'A Comment on Legitimate Expectations and the Duty to Give Reasons in Administrative Law' (1987) 25 *Alberta Law Review* 512.

[134] *Russell v Duke of Norfolk* [1949] 1 All ER 109 *per* Tucker LJ, 118; Arrowsmith, *Procurement and Judicial Review*, above n 23, ch 8.

[135] *R v National Lottery Commission ex parte Camelot* [2001] EMLR 3.

[136] S Shapiro and R Levy, 'Government Benefits and the Rule of Law: Towards a Standards Based Theory of Due Process' (2005) 57 *Administrative Law Review* 107, 110; Arrowsmith, *Procurement and Judicial Review*, above n 23, 166–7.

implemented by a procuring authority during the procurement process may not need to be as detailed as measures not triggered by a conviction and imposed outside the procurement process.

5.3 TIME LIMITS FOR DISQUALIFICATION

As stated in the introduction, this chapter will also consider the time limits for disqualification. Clear and appropriate time limits give credence to the rationale behind disqualification and ensure that the measure is reasonable and proportionate to the offence committed; as an excessively long disqualification may be regarded as disproportionate, especially where a supplier has already been convicted for a relevant offence. Excessive time limits may also call into question the reasonableness of the disqualification, which may be grounds for judicial review.

Time limits are relevant to disqualification decisions in two ways: first, time limits are relevant where the disqualification is based on a conviction or offence to determine when the conviction or offence ceases to be relevant for the purposes of disqualification. This issue is not addressed in most of the jurisdictions and is likely to be dealt with by rehabilitative statutes or other national provisions on the non-disclosure of convictions. Secondly, time limits are relevant to the length of disqualification where the measure is intended to operate for a specified period of time. In most jurisdictions, legislative standards prescribe what this period should be, whilst also giving the disqualifying entity a measure of flexibility. The two ways in which time limits are relevant to disqualification are interlinked, as the time limit for the relevance of a conviction may invariably spell the length of a disqualification.

5.3.1 Time Limits in the EU and the UK

In relation to the mandatory disqualifications in the EU, the directives do not indicate the length of the disqualification or when an offence ceases to be relevant for disqualification purposes, which is left to the discretion of Member States. However, as will be seen from the UK, not all Member States have provided time limits for disqualification and this approach has unfortunately led to differences in the time limits specified by Member States, which may lead to differences in the treatment of suppliers across the EU.[137] It will be seen that some of the other jurisdictions provide either

[137] T Medina, 'EU Directives as an Anti-Corruption Measure: Excluding Corruption-Convicted Tenderers from Public Procurement Contracts' in KV Thai (ed), *International Handbook of Public Procurement* (Boca Raton, CRC Press, 2009).

for maximum time limits for disqualification (US) or for both minimum and maximum time limits for disqualification (South Africa).

Although the EU directives do not mention when a relevant conviction would cease to be relevant for disqualification purposes, the initial proposals on the public sector directive provided that disqualification would apply to convictions obtained in the five-year period preceding contract award procedures.[138] However, this reference to time limits disappeared from the directives as adopted, as some Member States felt that a mandatory five-year disqualification period was too long.[139] The preparatory documents on the directives also required Member States to specify the 'maximum length of time prior to the start of the contract award procedure during which account must be taken of the conviction'.[140] This requirement was also deleted from the directives as adopted and substituted with the general provision in the present text which requires Member States to specify in accordance with national law, the implementing conditions for the disqualifications. The reasons behind this substitution are, however, not clear from the preparatory documents.[141]

Member States thus have the discretion to decide on the length of disqualification and/or when a conviction ceases to be relevant. Some Member States have adopted the five-year rule present in initial proposals and others have left the issue to be determined under national rules relating to the disclosure and relevance of convictions.[142] However, the absence of EU guidelines on this issue may mean that the same conviction might be treated differently in different Member States, where differences exist in national rules on the non-disclosure of convictions.[143] The absence of a time limit for disqualification in the EU may also call into question the proportionality[144] and the fairness of the disqualification measure in certain contexts. For instance, should a procuring authority disqualify a

138 Proposal for a Directive of the European Parliament and of the Council on the coordination of procedures for the award of public supply contracts, public service contracts and public works contracts [2001] OJ C29E/11, art 46(1).

139 Council of the EU, Brussels, 19/10/2000 (31.10) SN4075/00 Presidency Document. Proposal for a Directive of the European Parliament and of the Council on the co-ordination of procedures for the award of public supply contracts, public service contracts and public works contracts. Reproduced in JM Hebly, *European Public Procurement: Legislative History of the Classic Directive 2004/18/EC* (Alphen aan den Rijn, Kluwer Law International, 2007) 1109.

140 Proposal for a directive of the European parliament and of the council on the coordination of procedures for the award of public supply contracts, public service contracts and public works contracts, DG C II, SN 2325/1/01/Rev 1 (MAP) Working document, Brussels, 31 May 2001. The various Member States have different approaches to this issue. See Medina, 'EU Directives as an Anti-Corruption Measure', above n 137.

141 Outcome of Proceedings from Working Party on Public Procurement, 22/02/2002. Reproduced in Hebly, *European Public Procurement*, above n 139, 1139.

142 Medina, 'EU Directives as an Anti-Corruption Measure', above n 137.

143 Annex, White paper on exchanges of information on convictions and the effect of such convictions in the EU COM(2005)10 final.

144 In Case C-213/07 *Michaniki* [2008] ECR I-9999, AG Maduro stressed the requirement of proportionality in exclusion measures.

supplier for convictions obtained in the 5, 10 or 20 years prior to the contract award procedure? Disproportionate time limits may also go against the non-punitive rationale for the mandatory disqualifications in the EU.

Time limits are also relevant to the discretionary disqualifications, and the EU directives are similarly silent here. However, the CJEU has provided guidance as to the importance of time limits in relation to the discretionary disqualifications, which principles may also apply to the mandatory disqualifications. Thus, in *La Cascina*, it was held that one of the factors which need to be clearly defined was the time limits for when the supplier ought to be in compliance with his obligations.[145] In this case, suppliers were disqualified from the procurement procedure on the grounds that they were in breach of social security and tax obligations, and they challenged the disqualification on the basis that the breaches had subsequently been regularised. The questions put to the CJEU included whether persons who were not in compliance with the relevant obligations, but who could show that they would comply with those obligations before the contract was awarded could be permitted to participate in the procurement procedure. In other words, at which point in time did suppliers need to have complied with their obligations under the relevant legislation? The CJEU refused to be prescriptive about the time when the relevant obligations should have been met, preferring to leave this to national discretion, but stated that irrespective of the approach adopted by national legislation, the time limits for when the supplier ought to be in compliance with its obligations and other requirements for disqualification should be clearly defined and made public in the interests of transparency and equal treatment.[146] It is arguable by extension that the CJEU may also require Member States to set clear time limits for the mandatory disqualifications.

In implementing the EU directives, the UK did not go any further on this point than the detail in the directives and did not indicate time limits for both the mandatory and the discretionary disqualifications. As the issue was left to Member States discretion, it would have been preferable for the UK regulations to specify clear time limits. By not specifying limits, the UK may run counter to future CJEU interpretation of the mandatory disqualifications, as evidenced by the CJEU's approach to requiring clearly-defined time limits for discretionary disqualifications in *La Cascina*.

Although the UK regulations are silent as to the time limits for disqualification or when a conviction ceases to be relevant, the Rehabilitation of Offenders Act 1974 provides this information in relation to criminal offences. Under this Act, certain convictions become 'spent' and do not need to be admitted by the offender after a period of time known as the

[145] Case C-226/04 *La Cascina*, above n 26, paras 31–2.
[146] ibid.

'rehabilitation period'. The 'rehabilitation period' depends on the type of sentence given and not the offence committed, and custodial sentences of more than two and a half years can never become spent.[147] In the disqualification context, procuring authorities may feel bound to disqualify a supplier with a corruption conviction that can never be spent, meaning such a person may in reality be permanently denied access to public contracts.

The extreme consequences of this possibility were illustrated in *R (on the application of A) v B Council*,[148] where the applicant was an independent bus driver employed by a firm which provided school transport to a local authority. In response to Council requirements, all drivers were assessed to ensure that they did not have convictions precluding them from working with children. The applicant had been convicted of very serious violence offences 30 years previously, and the convictions could never become spent. As a result, the applicant was denied employment on the school transport subcontracts. In an application for judicial review, the court held that the Council had rightly exercised its discretion and dismissed the application. This case illustrates the difficulties that could be faced by a supplier convicted of an offence that could never become spent, even if the supplier had not committed any offence for an extended period as occurred in this case.

While it seems clear that a supplier will be disqualified for an unspent conviction, since such a conviction must be disclosed where information on convictions is requested, there is little clarity on the status of a spent conviction. It must be noted that information on convictions obtainable from the Criminal Records Bureau may include information on spent convictions and it is not clear whether a procuring authority in the UK will have to disqualify a supplier on the basis of a spent conviction under the mandatory provisions.

Apart from the adverse effects that an unspent conviction may have on a supplier, the absence of any time limits on disqualification may call into question the proportionality of a disqualification. However, if disqualification is challenged by a supplier before the CJEU, two outcomes are possible: first the CJEU may imply a certain minimum period for disqualification, or indicate when disqualification is regarded as too brief – in order to increase the effectiveness of the provisions. Secondly, specific direction from the CJEU on this issue may lead the EU to include a specific period for disqualification – either a uniform period or, at the very least, a minimum period – in future revisions of procurement legislation.[149]

[147] Rehabilitation of Offenders Act 1974, s 5(1). The penalty for corruption on indictment under the Bribery Act 2010, s 11 is imprisonment for a term not exceeding 10 years or a fine or both.

[148] *R (on the application of A) v B Council* [2007] EWHC 1529.

[149] Arrowsmith, *Public and Utilities Procurement*, above n 123, ch 19.84.

5.3.2 Time Limits in the US

The US FAR specifies the lengths for both the shorter and longer disqualifications. The shorter disqualifications are imposed to protect the government pending the completion of an investigation or legal proceedings against a supplier,[150] and cannot last longer than 12 months,[151] unless an extension is requested or legal proceedings against the supplier are underway, in which case, the shorter disqualification will last as long as the legal proceedings. The strict imposition of a time limit for the shorter disqualification where there are no legal proceedings reinforces its purpose as a non-punitive remedy that is directed at protecting the government. In relation to the longer disqualifications, a disqualifying official has a measure of flexibility in determining the length of the disqualification, which shall be commensurate with the seriousness of the offence but should generally not exceed three years.[152]

The absence of a mandatory minimum period for disqualification reflects the fact that disqualification is not intended to be punitive,[153] but should last for as long as is required to protect the government from the erring supplier. The US disqualifications also take into account the proportionality of the measure, and the disqualifying official is permitted to extend the disqualification where necessary to protect the government's interest,[154] but may also reduce the period of a disqualification at the supplier's request, where new material comes to light, or a conviction or civil judgment on which the disqualification is based is quashed, or there is a bona fide change in the ownership or management of the supplier, or the causes for disqualification have been eliminated or for any other reason that is appropriate.[155]

5.3.3 Time Limits in the World Bank

The World Bank adopts a similar approach to the US and disqualification by the Bank is imposed for a defined period of time.[156] The current approach in which the Bank disqualifies for a set period of time is a result of evolution within the Bank, but at the inception of the Bank's disqualification process, most disqualifications were issued for an indefinite period,[157] and between 1999, when the first disqualification was imposed

150 FAR 9.407-4(a).
151 FAR 9.407-4(b).
152 FAR 9.406-4(a).
153 Gordon, 'Suspension and Debarment', above n 52, 589.
154 FAR 9.406-4(b); *SAFE Export Corp*, 65 Comp Gen 530 (B-222308), 86-1 CPD ¶ 413.
155 FAR 9.406-4(c).
156 BPG, para 1.16(d); WBSP, art IX.
157 *Thornburgh Report*, 58.

and 2001, all the firms disqualified by the Bank were disqualified permanently.[158] However, the Bank subsequently relaxed the severity of these sanctions and since 2010, requires in most cases, a three-year disqualification as the base sanction for all misconduct.[159]

In determining the length of a disqualification, the World Bank adopts a similar approach to the US and the Sanctions Board may take various mitigating or aggravating factors into account, including the severity of the misconduct; the magnitude of the harm caused; interference in the investigation; past history of misconduct; cooperation in the investigation; and any other factor.[160]

Finally, it must be noted that the Bank imposes limits on the period within which an offence should have been committed and the Bank will not disqualify a supplier where an offence was committed within a contract that was executed more than 10 years previously.[161]

5.3.4 Time Limits in South Africa

In South Africa, the length of the disqualification is also specified in the legislation, and some of the South African provisions specify both minimum and maximum time limits. Requiring minimum time limits further reinforces the punitive rationale for disqualification in South Africa.

The Corruption Act provides that the length of disqualification should be between five and 10 years.[162] Under the Act, although it is the court that is empowered to disqualify, the power to determine the length of the disqualification is reserved to the National Treasury,[163] which also has the power to amend or vary the length of disqualification.[164] Unlike the US and World Bank provisions, the Corruption Act is silent on the factors to be taken into account in determining the length of disqualification or in deciding to amend the same.

The South African PPPFA regulations, like the US provisions, provide for a maximum but no minimum time limit for disqualification, which is not to exceed 10 years.[165] Similar to the Corruption Act, the regulations are also silent on the factors that need to be taken into account in determining the length of the disqualification and this has been left to the discretion of individual disqualifying entities. A consequence of the lack of a standardised approach to disqualification is that since the decision and the criteria

[158] List of Debarred Firms. Available at: www.worldbank.org .
[159] World Bank Sanctioning Guidelines (2010), art I.
[160] WBSP, art IX.
[161] WBSP, art IV.
[162] Corruption Act, 2004, s 28(3)(a)(ii).
[163] Corruption Act, 2004, s 28(3)(a)(ii).
[164] Corruption Act, 2004, s 28(4)(a).
[165] PPPFA reg 13(2)(d).

for disqualification are at the discretion of the procuring authority, this could lead to a situation where procuring authorities prescribe different time limits in similar cases. Such inconsistencies in application are not desirable and may open a procuring authority to a legal challenge to justify why suppliers have been subject to different time limits in similar circumstances. In addition, the potential discrimination that suppliers may be subject to may be unconstitutional.[166]

5.3.5 Time Limits, Proportionality, Reasonableness, Fairness and Transparency

As can be seen, the jurisdictions adopt differing approaches to the issue of time limits – with some jurisdictions specifying clear minimum or maximum time limits and others being silent on the issue. Time limits may affect the perception of a disqualification system as proportionate, reasonable, fair and transparent. To be regarded as proportionate, a disqualification system should not seek to penalise a supplier (unless the purpose of disqualification in the jurisdiction is punitive).[167] The length of disqualification should also not be longer than necessary to achieve the purpose of disqualification in the jurisdiction. Proportionality is thus tied to the circumstances requiring disqualification, whether the supplier has been previously sanctioned for the same offence, and the rationale for the disqualification. To ensure proportionality, disqualification for criminal infringements must take into account previous penalties as well as the express or implied purpose of the disqualification system. A lack of proportionality in a disqualification decision may call into question the reasonableness of the decision and may be a ground for judicial review.

In the EU and the UK where the legislation does not provide time limits for disqualification, this may lead to disproportionate disqualifications and disqualification decisions that go too far in achieving the policy rationale behind EU disqualifications. This was seen in the UK case of *R (on the application of A) v B Council*,[168] discussed above, where the applicant was disqualified from working as a subcontractor for offences committed 30 years prior to the contract award procedure.

In South Africa, the issue of proportionality arises in relation to the excessive time limits for disqualification in some of the legislation. The PPPFA regulations and the Corruption Act both specify 10 years as the maximum length for disqualification, with the Corruption Act further imposing a minimum time limit of five years. This is arguably an

[166] Constitution of the Republic of South Africa (Act 108 of 1996) s 217(1).

[167] E Tomko and K Weinberg, 'After the Fall: Conviction, Debarment and Double Jeopardy' (1992) 21 *Public Contract Law Journal* 355.

[168] *R (on the application of A) v B Council* [2007] EWHC 1529.

unduly long period of time, if one considers the approach in other jurisdictions – the EU procurement directives dropped the five-year time limit because Member States felt it was too long and the general maximum limit in the US is three years. The emerging jurisprudence on disqualification in South Africa shows that some procuring authorities impose the maximum disqualification period on suppliers[169] and do not use their discretion to impose shorter time limits. Although the South African disqualification system is punitive, these time limits may still be regarded as excessive and disproportionate.

Time limits may also affect the fairness and transparency of disqualification. Where there are no clear time limits for disqualification, this may lead to decisions that may not be justified by reference to the offence or may lead to the different treatment of suppliers in similar cases. Transparency in public procurement requires publicity of the rules governing the procurement process. An aspect of transparency in the disqualification process is the presence of rules which specify the time limits for disqualification or expressly link time limits to domestic rules on non-disclosure of convictions. Although domestic rehabilitative statutes may provide information on when convictions become spent or expunged from the record, it is suggested that this information ought to be included in legislative provisions on disqualification. This will increase transparency by ensuring that suppliers are aware of the requirements of the disqualification process, will ensure that there is uniformity in relation to time limits, reduce the scope for discriminatory decisions and ensure that the disqualification is relevant to the supplier's present status, especially when disqualification has a non-punitive rationale.

5.4 SUMMARY AND ANALYSIS OF MAIN ISSUES

This chapter has examined the very complex procedural issues arising from disqualification. As can be seen from the forgoing discussion, legislative provisions on procedural issues in the disqualification context are lacking in some jurisdictions and this may affect the quality of disqualification decision-making and create problems in practice for entities implementing disqualification provisions.

5.4.1 The Existence of a Clear Procedure for Disqualification

It was seen that apart from the US, the World Bank, and the South African PPPFA regulations, the jurisdictions do not generally specify a procedure

[169] *Chairman, State Tender Board v Supersonic Tours (Pty) Ltd*, above n 61.

for disqualifying suppliers. In the context of the EU, it is important for clarity in the sense of minimum procedural requirements to ensure that the disqualification procedure in Member States meets EU requirements for transparency and fairness. As was seen from the jurisprudence, although domestic administrative law in Member States such as the UK requires procedures for administrative decision-making, disqualifying entities have not always conducted the disqualification process in accordance with these requirements by providing notice of a proposed disqualification and the factors on which disqualification is based, an opportunity to make representations and adequate reasons for the decision. Similarly, in South Africa, the available jurisprudence suggests that in some cases, despite the existence of the procedural requirements of the PAJA in relation to administrative decisions, disqualifying entities do not always meet these standards.

The absence of clear rules for decision-making in the disqualification context may affect the transparency of the measure and the ability of the disqualified supplier to challenge its disqualification. Clear rules are of grave importance in jurisdictions where disqualifications may be imposed in the absence of a conviction. It is thus suggested that at the very minimum, states should include in their legislation rules on the giving of notice and an opportunity to make representations depending on the nature and context of the disqualification measure.

5.4.2 Time Limits

As has been discussed, clear time limits for disqualification are absent in the jurisdictions excepting the US and World Bank. Although South Africa provides maximum time limits for disqualification under the PPPFA regulations, the lack of a standardised approach may lead to a situation where procuring entities prescribe different limits in similar cases. Similar criticisms may be made about the EU/UK mandatory disqualification provisions, in which there is a lack of clarity on the issue of time limits, both in the sense of when convictions cease to be relevant and the length of disqualification. Whilst the EU directives appear to have left the issue of time limits to the discretion of Member States, this approach will lead to differences in the treatment of suppliers in the different Member States and possibly also differences in the treatment of suppliers within the same state. Also, should Member States specify excessive time limits for disqualification this might go beyond the protective and policy rationales for the mandatory disqualifications in the EU. Whilst domestic statutes on the non-disclosure of offences may provide an indication of when convictions cease to be relevant, procuring authorities may not be aware of the details of such statutes, especially where they are faced with suppliers from other Member States. To prevent the potential discrimination which EU suppliers may face in this regard, it is suggested that the EU adopts a coherent approach to the issue of time limits. It is suggested that the US approach which provides maximum but not minimum time limits (to give procuring entities some flexibility) and the World Bank approach that specifies a limitation period for offences that may lead to disqualification provide the necessary clarity and proportionality in this difficult aspect of the disqualification decision.

6

Disqualifying Entities and the Scope of Disqualification

6.1 INTRODUCTION

THIS CHAPTER CONSIDERS the types of entities involved in the disqualification process and the scope of disqualification once imposed, ie whether disqualification will apply to procuring authorities beyond the entity that disqualifies the supplier. A disqualifying entity may be a procuring authority, an external administrative body, a court or the legislature, to a limited extent. The type of disqualifying entity affects the nature of the decisions that the entity can take, the discretion available to the disqualifying entity and the limits of the disqualifying entity's powers to bind other entities with a disqualification decision.

The decision to disqualify involves many different elements and in some cases, elements of the decision may be split between different disqualifying entities. The kinds of decisions that an entity may take may be understood as different points on the continuum of disqualification. For instance, where legislation imposes a mandatory disqualification on corrupt suppliers, the procuring authority may simply be required to decide if there is a relevant conviction or offence, and disqualify a supplier once this is established. At the other end of the continuum, a procuring authority may have to make more involved decisions. For instance, in cases where the procuring authority has a discretion in deciding whether to disqualify, the authority may be required to decide if the offence was committed and a case for disqualification exists, or if there are mitigating circumstances making disqualification inappropriate in the particular instance. In between these two extremes, the legislation may also grant procuring authorities the discretion to derogate from or waive a mandatory requirement to disqualify.

In most jurisdictions, the different elements of a disqualification decision are split between different disqualifying entities. The stages of the disqualification process analysed in chapter five revealed the four substantive elements of a disqualification decision that need to be addressed by a disqualifying entity. The first is whether a supplier is guilty of having committed a relevant offence. The supplier's guilt may be determined by judicial process or a professional organisation exercising a judicial function, whilst a procuring authority considering disqualification will require proof of a conviction/offence. The second element of a disqualification decision is whether disqualification is justifiable on the basis of the supplier's guilt, or whether there are public interest factors or the supplier's rehabilitation, which make disqualification inappropriate in a particular circumstance. This may be determined by a court imposing disqualification as part of a sentence for corruption, by an administrative body or procuring authority. The legislature may also have specified in the law what public interest factors ought to be considered by the disqualifying entity. The third element of a disqualification decision is the length of the disqualification. This may also be determined by a court, an administrative body, a procuring authority or the legislature, where the law specifies the time limits for disqualification. The fourth element is the applicability of the disqualification to related persons. This may be decided by the entity that imposes the disqualification or the lawmaker, where there is a legal or policy requirement to disqualify named related persons.

It is also possible for all the elements of the decision to be determined by one entity such as a court or an administrative body and for individual procuring authorities to merely be required to give practical effect to the decision of this entity. In other cases, especially in relation to the decisions which involve policy considerations such as public interest waivers or the disqualification of related persons, it is also possible for the lawmaker to have enumerated the instances in which such waivers or disqualifications may be appropriate and for a disqualifying entity such as a procuring authority or administrative body to apply this policy to individual cases, giving different entities jurisdiction over one aspect of the decision.

The issue of the scope of disqualification deals with whether once an entity has disqualified a supplier, other entities or procuring authorities may or must also apply the disqualification decision.

6.2 DISQUALIFYING ENTITIES

6.2.1 Courts

The role of the courts in the disqualification process is often limited to determining the guilt of a supplier for relevant offences. Where disqualification relates to an offence of professional misconduct, a professional organisation may perform a judicial function in determining the supplier's guilt. As an impartial institution, a court is the best forum for deciding whether a supplier is guilty of an offence, since it has the power to obtain evidence and summon witnesses.

Apart from deciding whether an offence was committed, a court may also be charged with determining other elements in a disqualification decision. Thus, legislation may give a court power to disqualify a supplier as part of the sentence for the offence committed. Whilst a court may be competent to decide if disqualification is an appropriate sanction on a supplier, especially where disqualification is intended to be punitive, it is less clear if a court will be able to come to a satisfactory decision on the second element of the disqualification decision, which is deciding whether there are public interest or other factors making disqualification inappropriate. This is because a court may be unable to foretell the circumstances that will face procuring authorities that are required to apply the disqualification decision of the court. This element of the disqualification decision is best left to procuring authorities, who are best able to determine their requirements in relation to a disqualified supplier.

The third element of a disqualification decision is the duration of the disqualification. This decision may be reserved to the courts where the court is given the power to disqualify corrupt suppliers. In such cases, a court may rely on the legislation on disqualification or general sentencing guidelines to determine an appropriate length of disqualification.

The fourth element of a disqualification decision is determining the position of persons/firms related to the corrupt supplier. It is suggested that the courts may not be the appropriate forum for this decision unless the courts are willing to examine the networks of company ownership to ensure that that a related firm is not unduly prejudiced.

Using the courts as the forum for disqualification has certain advantages: the disqualification process will benefit from the procedural safeguards that accompany criminal trials, and investigations into the commission of the offence will be conducted by the prosecution, who may be more thorough than a procuring authority as they possess better investigatory tools and expertise. Also, domestic prosecutorial authorities may provide a central source of information on completed investigations, making the dissemination of this information much easier. Although the courts are not generally used as a disqualifying entity, the courts have the power to review the different aspects of a disqualification decision under their power of judicial review of administrative decisions.

Where disqualification is triggered by a conviction or civil judgment, the courts or similar adjudicatory bodies will be used to determine if the supplier is guilty of the relevant offence. Thus in the EU a supplier will be disqualified under the mandatory disqualifications where he has been convicted 'by final judgment' and under the discretionary disqualifications where he has been convicted 'by a judgment which has the force of res judicata'.[1] A similar approach applies in the UK, the US and in South

[1] PSD, art 45(1) and (2).

Africa under the Corruption Act, and in these jurisdictions a supplier also needs to have been convicted (or incurred a civil judgment) for disqualification to be considered against the supplier.

In relation to determining the other elements of a disqualification, such as whether disqualification is appropriate in a given case, the length of disqualification and the position of related persons, none of the jurisdictions, except South Africa give the courts this power. In South Africa, the Corruption Act gives the courts the discretion to disqualify a supplier as part of the sanctions for procurement-related corruption offences,[2] and the courts also decide whether the disqualification will apply to persons and firms related to the corrupt supplier.[3] However, under the Corruption Act, the third element of a disqualification, determining the length of the disqualification, is reserved to an administrative entity – the National Treasury.[4]

As discussed above, it is not clear whether the courts are the appropriate forum for determining most elements of the disqualification decision. In South Africa, the courts have exhibited an unwillingness to exercise their discretion to disqualify corrupt firms, and between 2004 and October 2011 only two persons were disqualified under the Corruption Act. This is in contrast to the scores of suppliers who have been disqualified by procuring authorities under the PPPFA and PFMA regulations.

6.2.2 Procuring Authorities

Procuring authorities are the most common forum for disqualification determinations and are the disqualifying entity in the EU, UK, US and under the South African PPPFA and PFMA regulations. In most jurisdictions, procuring authorities are given the power to decide on all the substantive elements of the disqualification decision, except determining if the supplier is guilty of a criminal offence where disqualification is based on a conviction.

Where disqualification is triggered by evidence short of a conviction, a procuring authority may be required to either decide or obtain sufficient proof that the supplier committed the offence. The ease by which a procuring authority will achieve this may depend on what is regarded as sufficient proof and how much time and resources a procuring authority devotes to obtaining this proof and the extent of the procuring authority's investigative powers.

In relation to the first element of a disqualification decision – determining that an offence was committed; procuring authorities may not be the

[2] Corruption Act, 2004, s 28(1).
[3] Corruption Act, 2004, s 28(1).
[4] Corruption Act, 2004, s 28(3).

most appropriate forum for this, as such decisions will normally involve a level of investigation for which the procuring authority may not have the expertise, time or resources to carry out efficiently. As is discussed in chapter seven, most procuring authorities have not been given express powers of investigation and are limited to considering disclosures by a supplier as proof that an offence was not committed. Also, where a procuring authority has to determine whether the supplier has committed a relevant offence, where the offence was committed against the procuring authority, such as where corruption occurs in an on-going procurement procedure, this puts the procuring authority in a position where it may be contravening the rule against bias,[5] since the procuring authority will be a person with an interest in the proceedings.[6]

In relation to the second element of a disqualification decision – deciding if disqualification is appropriate in a particular case – a procuring authority may be the most appropriate forum for this, as a procuring authority will be able to determine whether disqualification is in its best interest. However, this is not true in all cases and where a supplier argues that disqualification is not warranted because it has eliminated the cause for disqualification, a procuring authority may not be able to satisfactorily decide if the supplier's rehabilitation is sufficient to avoid disqualification as it may not fully appreciate the nuances of company law and ownership that may be presented by a supplier's rehabilitation. Thus, the procuring authority may find that its decision is challenged on the basis that its discretion has not been properly exercised because it is unable to sufficiently address the issues raised.[7]

The third element of a disqualification decision – determining the length of the disqualification – is reserved by most jurisdictions to procuring authorities. Arguably a procuring authority is the most appropriate entity to make this decision, as the procuring authority will be able to decide how long the disqualification is required to protect itself from the corrupt supplier, especially where disqualification has a protective rationale.

The fourth element of the disqualification decision – determining the 'fate' of related persons – is also often left to the discretion of procuring authorities. The appropriateness of a procuring authority for taking this decision may depend on whether the supplier is well known to the procuring authority and/or whether the procuring authority is able to sufficiently devote resources to examining the relationships between the

[5] However, the US Supreme Court has held that combining investigative and adjudicative functions does not necessarily constitute a due process violation: *Withrow v Larkin* 412 US 35, 58 (1975).

[6] Arrowsmith, *Procurement and Judicial Review*, 173, argues that the rule against bias may not apply with the same force to administrative proceedings.

[7] *Padfield v Ministry of Agriculture, Fisheries & Food* [1968] AC 997 *per* Lord Upjohn; R Pierce, 'Judicial Review of Agency Actions in a Period of Diminishing Agency Resources' (1997) 49 *Administrative Law Review* 61.

disqualified supplier and related persons. As has been detailed by Anechiarico and Jacobs, the expense of doing this may mean that it may not always be appropriate for a procuring authority to be involved in making this decision.[8]

The jurisdictions adopt different approaches to the taking of disqualification decisions by procuring authorities. In relation to the first element of disqualification, deciding if an offence has been committed, all the jurisdictions leave it to a procuring authority to decide if an offence was committed where a conviction is not required for disqualification. In the EU, a procuring authority is required under the discretionary disqualification provisions to disqualify a supplier who is 'guilty . . . by any means which the procuring authority can demonstrate'.[9] Similarly, in the UK, a procuring authority may disqualify a supplier who has 'committed an act of grave misconduct'.[10] In the US, a procuring authority may temporarily disqualify a supplier 'upon adequate evidence'[11] and an indictment for a relevant offence constitutes 'adequate evidence'.[12] Under the South African PPPFA and PFMA regulations, a procuring authority may disqualify a supplier who has committed a relevant offence.[13] As is discussed further in chapter seven, all the jurisdictions apart from South Africa give an indication into the kind of evidence or proof that a procuring authority may rely on in deciding that an offence was committed.

In relation to the second element of a disqualification decision, determining if disqualification is appropriate or if there are factors precluding disqualification in a particular case, this decision is also reserved to procuring authorities in the jurisdictions. Thus, the EU and UK reserve the power to decide if disqualification is appropriate to the procuring authority, which also determines if there are public interest considerations which mean the supplier should not be disqualified. Both the EU and the UK give a large measure of discretion to procuring authorities in relation to this decision as the law defines public interest in very broad terms. A similar approach is adopted by the US where a procuring authority may derogate from disqualifications imposed by other entities where there are compelling reasons for doing so. In South Africa, there is no possibility for procuring entities to derogate from a general disqualification that is imposed by the courts or another procuring authority and a procuring entity may only amend a disqualification order imposed by it.[14]

[8] F Anechiarico and J Jacobs, 'Purging Corruption from Public Contracting: The Solutions are now Part of the Problem' (1995) *New York Law School Law Review* 162–72.

[9] PSD, art 45(2)(d).

[10] Public Contracts Regulations 2006 reg 23(4)(e).

[11] FAR 9.407-2(a).

[12] FAR 9.407-2(b).

[13] PPPFA reg 13 and PFMA reg 16.A9.1.

[14] National Treasury Supply Chain Management Office Practice Note Number SCM 5 of 2006, Restriction of Suppliers, 9 October 2006, para 2.4.

In jurisdictions where the disqualification is imposed by a central authority, the decisions of a procuring authority may be limited to determining, where discretion exists, whether the authority should apply the disqualification decision. Where there is no discretion, a procuring authority will merely be required to give practical effect to the disqualification decision. This is the case in relation to disqualifications under the South African Corruption Act (imposed by the courts) and disqualifications in the World Bank (imposed by the EO/Sanctions Board).

In relation to the third element of a disqualification decision, the length of the disqualification, there are differing approaches to this issue. In the EU, the UK, the US, and the South African PPPFA regulations, this issue has been left to the discretion of procuring authorities, who determine the time limits for disqualification within the limits set by law, where applicable.

The fourth element of disqualification – the position of related persons – is also usually reserved to procuring authorities, after the legislation may have determined what categories of related persons ought to be disqualified. In the EU, a procuring authority is required to disqualify 'any candidate or tenderer' from public contracts, whilst the UK regulations provide that the procuring authority must disqualify 'the economic operator or its directors or any other person who has powers of representation, decision or control of the economic operator'. Similarly, the US and the South African provisions provide that the procuring authority may also disqualify various persons and firms related to the disqualified supplier.[15] The position of related persons is discussed in chapter eight.

6.2.3 Administrative Bodies

Where administrative bodies are used to disqualify suppliers, the body may issue a general disqualification against a supplier, which individual procuring authorities may give effect to. As a forum for taking disqualification decisions, administrative bodies possess a number of advantages over the courts and procuring authorities. First, an administrative body may eliminate the delays to the procurement process that disqualification may cause where a procuring authority conducts the disqualification procedure within the procurement process. Secondly, an administrative body may lead to the centralisation of expertise, which may eventually lead to quicker, fairer and more transparent decisions as the body learns from past mistakes and challenges to its decisions. Thirdly, an administrative body may serve as a central source of statistical information on disqualification, which may be used to analyse the efficacy of the disqualification regime. Fourthly, an administrative body will save the time and resources

[15] FAR 9.406-5; PPPFA, reg 13; PFMA reg 16.A9.

procuring authorities would have used in making multiple disqualification decisions over the same supplier in jurisdictions which do not maintain central databases of disqualified firms.

In spite of the advantages of an administrative body over the courts and procuring authorities, few jurisdictions utilise such bodies for disqualification and they are only used in limited contexts for some elements of the disqualification decision

In relation to the first element of a disqualification decision – determining the guilt of a supplier, an administrative body involved in disqualification may be required to conduct a judicial function and decide if an offence was committed or obtain information on the guilt of a supplier that has been established by a court or other entity. Where an administrative body performs a judicial function by establishing the guilt of a supplier, it may be necessary for the body to possess a certain level of investigative power. Such a body may also need to establish procedures to ensure fairness in its determination of the supplier's guilt.

In relation to the second element of a disqualification decision – determining if disqualification is appropriate – similar arguments made in relation to the courts may be advanced and it is not clear whether an administrative body is the best forum for determining whether public interest concerns make disqualification inappropriate. As discussed in the context of courts, entities external to a procuring authority may be unable to foretell if derogating from a disqualification is in the best interests of a procuring authority in a particular case and the administrative body may not always be aware of the reasons why a procuring authority may need to contract with a supplier even though a cause for disqualification might exist.

In relation to the third element of the disqualification decision – the length of the disqualification – an administrative body may be able to decide an appropriate length for disqualification in order to protect the government from the corrupt supplier, or fulfil the government's policy in relation to disqualification. This is because an administrative body may possess a macro-understanding of the procurement system and can thus take appropriate decisions for the benefit of the system as a whole.

Determining the fourth element in a disqualification decision – the position of related persons – may be easier for an administrative entity than a procuring authority, especially where an administrative entity has disqualification as one of its main functions, as it may be able to devote parts of its budget to investigating the networks of company ownership relevant to the disqualification of related persons.

As mentioned above, most of the jurisdictions do not rely on administrative bodies for disqualification. In relation to the first element of a disqualification decision – determining if an offence was committed – the only jurisdiction that uses an administrative entity to make this decision is the World Bank. The Bank's INT determines whether an offence was committed. Although the Bank does not possess the same kind of investigative powers as national authorities, the Bank is able to rely on contractual provisions, which give the Bank access to the relevant documentation of suppliers.[16]

In respect of the second element of disqualification – determining if disqualification is appropriate – again, the World Bank relies on its Evaluations Officer to decide whether there are factors which mean the supplier should not be disqualified. Although the Bank does not take public interest considerations into account, the Bank may take mitigating factors into account and impose a lesser sanction on the supplier.[17]

Thirdly, in relation to the length of the disqualification, this power is again within the remit of the Evaluations Officer, within the limits provided by the Bank's sanctioning guidelines. The use of an administrative entity external to the procurement process for disqualification is due to the nature of Bank procurement, in that since the Bank does not conduct the procurement process for funded projects, it is unable to utilise procuring authorities to disqualify suppliers. South Africa also adopts an approach whereby in relation to disqualifications under the Corruption Act, it is an administrative entity, the National Treasury, that determines the length of a disqualification.[18]

The fourth element in a disqualification decision – determining the position of related persons – is again left to the Evaluations Officer in the World Bank context, whilst as discussed above; the other jurisdictions leave this to procuring authorities or the court under the South Africa Corruption Act.

6.2.4 The Legislature

As a disqualifying entity, the legislature's role is limited to passing statutes that prescribe the framework for the disqualification process. These laws will in turn be interpreted and applied by other entities such as the courts, procuring authorities and administrative bodies. In the jurisdictions, the disqualification regime is governed to various extents by binding laws and regulations, which give different entities various measures of discretion over specific aspects of the disqualification process.

Where parliament has issued legislation on disqualification, disqualifying entities are required to give practical effect to the law by disqualifying the suppliers identified as liable to disqualification by the law. The exist-

[16] BPG, para 1.16(e).

[17] WBSP, art IX; S Williams, 'The Debarment of Corrupt Contractors from World Bank-Financed Contracts' (2007) *Public Contract Law Journal* 277, 299.

[18] Corruption Act 2004, s 28(3).

ence of clear laws governing the disqualification process promotes transparency, certainty and clarity in the disqualification system.

In relation to the first element of a disqualification decision – determining the guilt of a supplier, the legislature's role is to enumerate the offences, which may lead to disqualification and possibly the standard of proof required for such offences, either a conviction or a determination of guilt by another entity. This is the case in all the jurisdictions and the offences that may lead to disqualification are enumerated in the legislation.

In relation to the second element of a disqualification decision – determining if disqualification is appropriate, again, the legislature's role is limited to specifying the public interest concerns or the factual situations such as the suppliers rehabilitation that make disqualification inappropriate in a particular case. In such situations, clarity in the law is of the utmost importance to prevent such waivers from being abused. In the jurisdictions, however, this issue is one in which the most amount of discretion has been left to the other entities in the disqualification process. Thus, the US and the EU/UK all in broad terms state that a disqualifying entity may waive a requirement to disqualify where it is in the general interest or there are compelling reasons for doing so without going into further detail. Disqualifying entities thus have to determine and interpret the meaning of public interest within what they consider to be the limits of the law.

In relation to the third element of the disqualification decision – the length of the disqualification – again, the law-makers may prescribe either specific time limits for various offences, or give other disqualifying entities discretion to set limits within a prescribed minimum or maximum time limit as is the case for the US, the World Bank and South Africa.

The fourth element in a disqualification decision – the position of related persons – may also be determined by the legislature, where it requires the disqualification of certain categories of related persons. As will be seen in chapter 8 the law on disqualification in all the jurisdictions specifies to differing extents, the related persons that are liable to be disqualified.

6.3 THE SCOPE OF DISQUALIFICATION

The issue here is whether a disqualification is applicable beyond the entity that imposed the measure. A disqualification may affect other entities, or it may not have any effect beyond the entity that imposed the disqualification. Where an administrative entity or a court imposes disqualification, the disqualification may be applied by procuring authorities required to give practical effect to the decision of this entity. Where a procuring authority imposes disqualification it is not in every case that other procuring authorities will be required to apply the disqualification decision. It will be seen that not all the jurisdictions are clear as to whether a disqualification decision should be implemented by other entities. Thus, as will be seen, whilst the US, the World Bank and South Africa are clear that disqualification imposed by a relevant entity should be applied by other procuring entities, the EU and the UK provisions are silent on this issue.

There are advantages and disadvantages to having a relatively wide scope of disqualification. First, extending disqualification to other entities beyond the disqualifying entity may be necessary in certain contexts to secure the effectiveness of the disqualification measure and also because the increased opening of procurement markets due to the EU directives, the GPA and other trade agreements[19] means that disqualification measures limited to one procuring authority or even one jurisdiction may have a limited impact. Secondly, extending disqualification may also be efficient in that resources are not wasted by other entities taking similar decisions over the same supplier. However, extending disqualification to a wide range of procuring authorities may be disproportionate to the aims sought to be achieved by a disqualification system, may be potentially devastating to suppliers and may turn a non-punitive disqualification into a punitive measure. This reinforces the need for adequate procedural safeguards.

Where disqualification is designed to affect other entities, two issues are raised: first, how do other entities discover that the supplier has been previously disqualified, and secondly, what elements of the disqualification decision are left to the discretion of the non-disqualifying entity applying the disqualification?

6.3.1 A Requirement that Disqualification be Extended and Discovering Previous Disqualifications

The US, South Africa and the World Bank are clear on the fact that disqualification should be applied by entities beyond the disqualifying entity and they also provide for how such procuring authorities discover the existence of previous disqualifications.

The most common method of enabling entities to discover previous disqualifications is for a jurisdiction to create a database of disqualified firms, which will be examined by procuring authorities during the procurement process. Such a database may be open to the public at large, or may be restricted to procuring authorities. For instance, South Africa and the World Bank maintain internet-based databases that are open to the public.

[19] A Davies, 'Government Procurement' in S Lester and B Mercurio (eds), *Bilateral and Regional Trade Agreements: Commentary and Analysis* (Cambridge, Cambridge University Press, 2009).

The US maintains a similar database that is also open to the public, with sensitive information being restricted to procuring authorities. A jurisdiction will also have to provide for the management of the database, which includes recording the information on disqualifications and removing this information once the disqualification expires.

In the US, the FAR provides that a disqualification shall be 'effective throughout the executive branch of the government' unless the disqualification is waived by the head of an agency.[20] Thus, once a supplier is disqualified, all federal procuring authorities are obliged to abide by this decision. For other procuring authorities to discover the previous disqualification, the General Services Administration maintains an internet-based register of disqualified firms called the Excluded Parties List System (EPLS), which is publicly available.[21]

South Africa adopts a similar approach to disqualification under the Corruption Act. Both the Corruption Act[22] and the PFMA regulations[23] provide that all procuring authorities and government departments must either ignore any tender made by a disqualified supplier or otherwise disqualify the supplier from accessing contracts in that procuring authority. This approach is made possible by the inclusion of the supplier's details in either the Database of Restricted Suppliers (for disqualifications under the PPPFA and PFMA regulations) or the Register for Tender Defaulters (for disqualifications under the Corruption Act), both internet-based databases of disqualified suppliers are maintained by the National Treasury. The PFMA regulations, which apply to all national and provincial authorities, oblige public bodies to consult the Register before awarding a contract to ensure that a bidder for a public contract has not been disqualified.[24]

The South African PPPFA regulations also require disqualifications to be implemented by a wide range of procuring authorities by providing that a procuring authority may disqualify a supplier from obtaining business from any 'organ of state' for the duration of the disqualification.[25] 'Organ of state' means a national or provincial department; a municipality; a constitutional institution; Parliament; a provincial legislature; and *any* other institution or category of institution included in the definition of 'organ of state' in section 239 of the Constitution.[26] Thus, disqualifications under the PPPFA are required to be implemented by local, provincial and national authorities, constitutional institutions and perhaps, government parastatals.[27]

[20] FAR 9.407-1(d); FAR 9.406-1(c).
[21] FAR 9.404; 9.405(a).
[22] Corruption Act 2004, s 28(3)(a)(iii).
[23] PFMA reg 16A9.1(c).
[24] PFMA reg 16A9.1(c).
[25] PPPFA reg 13.
[26] PPPFA s 1.
[27] *Fidelity Springbok Security Services (Pty) Ltd v South Africa Post Office Ltd* [2004] JOL 13215 (T); Bolton, *Law of Government Contract*, 268.

The World Bank has adopted an approach similar to that of the US and South Africa. The diversity of the Bank's operations means that the procuring authorities that are required to abide by the Bank's disqualification measures are located worldwide in Borrower countries. Once the Bank disqualifies a supplier, the fact and duration of the disqualification is listed on the Bank's 'List of Debarred Firms', a publicly available database of disqualified firms, and any agency conducting procurement using Bank funds must examine this database to ensure that persons bidding for the contract have not been previously disqualified.[28] Where a previously disqualified firm tenders for a Bank contract, the Borrower or its agencies must inform the supplier that it is not eligible to tender for the contract.[29]

6.3.2 No Clear Requirement that Disqualification be Extended

As mentioned above, the EU and UK provisions are both silent as to whether a disqualification imposed by one procuring authority will affect other procuring authorities. This issue is particularly important in the context of the EU where one of the purposes of disqualification is to prevent the cross-border effects of corruption. Although the directives do not address this issue, it has been recognised that the increasing free movement within the EU requires greater exchange of disqualification information in the EU,[30] and there have been several attempts made towards measures that would eventually lead to coordination in disqualification matters.[31]

There are two issues that arise in the context of the EU: first is whether a *conviction* obtained in one Member State will lead to disqualification in another Member State and the second is whether a *disqualification* decision in one Member State will be applied by procuring authorities in other Member States. As discussed earlier, based on the definition of corruption imported into the mandatory disqualification provisions, it appears that a procuring authority may disqualify for a *conviction* obtained in another Member State, if the procuring authority is able to obtain information on

[28] BPG, appendix 1, para 8.

[29] BPG, para 1.8. See generally, T Canni, 'Debarment is No Longer Private World Bank Business: An Examination of the Bank's Distinct Debarment Procedures used for Corporate Procurements and Financed Projects' (2010) 40 *Public Contract Law Journal* 147.

[30] Communication from the Commission to the Council and the European Parliament: Disqualifications arising from criminal convictions in the EU, COM(2006) 73 final; Initiative of the Kingdom of Denmark with a view to adopting a Council Decision on increasing cooperation between European Union Member States with regard to disqualifications [2002] OJ C223/17.

[31] Initiative of the Kingdom of Denmark, ibid; White Paper on exchanges of information on convictions and the effect of such convictions in the EU, COM (2005) 10 final; Council Decision 2005/876/JHA on the exchange of information extracted from the criminal record.

the conviction.[32] It is of course difficult for a procuring authority to determine whether a supplier has been convicted in another Member State,[33] although there are various initiatives underway to improve the dissemination of criminal information in the EU, as discussed in chapter seven. The European Commission has also provided assistance in the form of a list of the kind of documents relating to convictions that are issued by Member States and the names of the institutions that issue these documents,[34] and Member States are required to assist by designating the authorities competent to issue information on convictions.[35]

Although there is no information on whether a disqualification by one procuring authority in the EU should be applied by other procuring authorities (eliminating the necessity for the other procuring authority to come to a separate decision to disqualify the same supplier), it is suggested that once a procuring authority in one Member State has disqualified a supplier, procuring authorities in other Member States are not bound by the disqualification decision. Thus, each EU procuring authority has a separate obligation to disqualify and this obligation is not diminished by the fact that the supplier may previously have been disqualified elsewhere. This is because the text of the mandatory provisions in the directives makes disqualification mandatory upon a relevant *conviction*, not a relevant *disqualification*.

In implementing the EU directives, the UK procurement regulations did not go much further than the text in the directives and whilst there is information on relying on convictions from other Member States, there is no information on the position of a disqualification from another Member State, in terms of being applied by procuring authorities in the UK. Further, there is also no information on whether a disqualification by one UK procuring authority can be relied on by other UK procuring authorities.

In relation to convictions, the UK regulations and the OGC Guidance suggest that a UK procuring authority may disqualify a supplier for a conviction obtained in another EU Member State or third country.[36] The regulations state that where a supplier is based in another Member State, procuring authorities may apply to the competent authorities of that State for the relevant information.[37] However, it may be difficult, without access to national databases of convicted firms or a central EU register of convicted firms, for a procuring authority in the UK to access information on convictions obtained outside the UK, in the absence of cooperation from

[32] PSD art 45(1).

[33] White Paper on exchanges of information on convictions and the effect of such convictions in the EU, COM (2005) 10 final.

[34] See: ec.europa.eu/internal_market/publicprocurement/2004_18/index_en.htm .

[35] PSD, art 45(4).

[36] PCR reg 23(1)(f); OGC Guidance, para 3.

[37] PCR reg 23(3); P Trepte, *Public Procurement in the EU: A Practitioner's Guide*, 2nd edn (Oxford, Oxford University Press, 2007) 340.

the authorities of the country where the conviction was obtained. As was discussed in chapter four, the difficulty of obtaining information on convictions obtained in other Member States and third countries was highlighted in relation to the issue of checking the criminal records of foreign 'airside' airport workers in the UK.

In relation to the issue of a disqualification from one procuring authority in the UK being implemented by another procuring authority, the UK regulations are also silent, but the absence of a national register of disqualified firms leads to the conclusion that procuring authorities in the UK are not bound by the disqualification decisions of other UK procuring authorities.

If the EU and/or the UK decide to implement a system where a disqualification by one procuring authority affects other procuring authorities, two approaches are possible. First, since disqualification is tied to a conviction, the best approach would be to maintain a register of convicted suppliers. This register should be accessible to procuring authorities in Member States and should contain information on the date when the conviction will be spent in the jurisdiction where the conviction was obtained. Secondly, the EU could establish a system of notification of disqualifications.[38] This notification may be implemented through a website to which procuring authorities and the public may have access,[39] and may have the same practical effect as a database of disqualified suppliers. The disadvantages of this approach, however, are that although disqualification by one procuring authority may signify that the supplier has been convicted of a relevant offence, the conviction may have become spent in the interim, thereby possibly ceasing to be relevant in some jurisdictions for disqualification purposes. The notification system would need to contain information on the conviction/offence for which the supplier was disqualified and when the conviction would become spent.

6.3.3 The Elements of the Disqualification Decision Left to the Non-disqualifying Entity

Where disqualification affects procuring authorities beyond the disqualifying entity, one issue that arises is whether such authorities have discretion to decide on any of the elements of the disqualification decision. Two approaches are possible: the non-disqualifying entity may be required to apply the disqualification decision *in toto* without being permitted to deviate from any elements of the decision; or a procuring authority may

[38] Convention on Driving Disqualification [1998] OJ C216/01, art 3 utilises such a notification system and the competent authorities where the disqualification was obtained are required to notify the authorities in the driver's state of residence.

[39] Initiative of the Kingdom of Denmark, above n 30, art 2.

be permitted to determine certain elements of the disqualification decision such as whether disqualification is inappropriate because of public interest concerns or the supplier's rehabilitation. Both approaches are utilised by the jurisdictions where disqualification is extended to other procuring authorities.

For instance, in the US, although disqualification applies to all federal procuring authorities as discussed above, individual procuring authorities are still able to exercise discretion to decide if there are reasons making disqualification inappropriate for that authority. Under the FAR, the head of a procuring authority may contract with a disqualified supplier where there are 'compelling reasons' for doing so.[40] This issue is discussed in chapter ten, but it suffices to say that US procuring authorities have discretion to derogate from the disqualification in limited contexts.

South Africa and the World Bank both adopt a similar approach and there is no discretion for a procuring authority to derogate from a disqualification imposed by the disqualifying entity. In South Africa none of the legislation gives procuring authorities the discretion to avoid a disqualification imposed by the court under the Corruption Act or a disqualifying entity under the PPPFA regulations. As was discussed earlier, the World Bank also does not permit procuring authorities in Borrower countries to derogate from a disqualification or vary it in any way.

6.4 SUMMARY AND ANALYSIS OF MAIN ISSUES

This chapter has examined the kinds of entities used in the disqualification context and whether a disqualification decision by one entity is binding on other procuring entities.

From the previous analysis, it may be said that it will always be the case that different elements of a disqualification decision will be split between different entities, especially as disqualification measures in most jurisdictions are based on a conviction. However, as was seen, some entities that are currently involved in disqualification decision-making may not be able to take appropriate decisions owing to their inherent institutional limitations. It is suggested that the most appropriate entity for disqualification decision-making is an independent administrative entity, with procuring entities being given the discretion to waive the disqualification decision of such an entity in limited circumstances. As was discussed, administrative entities may take quicker, fairer disqualification decisions, reduce the delays to the procurement process disqualification may cause and provide a central source of statistical information on disqualification in a jurisdiction.

[40] FAR 9.406-1(c).

In relation to the issue of extending the scope of disqualification, this may lead to a more efficient use of resources and possibly increase the deterrent effect of disqualification in jurisdictions where disqualification is applied by a wide range of procuring authorities. However, extending the scope of disqualification is only possible and appropriate where a jurisdiction devotes the resources to building and maintaining a mechanism, such as a database which permits procuring entities to quickly and accurately discover the previous disqualification of a proposed supplier.

7

Investigations

7.1 INTRODUCTION

THIS CHAPTER WILL consider in detail whether the disqualifying entity is required to conduct investigations into whether an offence was committed or a conviction exists; the extent of the entity's investigative powers and the kind of evidence that may be relied on by a disqualifying entity. This chapter will focus on investigations conducted by a procuring authority or an administrative authority, and not the investigations conducted by the police where the disqualifying entity is a court.[1]

The purpose of an investigation is to obtain the information required to come to an appropriate decision to disqualify. The extent and limits of an investigation are informed by: the legislative provisions on disqualification; the kinds of offences leading to disqualification; the nature of the disqualifying entity (a court, a procuring authority or an administrative entity); the kind of disqualification – whether a general disqualification or one limited to a specific contract award and whether the disqualification is tied to a conviction; and the stage of the procurement process in which the decision to disqualify is taken. Where the measure is based on a conviction, investigations by a disqualifying entity are limited to discovering the existence of the conviction but where the measure is not based on a conviction, the disqualifying entity may need to determine whether the supplier committed the relevant offence. Investigations may also be relevant to the issue of whether persons related to the corrupt supplier may also be disqualified. This issue will be further examined in chapter eight.

[1] Police investigative powers are very different in nature and in scope from the powers of a disqualifying entity and have been covered elsewhere. See P Stelfox, *Criminal Investigation: An Introduction to Principles and Practice* (Cullompton, Willan, 2009); J Graham 'Suspension of Contractors and Ongoing Criminal Investigations for Fraud: Looking for Fairness from a Tightrope of Competing Interests' (1984) 14 *Public Contract Law Journal* 216.

7.2 THE EXISTENCE OF A REQUIREMENT OR OBLIGATION TO INVESTIGATE

Imposing an obligation on disqualifying entities to investigate is difficult because such an obligation could easily turn a discretionary disqualification into something more mandatory. It is thus not surprising that in the selected jurisdictions, there is no requirement to investigate the commission of relevant offences or the existence of relevant convictions for the purposes of disqualification. Whilst this approach is appropriate for the discretionary measures, it is less clear why mandatory measures are designed without an investigative requirement.

This section will examine the requirement to investigate depending on whether the measure is tied to a conviction or not, since the approach to investigations will differ depending on whether a conviction establishing the offence exists.

7.2.1 The Requirement to Investigate for Disqualification Measures Based on a Conviction

Where disqualification is based on a conviction, investigations by a procuring or administrative authority are limited to determining whether the supplier has been convicted for a relevant offence. This information may be obtainable from a judicial extract or a police or similar database. In the jurisdictions that utilise conviction-based measures (the EU, UK, US and South Africa) there is no obligation on disqualifying entities to discover the existence of a conviction. This is the approach, irrespective of whether the measure is discretionary or mandatory.

In relation to discretionary measures, an obligation to investigate is unnecessary as the disqualifying entity retains the discretion to disqualify, and consequently, to investigate. However, in relation to mandatory measures, it is less clear why an obligation to investigate does not exist. In the EU and UK, the absence of an investigative obligation on procuring authorities in relation to the mandatory disqualification provisions has been criticised as anomalous and ambiguous, as although the requirement to disqualify is mandatory, procuring authorities are not *required* to obtain the information necessary to disqualify.[2] This ambiguity can be traced to the preparatory documents[3] on the directives, where several Member

[2] P Trepte, *Public Procurement in the EU: A Practitioners Guide*, 2nd edn (Oxford, Oxford University Press, 2007) 339–41.

[3] Proposal for a Directive of the European Parliament and of the Council on the co-ordination of procedures for the award of public supply contracts, public service contracts and public works contracts 10345/00 MAP 5 CODEC 550 – COM(2000) 275 final, 26/10/2001. Reproduced in Hebly, *European Public Procurement*, 1133.

States expressed discomfort with the mandatory nature of the disqualifications. In response to these concerns, the Commission clarified that the obligation on Member States to disqualify convicted contractors was one of due diligence and not 'an absolute obligation to achieve a result'; a procuring authority only had to show due diligence in investigating or verifying the situation of a supplier and the obligation to disqualify only arose where the procuring authority was informed of the conviction.[4]

Whilst one agrees that procuring authorities should not be under an obligation to 'achieve a result', given the difficulties that procuring authorities may face in obtaining information on convictions, it has been suggested by Arrowsmith that the EU directives ought to be interpreted as imposing an obligation on procuring authorities to request information on convictions,[5] as without such an approach, the disqualifications may be ineffective in practice. However, even if the directives are interpreted as imposing an obligation on procuring authorities to request the necessary information from suppliers, it must be noted that where there are doubts over the information provided by a supplier, it will be extremely difficult for procuring authorities to verify information on convictions without measures to improve the ease of access to this information, especially in relation to convictions obtained in other Member States.[6] Although there have been attempts made to improve the access to this information through a harmonised system of the sharing of criminal information,[7] there is as yet no central registry from which procuring

[4] Progress report on the Proposal or a Directive of the European Parliament and of the Council on the co-ordination of the procedures for the award of public supply contracts, public service contracts and public works contracts 10345/00 MAP 5 CODEC 550 – COM(2000) 275 final 21/11/2001. Reproduced in Hebly, *European Public Procurement*, 1134. See also Recital 43 PSD.

[5] S Arrowsmith, 'Implementation of the new EC Procurement Directives and the Alcatel Ruling in England and Wales: A Review of the New Legislation and Guidance' (2006) 3 *Public Procurement Law Review* 86, 89.

[6] J Jacobs and D Blitsa, 'Major "Minor" Progress under the Third Pillar: EU Institution Building in the Sharing of Criminal Information' (2008) 8 *Chicago-Kent Journal of International and Comparative Law* 111.

[7] See Action Plan of 3 December 1998 of the Council and the Commission on how best to implement the provisions of the Treaty of Amsterdam on an area of freedom, security and justice Point [1999] OJ C19/1, para 45(f); Conclusion 33–37 Tampere Special European Council on Justice and Home Affairs Matters (October 1999); Council Decision 2009/315/JHA on the organisation and content of the exchange of information extracted from criminal records between Member States [2009] OJ L93/23; Council Decision 2009/316/JHA on the establishment of a European Criminal Records Information System [2009] OJ 193/33; Communication from the Commission to the Council and the European Parliament- Mutual recognition of final judgments in criminal matters COM (2000) 0495 final; Council Decision 2005/876/JHA on the exchange of information extracted from the criminal record; Communication from the Commission to the Council and the European Parliament on measures to be taken to combat terrorism and other forms of serious crime, in particular to improve exchanges of information; White paper on exchanges of information on convictions and the effect of such convictions in the EU COM(2005)10 final; Convention on Mutual Assistance in Criminal Matters (2000).

authorities in one Member State may obtain information on criminal convictions in another Member State. While Member States' access to this information has been improved through harmonising the system of record keeping, the ultimate aim of the EU is to create a European Criminal Record (or register of convictions), where the details of persons convicted of criminal offences in Europe may be stored and used to fight crime in the EU.[8] However, serious challenges will have to be overcome before such a record can become a reality. These challenges have been detailed by Xanthaki and Stefanou and include the divergences in the definition of offences, the different approaches in recording the convictions of legal persons and recording offences committed by EU nationals overseas, and divergences in the rehabilitation period of convictions in Member States.[9]

Where a jurisdiction requires disqualification to be applied to a wide range of entities, investigations will be relevant for those entities to obtain information on the prior disqualification. As discussed in chapter six, the simplest way of achieving this is for a procuring authority to consult a database of disqualified contractors where one exists. In the jurisdictions which maintain such a database, there is an obligation for procuring authorities to consult such databases and a corresponding obligation for a procuring authority not to award contracts to such listed, disqualified contractors. Thus, the US FAR provides that procuring authorities must ensure they do not award contracts to persons listed in the database of disqualified firms.[10] A similar approach is adopted by the World Bank and South Africa. The World Bank procurement guidelines provide that a Borrower must not award a contract to a disqualified supplier[11] and under the South African Corruption Act and PFMA regulations, procuring authorities must ignore tenders from disqualified contractors.[12]

In these jurisdictions, the obligation placed on procuring authorities to examine these databases is not onerous as these databases are publicly accessible. It is instructive that none of the selected jurisdictions include any penalty in the legislation where a procuring authority fails to consult the database and awards a contract to a disqualified firm. In the US and South Africa, it is not clear what the consequence of a failure to consult the database and a corresponding award of a contract to a disqualified firm might be. In the US, the GAO has documented several instances where contracts were awarded to disqualified firms because procuring authorities failed to check the database of listed firms.[13] It is possible, however,

[8] C Stefanou and H Xanthaki, *Towards a European Criminal Record* (Cambridge, Cambridge University Press, 2008).

[9] Stefanou and Xanthaki, *European Criminal Record*, ibid, chs 1 and 2.

[10] FAR 9.404(c)(7); 9.405(d).

[11] BPG, para 1.8.

[12] Corruption Act 2004, s 28(3)(a)(iii); PFMA reg 16A9.1(c).

[13] GAO, Suspended and debarred businesses and individuals improperly receive federal funds (GAO 09-174 Feb 2009).

that such awards may be challenged by other suppliers, by way of analogy with the situations in which losing competitors have challenged affirmative determinations of responsibility against other suppliers.[14]

In the World Bank, a failure to consult the database by a Borrower and the proposed award of a contract to a disqualified firm would be caught by the Bank where the Bank is asked to assent to the proposed award of a contract by providing a no-objection notice. In such cases, the Bank will clearly not assent to the award of a contract to a disqualified firm.

7.2.2 The Requirement to Investigate for Disqualification Measures Not Based on a Conviction

Where disqualification is not based on a conviction, the disqualifying entity is faced with potentially more involved investigations than merely confirming the existence of a relevant conviction and the disqualifying entity needs to be satisfied to an adequate standard that the supplier committed the offence. As stated, none of the jurisdictions provide for an obligation to investigate or the nature of such investigations. The potential for disqualification decisions based on insufficient evidence makes it preferable for a jurisdiction to establish a framework for investigations. Such a framework should include the procedure that a procuring authority may use to undertake investigations, the extent of the obligation to investigate, and the limits to the disqualifying entity's investigative powers. This ought to be the case whether disqualification is for past offences or offences committed in the specific contract award procedure.

In the EU, the discretionary disqualification provisions that are not based on a conviction are silent on the issue of an obligation to investigate. As mentioned earlier, this is understandable, given that procuring authorities possess discretion with respect to all decisions within the disqualification process. Whilst being silent on an obligation to investigate, the EU directives give procuring authorities guidance on the nature of documents that may be relied on in seeking information on offences from contractors.[15]

In implementing the EU directives, the UK regulations clarified the obligation on procuring authorities in relation to the discretionary disqualifications by providing that a procuring authority 'may require an economic operator to provide such information as it considers it needs to make the evaluation', thus giving procuring authorities the power to request relevant documents from contractors in the conduct of investigations.[16]

[14] *Watts-Healy A JV v United States* 82 Fed Cl 614 (2008).
[15] PSD, art 45(3).
[16] PCR, reg 23(5).

In the US, procuring authorities are required to ensure that a contract is not awarded to a previously disqualified supplier, but since disqualification is discretionary, they are not under an obligation to investigate offences that could lead to disqualification.[17]

A similar approach is adopted by the World Bank and the South African provisions. In the Bank, the INT has the discretion to commence investigations into allegations of corruption in Bank-financed contracts, but is not under an obligation to do so.[18] In South Africa, neither the PPPFA nor the PFMA regulations impose an obligation on procuring authorities to investigate whether a supplier has committed an offence that may lead to disqualification.

7.3 THE ENTITY WITH THE POWER TO INVESTIGATE AND THE EXTENT OF THE ENTITY'S POWERS

Once it is determined whether a requirement to investigate exists, two further issues require consideration: identifying which entity has the power to investigate and determining the limits to the entity's investigative powers. The issue of identifying the investigating entity is not always directly addressed and it is often implied within the legislation that the disqualifying entity will conduct investigations. However, where the disqualifying entity is a procuring authority, it may not be competent to conduct the kinds of investigations required for disqualification, especially where it does not have powers to compel the production of relevant documents and evidence.[19]

In the EU and the UK, the legislation implies that the procuring authority will conduct the investigations by giving procuring authorities the discretion to request the necessary documents from the supplier.[20] In the US, the disqualifying official is expressly referred to as the person with the power to investigate.[21] For the non-judicial disqualifications in South Africa, the PFMA regulations designate the accounting officer within a procuring authority as the person who takes disqualification decisions and, in the absence of any other information, it seems likely that the accounting officer may also be responsible for conducting investigations. The PPPFA regulations also appear to imply that the procuring authority will conduct investigations to determine if an offence was committed.[22] In

[17] FAR 9.406-1(a); 9.407-1(a).

[18] WBSP, art II.

[19] J Moran, J Pope and A Doig, *Debarment as an Anti-Corruption Means: A Review Report* (Norway, U4, 2004) ch 5.

[20] PSD, art 45(1), (3); PCR reg 23(3) and (5).

[21] FAR 9.406-3(a).

[22] PPPFA reg 13(1).

the World Bank, investigations are conducted by the INT, which is the entity designated for this task.[23]

The extent or limits of the investigating entity's powers are not addressed by the legislation on disqualification. The extent of the investigative powers provided to a disqualifying entity depends on whether a conviction is required for disqualification and the nature of the disqualifying entity. Where disqualification is tied to a conviction, very limited investigative powers may be required as all the disqualifying entity needs to do is confirm that a conviction exists, although this may not be so simple where the conviction was obtained overseas. In relation to the nature of the disqualifying entity, where disqualification is a function of a judicial body, the powers of investigation will be those possessed by police/prosecutorial authorities. Where disqualification is the function of an external administrative body its investigative powers may be specified in the legislation establishing the body. Where the disqualifying entity is a procuring authority, the extent of the procuring authority's investigative powers may depend on the legislative provisions on disqualification and whether the procuring authority has been given express investigative powers. Where a procuring authority is not given express powers of investigation, it may not normally be competent or permitted to conduct investigations into the commission of offences unless this power is granted by legislation[24] or the core functions of the procuring authority include investigations.[25]

Where a procuring authority is not given express powers to investigate, this does not mean that it will be unable to obtain the relevant information, as suppliers are generally required to submit documentation to prove their suitability for a particular contract. Where information on offences is required as a part of such documentation and is withheld or shows that an offence was committed, the supplier may not be eligible for the contract or may be disqualified. Where a disqualifying entity is not given express powers to investigate, it may also rely on voluntary disclosures by suppliers. Such disclosures reduce the investigative burden on procuring authorities[26] and as discussed in chapter ten, voluntary disclosures are a facet of the attempts to maintain integrity in public procurement in some jurisdictions.[27]

[23] WBSP, art II.

[24] See generally, D Kirk and A Woodcock, *Serious Fraud: Investigation & Trial*, 3rd edn (London, Butterworth's, 2002); L Sealy and S Worthington, *Cases & Materials in Company Law*, 8th edn (Oxford, Oxford University Press, 2007) 595.

[25] For instance, authorities like the Revenue Department and Financial Services Authority in the UK are granted these powers in fulfilment of their core functions.

[26] I Rosen-Zvi and T Fisher, 'Overcoming Procedural Boundaries' (2008) *Virginia Law Review* 79, 122.

[27] Federal Acquisition Regulation; FAR Case 2007-006, Contractor Compliance Program and Integrity Reporting 72 Fed Reg 64019; C Zierdt and E Podgor, 'Back Against the Wall – Corporate Deferred Prosecution through the Lens of Contract Policing' (2009) 23 *Criminal Justice* 34; S Williams, 'The Debarment of Corrupt Contractors from World Bank-Financed

The selected jurisdictions adopt a similar approach to the extent or limits of the investigative powers of disqualifying entities and do not specify the extent or limits to investigative powers. This may be problematic, as a procuring authority may go too far in an attempt to gather information on a contractor's wrongdoing. For instance, in the US case of *Cubic Corp v Cheney*,[28] the supplier was able to successfully challenge the manner in which the information relied on for disqualification was obtained, where the procuring authority relied on wire-tap evidence in disqualification proceedings. The court held that if an agency relied on wire-tap evidence in rendering a reviewable decision, the agency had to be prepared to defend the legality of that evidence. Providing limits on the investigative powers of a disqualifying entity would serve to prevent such abuses in the disqualification context.

7.4 THE NATURE AND SOURCES OF INFORMATION AND EVIDENCE

Although there may not be an obligation to investigate, all the jurisdictions, except South Africa specify the nature and kinds of evidence that can be relied on in disqualification decision-making. This is important as without guidance on what kind of information is appropriate, there is a danger that a disqualifying entity may rely on insufficient evidence or 'mere suspicion, unfounded allegation or error'[29] or information that may not be reliable, leading to decisions that may not stand up to judicial scrutiny.

In the EU, the directives list the kinds of information that may be relied on by procuring authorities to prove that a conviction exists against a contractor.[30] These are: extracts from a judicial record; an equivalent document issued by a competent authority; a declaration on oath from the contractor; and a solemn declaration before a competent judicial or administrative authority or notary or competent professional or trade body in the contractor's country of origin.[31]

The adoption in 2009 of a EU Framework Decision[32] on the exchange of criminal information may also assist procuring authorities in obtaining this information, as Member States are under an obligation to designate a central authority for the dissemination of this information and have the option to include information on disqualifications arising from con-

Contracts' (2007) 36 *Public Contract Law Journal* 277; S Williams, 'World Bank Introduces New Measures to Fight Corruption in Bank-Financed Contracts and the Administration of Bank Loans' (2007) *Public Procurement Law Review* NA152.

[28] *Cubic Corp v Cheney* 914 F2d 1501 (DC Cir 1990).

[29] *Transco Security v Freeman* 454 US 820 (1981).

[30] PSD art 45(3).

[31] PSD art 45(3).

[32] Council Decision 2009/315/JHA on the organisation and content of the exchange of information extracted from criminal records between Member States [2009] OJ L93/23.

victions.[33] Whether Member States will use this option to assist in the dissemination of information on the mandatory disqualifications remains to be seen. Whichever option is chosen, the CJEU has held in the context of the discretionary exclusions for non-compliance with social security and tax obligations, that the means of assessing a supplier's compliance with these obligations must not involve excessive administrative charges, complicate or delay the procurement process, or be dissuasive to foreign suppliers.[34]

The UK regulations in implementing the directives adopted a similar approach to the directives and provide that the evidence that will suffice to prove the existence of a conviction includes an extract from a judicial record,[35] a document issued by a relevant judicial or administrative authority,[36] and a declaration on oath made by the supplier before a competent authority, notary public or Commissioner for Oaths.[37] Under the regulations, this information may be requested from suppliers, or the disqualifying entity may approach the relevant databases for information on the criminal record of the contractor.[38]

Although the UK regulations provide limited guidance on the kinds of information that will be sufficient, a clearer, more detailed approach would be preferable as such an approach would also create limits on the scope of the discretionary disqualifications. As discussed in chapter three, these disqualifications are quite broad and may be used to disqualify a supplier for criminal and non-criminal offences without the requirement of a conviction. Without detailed guidance on what kinds of documents are required to prove these breaches and without the power or competence to investigate the commission of offences, it may be very difficult in practice for a procuring authority to determine if a relevant offence has been committed for the purposes of the discretionary disqualifications. As will be seen below, similar arguments may be made in relation to the South African system, which does not provide any guidance to disqualifying entities on the nature and sources of appropriate information.

The US and the World Bank provide more details on the nature of the information that could be used to come to a disqualification decision. The FAR lists sources of information relevant for disqualification. These are the contractor's records and experience data, bid and proposal information, pre-qualification questionnaire replies, personnel information and other sources of information such as publications, suppliers, subcontractors,

[33] Council Decision 2009/315/JHA ibid, art 11.

[34] Case C-199/07 *Commission v Hellenic Republic* [2009] ECR I-10669; Case C-74/09 *Batiments et Ponts Contruction & WISAG Produktionsservice GmbH v Berlaymont 2000 SA* (unreported 15.07.10).

[35] PCR reg 23(5)(a)(i).

[36] PCR reg 23(5)(a)(ii).

[37] PCR reg 23(5)(c).

[38] PSD, art 45(1); PCR reg 23(5) and (3).

customers of the proposed contractor, financial institutions, government agencies and business and trade associations.[39] Unlike the EU and UK, the sources of information listed include a wide-range of non-official sources. Similar to the EU and UK, however, this information may be furnished by the supplier at the request of the procuring authority,[40] or furnished voluntarily by the supplier to satisfy the requirement that it is responsible.[41]

The World Bank procurement guidelines include a provision granting the Bank the right to require access to contractor's accounts, records, bid submission and contract performance documents and to permit these documents to be audited by the Bank.[42] Another rare source of information for the Bank is domestic corruption convictions. However, as discussed in chapter four, the Bank does not generally rely on domestic convictions as a basis for disqualifying contractors.[43]

The South African approach diverges from the approach of all the other selected jurisdictions and none of the South African provisions specify the kinds of information that could be relied on for disqualification. This means that disqualifying entities are not given any guidance on the strength or reliability of the information that may be used to disqualify. South Africa should have adopted an approach similar to the UK, where the disqualifying entity is given limited guidance on the kinds of evidence that would suffice. The South African approach may prove problematic in practice, especially where the disqualification is not based on a conviction, as it is possible that the disqualifying entity may disqualify on the basis of inadequate information or information which may not withstand judicial scrutiny.

7.5 SUMMARY AND ANALYSIS OF MAIN ISSUES

This chapter examined whether disqualifying entities are under an obligation to obtain information relevant to disqualification in relation to mandatory provisions. It was seen that in the jurisdictions with mandatory provisions, there is no requirement to obtain information on convictions or offences, and this may hamper the effectiveness of such measures. It is submitted that if disqualification measures are to be effective, disqualifying entities should at the very least be obliged to ask suppliers to submit information on convictions. In the EU context, as the

39 FAR 9.105-1(c).

40 J Cibinic and R Nash, *Formation of Government Contracts*, 3rd edn (Alphen aan den Rijn, Wolters Kluwer, 1998) 441.

41 FAR 9.103(c).

42 BPG para 1.16.

43 S Williams, 'World Bank Introduces New Measures to Fight Corruption in Bank-Financed Contracts and the Administration of Bank Loans' (2007) *Public Procurement Law Review* NA152.

sharing of criminal information progresses, disqualifying entities may be able to approach the relevant authorities in various Member States to verify this information. It is important that the EU continues to develop the systems and processes for the sharing of this information, as this will support the disqualification provisions and make them more effective.

Another issue that requires further discussion is providing disqualifying entities with a framework for conducting investigations and express powers to investigate where disqualification is not tied to a conviction. This will ensure that disqualifying entities are able to obtain the necessary evidence to disqualify, but will not disqualify on the basis of inadequate evidence. In addition, the legislation on disqualification in the jurisdictions should also place clear limits on these powers of investigation. Such limits are especially important where a conviction is not required for disqualification to prevent abuses of the disqualification process. It was seen in the context of the US that it is possible for a disqualifying entity to abuse its powers of investigation in a desire to see a supplier disqualified. It is worth mentioning here that as discussed in chapter five, the centralisation of disqualification through an administrative entity may also reduce the likelihood of such abuses as well as increase the effectiveness of a disqualification regime.

Finally, it was seen that in jurisdictions in which disqualification is applied by entities beyond the disqualifying entity, there do not appear to be penalties or consequences where a procuring authority fails to consult a database of disqualified contractors and awards a contract to a disqualified contractor. This is anomalous and the lack of such penalties may also limit the effectiveness of disqualification provisions.

8

The Disqualification of Persons Related to a Corrupt Supplier

8.1 INTRODUCTION

DISQUALIFICATION IS USUALLY directed at the person that committed the offence or received the conviction or civil judgment for corruption (the primary supplier), who may be a legal or a natural person. In certain contexts, persons related to the disqualified primary supplier may also be disqualified, although they may not necessarily have been involved in the commission of the offence. Disqualifying related persons may assist in meeting the rationales for disqualification and may be necessary to ensure the effectiveness of the measure, as it may be possible for the effects of disqualification to be avoided where a disqualified supplier is able to compete for public contracts through related entities, persons and subcontractors.[1] Disqualifying related persons may also be useful in jurisdictions reluctant to attach criminal liability to corporate entities, as a corporate entity may be disqualified for a conviction obtained by natural persons connected to the firm.[2] Although a full discourse on corporate criminal liability is beyond the scope of this book, the difficulties of convicting corporations of corruption and the often civil settlements that corporations enter into in the context of corruption allegations make the disqualification of related persons an important aspect of ensuring the effectiveness of disqualification measures.

A number of issues arise from the disqualification of related persons. First, a disqualifying entity will have to identify the related persons it wishes to disqualify. These persons may be determined by the legislation, or the disqualifying entity may exercise its discretion in this regard. Secondly, a disqualifying entity will need to determine the basis for the disqualification of related persons, which may be the related person's complicity in the commission of an offence or its association with the

[1] F Anechiarico and J Jacobs, 'Purging Corruption from Public Contracting: The Solutions are Now Part of the Problem' (1995) *New York Law School Law Review* 162–72.

[2] A Hamdani and A Klement, 'Corporate Crime & Deterrence' (2008) 61 *Stanford Law Review* 271.

primary supplier. This basis will determine the limits of such disqualifications in a jurisdiction.[3] The third issue is determining how to limit the practical problems of disqualifying related persons such as the expense and difficulties of investigating them, delays to the procurement process, ensuring that the disqualification of related persons is not disproportionate to the aims of the disqualification policy and providing adequate procedural safeguards to related persons.

8.2 RATIONALES FOR DISQUALIFYING RELATED PERSONS

The rationales justifying the disqualification of persons related to a corrupt primary supplier are essentially the same rationales behind a disqualification policy as discussed in chapter two. Thus, disqualifying related persons may be done for policy, protective or punitive/deterrent reasons. Where disqualification exists for policy reasons such as giving effect to the anti-corruption policies of the government, disqualifying related persons supports the government's policy to the extent that the government will avoid contracting with the corrupt supplier and persons related to him.

Where disqualification is aimed at protecting the government from dealing with unscrupulous contractors, disqualifying related persons may ensure the government is protected should the primary supplier attempt to avoid the effects of its disqualification by obtaining public contracts through related entities. Similarly, where the purpose of disqualification is punitive, the disqualification of related persons gives maximum weight to the primary disqualification and reinforces the punitive nature of disqualification.

Disqualifying related persons may also increase the effectiveness of a disqualification policy. Empirical evidence gathered by Anechiarico and Jacobs in relation to disqualification measures in New York suggests that unless persons related to a disqualified primary supplier are disqualified, the primary supplier may continue to bid for public contracts under different corporate identities or through different officers or subcontractors.[4] Thus, if disqualification is to be effective, it may be necessary to disqualify the 'alter-egos' of the disqualified primary supplier to prevent the primary supplier from using such entities to obtain public contracts.[5] Where the disqualification of related persons is intended to increase the effectiveness

[3] J Jacobs and F Anechiarico, 'Blacklisting Public Contractors as an Anti-Corruption and Racketeering Strategy' (1992) 11 *Criminal Justice Ethics* 64, 68.

[4] Anechiarico and Jacobs, 'Purging Corruption from Public Contracting', above n 1, 172.

[5] The GAO compiled evidence of firms avoiding disqualification through the use of new corporate identities – GAO, *Suspended and debarred businesses and individuals improperly receive federal funds* (GAO 09-174 Feb 2009).

of the measure, the disqualification must be conducted in a way that is proportionate[6] and does not result in convicting and punishing[7] companies and their employees for offences that they have not committed.[8]

Disqualifying related persons may also be intended to secure equal treatment of contractors and increase transparency in public procurement.[9] A level playing-field for contractors may be achieved where persons tainted by corruption because of their association with the primary supplier are denied access to public contracts. This will increase transparency in the disqualification system, since a disqualified primary supplier, who may be financially dependent on or otherwise connected to another company, will be unable to use such companies to obtain public contracts.

In the disqualification of related persons, care must be taken so that there is no overreach of the rationales behind disqualification, which may lead to 'over-breadth'[10] in the legal regulation of public procurement.

8.3 THE RELATED PERSONS

'Related persons' refers to natural and legal persons, and three categories of related persons will be examined in this chapter: natural persons; connected companies, defined to include sister, subsidiary and parent companies; and cooperating companies, defined as subcontractors and joint ventures.

The problems that are faced in disqualifying all categories of related persons are similar, but are not always anticipated by legislative provisions on disqualification and where anticipated, the problems are not amenable to simple solutions. First, the disqualifying entity has to identify the relevant related person. This may be difficult depending on the nature of the person in question. For instance it may be difficult to identify the parent company of a supplier where that parent is a holding company whose shares are in turn held by unidentifiable beneficiaries. Secondly, it will be necessary to determine the basis of the related person's disqualification. This may be the complicity of the related person in the commission of the offence, the proximity between the related person and the primary supplier, or the control exercised by the related person over the primary supplier and vice versa. The basis of the related person's disqualification may be specified or implied by the legislation, left to the

6 F Anechiarico, 'Prosecution as Corruption Control: Paradigms of Public Integrity in Context' (2007) 52 *Wayne Law Review* 1415.

7 Jacobs and Anechiarico, 'Blacklisting Public Contractors', above n 3, 65.

8 Hamdani and Klement, 'Corporate Crime & Deterrence', above n 2, 271–4.

9 Case C-213/07 *Michaniki AE* [2008] ECR I-9999, Opinion of AG Maduro.

10 Defined as a situation where 'a legal prohibition sanctions behaviour outside the class of wrongdoing or harm-creation that the rule is designed to address'. S Buell, 'The Upside of Overbreadth' (2008) 83 *New York University Law Review* 1491.

discretion of the disqualifying entity, or left to be determined by the courts. Thirdly, the disqualifying entity will have to determine whether the disqualification of a related person is warranted where the connection between the related person and the primary offender has been terminated.

8.3.1 Natural Persons

Two scenarios are relevant where a natural person is involved in disqualification proceedings: a firm may be disqualified for the corrupt activity of a natural person and a natural person related to a firm may be disqualified for the corrupt activity of the firm.

8.3.1.1 Disqualifying a firm for the corrupt activity of a natural person

The disqualification of a firm for offences committed by natural persons is an important tool in ensuring the effectiveness of disqualification measures. This is particularly so where disqualification is based on a conviction in jurisdictions that recognise the criminal liability of corporations only in limited statutory contexts[11] or not at all. Where a firm cannot be convicted of corruption, corrupt firms will avoid disqualification where a conviction is required. Even where criminal convictions against corporate entities are recognised,[12] convictions for corruption against corporations are notably rare,[13] which may mean that the disqualification of firms may have to be hinged on the conviction of a related natural person. Further, most corruption cases against firms result in civil and not criminal penalties, due in part to the difficulties of meeting the burden of proof and the leniency that is offered to firms who self-report and cooperate with prosecutors.[14]

There are a number of issues that arise in disqualifying a firm for the corrupt activity of a natural person. The first is determining the natural

[11] C Wells, *Corporations and Criminal Responsibility* (Oxford, Oxford University Press, 2001); G Stessens, 'Corporate Criminal Liability: A Comparative Perspective' (1994) 43 *International and Comparative Law Quarterly* 493; W Hetzer, 'Corruption as Business Practice? Corporate Criminal Liability in the European Union' (2007) 3–4 *European Journal of Crime, Criminal Law and Criminal Justice* 383; T Weigend, 'Societas Delinquere Non Potest? A German Perspective' (2008) 6 *Journal of International Criminal Justice* 927; G Ferguson, 'Corruption and Corporate Criminal Liability', Paper presented at International Colloquium on Criminal Responsibility of Collective Legal, Entities, May 1998. Available at: www.icclr.law.ubc.ca/Publications/Reports/FergusonG.PDF .

[12] A Pinto and M Evans, *Corporate Criminal Liability*, 2nd edn (London, Sweet and Maxwell, 2008) chs 2–4.

[13] C Nicholls, T Daniel, M Polaine and J Hatchard, *Corruption and Misuse of Public Office*, 1st edn (Oxford, Oxford University Press, 2006) 40–43.

[14] Serious Fraud Office, *Approach to Overseas Corruption* (2009); Crown Prosecution Service, Corporate Prosecutions available at: www.cps.gov.uk; Department of Justice, *Principles for Federal Prosecution of Business Organisations* (Revised 2008).

persons whose actions may lead to the disqualification of a firm. Identifying such persons may depend on the doctrine of corporate liability in the jurisdictions and, as will be seen, two approaches are possible based either on the identification doctrine or on the doctrine of vicarious liability (*respondeat superior*). Thus, such persons may be those with decision-making powers in the firm or persons who may be regarded as the 'directing mind and will' of the firm, and whose actions are identified as the acts of the company, as is the case in the UK.[15] However, in jurisdictions that adopt a *respondeat superior* doctrine of corporate criminal liability, such as the US and South Africa, or doctrines based on vicarious liability, the corrupt activity of any employee, irrespective of seniority may lead to the disqualification of the firm.[16]

However, it has been argued that approaches that penalise a corporation for the misconduct of employees irrespective of seniority may inversely reduce the incentives for the firm to monitor misconduct in the firm, since the firm will suffer regardless of the measures it takes to reduce misconduct.[17] Thus, it may be preferable for jurisdictions to adopt an approach that a firm may only be disqualified for the actions of decision-makers whose acts may be identified as the acts of the firm. As will be seen, this approach finds support in the legislative provisions on disqualification in the EU, the UK and South Africa.

In determining whose actions should lead to the disqualification of a firm, it has been suggested that disqualifying officials should 'distinguish between wrongdoing attributable to corporate policies or practices, or wrongdoing authorised by high-level corporate officials, and wrongdoing committed in blatant defiance of responsible corporate self-governance policies and practices', and disqualification should only occur in the first two instances.[18]

Where the disqualification of a firm for the corrupt activity of a natural person is proposed, a second issue is determining whether a firm should still be disqualified where the firm's connection with that person has been

[15] *Lennards Carrying Company v Asiatic* [1915] AC 705; *Tesco Supermarket v Nattrass* [1972] AC 153; E Mugnai and J Gobert, 'Corporate Criminal Responsibility: Some Lessons from Italy' [2002] *Criminal Law Review* 619. For a corporation to be liable for corruption in the UK, the prosecution needs to prove that the official had the necessary status and authority to make his acts the acts of the company. See *R v Andrews-Weatherfoil Ltd* (1972) 56 Cr App R 31. See Pinto and Evans, *Corporate Criminal Liability*, above n 12, 306.

[16] *Standard Oil of Texas v United States*, 307 F2d 120 (5th Cir 1962), where the misconduct of 'menial' employees was imputed to the corporation. C Green, 'Punishing Corporations: The Food-Chain Schizophrenia in Punitive Damages and Criminal Law' (2008) 87 *Nebraska Law Review* 197, 199; Weigend, 'Societas Delinquere', above n 11, 933. C Nana, 'Corporate Criminal Liability in South Africa: The Need to Look Beyond Vicarious Liability' (2011) 55 *Journal of African Law* 86.

[17] Hamdani and Klement, 'Corporate Crime and Deterrence', above n 2, 271.

[18] R Bednar, 'Emerging Issues in Suspension and Debarment' (2004) 13 *Public Procurement Law Review* 223.

terminated.[19] Three approaches are possible: (i) that the dismissal of the person or persons who carried out or authorised the corrupt acts eliminates the necessity for the disqualification of the firm; (ii) that the dismissal of the corrupt natural person may be insufficient to eliminate a culture of corruption, which may be endemic within the firm and as such the firm still ought to be disqualified;[20] or (iii) one could argue that where the natural person did not act for his own account and his actions were intended to benefit the firm, the firm should still be disqualified, even if the person's employment has been terminated.

A third issue in the disqualification of firms for the offences of a natural person is whether such a disqualification should apply to firms that are yet to be established or controlled by the natural person. In other words, should disqualification apply to the future business entities of the natural person? As will be seen, two of the jurisdictions extend disqualification to the future business entities of the natural person.

The final issue that arises is determining the basis of the firm's disqualification. This may either be the firm's complicity in the offences committed by the natural person (or because the corrupt activity was intended to benefit the firm) or the level of control and/or decision-making power which the natural person wields over the firm. Determining the decision-making power of a natural person may not be straightforward and a disqualifying entity may need to examine the organisational structure of a firm.

The approach to these issues in the jurisdictions varies and some jurisdictions are silent, whilst others provide extensive rules on the issues. In the EU, the procurement directives are silent on the disqualification of a firm for an offence committed by a natural person and do not identify relevant natural persons or establish the basis for the disqualification of such persons. This omission relates to the mandatory and discretionary disqualifications. However, in relation to the mandatory disqualifications, the directives may possibly be interpreted as permitting the disqualification of a firm for the conviction of a natural person. This is because the text of the directives provides that in obtaining information on convictions, a procuring authority may obtain information relating to 'legal and/or natural persons, including, if appropriate, company directors and any person having powers of representation, decision or control in respect of the candidate or tenderer'.[21] This may mean that the convictions of these persons may lead to the disqualification of the firm. However, not all Member States are willing to

[19] S Arrowsmith, HJ Priess and P Friton, 'Self-Cleaning as a Defence to Exclusions for Misconduct: An Emerging Concept in EC Public Procurement Law' (2009) 6 *Public Procurement Law Review* 257.

[20] Weigend, 'Societas Delinquere', above n 11.

[21] PSD, art 45(1).

disqualify a firm for the activity of natural persons and a study by Medina[22] shows that only a few Member States' legislation[23] required the disqualification of a firm for the conviction of a natural person under their mandatory disqualification provisions.

In relation to the discretionary disqualification provisions, as the directives omitted to mention the convictions of natural persons as was done in the mandatory provisions, this may be an indication that the discretionary provisions do not contemplate that a firm can be disqualified for the offences of natural persons. Alternatively, it is possible that this issue has been left entirely to the discretion of Member States. Further, the nature of some of the offences under the discretionary provisions makes it appropriate that the EU did not adopt a blanket provision requiring extension of the disqualifications.

Neither the EU directives nor the UK regulations address the situation where the cause for disqualification has been eliminated, such as where the employment of the natural person has been terminated, but it seems to be accepted as a general principle in the EU that this could lead to a firm avoiding disqualification altogether.[24] In addition, neither the EU directives nor the UK regulations address the issue of the disqualification of the future business entities of the natural person. This is legislated for by the South African Corruption Act, and may be informed by the punitive nature of South African disqualifications. In jurisdictions like the EU and the UK, which utilise disqualifications for policy and protective reasons, an approach that targets the future business activities of a natural person may be disproportionate to the aims of the disqualification policy.

In transposing the directives, the UK regulations went slightly further than the EU directives and provided that a firm will be disqualified under the mandatory disqualification provisions where directors[25] or other persons with powers of representation, decision and control have been convicted of corruption.[26] The OGC Guidance has interpreted this as including partners or senior managers in a firm.[27] This approach accords with the common law identification doctrine of corporate liability, where a firm will be liable when its 'directing mind and will' commit an offence.[28] However, a procuring authority may have the flexibility to adopt a wider definition of natural persons, as the identification doctrine has been

[22] T Medina, 'EU Directives as an Anti-Corruption Measure: Excluding Corruption-Convicted Tenderers from Public Procurement Contracts' in KV Thai (ed), *International Handbook of Public Procurement* (Boca Raton, CRC Press, 2009).

[23] These are Austria, Estonia, Germany, Italy, Latvia, Slovakia, Slovenia, and the UK.

[24] Arrowsmith, Priess and Friton, 'Self Cleaning', above n 19.

[25] Directors are natural persons in UK law – Companies Act 2006, s 155.

[26] Public Contracts Regulations 2006, reg 23(1).

[27] OGC Guidance, para 4.1; S Williams, 'The Mandatory Contractor Exclusions for Serious Criminal Offences in UK Public Procurement' (2009) 15 *European Public Law* 436.

[28] *Lennards Carrying Company v Asiatic*, above n 15; *Tesco Supermarket v Nattrass*, above n 15.

relaxed in some judicial[29] and statutory contexts, due to its narrow constraints.[30] For instance, under the Bribery Act 2010, a firm may be convicted of bribery where a person who performs services for or on behalf of the firm gives a bribe, even though the person is an agent, employee or subsidiary.[31] Thus, by way of analogy, a procuring authority may choose to interpret the regulations as permitting the disqualification of a firm where a person that is not the alter-ego[32] of the company but one who represents the company, such as an employee or agent, has been convicted or is guilty of a relevant offence. In other words, a procuring authority may base disqualification on the vicarious liability of the firm for the actions of its employees or agents acting within the scope of their employment. Such an approach is supported by *Meridian*, where the court denied the existence of an absolute identification doctrine and held that the rules of attribution should be tailored to fit particular cases.[33]

In relation to the discretionary disqualifications, the UK regulations adopt a different approach and mention individuals in relation to some offences (bankruptcy) and not in relation to others (winding-up). In relation to the disqualification for misconduct in the course of a business, the regulations do not mention the disqualification of natural persons at all, and this may either mean that a disqualifying entity may exercise its discretion or that the regulations do not contemplate the disqualification of a firm for these offences committed by a natural person.[34] Further, the fact that the discretionary disqualifications do not generally require a conviction may mean that a disqualifying entity may struggle to obtain proof of the commission of a relevant offence, making it inappropriate for such disqualifications to be extended.

The US approach to the disqualification of related persons is more comprehensive[35] than the EU/UK approach. The FAR identifies the persons whose offences may lead to the disqualification of the firm as well as the basis for the firm's disqualification. Under the FAR, a firm may be disqualified for the corrupt activity of an officer, director, shareholder, partner or other individual associated with the firm, when the conduct occurred in connection with the person's performance of his duties for the firm and the firm knew, approved or acquiesced in the conduct. Where the firm benefits from the improper conduct, this will be an indication of

[29] *Tesco Supermarket v Brent LBC* [1993] 1 WLR 1037; *Meridian Global Funds v Securities Commission* [1995] 2 AC 500.

[30] G Sullivan, 'The Attribution of Culpability to Limited Companies' (1996) 55 *Cambridge Law Journal* 515.

[31] Bribery Act 2010, ss 7 and 8.

[32] *Lennards Carrying Company v Asiatic* [1915] AC 705.

[33] *Meridian Global Funds*, above n 29, 507.

[34] PCR reg 23(4).

[35] FAR 9.406.5(a).

such knowledge, approval, or acquiescence.[36] The requirement that the firm will be disqualified where it knew, approved of or acquiesced in the conduct puts limits on the requirement to disqualify related persons as in US law; the knowledge that may be imputed to the firm where there is wrongdoing is either the knowledge of a person in a position of responsibility[37] or the aggregated knowledge of the company's employees.[38] In practice, in the context of responsibility determinations, the GAO has generally upheld the exclusion of a firm where the integrity of a key employee or an employee who may exercise significant influence in the performance of a contract was in doubt.[39]

There are two important differences between the UK and the US approach to this issue. First, in the UK, under the mandatory disqualification provisions, the test to determine whether a firm will be disqualified for the conviction of a natural person is an objective one, and merely looks to whether the relevant person has been convicted of a relevant offence. In the US, the disqualification of the firm is tied to its knowledge. As stated, this knowledge may be attributed to a person in senior management or may be the aggregated knowledge of the firm's employees[40] and the US provisions may be interpreted as requiring the disqualification of a firm where the employees as a collective were aware of the corrupt activity.[41] A firm may be held to have the required knowledge although different employees are aware of different aspects of the corrupt activity, since it is the aggregated knowledge that is taken into account.[42] In any event the test is a subjective one in the US.

The second area of difference between the UK and the US is that in the UK, the firm will be disqualified where a decision-maker has obtained a relevant conviction, but in the US, a firm may be disqualified for the corrupt activity of persons who are not key decision-makers. This is due to the *respondeat superior* doctrine of corporate liability adopted by the US.[43] The US thus requires a higher level of internal monitoring within an

[36] FAR 9.406-5.

[37] *United States v Sun-Diamond Growers of California*, 138 F3d 961 (DC 1998).

[38] *United States v Bank of New England*, 821 F2d 844, 826 (1st Cir 1987). Cf B Pollack, 'Time to Stop Living Vicariously: A Better Approach to Corporate Criminal Liability' (2009) 46 *American Criminal Law Review* 1393, 1394, who argues that the intent of a company should be based on the knowledge and intent of senior management.

[39] See for instance, *Speco Corp* B-211353 (Comp Gen Apr 26 1983).

[40] E Lederman, 'Models for Imposing Corporate Criminal Liability: From Adaptation and Imitation towards Aggregation and the Search for Self-Identity' (2000) 4 *Buffalo Criminal Law Review* 641, 663.

[41] F Borsch and F Dworschak, 'Criminal Liability of Corporations: A Primer for Procurement Fraud' (1991) 8 *Army Lawyer* 7.

[42] *United States v Bank of New England*, above n 38, 856.

[43] V Khanna, Corporate Criminal Liability: What Purpose does it Serve?' (1996) 109 *Harvard Law Review* 1477, 1499–1512; S Beale, 'Is Corporate Criminal Liability Unique?' (2007) 44 *American Criminal Law Review* 1503, 1522; K Brickey, 'Andersen's Fall from Grace' (2003) 81 *Washington University Law Quarterly* 917, 929.

organisation, as the corrupt activity of junior members of staff where such persons were acting for the benefit of the firm could lead to the firm's disqualification.[44] Further, the US regulations are not limited to disqualifying a firm for the actions of employees, as a firm could also be disqualified for the activity of 'any other individual associated' with the firm.[45] It is thus possible for a firm to be disqualified for the conduct of persons who are not employees, but consultants or agents where the firm is deemed to have approved the corrupt activity.

Unlike the EU and UK, the FAR also deals with the position where the natural person's employment has been terminated by the contractor, by providing that disqualification may not be appropriate where the firm has taken 'appropriate disciplinary action' against the individuals responsible for the corrupt activity[46] or has 'eliminated the circumstances' that led to the cause for disqualification.[47]

The differences in approach between the UK and the US may be traced to the different approaches to corporate liability, the differing rationales for disqualification as well as the historical evolution of procurement regulation in the jurisdictions. Thus, whilst the US adopts a *respondeat superior* doctrine of corporate liability, under which the employer is liable for the acts of an employee within certain limits,[48] the UK generally prefers to base corporate liability on the identification doctrine, where a firm is liable where persons whose actions may be identified as the actions of the firm commit an offence.[49] As was mentioned, the US disqualification policy is intended to protect the government from dealing with corrupt contractors and this may necessitate an approach that requires the disqualification of a firm controlled by corrupt persons. Although the UK disqualification policy is intended to give effect to the policy and protective rationales of EU legislation, the EU has left this issue to be determined by Member States, and the UK has consequently relied on the narrow identification doctrine at common law. In relation to the evolution of procurement regulation in both jurisdictions, US procurement evolved with a very strong anti-corruption element – a feature that is not shared by the UK system, which may also explain the more comprehensive nature of the US regime.

Similar to the UK, however, the US also does not extend disqualification to firms that the natural person may establish in future. As is the case in the EU/UK this may be due to the non-punitive nature of the US

[44] *Standard Oil of Texas*, above n 16.

[45] FAR 9.406-5(b).

[46] FAR 9.406-1(a)(6).

[47] FAR 9.406-1(a)(9).

[48] R Gruner, *Corporate Criminal Liability and Prevention* (Law Journal Press, 2004) chs 2–4.

[49] *Lennards Carrying Company v Asiatic*, above n 32; *Tesco Supermarket v Nattrass*, above n 15; *Meridian Global Funds v Securities Commission* [1995] 2 AC 500; Pinto and Evans, *Corporate Criminal Liability*, above n 12.

disqualification policy, as well as the difficulties that may be faced in implementing such an approach.

The World Bank's approach to extending disqualification contains elements of the US and UK approach. The Bank Sanctions procedures provide that where a sanction is imposed on a contractor, appropriate sanctions may also be imposed on an affiliate of the contractor.[50] An affiliate is defined as 'any legal or natural person that controls, is controlled by, or is under common control with the Respondent'.[51] Thus, a firm may be disqualified for the offences of a natural person if the firm either controls or is controlled by the natural person, or the same entity controls both the firm and the natural person. Although the Bank does not define the limits of the test of control, it is assumed that a natural person controls a firm when the natural person is a key-decision maker who is able to influence the activity of the firm. Further, and similar to the US approach, where a firm controls a natural person, such as where the natural person is an employee of the firm, the firm could also be disqualified on this basis. The Bank thus imports both the identification doctrine and vicarious liability into its procedures. The test of control used by the Bank is subjective and depends on the Bank's determination. Like the US, the Bank also deals with the position where a firm has terminated its connection with an individual implicated in corruption. The Bank may decide not to disqualify a firm that was only 'peripherally associated' with corruption, where the firm has taken measures against the employee.[52]

There are two areas of difference between the Bank and the UK/US. First, the Bank provides that a firm could be disqualified for the offences of a natural person where the same principal controls the natural person and the disqualified firm and secondly, the Bank extends disqualification to the future business entities of a disqualified person, by providing that any sanction shall also apply to the disqualified person's successors and assigns.[53] This provision will prevent a disqualified entity from re-inventing itself with its constituents. In the Bank context, the disqualification of future firms is understandable given that the Bank considers itself to be at the forefront of the fight against corruption in the development arena. Further, contracting with the Bank may be considered an option for suppliers, but as will be discussed in the context of South Africa, which contains similar provisions in the Corruption Act, it is less clear whether the disqualification of future firms is appropriate in a domestic jurisdiction.

In South Africa, the different legislation provides for the disqualification of a firm for the corruption of natural persons in different contexts. The Corruption Act provides for the disqualification of firms related to a

[50] WBSP, art IX s 9.04.
[51] WBSP, art I s 1.02.
[52] WBSP, art IX s 9.02.
[53] WBSP, art IX s 9.05.

convicted natural person, where the firm is owned or controlled by that person and the firm is involved in the offence.[54] This aspect of the test requiring the involvement of the firm has parallels in the US provisions.

Interestingly, and similar to the World Bank, the Corruption Act also provides for the disqualification of firms that may be established in future by the convicted natural person.[55] This has been criticised as stifling commerce, as it essentially cripples the future business activity of the convicted person, possibly beyond the length of the conviction[56] and the rehabilitation period and may be disproportionate in certain contexts. However, the punitive nature of disqualification in South Africa may inform this approach.

Unlike the US and World Bank, the Corruption Act is not clear on the position where the natural person's employment in the firm has been terminated. However, as the National Treasury has the power to vary or amend the terms of a disqualification,[57] it may be possible for the National Treasury to amend a disqualification where the natural person's connection with the firm has ceased.

The PFMA regulations adopt two approaches to the disqualification of a firm for the activity of a natural person. The mandatory PFMA disqualifications do not provide for the disqualification of a firm for the offence of a natural person, whilst the discretionary disqualifications provide that a firm may be disqualified where the firm or any of its directors have committed a relevant offence. This approach has its parallels in the UK where a firm will be disqualified for offences committed by decision-makers. Similar to the UK, the PFMA regulations are silent as to whether a firm will be disqualified where the director's employment with the firm has been terminated and establish the basis of the firm's disqualification as the commission of an offence by the director.

As is discussed below, the PPPFA regulations provide that natural persons may be disqualified for the corrupt activity of a firm, but do not provide for the disqualification of a firm for the corrupt activity of a natural person.

8.3.1.2 Disqualifying a natural person for the corrupt activity of a firm

The provisions imputing the conduct of a firm to a natural person are intended to prevent persons who have participated in corrupt practices or have powers of control or management over a firm from escaping the consequences of their actions by hiding behind the corporate veil.[58] The

[54] Corruption Act 2004, s 28(1)(c).
[55] Corruption Act 2004, s 28(1)(d).
[56] S Williams and G Quinot, 'Public Procurement and Corruption: The South African Response' (2007) 124 *South African Law Journal* 339.
[57] Corruption Act 2004, s 28(4)(a).
[58] See for example, *Robinson v Cheney*, 876 F2d 152 (DC Cir 1989).

approach is to disqualify natural persons who are regarded as being responsible for the corrupt activity in a firm, so that they are unable to obtain public contracts either in a personal capacity or through a new corporate identity. This may also increase the effectiveness of a disqualification measure as the culpable natural person will be unable to evade the effects of the disqualification. Also, where a jurisdiction is reluctant to impute criminal liability to a firm,[59] or it is difficult to convict a firm for corruption,[60] the disqualification of natural persons may be the only manner by which disqualification may be implemented.

The issues posed by the disqualification of natural persons for the offences of a firm are determining who the relevant natural persons are and the basis for the natural person's disqualification. This basis may be complicity in the commission of the offence, control, or the position of the person within the firm. In the jurisdictions, the relevant natural persons are sometimes, but not always those with decision-making powers in the firm such as directors, partners and senior managers.[61] However, the decision-making powers of such persons may vary with the size and nature of the firm in question, and a titled post may not necessarily be determinative of actual power exercised.[62]

Where a natural person is disqualified for the corrupt activity of a firm, the disqualification may be limited to the natural person in a personal capacity or may further prevent the natural person from obtaining public contracts through a new or existing corporate identity by extending the disqualification to other firms in which the natural person is involved.

As discussed above, the EU directives are silent on the disqualification of related persons and this also applies to the disqualification of a natural person for offences attributable to a firm. This silence relates both to the mandatory and discretionary disqualifications. Although the directives permit a procuring authority to obtain information on the convictions of directors and persons with powers of 'representation, decision and control' in the disqualification process, it is not clear whether a natural person who has not been convicted, but is a person with such powers over a firm may be disqualified for an offence attributed to a firm. The UK regulations, in implementing the directives, adopted a similar approach to the directives and do not mention the disqualification of a natural person for

[59] S Beale, 'A Response the Critics of Corporate Criminal Liability' (2009) 46 *American Criminal Law Review* 1481.

[60] The UK's SFO has admitted that it finds it difficult to prove corporate responsibility in corruption cases. Law Commission, Reforming Bribery Consultation Paper 313 (October 2008) 68.

[61] Pinto and Evans, *Corporate Criminal Liability*, 306. For instance, for a corporation to be liable for corruption in the UK, the prosecution needs to prove that the official had the necessary status and authority to make his acts the acts of the company. See *R v Andrews-Weatherfoil Ltd* (1972) 56 Cr App R 31.

[62] See for example, *Stone & Rolls Ltd v Moore Stephens* [2009] UKHL 39.

the conviction or offences of a firm.[63] Although the UK regulations require the disqualification of a firm where a relevant natural person has been convicted, the fact that the regulations are silent on the disqualification of a natural person for the offences of a firm may indicate that the UK regulations did not intend this to be the case. This omission may not be too problematic in practice as many corruption cases involving UK companies show that the courts are more likely to convict the natural persons in control of a firm and not the firm itself.[64] In other words, the courts often pierce the corporate veil where there is corruption or fraud. However, it must be stated that if this is indeed the UK approach, it runs counter to the Serious Crime Act 2007, which applies to corruption offences and provides that where an offence committed by a 'body corporate' is committed with the consent or connivance of an officer (defined to mean a director, manager or secretary), that person is also guilty of the offence.[65] Thus under the Serious Crime Act, where a firm is guilty of corruption, its culpable officers will also be guilty where they consented or connived in the commission of the offence.

In relation to the discretionary provisions in the EU and the UK, as stated, the legislation is silent on the extension of these disqualifications. As discussed above, some of the offences and circumstances that may lead to disqualification may only be committed by individuals (eg bankruptcy) and some may only be committed by firms (eg winding-up), and it is thus appropriate that the provisions do not contain blanket rules requiring extension in circumstances where this may not be appropriate. It seems likely therefore that procuring authorities have the discretion to decide if a natural person will be disqualified for the offences of the firm.

Finally, neither the EU nor the UK provisions extend the disqualification to other firms in which the natural person is involved. A similar approach is adopted by the US but the World Bank and South Africa extend disqualification to the successors and assigns of the offender and future businesses of a disqualified natural person respectively.

Unlike the position in the EU and UK, the US FAR provides for the disqualification of a natural person for offences committed by a firm.[66] Under the FAR, a person who is an officer, director, shareholder, partner, employee or other individual associated with a firm may be disqualified for the actions of the firm where the person participated in, knew of, or had reason to know of the firm's improper conduct.[67] The test to determine whether an

[63] *DPP v Kent & Sussex Contractors* [1944] KB 146.

[64] *R v Welcher & Others* [2007] EWCA 480; *R v Tumukunde & Tobiasen* (unreported 09.08); *R v Bush* [2003] EWCA Crim 1056; *R v Hinchliffe* [2002] EWCA Crim 2447; *R v Godden-Wood* [2001] EWCA Crim 1586; *R v Forsyth*, [2011] UKSC 9. See, however, *R v Mabey & Johnson* (unreported 25.9.09); *R v Innospec* [2010] Lloyds Rep FC 462.

[65] Serious Crime Act 2007, s 30.

[66] FAR 9.406-5(b).

[67] FAR 9.406-5(b); *Novicki v Cook*, 946 F2d 938 (DC Cir 1991).

individual 'had reason to know' of the cause for disqualification is not a strict liability test, and the duty imposed on the disqualifying official is to draw reasonable inferences from the information known to him.[68] This is a subjective test,[69] and without actual or 'blind-eye' knowledge, the conduct of a firm will not affect natural persons.[70] This approach is informed by the *respondeat superior* doctrine of corporate liability and is supported by the Department of Justice Principles for the Federal Prosecution of Business Organizations,[71] which require prosecutors to pursue action against a firm and the culpable individuals where an offence is committed by a firm.

As discussed above, the World Bank provides for the disqualification of affiliates, which includes natural persons who control or are controlled by disqualified companies.[72] The Bank is the only jurisdiction that appears to disqualify employees (natural persons controlled by a firm) without basing this on the employee's culpability and it is difficult to see why the disqualification of employees is warranted, unless there is evidence to show their complicity in the commission of the relevant offences, as is the case in the US. In the World Bank, a natural person may also be disqualified for the offences of a firm where the person exercises control over the firm. This may apply to decision-makers in the firm and Bank practice is that the Bank normally disqualifies directors, partners and senior personnel who control the disqualified company. This approach is similar to that of the US, except that in the Bank there is no requirement that the natural person knows of or participates in the corrupt activity, and compared to the US, a wider range of persons may be caught by the Bank's provisions.

South Africa also provides for the disqualification of a natural person for offences committed by a firm. The South African approach is similar to the US approach in that senior personnel may be disqualified where such personnel were involved in or knew of the corrupt activity. Thus, the Corruption Act provides for the disqualification of specified natural persons related to a convicted firm where the natural person's complicity in the offence is established. Under the Act, where a firm is convicted and disqualified by the court, the disqualification may be extended to any partner, manager, director or other person who wholly or partly exercises control over that firm, who was involved in the offence, or who knew or ought reasonably to have known or suspected that the firm committed the offence.[73] The Act thus uses the tests of control, complicity and know-

[68] *Novicki v Cook*, ibid, 941.

[69] FAR 9.406-5.

[70] J Cibinic and R Nash, *Formation of Government Contracts*, 3rd edn (Alphen aan den Rijn, Wolters Kluwer, 1998) 474; In *Facchiano Constr Co v Department of Labour*, 987 F2d 206 (3rd Cir 1993), the court held that the agency could disqualify 'responsible officers' of a contractor, but not officers who did not know about the misconduct.

[71] Available at: www.justice.gov.

[72] WBSP, art I s 1.02 and art IX s 9.04.

[73] Corruption Act 2004, s 28(1)(b)(ii).

ledge. The Corruption Act also applies the disqualification to every future firm of the disqualified natural person, if such firm is wholly or partly controlled or owned by the disqualified person.[74] As argued above, this may jeopardise the commercial future of such a person, and may be unduly punitive and disproportionate.

The PPPFA regulations also extend disqualification to natural persons and provide that where corruption has occurred in bidding for a public contract, the procuring authority may disqualify the supplier, its shareholders and directors or only the shareholders and directors involved in the fraudulent conduct. On the basis that directors of firms are required to be natural people,[75] this means a natural person may be disqualified for the offences of the firm The regulations are quite odd in designating on one hand the basis of the disqualification of the directors and the shareholders as their complicity in the offending conduct and in the same sentence also providing that the directors and shareholders can be disqualified without providing any basis for this. In such cases, it is not clear whether directors will be disqualified because they are directors (and control the activities of firm). However, a directive from the National Treasury suggests that such persons will be disqualified on the basis of the control exercised over the supplier.[76]

The extension of disqualification to shareholders is not found in the other jurisdictions and is quite odd, if one considers that a publicly-listed company may have thousands of shareholders, some of whom may be nominees who will only have a limited say in the company's affairs.[77] However, as the PPPFA regulations provide that a procuring authority may either disqualify the shareholders or only disqualify the shareholders who acted on a fraudulent basis,[78] it is suggested that procuring authorities should rely on the narrower, alternative provision and only disqualify where the shareholder was complicit in the commission of the offence. Although the regulations are silent on the basis of the shareholders' disqualification, the National Treasury directive provides some guidance and suggests that persons who have control over the firm may be disqualified.[79]

[74] Corruption Act 2004, s 23(1)(d).

[75] Companies Act 2008 (South Africa), s 69(7)(a).

[76] National Treasury Supply Chain Management Office Practice Note Number SCM 5 of 2006, Restriction of Suppliers, 9 October 2006, para 2.3.

[77] L Sealy and S Worthington, *Cases & Materials in Company Law*, 8th edn (Oxford, Oxford University Press, 2007) 170.

[78] PPPFA reg 13(2)(d).

[79] National Treasury Supply Chain Management Office Practice Note Number SCM 5 of 2006, Restriction of Suppliers, 9 October 2006, para 2.3.

8.3.1.3 Summary and Analysis

As can be seen, the jurisdictions adopt different approaches to the disqualification of a firm for the offences of a natural person and vice versa. However, there are certain issues which merit further discussion. The first issue is determining who are the natural persons whose convictions/offences ought to lead to the disqualification of a firm and similarly, which natural persons should be disqualified for the offences/conviction of a firm. In some jurisdictions, such as the US, the legislation has spelt this out with sufficient clarity, whilst in other jurisdictions a disqualifying entity is given the discretion to determine who these natural persons should be. Where the discretion rests with a disqualifying entity, the following guidelines may be adopted in determining whether a natural person ought to be disqualified.

- As a general rule, it is suggested that a firm should always be held responsible for the corrupt activities of its decision-makers, to provide an incentive for internal monitoring within the firm and also because in some instances, this may merely be a case of piercing the corporate veil to hold the firm liable for the actions of its decision-makers. Elements of this approach are found in all the jurisdictions under study and the importance of adopting such an approach was seen in a US case where a natural person was disqualified and the disqualification was not extended to the firm, the natural person merely transferred ownership of the firm to a family member in order to continue receiving government benefits.[80]
- Secondly, the offences or conviction of an employee should affect the firm where it is determined that the corrupt activities were primarily intended to benefit the firm. This approach is also reflected to a limited extent in the US and South Africa.
- Thirdly, a firm could be disqualified for the conviction of an employee where the conviction revealed an active and unchanged culture of corruption in the firm.[81] However, where a firm has terminated its connection with the corrupt and convicted employees, then as is discussed in chapter nine, the disqualification of the firm may no longer be necessary.

These guidelines may ensure that a jurisdiction does not go too far in extending disqualification but ensure also that firms cannot avoid the responsibility of implementing adequate internal anti-corruption processes. The use of these guidelines will, however, depend on whether a disqualification regime is mandatory or discretionary and the limits of the disqualifying entity's discretion in the disqualification of related persons.

[80] GAO, *Suspended and debarred businesses and individuals improperly receive federal funds* (GAO 09-174 Feb 2009) 4.

[81] Hetzer, 'Corruption as Business Practice', above n 11, 383; Ferguson, 'Corruption and Corporate Criminal Liability', above n 11.

The second issue requiring further discussion is guidance on determining whether a firm is controlled by a natural person. As has been seen, most jurisdictions rely on the test of control to determine whether a natural person ought to be disqualified for the offences of a firm. However, it is not clear what criteria a disqualifying entity may use to determine whether a natural person is indeed in control of a firm. Thus, can a natural person be said to be in control of a firm because that person is the main shareholder, or because the person holds a position of power or authority and is the/a main decision-maker, or is control based on an identity of interest between the natural person and the firm? This may not be easily determined. For instance, in the UK, although the directors of a company have day-to-day control over the company, it is arguable that it is the shareholders who really control a company,[82] as they appoint the directors and can remove them[83] and may also give the directors direction by means of a special resolution.[84] In a small company, the directors will often be majority shareholders and owners of the company, but in a large corporation, there may be a clear division between the directors and the shareholders. In such cases, how will a disqualifying entity determine who is in control of a firm? Will it be those in day-to-day control of the company, or those who have overall supervision over the decision-makers? Further, will a disqualifying entity take into account the position of de facto and shadow directors in determining who controls a company?[85]

One approach that may be relied upon by a disqualifying entity is to disqualify the natural persons who directly authorised/approved the actions that led to the commission of the offence or the conviction of the firm. This approach finds support in the UK Enterprise Act 2002, which provides that a person controls a company where he can materially influence its policy, even if he does not have a controlling interest in it.[86] Of course this criterion may not always work, as in a large multinational it may not always be possible to identify this person and it has in fact been argued that some firms contrive to avoid this type of liability by decentralising responsibilities to make it impossible to identify a person in charge of any matter.[87]

[82] See however, *Automatic Self-Cleansing Filter Syndicate Co Ltd v Cunninghame* [1906] 2 Ch 34.

[83] Companies Act 2006 (UK), s 168.

[84] Draft articles of association, art 70, Table A Companies Act 2006.

[85] In the UK, a de facto director is one who has not been formally appointed but in fact acts as a director: *Re Kaytech International Plc* [1999] BCC 390 (CA); a shadow director is usually a shareholder who in order to avoid the duties of a director avoids a formal appointment, but controls the decisions of the formally appointed board: *Re Hydrodam (Corby) Ltd* [1994] BCC 161.

[86] Enterprise Act 2002, s 26.

[87] E Ferran, 'Corporate Attribution and the Directing Mind and Will' (2011) 127 *Law Quarterly Review* 239.

A third issue is the extent of disqualification where a natural person such as a director is disqualified for the offences of a firm. Should other firms or future firms in which this natural person is/may be interested also be affected by the disqualification? If these other companies are not disqualified, the disqualification of the director may have little effect, as he may still be able to access public contracts using his other corporate entities. However, an approach that disqualifies these other entities or firms may be problematic for three reasons. First because of the extensive investigations that a disqualifying entity may need to conduct to discover the companies which are related to the director, especially where future business is concerned. Secondly because the basis of these firms' disqualification will need to be determined – will it be the control or ownership the director exercises over them? Thirdly, the disqualification of these firms may be too remote from the commission of the initial offence and their disqualification may penalise employees and investors that may not be related to the original disqualified firm, except through their connection with the director and thus may be disproportionate to the aims of the disqualification policy.

8.3.2 Connected Companies

Connected companies are defined in this book to mean sister, parent, and subsidiary companies. A connected company is one that is related to another through shared ownership or control in the sense that the same entity controls two separate companies, or one entity controls another, or two or more entities share a management structure.[88] Connected companies are often included in the list of related persons to be disqualified alongside the primary supplier. The basis for the disqualification of a connected company may be the complicity of the connected company in the commission of the offence; the level of control which the connected company wields over the disqualified company or vice versa; inter-connected ownership structures such as where a third entity controls both the disqualified primary supplier and the connected company; or because there is an identity of management and operations and the connected company is an integral part of the disqualified supplier.

The issues presented by the disqualification of connected companies are similar to the issues presented in the case of natural persons, however as will be discussed, trying to ascertain the relationship between connected companies can often be a daunting task, especially where a company has undergone restructuring following corruption issues or disqualification proceedings.

[88] Companies Act 2008 (South Africa), s 2; Companies Act 2006 (UK), s 1159.

8.3.2.1 Disqualifying a parent company for the offences of a subsidiary

A parent company may be defined as a company that owns enough voting stock in another firm to control the management and operations of that firm (the subsidiary). The definition of a parent company may differ between jurisdictions, but it is usually defined by reference to factors such as the parent being able to determine the composition of the board of directors of the subsidiary; controlling the voting power of the subsidiary or owning more than half of the issued share capital of the subsidiary.[89]

A parent company may be disqualified from public contracts for offences committed by a subsidiary on the basis of the level of control exercised by the parent over the subsidiary, which makes the parent responsible for the offences of the subsidiary. However, a parent may not always exercise the kind of control over the subsidiary that would justify the imposition of disqualification, since the directors of a subsidiary are required to act independently for, and in the interests of the subsidiary.[90] To disqualify a parent, a disqualifying entity will first need to identify the parent company. This may not always be easy, as a parent may be a holding company whose shares may be owned by the beneficial owners of the company or a trust company, making it difficult to determine the precise entities controlling the subsidiary. Secondly, the disqualifying entity will have to determine the basis of the parent's disqualification. If the basis is complicity in the commission of the offence and not control/ownership, the extent of this complicity may need to be determined by an investigation into the parent's role in the offence.

In the EU, the directives are silent on the issue of connected companies in relation to the mandatory and the discretionary provisions and this may mean the issue is left to Member States discretion. One indication that Member States may rightly exercise this discretion in relation to the mandatory provisions is the provision permitting Member States to obtain information on convictions from legal and natural persons, including company directors and persons having powers of representation, decision and control of the contractor.[91] In relation to the discretionary disqualification provisions, as the directives omitted to mention the convictions of other persons, including legal persons, in the same manner as was done for the mandatory provisions, this may either mean that connected persons are not intended to be disqualified under the discretionary provisions or that this issue has been left to the discretion of Member States. As it is not clear in relation to the mandatory provisions whether or in what contexts a procuring authority may disqualify a parent, limited guidance

[89] Companies Act 2008 (South Africa), s 3; Companies Act 2006 (UK), s 1162.
[90] For instance, in the UK see *Charterbridge Corp v Lloyds Bank* [1970] Ch 62, 74.
[91] PSD, art 45(1).

may be found from EU jurisprudence in other contexts which has held parent companies liable for the legal infringements of a subsidiary.

It should be noted that the directives permit the use of subsidiary companies in public contracts under provisions allowing a supplier to rely on the capacities of other entities, regardless of the nature of the legal links it has with them.[92] These provisions require a procuring authority to look beyond the corporate shell where a parent relies on the assets of a subsidiary to qualify for a contract. In *Ballast Nedam Groep I*[93] the CJEU held that account must be taken of the companies belonging to a holding company where it applies for a public contract, provided that it actually has the resources of the subsidiaries available to it.

EU law is also acquainted in other contexts with going behind the corporate veil to hold a parent company liable for the actions of its subsidiary.[94] In *Tokai Carbon*,[95] the CJEU held a parent company and its subsidiary jointly liable for alleged anti-competitive acts, imputing the acts of one company to the other.[96] Similarly, it is possible for a disqualifying entity to look beyond the corporate shell in deciding whether to disqualify a parent for a subsidiary's convictions.

The factors which the CJEU has taken into account in determining that a parent and subsidiary consist of a single economic entity so as to hold the parent responsible for the actions of the subsidiary include the fact that the companies form part of a 'unitary organisation of personal, tangible and intangible elements' pursuing specific economic aims that are determined in the same way.[97] The CJEU will also find a parent responsible for the actions of a wholly-owned subsidiary, as a presumption exists that the subsidiary follows instructions given by the parent, without actually confirming whether the parent exercised this power.[98] However, the court will also consider whether the parent has itself committed an infringement of the rules, either in its own right or through the subsidiary, before holding it liable for the actions of its subsidiary.[99] In *Tokai Carbon*, the Commission argued that a parent's responsibility for the acts of the subsidiary is based on the theory of economic unity and not on any separate legal concept of 'attribution'.[100] In other words, a parent company is not liable because it is a parent, but rather where specified criteria are satisfied in relation to its interaction with the subsidiary.

[92] PSD, art 48(3).

[93] Case C-389/92, *Ballast Nedam Groep NV v Belgian State* [1994] ECR I-1289, para 17.

[94] Joined Cases T-71/03, T74/03, T-87/03 and T-91/03, *Tokai Carbon v Commission* [2005] 5 ECR II-10.

[95] *Tokai Carbon*, ibid.

[96] Case T-9/99, *HFB v Commission* [2002] ECR II-1487 para 54, 524–5.

[97] *HFB v Commission*, above n 96, paras 53–54.

[98] *Tokai Carbon*, above n 94. Case C-294/98P *Metsa-Serla Oyj & Others v Commission* [2000] ECR I-10065. Opinion of AG Mischo para 60.

[99] Case T-65/89 *BPB Industries & Another v Commission* [1993] ECR II-389, paras 149, 153.

[100] *Tokai Carbon*, above n 94, para 384.

From the above, one can arguably extrapolate the following principles in suggesting an EU approach in relation to the mandatory disqualifications. First, if the subsidiary is an agent of the parent, its actions will be imputed to the parent in so far as the subsidiary was acting within the scope of its authority.[101] However, this may be very difficult for a procuring authority applying the disqualifications to establish in any particular case. Secondly, if the subsidiary is not an agent, but is controlled by the parent to the extent that the two units consist of a single business enterprise, the subsidiary's conviction may be imputed to the parent. Thirdly, if the subsidiary operates independently of the parent company, there is no basis for imputing the conviction to the parent, unless one accepts the argument that a parent corporation should know and be liable for whatever is being done in its name.[102]

The UK regulations in implementing the directives do not explicitly mention the position of parent companies, but provide that the supplier will be disqualified for its own convictions as well as where 'any other person who has powers of representation, decision or control' has been convicted. Since the meaning of 'person' in UK law includes legal persons,[103] this provision may be interpreted as applying to parent companies (legal persons with powers of decision or control). In relation to imposing liability on a parent for acts of a subsidiary, UK jurisprudence has established, similar to EU jurisprudence discussed above, that a parent may be responsible for the actions of a subsidiary where the subsidiary is subservient to the will of the parent and is essentially its alter-ego.[104]

Although a literal interpretation of the UK procurement regulations may give rise to an interpretation that parent companies may be disqualified for the offences of a subsidiary, the OGC Guidance is against this interpretation and states that the convictions of 'persons with powers of representation, decision or control' relates to natural persons and not parent or subsidiary companies that are separate legal entities.[105] Although the OGC Guidance is not prescriptive, in the absence of any other direction, procuring authorities are likely to follow the Guidance. Whilst the OGC's approach is realistic, given that it may be prohibitively expensive for a procuring authority to investigate the networks of company ownership,[106] and such investigations may also delay the procurement

[101] Joined Cases T 339/94–342/94, *Metsa-Serla v Commission* [1998] ECR II-1727, paras 58–59 and Case C-294/98P, *Metsa-Serla Oyj v Commission* [2000] ECR I-10065, para 27.

[102] G Caiden, 'A Cautionary Tale: Ten Major Flaws in Combating Corruption' (2004) 10 *South Western Journal of Law and Trade in the Americas* 269, 276.

[103] Schedule 1, Interpretation Act 1978.

[104] *Lonrho Ltd v Shell Petroleum Ltd* [1980] 1 WLR 627; *Greene King Plc v Harlow District Council* [2003] EWHC 2852.

[105] OGC Guidance, para 4.1.

[106] Anechiarico and Jacobs, 'Purging Corruption from Public Contracting', above n 1, 162–72.

process, this approach may affect the effectiveness of the disqualifications in practice.[107] Further, the OGC's limitation of persons in control of a supplier to natural persons may run counter to the provisions of the Enterprise Act 2002, which provides that enterprises will not be regarded as being distinct entities if they are brought under common control or common ownership and further, that a person or group of persons who is able, directly or indirectly, to control or materially influence the policy of a body corporate, but without having a controlling interest in that body corporate or in that enterprise, will be regarded as having control of it.[108] Thus, if the meaning of entities under the Enterprise Act were applied to the disqualification provisions, parent companies in some instances may be regarded as being in control of subsidiaries, making them liable to disqualification.

As will be seen, the US, the World Bank and South Africa provide for the disqualification of a parent company for the actions of its subsidiary and use the test of control to determine whether the parent ought to be disqualified. The US approach is, however, more comprehensive than the approach in the other jurisdictions. In the US, the FAR provides that disqualification affects all divisions or other organisational elements of the contractor, unless the disqualification is limited to specific divisions/elements.[109] Some of the factors that may determine whether entities such as parent companies will be disqualified include 'whether the level and extent of the misconduct is an isolated incident or a systemic problem . . . the corporate culture; and the relationship among the company's various units'.[110]

A disqualifying entity also has the discretion to disqualify the contractor's affiliates,[111] which is defined as an organisation that controls or is controlled by a supplier, or a third party that controls both the supplier and another organisation. Thus, a parent company comes within the definition of affiliate. The basis of the parent's disqualification in the US is the control it exercises over the disqualified supplier and not ownership. The adoption of control and not ownership as the basis for disqualification stems from a recognition that it is possible to control the activities of a separate firm without owning a majority interest in that firm. The FAR also lists the factors indicating one entity controls another.[112] These include interlocking management or ownership;[113] an identity of interests amongst

[107] ibid.

[108] Enterprise Act 2002, s 26.

[109] FAR 9.406-1(b).

[110] R Bednar (ed), *The Practitioner's Guide to Suspension and Debarment*, 3rd edn (American Bar Association, 2002) 86.

[111] FAR 9.406-1(b).

[112] FAR 9.403.

[113] *Detek Inc*, Comp Gen Dec B-261678, 95-2 CPD ¶ 177.

family members;[114] shared facilities and equipment; common use of employees or the reorganisation of a business following a disqualification where the management, ownership or principal employees are similar to that of the disqualified supplier.[115]

In the US, the disqualification of a parent company is not based on the parent's participation/knowledge of the corrupt activity but is a matter of objective assessment once it is established that the parent wields the required control over the subsidiary. However, knowing whether a parent ought to be disqualified in such cases is not always simple and in *Bilfinger Berger v United States*,[116] the procuring authority excluded a parent and another related company from a public contract based on the prior disqualification of a subsidiary. The companies had undergone an inter-group transfer and restructuring in which the contracts being performed by the disqualified subsidiary were transferred to a 'branch' of the parent company. In making its decision, the procuring authority complained that it could not identify the 'lines of authority' between the companies. The GAO accepted the determination of the procuring authority to exclude the parent, but this decision was ultimately overturned by the Court of Federal Claims (COFC).

The World Bank adopts an approach similar to that of the US, and uses the test of control to determine if a parent company should be disqualified. The Bank may disqualify any 'affiliate', which is defined to include any legal person that controls the offender.[117] Thus, a parent company which controls a disqualified subsidiary may also be disqualified. Similar to the US, the World Bank does not include any subjective criteria such as the knowledge or participation of the parent for the disqualification of the parent.

Similarly, in South Africa, the Corruption Act provides that in addition to the primary offender, a court may disqualify any other person who wholly or partly exercises or may exercise control over that firm and who was involved in the offence concerned; or who knew or ought reasonably to have known or suspected that the firm committed the offence.[118] This may be interpreted as providing for the disqualification of parent companies, as section 28(7) of the Corruption Act defines a person to include legal persons. The basis of a parent's disqualification is the control the parent wields over the subsidiary or the parent's knowledge/complicity in the offence.

Unlike the Corruption Act, the PPPFA regulations are not clear on the issue of parent companies being disqualified for the offences of a

114 *ALB Indus, Inc*, Comp Gen Dec B-207335, 82-2 CPD ¶ 119.
115 FAR 9.403; *Solid Waste Servs Inc*, Comp Gen Dec B-218445, 85-1 CPD ¶ 703.
116 *Bilfinger Berger v United States* 94 Fed Cl 538 (2010).
117 WBSP, art I s 1.02 and art IX s 9.04.
118 Corruption Act 2004, s 28(1)(b).

subsidiary. However, the PPPFA regulations provide that a disqualifying entity may disqualify the supplier and its culpable and non-culpable shareholders (and directors) from public contracts where a relevant offence is committed. This may be interpreted as providing for the disqualification of parent companies who are shareholders in the offending company. However, as was discussed in the context of natural persons, the basis of the non-culpable shareholder's disqualification is not treated under the regulations, but is contained in a practice note issued by the National Treasury, which practice note also provides for the disqualification of persons in control of a supplier, where that person or firm is 'actively associated' with the supplier.[119]

The PFMA regulations only permit the disqualification of the supplier and its directors and do not provide for the disqualification of parent companies.

8.3.2.2 Disqualifying a subsidiary company for the offences of a parent

Apart from the possibility of disqualifying a parent for offences committed by a subsidiary, a subsidiary may be disqualified for offences committed by the parent. A subsidiary is defined as a company in which another entity (the parent) owns more than 50 per cent of its voting stock.[120] The disqualification of a subsidiary may ensure that the disqualified parent is unable to avoid the effects of the disqualification by relying on an entity it controls for public contracts. Again, for the disqualification of a subsidiary, a disqualifying entity will need to identify the subsidiary and the basis for the subsidiary's disqualification, although this will usually be the control which the disqualified parent exercises over the subsidiary.

The legislative provisions on disqualification in the EU are silent on whether a subsidiary company will be disqualified for the offences of its parent, and as previously mentioned, this issue has been left to Member States' discretion. Relying on the EU jurisprudence discussed above, it is suggested that Member States may adopt an approach similar to what obtains in relation to parent companies. Thus, a subsidiary may be affected by the conviction of a parent where it is decided that the two units comprise a single business unit and because of the level of control which the parent is deemed to exercise over the subsidiary.[121]

The US and the World Bank adopt a similar approach and disqualification extends to the affiliates of the disqualified firm, which includes any

[119] National Treasury Supply Chain Management Office Practice Note Number SCM 5 of 2006, Restriction of Suppliers, 9 October 2006, para 2.3

[120] Companies Act 2008 (South Africa), s 3; Companies Act 2006 (UK), s 1162.

[121] S Williams, 'The Mandatory Exclusions for Corruption in the new EC Procurement Directives' (2006) 31 *European Law Review*, 711, 724.

firm controlled by the disqualified firm.[122] Also, in the US, in the context of responsibility determinations, the COFC has held that a procuring authority could exclude a subsidiary based on the violations of a parent company, although another procuring authority had previously elected not to disqualify the parent for its offences.[123]

In the UK, as discussed above, the procurement regulations have been interpreted by the OGC Guidance as precluding the disqualification of subsidiaries or other legal persons that are legally distinct from the primary contractor.[124] Although procuring authorities are likely to follow this Guidance, they are not bound by it and may adopt an approach that accords with UK jurisprudence, under which companies may be liable for each other's actions where the companies are in essence each other's alter egos.[125]

In the South African system, only the Corruption Act permits the disqualification of a subsidiary by permitting the courts to disqualify any firm which is owned or controlled by the convicted supplier.[126] The Corruption Act goes further than the other jurisdictions by permitting a court to also disqualify a firm established in the future by the convicted parent, if that future firm is wholly or partly controlled or owned by the person convicted.[127]

8.3.2.3 *Disqualifying a firm for the offences of a sister company*

A sister company is an entity that is owned by the same principal that owns the disqualified firm. The disqualification of a firm for offences committed by its 'sister' is not particularly favoured by the jurisdictions but where sister companies are disqualified, the rationale for doing so is to prevent the principal of the disqualified firm from assisting it to avoid the effects of its disqualification by bidding through a sister company.

In the EU, as previously mentioned, the procurement directives are silent on this issue, but direction on the EU's future approach may be found in its jurisprudence. Current European jurisprudence is not wholly in favour of imputing the actions of sister companies to each other, unless strong grounds exist for doing so. In *HFB v Commission*, it was held that where there was no holding company co-ordinating the activity of a group of companies the component companies could be held jointly and severally liable for a legal infringement.[128] However, this would only occur where there was

122 *Bilfinger Berger*, above n 116; FAR 9.403; WBSP, art I s 1.02 and art IX s 9.04.
123 *OSG Product Tankers v United States* 82 Fed Cl 570 (2008).
124 OGC Guidance, para 3 2.
125 *Lonrho*, above n 104.
126 Corruption Act 2004, s 28(1)(a).
127 Corruption Act 2004, s 28(1)(d).
128 Case T-9/99, *HFB v Commission* [2002] ECR II-1487, para 66.

either no person at the head of the group to which the violations of the group might be imputed or it was 'impossible or excessively difficult to identify the person at the head of the group'.[129] Thus, by way of analogy, it is arguable that in the disqualification context, the conviction of a sister or related company will not affect the primary supplier as long as the convicted company is not participating in the contract; unless it is determined that the companies constitute a single business enterprise.

As has been discussed above, the UK regulations as interpreted by the OGC, limit disqualification to natural persons. However, as discussed earlier, the OGC Guidance is not prescriptive and procuring authorities may adopt an approach in line with UK jurisprudence in which the veil of incorporation may be pierced where necessary.[130]

Unlike the EU and UK, the US and World Bank regulations expressly permit the disqualification of sister companies. The FAR and the World Bank Sanctions Procedures extend disqualification to 'affiliates' of the disqualified company, which are defined to include sister companies or entities controlled by the same entity that controls a disqualified contractor.[131] The US regulations provide more detail than the World Bank provisions and provide that a sister company may be disqualified for the offence of a primary supplier where the necessary connection exists between the entities.[132] A necessary connection will exist where there is interlocking management or ownership;[133] an identity of interests amongst family members;[134] shared facilities and equipment; or common use of employees.[135]

The South African provisions do not contemplate the disqualification of sister companies. In South Africa, it is not clear why a firm established in the future will be disqualified under the provisions of the Corruption Act, whilst a sister firm will retain access to public contracts, since the only difference between a sister company and a firm established in future, where both are owned by the same principals that own the convicted firm, is in their respective dates of establishment.[136]

8.3.2.4 Summary and Analysis

As can been seen, there are varied approaches to the disqualification of connected companies. The disqualification of related connected companies is a complex issue which creates several problems, which are not all addressed by the jurisdictions.

[129] ibid.
[130] *DHN Food Distributors Ltd v Tower Hamlets London Borough Council* [1976] 1 WLR 852.
[131] FAR 9.403; WBSP, Art I s 1.02.
[132] FAR 9.406-1(b).
[133] *Detek Inc*, Comp Gen Dec B-261678, 95-2 CPD ¶ 177.
[134] *ALB Indus, Inc*, Comp Gen Dec B-207335, 82-2 CPD ¶ 119.
[135] FAR 9.403; *Solid Waste Servs, Inc*, Comp Gen Dec B-218445, 85-1 CPD ¶ 703.
[136] Williams and Quinot, 'Public Procurement and Corruption', above n 56, 353.

One issue that may prove problematic is the application of the test of control, which is relied on to determine whether a parent, subsidiary or sister company ought to be disqualified alongside a primary supplier. Apart from the US, none of the jurisdictions provide disqualifying entities with any guidance on how to determine whether the necessary connection exists between related companies for the purpose of disqualification. This is particularly so where the test of control is used in parent/subsidiary cases. It is suggested, therefore, that disqualifying entities in other jurisdictions may rely on similar criteria to the US to determine if the necessary level of control exists. Criteria such as interlocking management (such as where the same persons are directors in both companies) or ownership may assist in properly determining whether one company controls another. In practice, it may be difficult where the parent is a holding company whose shares are in turn held by another entity to determine whether one company is ultimately in control of another.

Where the disqualification of a related company is based on the knowledge or complicity of the related company in the commission of the offence, as is the case in South Africa, the disqualifying entity may be required to investigate the connected company's involvement in the commission of the offence. Determining the connected company's knowledge of the offence will also be difficult, as the disqualifying entity may be required to discover the persons in connected firms whose knowledge may be identified as the knowledge of that firm.

Another issue that merits discussion is the proportionality of disqualifying related firms where these firms were not implicated in any wrongdoing, especially where disqualification is not intended to be punitive. As was discussed, the disqualification of related firms may affect the business, investors and employees of a firm that has not committed any wrongdoing and in the long term may discourage investment in firms specialising in government business.

Finally, none of the jurisdictions apart from the US are clear on the position where a related company terminates its connection with the offending company, such as where it divests itself of the offending company.[137] This is similar to the issue of the termination of the employment of the offender in the context of natural persons. A jurisdiction may consider such divestment as precluding the necessity to disqualify the related person[138] but such divestment may not always mean that the related company will be readmitted to a procurement process.[139] Thus in the US, the courts have held that where a supplier was disqualified based on its relationship to another disqualified firm, the procuring authority was not required to readmit the supplier to the procurement process although

[137] FAR 9.406-4(c).

[138] *Bilfinger Berger*, above n 116.

[139] FAR 9.405(d)(3).

the disqualification was lifted prior to the conclusion of the procurement process.[140]

8.3.3 Cooperating Companies

The final category of related persons that may be disqualified alongside a primary supplier is cooperating companies. Cooperating companies are defined here as subcontractors and joint venture partners who are connected by virtue of a voluntary business arrangement. In relation to cooperating companies, a disqualifying entity will need to identify the relevant cooperating company and determine the basis for the disqualification of the cooperating company. The issues that affect cooperating companies are whether a primary supplier will be disqualified for an offence committed by a subcontractor and whether joint venture partners will be disqualified for each other's offences. The disqualification of subcontractors and joint venture partners is given the least attention in the jurisdictions and where this is the case, it may be necessary to consider the approach to the liability of cooperating companies in other contexts.

8.3.3.1 Subcontractors

A subcontractor is a person hired by a primary supplier to perform part or even all of the obligations of the supplier under a public contract. The issue here is whether a primary supplier will be disqualified where it intends to utilise a subcontractor that has been disqualified, or has committed or been convicted of relevant offences. For the disqualification of a primary supplier on the basis of the subcontractor's offences, two hurdles must be overcome. First, the disqualifying entity will need to know in advance the identity of the subcontractor and secondly, the disqualifying entity may need to have reserved a right to approve or veto the subcontractors that will participate in a contract. This may be difficult, as a primary supplier is not always required to reveal the details of subcontractors when it bids for a public contract.

The EU procurement directives are silent on the issue of subcontractors, in relation to both the discretionary and the mandatory disqualifications and it is thus necessary to consider the treatment of subcontractors in European jurisprudence to determine whether a primary supplier will be disqualified if it intends to use a convicted subcontractor under the mandatory provisions. Although the directives generally permit contractors to insist on the use of subcontractors, the fact of subcontracting will not limit

[140] *FAS Support Services LLC v United States* 93 Fed Cl 687 (2010).

the primary supplier's liability under the contract[141] and restrictions on subcontracting may be justified where the procuring authority cannot verify the ability of the subcontractor to perform.[142] In relation to the disqualifications, if a procuring authority is aware of the subcontractor's conviction, the subcontractor will of course be disqualified since the text of the directives disqualifies convicted persons from *participation* in a public contract. Where a primary supplier insists on the use of a convicted subcontractor, this should be regarded as indicating the incapability of the primary supplier to perform on the contract,[143] prejudicing its ability to participate in the procurement, especially where the primary supplier relies on the subcontractor's qualifications as a means of fulfilling the technical/financial requirements under the contract.[144] Where procuring authorities reserve the right to approve or veto subcontractors,[145] Piselli suggests that procuring authorities should use this power to prevent convicted companies avoiding public control by working as subcontractors on public contracts.[146]

In relation to the discretionary disqualifications, similar considerations may apply. Where the subcontractor has been convicted or is guilty of a relevant offence, that subcontractor may be precluded from participating in a public contract under the EU directives and may prejudice a primary supplier's participation in the contract.

Thus, although the EU directives are silent on the issue, European jurisprudence provides grounds to establish that a proposed subcontractor's conviction may affect the primary supplier, in which case, the primary supplier may not be disqualified,[147] but rather denied the contract on the grounds that it does not meet the technical/financial requirements to qualify for the contract because of the presence of a disqualified subcontractor.[148] However, where a procuring authority is not aware of the identity of proposed subcontractors and does not reserve a power to approve or veto them at a later date, there may be no way of preventing the participation of a convicted subcontractor in a public contract.

[141] PSD, art 25.

[142] Case C-176/98, *Holst Italia SpA v Comune di Cagliari* [1999] ECR I-8607 paras 28–29; Case C-314/01, *Siemens AG Osterreich, ARGE Telekom & Partner v Hauptverband der Osterreichischen Sozialversicherungstrager Bietergemeinschaft EDS*/ORGA [2004] ECR I-2549.

[143] PSD, art 48.

[144] Arrowsmith, *The Law of Public and Utilities Procurement*, 2nd edn (London, Sweet & Maxwell, 2005) ch 12; P Trepte, *Regulating Procurement: Understanding the Ends and Means of Public Procurement Regulation* (Oxford, Oxford University Press, 2004) 319.

[145] Arrowsmith, *Public and Utilities Procurement*, above n 144, ch 6.190.

[146] E Piselli, 'The Scope for Excluding Providers who have Committed Criminal Offences under the EU Procurement Directives' (2000) 6 *Public Procurement Law Review* 267, 281.

[147] ibid.

[148] Case C-5/97, *Ballast Nedam Groep NV v Belgian State* [1997] ECR I-7549, para 13; B Shannon, 'Debarment and Suspension Revisited: Fewer Eggs in the Basket' (1995) 44 *Catholic University Law Review* 363, 382.

The UK regulations did not go any further than the EU directives and do not mention the disqualification of subcontractors. In the UK, a supplier may be required to reveal the part of the contract which is intended to be subcontracted as well as the identity of its subcontractors.[149] In relation to the mandatory and the discretionary provisions, where the procuring authority is aware of the identity of the subcontractor and is aware that the subcontractor has been convicted or is otherwise guilty of corruption, the subcontractor may be prevented from participating in a public contract. In *R (On the application of A) v B Council*,[150] the court held that a local Council could deny a supplier permission to use a convicted subcontractor on a public contract. The OGC Guidance document also suggests that procuring authorities may ask an economic operator not to use a subcontractor that has a relevant conviction.[151] Thus, a procuring authority has the power to veto the use of a convicted subcontractor on a public contract. This does not necessarily mean that the primary supplier will be disqualified, but it will not be permitted to use the convicted/guilty subcontractor, and where it insists on the use of that subcontractor, then as was discussed in the context of the EU above, the primary supplier may not qualify for the contract on this basis.

Unlike the EU and the UK, in the US, the presence of a disqualified subcontractor may not necessarily prevent a primary supplier from obtaining a public contract but there are certain restrictions on the use of disqualified subcontractors. It used to be the case that a disqualified firm could be used as a subcontractor where the contract was not over a certain threshold and did not require government consent. However in 2010, Congress amended the Federal Acquisition Streamlining Act 1994 to require that disqualification be extended to all subcontracts at any tier, except where commercial items are concerned, in which case, disqualification will extend only to first tier subcontracts.[152] The FAR was subsequently amended to reflect this change.

The FAR provides restrictions on subcontracting with a disqualified contractor in two instances. First, a disqualified firm may be not be used as a subcontractor where the subcontract requires government consent unless the head of the procuring authority states in writing 'compelling reasons' for approving the subcontract.[153] Secondly, unless the subcontract is one for 'commercially available off-the-shelf items', a primary contractor may not enter into a subcontract with a value in excess of US$30,000 with a disqualified subcontractor unless there is a compelling reason to do

[149] PCR reg 45.
[150] *R (on the application of A) v B Council* [2007] EWHC 1529 (Admin).
[151] OGC Guidance, para 4.1.
[152] National Defence Authorization Act 2010, s 815.
[153] FAR 9.405-2(b). A subcontract may require consent depending on the type, complexity, or value, or because the subcontract needs special surveillance. See FAR 44.201-1.

so.[154] Where a primary contractor proposes to enter into a subcontract with a disqualified contractor for non-commercially available goods, the primary contractor must notify the procuring authority before concluding such subcontracts, stating the compelling reasons for doing so and the measures it has taken to protect the government's interest in view of the reasons behind the subcontractor's disqualification.[155] However, a primary supplier runs the risk of being declared non-responsible if significant purchases are to be made from a disqualified subcontractor, or the disqualified subcontractor will play an excessive role in the performance of the contract.[156]

The World Bank procurement guidelines require the highest standard of ethics from suppliers and subcontractors[157] whose details are included in a bid for a Bank-funded contract.[158] In the context of the Bank's one-off disqualification measure, where the proposal for the award of a contract is rejected by the Bank, the Bank procurement guidelines provide that all the bidders, including subcontractors, will be disqualified from the contract.[159] This is because where a bid included the particulars of subcontractors[160] and the bid is rejected, any subcontractors included in that bid will also be affected as it is impossible to separate the contactors who are reliant on each other's expertise to submit a successful bid. A supplier disqualified by the Bank cannot act as a subcontractor in future contracts as such a person is not permitted to participate in any Bank-funded contracts for the period of its disqualification.[161]

The South African legislation is silent as to the disqualification of subcontractors, but the South African approach may be similar to that of the EU and the UK and a subcontractor who is guilty of a relevant offence will be precluded from participating in a public contract.[162] In South Africa, the use of subcontractors is permitted in public contracts,[163] in so far as the subcontracting is done in accordance with the terms of the contract. Although the Corruption Act is silent on the issue of subcontractors, where a procuring authority is presented with a primary supplier wishing to rely on a disqualified subcontractor, the procuring authority will be

[154] FAR 9.405-2; 52.209-6.

[155] FAR 9.405-2(b); 52.209-6.

[156] Cibinic and Nash, *Formation,* above n 70, 486; Shannon, 'Debarment and Suspension Revisited', above n 148, 382.

[157] BPG, para 1.16.

[158] World Bank, Standard Procurement Document: Prequalification Document for Procurement of Works and Users Guide (2004), cll 4 and 24 [hereafter Prequalification Document for Works].

[159] BPG, para 1.16(b).

[160] Prequalification Document for Works, ibid cl 25.

[161] BPG, para 1.16(d).

[162] Cf P Bolton, 'The Exclusion of Contractors from Government Contract Awards' (2006) 10 *Law, Development, Democracy* 25.

[163] PPPFA reg 1(n).

required to refuse a contract to such a primary contractor, where the identity of the subcontractor is known to the procuring authority. This is because the Corruption Act obliges procuring authorities to ignore *any offer* tendered by a person who is disqualified and prohibits procuring authorities from making any offer to or obtaining any *agreement* from a disqualified person.[164] This may be interpreted as prohibiting a public body from entering into a contract that involves a disqualified subcontractor. A subcontractor's disqualification will come to light when a procuring authority examines the Register of Tender Defaulters before awarding a contract, in cases where the identity of the subcontractor is revealed to the procuring authority during the procurement process.

The PPPFA Regulations are also silent on the issue of subcontractors. However, a firm disqualified under the PPPFA regulations may not act as a subcontractor in another contract, as the disqualified person is prevented from 'obtaining business' from any procuring authority for the period of its disqualification. As is the case under the Corruption Act, the subcontractor's disqualification will come to light where the procuring authority examines the Database of Restricted Suppliers in cases where the subcontractor's details have been revealed to the procuring authority.

The PFMA regulations are similarly silent on the issue of subcontractors. Whilst the disqualification of a bidder under the PFMA will affect all subcontractors included in that bid, the disqualification will not affect the ability of the disqualified primary supplier and any subcontractors from obtaining public contracts in future, since the disqualifications are limited to a particular procurement process.

8.3.3.2 *Joint ventures*

A joint venture (JV) denotes cooperation between commercial entities that is not a partnership, and is defined by reference to factors such as an agreement to associate for joint profit; a contribution of money, property, knowledge or skill to a common undertaking; a right to participate in the management and profits of the enterprise; a duty to share in losses; and a limitation to a single undertaking.[165] The World Bank defines a JV as an 'ad-hoc association of firms that pool their resources and skills to undertake a large or complex contract'.[166] A JV arrangement may involve the creation of a new company, the JV company or may merely be a contractual agreement between existing parties.[167]

[164] Corruption Act 2004, s 28(3)(a)(iii).
[165] I Hewitt, *Joint Ventures*, 4th edn (London, Sweet and Maxwell, 2008) ch 1.
[166] Glossary to World Bank Prequalification Document for Works, above n 158.
[167] P Trepte *Public Procurement in the EU: A Practitioner's Guide*, 2nd edn (Oxford, Oxford University Press, 2007) 49.

Two scenarios are possible in relation to JVs. First, where there is the creation of a separate JV company, and one of the principal's of the new JV company has been convicted or is guilty of corruption, will this affect the ability of the new JV company to obtain public contracts? In such cases it seems likely that a JV will be treated under the rules applying to connected companies.

Secondly, where there is no new company, but merely a contractual arrangement between existing companies and one of these companies has been convicted or disqualified for corruption, what effect will this have on the other JV partner? In disqualifying JV partners or companies, the disqualifying entity will need to determine the basis of the JV's disqualification. This may either be the complicity in the commission of the offence, or the reliance of the innocent JV partner on the skills/expertise of the guilty partner.

The EU procurement directives are silent on the issue of disqualification and JVs and it is again necessary to examine such relationships under European law. The directives permit contractors to tender in groups, without requiring them to be in any specific legal form[168] and European jurisprudence has established that companies may rely on each other's expertise where a joint tender is made.[169]

In the context of the mandatory disqualifications, where there is the formation of a separate JV company and the new company is convicted of corruption, the JV company will be disqualified in that form from public contracts under the directives. Further, the conviction of the new JV company may affect the future ability of its principals to obtain public contracts. This approach finds support in European jurisprudence in the context of anti-competitive agreements. Thus in *Avebe*,[170] the CJEU held that where a separate company had been formed for the purpose of carrying out a JV, the two companies who were the shareholders in the JV company (ie the principals of the JV company) would be jointly responsible for the infringements committed by the JV company. Thus, it is arguable by way of analogy that in the context of both mandatory and discretionary disqualifications, where a separate JV company is convicted/guilty of an offence, the separate principals of the JV company may also be disqualified from public contracts. Alternatively, such principals may be disqualified where they are regarded as the parents of the JV company, as discussed in the context of connected companies.

Where there is a JV arrangement without the formation of a separate company and one of the partners has been convicted of corruption, this will affect the ability of the innocent partner to tender for a contract, where

[168] PSD, art 4.

[169] *Ballast Nedam Groep NV*, above n 148; *Holst Italia*, above n 142.

[170] Case T-314/01 *Cooperatieve Verkoop- en Productievereniging van Aardappelmeel en Derivaten Avebe BA v Commission* [2006] ECR II-3085.

it would have been relying on the resources, skills or expertise of the convicted/disqualified partner. Where the innocent partner was not reliant on the convicted/disqualified partner or is able to find an alternative JV partner, then the innocent partner may be permitted to tender for a public contract. This may, however, depend on how the jurisdiction deals with the loss of joint venture or consortium partners during the tendering process.[171]

In implementing the EU directives, the UK provisions are also silent on the issue of JVs. The UK regulations similarly permit suppliers to tender in groups without requiring them to be in any specific legal form.[172] The approach to the disqualification of JVs may depend on the form or nature of the JV arrangement, which determines how the JV will be treated in UK law. Under UK law, a JV may take the form of a contractual agreement between the JV partners, the creation of a new company, or the formation of a partnership agreement between the JV partners.[173]

Where there is the formation of a new JV company, which is convicted of corruption, this company will be disqualified under the UK regulations. The principals of this company will also be disqualified where they are natural persons and fall within the definition of persons with powers of representation, decision and control of the new JV company, as discussed in the context of natural persons above. Where there is no separate company, and the JV operates as a contractual agreement between the partners, it is likely that the conviction of one JV partner will not lead to the disqualification of the other partner. However, the innocent partner may not be awarded the contract where it is relying on the skills/expertise of the convicted partner. Where the JV takes the form of a partnership under UK law, then it is likely that the innocent partner may be disqualified alongside the convicted/guilty partner, since in UK partnership law, partners are jointly liable for the liabilities of the partnership and disqualification may be regarded as one such liability.[174]

Unlike the EU and UK approach, the US FAR clearly spells out the JV position. Under the FAR, the improper conduct of one JV partner may be imputed to the other participating partners where the conduct was intended to benefit the JV, or occurred with the knowledge, approval or acquiescence of the JV partners.[175] Accepting the benefits of the improper conduct will constitute sufficient knowledge, approval and acquiescence of the improper conduct. Thus, if one JV partner offers a bribe or other

[171] Arrowsmith, *Public and Utilities Procurement*, above n 144, ch 12.56. In the EU, the loss of a consortium partner or subcontractor after the award of a contract may give rise to a new award procedure where that loss constitutes a material amendment to the contract – Case C-454/06 *Pressetext GmbH v Austria* [2008] ECR I-4401.

[172] PCR reg 28.

[173] Hewitt, *Joint Ventures*, above n 165, ch 3.

[174] Partnership Act 1890, ss 9 and 10.

[175] FAR 9.407-5, 9.406-5(c).

inducement to a public official to secure the award of a contract to the JV, this may lead to the disqualification of the other JV partners.

Although the US approach to JVs is clearer and thus more preferable than the EU and UK approach, it is suggested that intending to benefit the JV may not be a sufficient test to impose liability on the other JV partners and a preferable test is subjective knowledge, as one JV partner may carry out the prohibited actions for the benefit of the JV, but against the knowledge or ethos of the other JV partners and these other partners should not be disqualified unless it can be shown that they did in fact acquiesce in the prohibited conduct.[176]

In the World Bank context, foreign bidders may enter into a JV with a domestic supplier, since it is believed that such JVs increase the chances of obtaining the contract as Borrowers prefer them, believing that local participation will benefit the domestic economy.[177] Research has also shown that in a corrupt environment, foreign investors prefer JVs as the vehicle of investment, to assist them in negotiating the corrupt bureaucracy.[178] Also, as many Bank contracts are large development projects, the size and complexity of these projects means that the formation of a JV arrangement may be necessary to pool the resources and expertise needed to secure a complex contract.

In relation to the Bank's one-off disqualification measure, the position of JV partners is similar to the position of subcontractors, and the rejection of a bid will affect all the persons included in the bid including JV partners. This is because under the Bank's procurement guidelines, the liability of the partners in a JV in relation to the bid and the contract is joint and several.[179] Thus, all the partners will share any liability faced in respect of the bid, such as disqualification In addition, in bidding for the contract, the joint venture partners would have submitted only one bid[180] and if that bid is disqualified, all the parties included in the bid will be affected by the disqualification, irrespective of their complicity in the offence.

In relation to the Bank's longer disqualification measures, the position is slightly different and where a Bank contract is performed by a JV arrangement and a Bank investigation reveals that either one or both of the partners in the JV engaged in corruption within that project, the Bank may disqualify the firm(s) involved in the corruption.[181] Where only one

[176] Corporate cultural differences have been highlighted as one of the problems of JV's. See Hewitt, *Joint Ventures*, above n 165, 13–14; C Shapiro and R Willig, 'On the Antitrust Treatment of Production Joint Ventures' (1990) 4 *Journal of Economic Perspectives* 113,114.

[177] cf B Aitken and A Harrison, 'Do Domestic Firms Benefit From Direct Foreign Investment? Evidence from Venezuela' (1999) 89 *American Economic Review* 605.

[178] B Smarzynska and S-J Wei, 'Corruption and Composition of Foreign Direct Investment: Firm Level Evidence' (2000) Available at: www.worldbank.org; G Ware and G Noone, 'The Anatomy of Transnational Corruption' (2005) 14 *International Affairs Review* 29, 34.

[179] BPG, para 1.12; Prequalification Document for Works, cl 4.1

[180] Prequalification Document for Works, cl 4.5.

[181] BPG, para 1.16(d).

of the JV partners participated in the corruption, then that firm alone will be disqualified from future Bank contracts and the innocent joint venture partner would not be affected.

The South African legislation is silent on the position of JV partners. The position of JVs under the Corruption Act may be similar to the position of subcontractors. Although the Act does not expressly mention the position of JVs, where a JV partner or a new JV company has been convicted of corruption, that firm may be disqualified by the court. Whether a JV partner that is not convicted of corruption under the Act will be disqualified for the conviction of its JV partner will depend on whether the innocent JV partner falls within the categories of related persons who may be disqualified alongside a convicted person under the Act. As was discussed earlier, these are parent and subsidiary companies as well as firms to be established in the future.[182] Thus if the innocent JV partner falls into one of these categories, it will be disqualified for the conviction of a partner, where it exercises control over the convicted partner and was involved in the offence or knew the convicted partner committed the offence.

Like the Corruption Act, the PPPFA regulations are also silent as to the possible disqualification of JV partners. However, where a JV arrangement is involved in corruptly obtaining a preference under the regulations, all the partners will be disqualified under the regulations as the partners fall within the definition of the 'contractor' who is to be disqualified. Where the JV involved the formation of a separate company, that company may be disqualified, and its principals may also be disqualified where those principals are shareholders in the joint venture, since as discussed earlier, the PPPFA regulations call for the disqualification of a contractor, its shareholders and directors.[183]

The PFMA regulations are silent on the position of JV partners. However, where a JV commits an offence, apart from the disqualification of the company, the principals of the JV may be disqualified where it is deemed that they fall within the definition of the 'bidder' who is to be disqualified under regulations.[184]

8.4 SUMMARY AND ANALYSIS OF MAIN ISSUES

Disqualifying related natural and legal persons raises several issues, which are not always considered by the legislative provisions on disqualification. Many of these issues have been highlighted and discussed in the preceding sections, but a number of issues require further discussion.

182 Corruption Act 2004, s 28(1)(b)(ii).
183 PPPFA reg 13(2)(d).
184 PFMA reg 16A9.2(a).

8.4.1 Discovering the Existence and Complicity of Related Natural and Legal Persons: the Expense and Difficulty of Investigations

One problem accompanying the disqualification of related persons is the difficulty that may be faced by a disqualifying entity in discovering the relevant related persons for the purposes of disqualification. This is especially so in the context of connected companies, natural persons and subcontractors. Where the related persons are identified and the basis for their disqualification is their complicity in the offence, the disqualifying entity may be required to investigate whether those persons were implicated in any wrongdoing.

In relation to discovering the identities of connected companies ie subsidiaries, parent and sister companies, the often complex networks of company ownership may make it difficult and expensive to discover whether one firm is related to another. Research from the US suggests that it typically costs between US$2000 and US$10,000 to investigate a typical applicant for a public sector contract.[185] This is a steep sum, and certainly not an amount that may be spent by the disqualifying entity in every case. The cost of conducting these investigations will place a financial burden on the procurement system where disqualifying related persons is required and the amount spent on investigating related persons may not be justified on the balance of costs and benefits and further may not be worth the expense where it turns out to be extremely difficult to prove that a new firm is the alter-ego of one previously disqualified.[186] In the context of subcontractors, a procuring authority may not be aware of the identity of subcontractors and there may be no way of discovering whether a primary supplier intends to use a guilty or convicted subcontractor in a public contract. In the context of parent companies and natural persons, it may be too difficult for a procuring authority to determine the level of control that a parent company wields over a subsidiary or the precise decision-making powers of a natural person for the disqualification of such persons to be justified.

Where the related persons have been identified, a procuring authority may need to go further, as is the case in the US and South African legislation, to determine whether the related person was implicated in the corrupt activity. This may also be difficult as it may involve investigations of a criminal nature, which the disqualifying entity may not be authorised, competent or equipped to conduct.

[185] Anechiarico and Jacobs, 'Purging Corruption from Public Contracting', above n 1, 162–72.

[186] Anechiarico and Jacobs, ibid, 172.

8.4.2 Procedural Burden and Delays to the Procurement Process

Apart from the expense involved, discovering the existence and the extent of the relationship between the primary supplier and related persons may impose a significant burden on the procurement process, especially where the disqualifying entity is a procuring authority. The task of investigating the relationships between related persons will fall to the disqualifying official, who may also be the procurement official. Such investigations may place an unnecessary burden on these officials and result in a deflection of organisational competence away from their primary goal,[187] which is to conduct and manage public procurement. Further, these investigations will result in delays to the procurement process, where the procurement process is halted pending the completion of the disqualification process. This will impact on the efficiency of the procurement process and may cause delays to the delivery of public services.

8.4.3 The Absence of Procedural Safeguards

Clear procedural safeguards for related persons in the disqualification process are lacking in the jurisdictions excepting the US, the World Bank and South Africa under the PPPFA regulations. This omission is indicative of the lack of a coherent approach to disqualification, especially in the EU/UK and the gaps that exist in the legislation. Adequate procedural safeguards are an important aspect of the disqualification process and are necessary to ensure that disqualification decisions are fair, non-discriminatory, justifiable and transparent. Similar arguments may be made in relation to the disqualification of related persons and procedural safeguards in relation to related persons are important given that some related persons may not have been involved in corrupt activity.

Without repeating the discussion in chapter five, it is important that related persons are given adequate procedural rights in the disqualification process to ensure they are able to challenge the disqualification decision if desired. The approach of the US and World Bank – which give related persons the same procedural rights as the primary offender and consolidate the disqualification hearing of the primary offender and the related person[188] – may be relied on by other jurisdictions to meet the procedural requirements in relation to related persons.

[187] Klitgaard, *Controlling Corruption* (California, University of California Press, 1988) 27.
[188] WBSP, art IX s 9.04; FAR 9.406-1(b).

8.4.4 The Lack of Clarity in the Legislation

As can be seen from the preceding discussions, there are varying degrees of clarity in the legislation on related persons in the jurisdictions. In jurisdictions where there is a lack of information on the position of related persons, a clearer approach is necessary for two reasons.

First, a clearer approach may provide limits on the disqualification of related persons. Where the legislation is not sufficiently clear on which related persons ought to be disqualified, a disqualifying entity may use its discretion in a manner that may be disproportionate to the aims sought to be achieved by the jurisdiction's disqualification policy. Where the legislation grants discretion to the disqualifying entity, the disqualification of related persons ought to be limited to cases where the related persons were implicated in the corrupt activity. This approach will minimise both the burden that a rigorous extension of disqualification may place on a disqualifying entity and limit the potential for abuse of the measure or an excessive reliance on the measure.

Secondly, the tests that are used to determine the basis for the disqualification of related persons ought to be spelt out with sufficient clarity for the benefit of the disqualifying entity and the related persons. As discussed, the limits of the test of control are not elaborated upon in any jurisdiction except the US. Whilst the proximity of the World Bank to the US may result in a reliance by the Bank on the guidance offered by the US approach, South Africa provides little clarity on what a disqualifying entity may take into account in determining that one firm controls or is controlled by another. Similar comments may be made about the EU and UK systems. The absence of any indication in these jurisdictions whether and to what extent related persons may also be disqualified means that disqualifying entities will have to determine what they think is appropriate within the confines of what they believe the legislation permits them to do. This may lead to differences in the treatment of related persons between the Member States and even within the same State. Such disparities may however lead to legal challenges, which may eventually lead to a more coherent approach in the EU.

9

The Effect of Disqualification on Existing Contracts

9.1 INTRODUCTION

THIS CHAPTER WILL examine the effect disqualification may have on the continuation of existing contracts between the disqualified supplier and a procuring authority. The issue is whether, where disqualification occurs during the pendency of a public contract, the disqualification will lead to the termination of the on-going contract, where that contract is not itself tainted by corruption. The termination of existing contracts may depend on whether disqualification is prospective or retrospective, and where the legislation is silent on this issue, it may depend on the circumstances in which the legislation calls for the termination of public contracts and whether disqualification falls within these circumstances as well as whether the rationales for disqualification in the jurisdiction support the case for termination.

The termination of on-going contracts where a supplier has been disqualified is a known, but not widely used concept in public procurement.[1] The reluctance of procurement systems to terminate existing contracts is reflected in the UNCITRAL Model Law, which does not provide for the cancellation of a contract as part of the remedies where there has been a breach of the procurement process prior to the conclusion of a contract,[2] although the guidance notes accompanying the Model Law contemplate that national systems might utilise contractual termination in cases of fraud or corruption.[3] As will be seen, the domestic jurisdictions under study also have mechanisms for terminating contracts where that contract is affected by corruption. The unwillingness of procurement systems to

[1] S Arrowsmith, J Linarelli and D Wallace, *Regulating Public Procurement: National and International Perspectives* (The Hague, Kluwer Law, 2000) 785–95.

[2] UNCITRAL Model Law on the Procurement of Goods, Construction and Services with Guide to Enactment 34 ILM 718 (1995), art 54; see also UNCITRAL Model Law on the Procurement of Goods, Construction and Services (2011), art 67.

[3] Guide to enactment of UNCITRAL Model Law, art 54, para 12, above n 2; D Wallace, 'UNCITRAL Model Law on Procurement of Goods, Construction and Services' (1994) 1 *Public Procurement Law Review* CS2.

provide for contractual termination is due to the far-reaching consequences of termination. As stated in the UNCITRAL Model law, 'annulment of procurement contracts may be particularly disruptive of the procurement process and might not be in the public interest'.[4]

Contractual termination raises several difficult issues, which may account for the disinclination of national systems to utilise termination in disqualification cases. The first issue is determining whether termination is prospective or retrospective. In other words, will the termination be retroactive and affect completed actions under the contract or will the termination only affect future actions under the contract. The approach to this issue also affects the outcome of the second problem, which is the restitutionary aftermath of termination and the apportionment of losses. Where a contract is terminated for disqualification, whether the supplier will be paid for work completed or for benefits the procuring authority has received and whether the procuring authority will be entitled to recover amounts paid out under the contract, including advance payments will need to be determined. Thirdly, contractual termination may be at odds with a non-punitive rationale behind disqualification, as termination may be considered punitive and disproportionate, and may also offend the rule against double jeopardy. Fourthly, contractual termination may not be economically efficient due to the waste that may result. For instance the supplier may have commenced the delivery of specialised goods, which may be useless if the contract is not completed. Another area of waste is in relation to the procurement procedure and where a contract is terminated, a procuring authority may need to restart the procurement process and it may be necessary to decide who bears the costs of the wasted procurement procedure and the costs of a new procedure. Fifthly, contractual termination may cause significant problems for the procuring authority and the public by affecting the delivery of public services and may also cause problems for third parties such as subcontractors and financiers.

Apart from the outright termination of contracts, a jurisdiction may also legislate against a disqualified supplier obtaining extensions to existing contracts or obtaining work under framework contracts. Termination is generally not favoured by the jurisdictions and different approaches to the issue are adopted. This chapter will examine the rationales for contractual termination, whether termination is permitted and the problems that arise with contractual termination.

[4] Guide to enactment of UNCITRAL Model law 1994, art 54 para 12, above n 2.

9.2 RATIONALES FOR CONTRACTUAL TERMINATION

The reasons for adopting a policy that requires or permits contractual termination for disqualification are related to the rationales for disqualification in a jurisdiction. In the first place, terminating existing contracts may fulfil the policy requirement for disqualification. Thus where disqualification is intended to support the anti-corruption policies of the government and show a lack of tolerance for corruption, terminating existing contracts ensures that the government is not associated with unlawful behaviour[5] by ending the government's interaction with the supplier proven to be corrupt and illustrates the extent to which the government will go in fulfilment of its policy of refusing to engage with corrupt contractors.

Secondly where disqualification is intended to punish contractors and act as a deterrent against unlawful behaviour, terminating existing contracts may serve as a further penalty towards this end. Contractual termination may provide an 'additional enforcement tool for securing compliance with the general law'.[6] A supplier likely to lose future as well as present government business if guilty of corruption may be more inclined to comply with anti-corruption law, and termination may thus act as a powerful deterrent against corruption.

Thirdly, where disqualification has a protective rationale and is intended to protect the government from corrupt contractors, terminating existing contracts will protect the government by ensuring that the supplier is unable to act corruptly within existing contracts.

9.3 IS THERE A DUTY TO TERMINATE EXISTING CONTRACTS FOR DISQUALIFICATION?

Most jurisdictions do not require contractual termination on disqualification and in some jurisdictions the legislation is silent as to whether there is even discretion to terminate. Where the legislation is silent, the existence of a duty to terminate for disqualification may depend on the circumstances in which procuring authorities are permitted or required to terminate contracts with suppliers and whether disqualification may be regarded as falling within these circumstances.

The existence of a duty or discretion to terminate existing contracts for the disqualification of a supplier depends in part on the rationale for disqualification in a jurisdiction. As was discussed in chapter three, the

[5] Arrowsmith, 'A taxonomy of horizontal policies in public procurement' in S Arrowsmith and P Kunzlik (eds), *Social and Environmental Policies in EC Procurement Law: New Directives and New Directions* (Cambridge, Cambridge University Press, 2009) 112.

[6] ibid.

mandatory disqualifications in the EU are intended to give effect to EU anti-corruption policy and protect the EU from the cross-border effects of corruption. Contractual termination may thus be necessary in certain instances to give effect to these rationales.

The EU procurement directives are, however, silent as to whether disqualification will affect on-going contracts. This is the case in relation to the mandatory and the discretionary disqualifications. Although EU law gives Member States the freedom to terminate concluded contracts in various contexts,[7] and requires termination in other contexts, it is silent as to whether contracts should be terminated for disqualification. However, the fact that disqualification is not retrospective and the EU's general approach to contractual termination discussed below indicate that there is no duty on Member States to terminate existing contracts for the disqualification of a supplier.

At present, there is also no principle of EU law which requires contractual termination in order to comply with EU law or Treaty principles. In the context of public service concessions, which are not governed by the procurement directives, the CJEU held that Member States are not required to terminate concluded contracts in order to comply with the obligation of transparency in the Treaty.[8] This may mean that the EU does not presently require contractual termination as a general principle to give effect to any EU policy, including its disqualification policy, except in situations where termination is expressly required. As will be seen, the EU requires Member States to terminate contracts where there have been procedural violations of the procurement rules in limited contexts. Contractual termination is also permitted in the context of procurement by EU institutions. Thus it is likely that whilst the EU does not require Member States to terminate existing contracts for disqualification, Member States are free to adopt such a policy.[9]

There are two contexts in which contractual termination is provided for by EU legislation. First, the 2007 amendments to the procurement remedies directive[10] impose an obligation on Member States to terminate contracts concluded in breach of EU law in certain cases. These provisions have implemented a shift from the previous position in the old remedies

[7] Case C-91/08 *Wall AG v Stadt Frankfurt am Main* [2010] ECR I-2815.

[8] Case C-91/08 *Wall AG*, ibid.

[9] S Arrowsmith, *The Law of Public and Utilities Procurement*, 2nd edn (London, Sweet & Maxwell, 2005) ch 21.99.

[10] Directive 89/665/EEC on the laws, regulations and administrative provisions relating to the application of review procedures to the award of public supply and public works contracts [1989] OJ L395/33 as amended by Directive 2007/66/EC amending Council Directives 89/665/EEC and 92/13/EEC with regard to improving the effectiveness of review procedures concerning the award of public contracts [2007] OJ L335/31, arts 2d and 2e [hereafter remedies directive].

directive,[11] which did not require contractual termination where there were breaches of the procurement directives and a contract had been concluded.[12] The approach under the old remedies directive may partly have been informed by the difficulties that accompany the termination of contracts as well as the desire in some legal systems to maintain the sanctity of concluded contracts.[13] There has, however, been a shift away from this position both by the CJEU and European legislators. In *Commission v Germany*,[14] the CJEU decided that in failing to terminate contracts concluded in breach of the procurement directives, Germany had failed to comply with a previous decision of the CJEU establishing a breach of the directives.[15]

Whilst *Commission v Germany*[16] established that there may be a duty to terminate concluded contracts for the breach of the procurement directives in order to give effect to the directives and to act as a deterrent against breaches of EU law,[17] the decision gave no indication as to the *circumstances* in which termination may be appropriate, or whether termination is necessary in every case in which there has been a breach of the procurement directives. Treumer suggested that the obligation to terminate a concluded contract for a breach of the procurement directives should be interpreted in a narrow fashion and a decision to terminate should only be made after a consideration of the seriousness of the breach, the impact on the internal market if the contract is not terminated, the degree of completion of the contract and the public interest and the interests of the procuring parties.[18]

The 2007 amendments to the EU remedies directive specified the cases in which the termination of concluded contracts or the 'ineffectiveness' of a contract is required when a supplier seeks a remedy in proceedings in a national court.[19] The amendments to the remedies directive provide that

[11] R Williams, 'A New Remedies Directive for the European Community' (2008) 2 *Public Procurement Law Review* NA19; Council Directive 89/665/EEC on the coordination of the laws, regulations and administrative provisions relating to the application of review procedures for the award of public supply and public works contracts [1989] OJ L395/33, art 2 [hereafter old remedies directive].

[12] Old remedies directive, art 2; Case C448/01 *EVN AG, Wienstrom GmbH v Austria* [2003] ECR I-14527; Arrowsmith, *Public and Utilities Procurement*, above n 9, chs 21.98–21.103; Joined Cases C-20/01 and 28/01 *Commission v Germany* [2003] ECR. I-3609; S Arrowsmith (ed), *Remedies for Enforcing the Public Procurement Rules* (Winteringham, Earlsgate, 1993) 84–7; S Treumer, 'Towards an Obligation to Terminate Contracts Concluded in Breach of the EC Public Procurement Rules: The End of the Status of Concluded Contracts as Sacred Cows' (2007) 6 *Public Procurement Law Review* 371 and the articles cited therein.

[13] Arrowsmith, Linarelli and Wallace, *Regulating Public Procurement*, above n 1, 785.

[14] Case C-503/04 *Commission v Germany* [2007] ECR I-6153.

[15] Joined Cases C-20/01 and C-28/01 *Commission v Germany* [2003] ECR I-3609.

[16] Case C-503/04 *Commission v Germany* [2007] ECR I-6153.

[17] Case C-503/04 *Commission v Germany*, ibid, paras 76–77.

[18] Treumer, 'Towards an Obligation to Terminate Contracts', above n 12; See also Case C-328/96 *Commission v Austria* [1999] ECR I-7479, opinion of AG Alber.

[19] Remedies directive, arts 2d and 2e.

a contract shall be ineffective where there are specified breaches of EU procurement law.[20] These breaches are: awarding a public contract without prior publication where publication is required by the procurement directives;[21] awarding a public contract in breach of the mandatory standstill period, where this breach is accompanied by a breach of the public sector directives and deprives the supplier from obtaining a review to obtain the contract;[22] and where a contract is concluded in breach of the obligation to suspend the award procedure automatically, pending a review procedure by the procuring authority or a body independent of the procuring authority, and this breach is accompanied by a breach of the public sector directives and deprives the tenderer of the chance to apply for a review to obtain the contract.[23] Where these breaches occur in a Member State, the obligation exists for such contracts to be declared ineffective.

The termination provisions in the remedies directive give Member States the discretion to determine the consequences of a contract being ineffective: which may be the retroactive cancellation of all contractual obligations or the prospective cancellation of obligations which remain to be performed under the contract.[24] Member States also have the discretion to provide that a contract subsists where 'overriding reasons relating to a general interest require that the effects of the contract should be maintained'.[25] The remedies directive clarifies that the economic consequences linked to the contract such as the costs of the delay of the contract; the costs of a new procurement procedure; the legal costs of termination; and the costs of the change of supplier may not amount to 'overriding reasons in the general interest'.[26] However, economic interests not linked to the contract may be taken into account where ineffectiveness will lead to disproportionate consequences.[27] Thus, although the economic consequences of termination may not normally be used by Member States to defeat the requirement for termination,[28] the EU has left it to Member States to determine the circumstances in which the disproportionate effects of termination may justify the maintenance of a contract that ought to be declared ineffective.

[20] M-J Clifton, 'Ineffectiveness – The New Deterrent: Will the New Remedies Directive Ensure Greater Compliance with the Substantive Procurement Rules in the Classical Sectors?' (2009) 18 *Public Procurement Law Review* 165.

[21] Remedies directive, art 2d(1)(a).

[22] Remedies directive, art 2d(1)(b).

[23] Remedies directive, art 2d(1)(b) and art 2d(1)(c).

[24] Remedies directive, art 2d(2).

[25] Remedies directive, art 2d(3). The meaning of a similar phrase is considered in chapter 10 of this volume.

[26] Remedies directive, art 2d(3).

[27] ibid.

[28] J Golding and P Henty, 'The New Remedies Directive of the EC: Standstill and Ineffectiveness' (2008) 3 *Public Procurement Law Review* 146.

The second context in which contractual termination exists in the EU is in procurement by EU institutions. The Financial Regulations applicable to the general budget of the EU,[29] which governs procurement by EU institutions, permit the termination of contracts in some instances. Article 103 of the Financial Regulations provides:

> Where, after the award of the contract, the award procedure or the performance of the contract prove to have been subject to substantial errors, irregularities or fraud, the institutions may, depending on the stage reached in the procedure, refrain from concluding the contract or suspend performance of the contract or, where appropriate, terminate the contract. Where such errors, irregularities or fraud are attributable to the contractor, the institutions may in addition refuse to make payments, may recover amounts already paid or may terminate all the contracts concluded with this contractor, in proportion to the seriousness of the errors, irregularities or fraud.

This provision is explained by the Regulations Implementing the Financial Regulations which provide that a 'substantial error or irregularity shall be any infringement of a provision of a contract or regulation resulting from an act or an omission which causes or might cause a loss to the Community budget'.[30] Thus, reading Article 103 of the Financial Regulations with Article 153 of the Implementing Regulations, a contract may be terminated where there has been the commission of an act which amounts to a breach of the terms of the contract, amounts to a breach of EU legislation and is likely to cause loss to EU finances. The commission of a corrupt act in the particular procurement will trigger these provisions as such an act will be a breach of EU legislation against corruption[31] and is also likely to cause loss to the EU.

From the above, it is argued that the specific instances in which the EU requires termination and the approach of the CJEU in *Wall AG* may point to the fact that termination is not required in the disqualification context but Member States are free to adopt an approach terminating existing contracts once a supplier is disqualified.

The EU procurement directives are also silent on the position of concluded contracts where the concluded contract was tainted by corruption.

[29] Council Regulation (EC, Euratom) 1605/2002/EC of 25 June 2002 on the Financial Regulation applicable to the general budget of the European Communities, [2002] OJ L248/1, as amended by Council Regulation (EC, Euratom) 1995/2006/EC [2006] OJ L390/16 [hereafter Financial Regulations].

[30] Commission Regulation (EC, Euratom) No 2342/2002 of 23 December 2002 laying down detailed rules for the implementation of Council Regulation (EC, Euratom) No 1605/2002 on the Financial Regulation applicable to the general budget of the European Communities [2002] OJ L357/1, art 153 [hereafter Implementing regulations].

[31] Council Regulation (EC, Euratom) 2988/95 of December 18, 1995 on the Protection of the Communities Financial Interests [1995] OJ L312/1.

This issue has been left to the discretion of Member States but generally where an existing contract is affected by corruption, the presence of corruption within the contract may lead to the termination of that contract.[32]

The EU directives do not mention the situation where a procuring authority concludes a public contract with an option to extend or a framework agreement has been concluded with a supplier who is subsequently disqualified.[33] In the EU, some but not all framework agreements may involve a further competition between the previously selected suppliers.[34] Where this is the case, it may be possible for the disqualification to be taken into account as a basis for the refusal to select the supplier.

As there does not appear to be a requirement for procuring authorities in Member States to terminate existing contracts for the mandatory disqualification of a supplier but Member States are free to do so at their option, it is likely that in relation to the discretionary provisions, Member States also have the discretion to decide whether to terminate existing contracts in this context.

In implementing the EU procurement directives, the UK procurement regulations did not go any further than the directives and are also silent on whether disqualification will lead to the termination of existing contracts. This silence relates to both the mandatory and the discretionary disqualifications. As discussed, the EU does not presently require Member States to terminate existing contracts to give effect to the EU's disqualification policy, but Member States are free to adopt such a policy at their discretion. The UK has not adopted an express policy requiring termination for disqualification but procuring authorities are permitted to terminate concluded contracts depending on the provisions of the contract between the procuring authority and the supplier as well as the reasons for contractual termination under the general contract law, in public law, and under the procurement regulations.

In relation to the situations in which existing contracts must be terminated, the UK implemented the amendments to the EU remedies directive through the Public Contracts (Amendment) Regulations 2009,[35] which implemented the EU provisions on the termination of concluded contracts. Before the transposition of these provisions, the old remedies provisions in the UK procurement regulations provided that a court did not have

[32] J Arnould, 'Damages for Performing an Illegal Contract – The Other Side of the Mirror: Comments on Three Recent Judgments of the French Council of State' (2008) 6 *Public Procurement Law Review* NA274; Treumer, 'Towards an Obligation to Terminate Contracts', above n 12; A Rubach-Larsen, 'Damages under German Law for Breach of EU Procurement Law' (2006) *Public Procurement Law Review* 179; K Kruger, 'Action for Damages due to Bad Procurement: On the Intersection between EU/EEA Law, National Law, with Special Reference to the Norwegian Experience' (2006) *Public Procurement Law Review* 211

[33] PSD, art 32; Arrowsmith, *Public and Utilities Procurement*, above n 9, ch 11.

[34] PSD, art 32(4).

[35] Public Contracts (Amendment) Regulations 2009, SI 2009/2992 as amended by Public Procurement (Miscellaneous Amendments) Regulations 2011, SI 2011/2053.

the power to order any remedy other than an award of damages where a contract was concluded in breach of the procurement regulations.[36] This restriction was intended to protect the winning bidder (who may have had nothing to do with the breach of the procurement regulations) as well as the procuring authority.[37] In *Ealing Community Transport v London Borough of Ealing*,[38] the court suggested that in the absence of bad faith, a contract could not be set aside for a breach of the procurement regulations.[39] The traditional approach to concluded contracts discussed in the context of the EU was confirmed by the court in this case.[40]

However, there may have been an exception to this rule where the winning bidder was aware of the underlying breach or illegality in the procurement process. Arrowsmith suggests that the principle of effectiveness may require that where the winning bidder was aware of the illegality, this should provide an exception to the rule that concluded contracts may not be terminated for breaches of the procurement regulations.[41]

In implementing the contractual termination provisions of the EU remedies directive, the UK regulations substantially mirror the directive, and a contract will be declared ineffective: where the contract is awarded without prior publication of a contract notice where required;[42] where the contract is awarded in breach of the mandatory 10-day standstill period or during proceedings challenging the contract award decision;[43] where a contract is awarded pending a challenge to the procurement process;[44] and where the contract is based on a framework or dynamic purchasing arrangement and is awarded in breach of that arrangement.[45] The consequence of 'ineffectiveness' in the UK is a prospective discharge of the contract from the time when the declaration of ineffectiveness is made.[46] The provisions give the courts the power to determine the implications of the ineffectiveness of a contract in relation to 'consequential matters arising from ineffectiveness'[47] and compensation and restitution as between the parties to the contract.[48] The court is also required to give effect to any

[36] Public Contracts Regulations 2006, reg 47(9).

[37] *Ealing Community Transport v London Borough of Ealing* [1999] COD 492; Arrowsmith, *Public and Utilities Procurement*, above n 9, ch 21.68

[38] *Ealing Community Transport*, ibid.

[39] ibid.

[40] R Williams, 'When is a Contract not a Contract?: The Significance of Third Party Rights in Remedies Available in UK Law under the EU Public Procurement Regime' (2000) 1 *Public Procurement Law Review* CS27.

[41] Arrowsmith, *Public and Utilities Procurement*, above n 9, ch 21.69.

[42] PCR reg 47K(2).

[43] PCR reg 47K(5); *DR Plumbing & Heating Services v Aberdeen City Council* (unreported 2009).

[44] PCR reg 47K(5).

[45] PCR reg 47K(6) .

[46] PCR reg 47M(1).

[47] PCR reg 47M(3)(b).

[48] PCR reg 47M(4).

contractual arrangements between the parties dealing with the consequences of ineffectiveness.[49]

The provisions on contractual termination appear to be exhaustive and do not create an obligation for a procuring authority to terminate a contract for the disqualification of a supplier. However, the provisions do not in any way limit the right of a procuring authority to terminate a contract under a term of the contract; under the general contract law; or where there is a breach of legislation or public law such as where the contract as concluded is unlawful.[50]

As the principles governing public contracts in the UK are the general principles of the law of contract,[51] in the absence of any intention to the contrary in the procurement regulations, the rules for contractual termination in general contract law may apply to public contracts. In contract law, a contract may come to an end for a number of reasons.

- First, a contract may be terminated for a repudiatory breach of contract,[52] where the party in breach makes it clear that he will not perform the contract, or by his own act makes performance of the contract impossible, or there is a substantial failure to perform the contract.[53] A substantial failure of performance will justify termination where the failure attains a required degree of seriousness or it is a failure to comply with a condition of the contract.
- Secondly, a contract may be terminated where the parties mutually agree to release each other from performance of their obligations under the contract.
- Thirdly, a contract may be rescinded, where the contract was induced by means of fraud, corruption,[54] misrepresentation, mistake,[55] duress, undue influence or other unconscionable conduct. Rescission in contract law is not prospective, but operates as a retrospective unravelling of the contract and the substantive restoration of the parties to their pre-contractual positions, and will be unavailable where it is impossible to restore the parties to their pre-contractual positions.[56]

[49] PCR reg 47M(6).

[50] Arrowsmith, *Public and Utilities Procurement*, above n 9, ch 21.13.

[51] C Turpin and P Brown, *Government Procurement and Contracts* (London, Longman, 1989) chs1–4; Arrowsmith, *Public and Utilities Procurement*, above n 9, ch 2, C Lewis, *Judicial Remedies in Public Law*, 4th edn (London, Sweet & Maxwell, 2008) 470.

[52] *Dalkia Utilities Services Plc v Celtech International Ltd* [2006] EWCA 63.

[53] E Peel and G Treitel, *Treitel on the Law of Contract*, 12th edn (London, Sweet & Maxwell, 2007) 869.

[54] *Mahesan S/O Thambiah v Malaysia Government Officers Cooperative Housing Society* [1979] AC 374 PC; *Panama & South Pacific Telegraph Co v India Rubber, Gutta Percha and Telegraph Works* (1875) LR 10 Ch App 96; G Jones and R Goff, *Goff and Jones: The Law of Restitution* (London, Sweet & Maxwell, 1998) para 33-023; A Berg, 'Bribery-Transaction Validity and other Civil Law Implications' [2001] *Lloyds Maritime and Commercial Law Quarterly* 27, 34.

[55] *Shogun Finance v Hudson* [2003] UKHL 62.

[56] *Salford v Lever* [1891] 1 QB 168.

- Fourthly, a contract may be terminated pursuant to an express or implied term in the contract. In the UK, procuring authorities may reserve a power to terminate a contract by virtue of a contractual term for various reasons or for no reason at all.[57] These clauses are referred to as termination for convenience clauses and give the government the power to terminate public contracts without the necessity for a breach.[58] These clauses are justified on the grounds that a government may have to break a contract because of a change in policy.[59] Where such clauses exist and are sufficiently clear,[60] they may possibly be relied on to terminate contracts where the procuring authority becomes aware of the subsequent disqualification of a supplier. Although these clauses are generally very wide, the courts have put judicial limits on their use.[61] As a remedy, this termination is prospective and brings the contract to an end with the subsequent determination of rights and liabilities under the contract. As will be seen, such clauses exist in the US and are explicitly linked to the disqualification context. In addition, some UK procuring authorities include in their standard contractual terms a right to terminate a contract where a supplier has engaged in corruption in the procurement or execution of the particular public contract, or is otherwise in default.[62]
- Lastly, a contract may come to an end due to a supervening event which frustrates the contract and makes the contract impossible to perform or radically different from what the parties contemplated at the time of entering the contract.[63]

The reasons for which a contract may be rescinded or terminated in English contract law suggest that contracts may not be terminated without the agreement of the parties, unless there is a deficiency or abnormality in the formation or the execution of the contract or the contract is frustrated. However, a procuring authority may find it difficult to plead that an existing contract has become frustrated as a result of the subse-

[57] Arrowsmith, *Public and Utilities Procurement*, above n 9, ch 2.47.

[58] Turpin and Brown, *Government Procurement and Contracts*, above n 51, 243–6; *Hadley Design Associates v Westminster City Council* [2003] EWHC 1617.

[59] N Seddon, *Government Contracts: Federal, State and Local*, 4th edn (Annandale, Federation Press, 2009) 239.

[60] *Abbey Developments v PP Brickwork Ltd* [2003] EWHC 1987.

[61] *Rice v Yarmouth Council* [2000] All ER 902; *R (Birmingham & Solihull Taxi Association) v Birmingham International Airport* [2009] EWHC 1913 (Admin); M Hirst, 'Termination for Convenience Clauses – A Shield or a Sword in Times of Economic Downturn' (2010) 27 *International Construction Law Review* 419.

[62] See for instance, Leicester, Leicestershire and Rutland Combined Fire Authority (Standing Orders relating to contracts); Sefton Council Contracts Procedure Rules; Rother District Council Contract Procedure Rules. See also Berg, 'Bribery-Transaction Validity', above n 54, 34.

[63] *Davis Contractors v Fareham UDC* [1956] AC 696, *per* Lord Radcliffe; Peel and Treitel, *Law of Contract*, above n 53, ch 19.

quent disqualification, as the orthodoxy in relation to frustration is that the supervening event has to make the contract 'impossible, illegal or radically different' to what was in the contemplation of the parties at the time they entered into the contract.[64] Thus the fact that the supplier is disqualified from future contracts may not be said to affect the nature of the existing contract or make it impossible to perform. Accordingly, unless the existing contract is tainted with corruption or a procuring authority includes a termination for convenience clause in the contract it may not be possible for UK procuring authorities to rely on contract law principles to terminate public contracts for the disqualification of a supplier.

Another body of law which may be relevant to this issue is public law. It is possible that the breach of public law principles[65] or statute[66] will entitle a procuring authority to terminate a contract. However, where a public contract is terminated for the breach of a statute this occurs because the public contract is governed by the statute in question.[67] It may thus be possible to argue, where disqualification is based on a conviction for corruption, that the breach of anti-corruption legislation gives the procuring authority the discretion to terminate its contractual relationship with a supplier.

Similarly to the EU, the UK regulations are also silent as to whether a disqualified supplier may obtain work under framework agreements or agreements with options. As discussed in the context of the EU, where a framework agreement operates as a multi-provider agreement that is subject to further competition, the disqualification provisions may be applicable to the mini-tender.

From the above, it can be seen that the limitations on termination in the remedies provisions and the reluctance of general contract law to set aside concluded contracts without the agreement of the parties or where the existing contract is unaffected by corruption or other vitiating circumstances shows that UK procuring authorities are not under a duty to terminate existing contracts for disqualification. Whilst there is at present no duty under EU law to terminate existing contracts for disqualification, if the EU in future decides that the disqualification regime will be better served by the termination of existing contracts, the UK will be required to adopt a similar approach.

Unlike the position in the UK and the EU, the US provides for the termination of contracts for disqualification in limited circumstances and also deals with framework agreements and contracts with options. Although disqualification in the US is prospective and is not intended to affect existing contracts, once a supplier has been disqualified, procuring

[64] E McKendrick, *Contract Law*, 8th edn (Basingstoke, Palgrave Macmillan, 2007) 245.

[65] *R v Port Talbot Borough Council ex parte Jones* [1988] 2 All ER 207.

[66] *R v Basildon DC ex parte Brown* (1981) 79 LGR 655.

[67] *R v Basildon DC*, ibid.

authorities may not place orders exceeding the guaranteed minimum under indefinite quantity contracts, place orders under blanket purchase agreements, add new work or extend the duration or exercise other options under existing contracts.[68]

Whilst the termination of existing contracts is not automatic upon disqualification, and there is no duty to terminate, the FAR grants procuring authorities discretion in some cases to terminate existing contracts for the disqualification of the supplier.[69] There are two circumstances in which a procuring authority may terminate a public contract under the FAR.[70] These are where the supplier is in breach of contract (default termination) and where termination is in the government's interest (convenience termination).[71] Termination may follow a disqualification either where the reasons giving rise to disqualification also constitute a default in performance, or where the supplier presents a significant risk to the government in relation to his being able to complete the contract, making termination in the government's interest. Also, as is the case in the UK, termination may occur where the supplier is convicted of a corruption offence or is otherwise deemed guilty of such offences in relation to the particular contract.

A default termination[72] is a means of dealing with a supplier's failure to perform the contract in accordance with the contract specifications and schedule[73] and may be likened to the UK common law approach to termination of contracts for a substantial failure of performance. A default termination may occur where the supplier fails to deliver the goods or services within the stated time, fails to make progress in executing the contract,[74] or is otherwise in breach of contract.[75] Default terminations are based on breaches in relation to the contract,[76] and a subsequent disqualification will not necessarily lead to a default termination unless the reasons leading to the disqualification also constitute a default in the performance of the contract.

Similar to the UK, where termination is based on a reason unrelated to performance and is thought to be in the government's interest such termi-

[68] FAR 9.405-1(b); R Kramer, 'Awarding Contracts to Suspended and Debarred Firms: Are Stricter Rules Necessary?' (2005) 34 *Public Contract Law Journal* 539.

[69] FAR 49, FAR 52.249. A convenience termination clause is also implied into government contracts by virtue of *Christian & Assoc v United States* 312 F.2d 418 (1963).

[70] C Tiefer, 'Forfeiture by Cancellation or Termination' (2003) 54 *Mercer Law Review* 1031.

[71] FAR 12.403(b); FAR 52.212-4(m); J Cibinic and R Nash, *Formation of Government Contracts*, 3rd edn (Alphen aan den Rijn, Wolters Kluwer, 1998) 485; *Integrated Systems Group Inc v Dept of the Army* GSBCA 12613-P, 94-2 BCA ¶ 26, 618.

[72] M Norris, 'Terminations for Default' (2008) *Army Lawyer* 55.

[73] J Cibinic and R Nash, *Administration of Government Contracts*, 4th edn (CCH, 2006) ch 10.

[74] B Fagg, 'Default Terminations for Failing to Make Progress' (1995) 25 *Public Contract Law Journal* 113.

[75] FAR 49.402.

[76] C Tiefer and W Shook, *Government Contract Law*, 2nd edn (Durham, Carolina Academic Press, 2003) 516.

nation is referred to as a 'convenience termination'.[77] This is defined as 'the exercise of the Government's right to completely or partially terminate performance of work under a contract when it is in the Government's interest'.[78] Terminations for convenience have been criticised as giving the government complete authority to escape from contractual obligations,[79] since these terminations may be unrelated to the performance of the contract or default of the supplier in executing the contract. Although convenience terminations must be in the government's interest, the FAR provides no guidance on what factors may be considered in determining what is in the government's interest.[80] However, convenience terminations may not be done in bad faith,[81] or be arbitrary or capricious[82] and a contract may not be terminated for convenience so that the government may obtain a lower price from a different supplier.[83] Contracts have been terminated for convenience for various reasons including: the fact that the government no longer requires the work; where there is a shortage of funds to complete the contract;[84] where there are questions regarding the propriety of a contract;[85] and where there has been a cardinal change of circumstance.[86]

Procuring authorities have also sought to terminate public contracts for convenience because the supplier was subsequently disqualified.[87] Where termination is proposed on this basis it is not clear whether the supplier may challenge the termination if he has subsequently removed the cause for disqualification. However, because of the wide discretion possessed in terminating for convenience, it is possible that a supplier may not challenge the termination as long as it is done in good faith. When a procuring authority decides to terminate an existing contract for convenience following the imposition of disqualification, the termination must be in accordance with the established procedures for termination under the FAR,[88] which relate to the provision of a detailed notice of termination to

[77] FAR 12.403; M Pederson, 'Rethinking the Termination for Convenience Clause in Federal Contracts' (2001) 31 *Public Contract Law Journal* 83.

[78] FAR 2.101.

[79] Cibinic and Nash, *Administration of Government Contracts,* above n 73, ch 11; *Krygoski Construction Co v United States* 94 F3d 1537 (Fed Cir 1996).

[80] Cibinic and Nash, *Administration of Government Contracts,* above n 73, ch 11.

[81] *Krygoski Construction,* above n 79; *Kalvar Corp v United States* 543 F2d 1298 (Ct Cl 1976); *Allied Materials & Equipment Co v United States* 215 Ct Cl 192 (1978).

[82] *Gould Inc v Chafee* 450 F2d 667 (1971).

[83] *Torncello v United States* 231 Ct Cl 20 (1982); *Vibra-Tech Engineers Inc v United States* 567 F Supp 484 (1983).

[84] *Jacobs Engineering Group Inc v United States* 434 F3d 1378 (Fed Cir 2006).

[85] Cibinic and Nash, *Administration of Government Contracts,* above n 73, 1076.

[86] *T & M Distribution Inc v United States* 185 F3d 1279 (Fed Cir 1999).

[87] *Integrated Systems Group Inc v Dept of the Army* GSBCA 12613-P, 94-2 BCA ¶ 26, 618; *TMD USA Inc/Vincent Schickler v General Services Administration* GSBCA 15420-R.

[88] FAR 12.403 and FAR 49.102.

the contractor,[89] and the settling of outstanding claims under the contract. Once a contract is terminated for convenience, the government's liability for terminating the contract is admitted,[90] although termination does not amount to a breach by the government.[91]

The approach to convenience terminations seeks to strike a balance between the government's power to terminate contracts unilaterally and the contractor's right not to be unduly prejudiced by the termination. Where contracts are terminated for convenience, either for disqualification or for any other reason, such termination is subject to the decision of the procuring authority head, taken in consultation with relevant staff.[92] Similar to the UK, contractual termination is also subject to review by the courts, providing judicial limitations on the discretion to terminate for convenience.[93]

As is the case in the other jurisdictions, contractual termination is also permitted under the FAR where the existing contract is tainted with corruption. Where a person has been convicted of bribery or corruption offences, or bid information has been disclosed in exchange for a bribe,[94] the head of the procuring authority may rescind or cancel a contract with the contractor[95] and recover payments made under the contract.[96] The Supreme Court has affirmed that in such cases, the government may cancel the contract and need not pay for work done,[97] and other jurisprudence illustrates that the government may recover the full amount paid on a completed contract that is subsequently found to be tainted with corruption.[98]

The World Bank's approach to contractual termination differs from that of domestic jurisdictions. Disqualification by the World Bank is prospective and does not affect the completion of existing contracts. In fact, prior to the 2010 revision of the Bank's sanctions procedures, which now impose a temporary disqualification on contractors pending the conclusion of the disqualification process,[99] it used to be possible for a supplier to obtain a contract during the pendency of disqualification proceedings, and such

[89] FAR 49.102.

[90] Cibinic and Nash, *Administration of Government Contracts*, above n 73, 1076.

[91] Pederson, 'Rethinking the Termination for Convenience Clause', above n 77, 85.

[92] FAR 9.405-1.

[93] See *Krygoski Construction*, above n 79; *Kalvar Corp v United States* 543 F2d 1298 (Ct Cl 1976); *Allied Materials & Equipment Co v United States* 215 Ct Cl 192 (1978); *Gould Inc v Chafee* 450 F.2d 667 (1971); *Torncello v United States* 231 Ct Cl 20 (1982); *Vibra-Tech Engineers Inc v United States* 567 F Supp 484 (1983).

[94] FAR 3.700.

[95] FAR 3.702.

[96] FAR 3.704.

[97] *Pan American Petroleum & Transp Co v United States*, 273 US 456 (1927).

[98] *K & R Engineering Co v United States*, 222 Ct Cl 340, 616 F2d 469 (1980); *Godley v United States* 5 F3d 1473 (1993 US App); *JETS, Inc v United States*, 838 F2d 1196, 1200 (Fed Cir); *United States v Mississippi Valley Generating Co*, 364 US 520, 565, 5 L Ed 2d 268, 81 S Ct 294 (1961).

[99] WBSP, art II.

new contracts would not be affected by the subsequent disqualification.[100] The Bank's refusal to terminate existing contracts for disqualification is intended to prevent the adverse consequences that may result for the Borrower.[101] Terminating a contract for disqualification may mean that the Borrower does not obtain the intended benefit of the loan in the form of the contracted for goods or services, but will still be required to repay the loan to the Bank. As such, contractual termination is not appropriate in the Bank context.

However, although existing contracts will not be terminated, the Bank will not finance any modification to an existing contract signed with a disqualified person after the date of disqualification.[102] In other words, although disqualification will not affect existing contracts, the Bank will not permit any changes in the contractual relationship between a Borrower and a firm that is subsequently disqualified. This approach has parallels in the US, which does not permit changes or extensions to existing contracts with a disqualified supplier.

Apart from a desire not to cause undue hardship to its Borrowers, there is a practical limitation preventing the Bank from terminating existing contracts. As the Bank relies on the Borrower to conduct procurements for Bank-funded contracts, the Bank is in practice unable to cancel concluded contracts, as it does not have a contractual relationship with suppliers.[103] The power of contractual termination is reserved to the Borrower, who can cancel a contract: where there has been a breach of the contract (known as termination for default); where the supplier becomes insolvent; where the supplier has acted corruptly in competing for or in executing the contract and where the termination is in the Borrower's interest (known as termination for convenience).[104] Should the Bank in future choose to adopt an approach where it wishes a Borrower to terminate existing contracts with disqualified contractors, it may include an obligation to terminate in the Loan Agreement, which governs the conditions of the loan granted by the Bank to the Borrower. Although some jurisdictions may not permit contractual termination in order to maintain the sanctity of contracts, the Loan Agreement is regarded as a treaty in international law and will thus not be affected by domestic approaches to termination.

[100] Thornburgh, Gainer and Walker, *Report to Oversight Committee on Fraud and Corruption, The World Bank Concerning Mechanisms to Address Problems of Fraud and Corruption* (Washington, World Bank, 2000) 39; C Hostetler, 'Going from Bad to Good: Combating Corruption on World Bank-Funded Infrastructure Projects' (2011) 14 *Yale Human Rights and Development Law Journal* 231, 251.

[101] ibid.

[102] BPG appendix 1, para 8.

[103] S Williams, 'The Debarment of Corrupt Contractors from World Bank-Financed Contracts' (2007) 36 *Public Contract Law Journal* 277.

[104] World Bank, Standard Bidding Documents (Procurement of goods) General Conditions of Contract, cl 34.

Contractual termination in South Africa contains elements of the approaches from all the selected jurisdictions. Like the US, there is no duty to terminate, but the Corruption Act gives the National Treasury the discretion to terminate contracts for disqualification. Like the EU and UK, the PPPFA and the PFMA regulations are silent on the issue of whether contractual termination may accompany disqualification but they provide for contractual termination as stand-alone remedies where there has been corruption or fraud in the award or the execution of a particular contract.[105]

The Corruption Act permits the termination of existing contracts on disqualification. Where a supplier has been disqualified, the National Treasury may, after consultation with the relevant procuring authority, terminate any agreement with the disqualified supplier.[106] It is not clear whether the procuring authority may veto the National Treasury's decision to terminate the contract or whether the procuring authority may only make representations to the National Treasury, which may be taken into account. The National Treasury is required to take several factors into account before it terminates a contract to ensure that termination is not capricious or unduly prejudicial to the government. These factors are: the extent and duration of the agreement concerned; whether it is likely to conclude a similar agreement with another person within a specific timeframe; the extent to which the agreement has been executed; the urgency of the services to be delivered or supplied under the terms of the agreement; whether extreme costs will follow such termination; and any other factor which may impact on the termination of the agreement.[107] The National Treasury may terminate an existing contract irrespective of whether there are deficiencies in the existing contract. The powers granted to the Treasury are very broad and are similar to the powers given to UK and US procuring authorities to terminate contracts for convenience.

As stated, the PPPFA and PFMA regulations are silent as to whether a procuring authority will be required to terminate existing contracts with a disqualified supplier. However, the PPPFA regulations provide for contractual termination as an additional stand-alone remedy where there has been fraud in obtaining preferences for a public contract. Thus a procuring authority may 'cancel the contract and claim any damages which it has suffered as a result of having to make less favourable arrangements due to such cancellation'.[108] Similarly, the PFMA regulations provide that a procuring authority may cancel a contract awarded to a supplier of goods or services if (i) the supplier committed any corrupt or fraudulent act during the bidding process or the execution of that contract; or (ii) if any official or other role player committed any corrupt or fraudulent act

105 PFMA reg 16.A9.1; PPPFA reg 13(2)(c).
106 Corruption Act 2004, s 28(3).
107 Corruption Act 2004, s 28(3)(a)(i).
108 PPPFA reg 13(2)(c).

during the bidding process or the execution of that contract that benefited that supplier.[109] Under these regulations, the termination of existing contracts is in addition to, but not consequent upon disqualification.

The power to cancel contracts is thus utilised by procuring authorities where there is corruption in the procurement process[110] and in the execution of the contract.[111] This power may be derived from the procurement legislation, from the contract[112] or from common law.[113] Where the power to terminate a contract is derived from legislation, the power to terminate must be exercised in accordance with the PAJA,[114] and a procuring authority will be required to ensure the decision to terminate is accompanied by procedural safeguards such as the requirement of notice, a right to a hearing and a right to a decision that is reasonable and fair.[115] Where procedural requirements are not taken into account, this may open the government to a legal challenge by the supplier in question. In *Supersonic Tours*, the court set aside the procuring authority's decision to disqualify the supplier and terminate concluded contracts on the grounds that the decision was made without the necessary procedural safeguards.

However, where the power to terminate a contract derives from the contract or the common law, this does not amount to administrative action within the meaning of PAJA[116] and the decision to terminate need not accord with the procedural safeguards for taking administrative action under PAJA.

9.4 PROBLEMS WITH CONTRACTUAL TERMINATION

9.4.1 Determining if Termination is Prospective or Retrospective

Where a procuring authority wishes to terminate an existing contract with a disqualified contractor, it will have to determine whether the termination will operate prospectively or retrospectively. This may depend on the legislative provisions on termination, but may also depend on the reason for the termination of the contract. For instance, if the existing contract is tainted with corruption, the contract may be regarded as an illegal contract in most jurisdictions and will possibly be terminated retrospectively:

[109] PFMA reg 16A9.1(f).

[110] *Supersonic Tours (Pty) Ltd v State Tender Board* [2007] JOL 19891 (T).

[111] *Cape Metropolitan Council v Metro Inspection Services (Western Cape CC) and others* 2001 (3) SA 1013 (SCA).

[112] *Logbro Properties CC v Bedderson NO & Others* 2003 (2) SA 460 (SCA) paras 9 and 10.

[113] *Cape Metropolitan Council*, above n 111, para 18.

[114] *Supersonic Tours (Pty) Ltd*, above n 110.

[115] PAJA, ss 3 and 6; *Cape Metropolitan Council*, above n 111.

[116] *Temoso Emergency Equipment CC v State Tender Board* 17444/2006 TPD; cf *Cape Metropolitan Council*, above n 111.

in other words, the contract may be regarded as void,[117] and treated as if it never existed, or unravelled in its entirety.[118] Where the existing contract is not affected by corruption but is terminated in furtherance of a policy requirement, then it is likely that the contract will be terminated prospectively. This means that the contract will be terminated either as from the time of the disqualification, or from the time the procuring authority becomes aware of the disqualification, but all the activity that went before the termination will be regarded as valid and subsisting. Knowing whether a contract is to be terminated retrospectively or prospectively is important as this may affect the restitutionary consequences of termination and the manner in which losses may be apportioned. This section will examine this issue in relation to contracts that are not affected with corruption.

As most of the jurisdictions under study are silent on this issue, the nature of termination in other contexts may provide an indication on the likely approaches that a jurisdiction may adopt in future. As discussed, in the EU, the procurement directives are silent as to the possibility of termination on disqualification, and have left this to the discretion of Member States, who may adopt different approaches to deciding whether termination should be prospective or retrospective.[119] At present there is no consistent European law approach to guide Member States in deciding whether termination in such contexts ought to be prospective or retrospective. In *Commission v Germany*, the court was not clear as to whether the proposed termination ought to be retrospective or prospective, as the Commission, the Court and the Advocate-General used the terms rescission and termination interchangeably,[120] although they may not always mean the same thing in contract law.[121]

In the UK, if a procuring authority decides to terminate contracts for disqualification, it is likely that termination will be prospective. This view is supported by the UK's approach to termination under the 'ineffectiveness' provisions and the approach to termination under the general law of contract where there are no deficiencies in the formation of the contract.

In the US, the termination provisions of the FAR suggest that termination on disqualification is intended to be prospective. This is because the FAR requires the procuring authority to settle all outstanding claims of

[117] See generally, R Buckley, *Illegality and Public Policy* (London, Sweet & Maxwell, 2002); N Enonchong, *Illegal Transactions* (London, LLP, 1998).

[118] M Nell, 'Contracts Obtained by Means of bribery: Should they be Void or Valid?' (2009) 27 *European Journal of Law and Economics* 159.

[119] J Arnold, 'Damages for Performing an Illegal Contract – The Other Side of the Mirror: Comments in Three Recent Judgments of the French Council of State' (2008) 17 *Public Procurement Law Review* NA274; A Chong, *Void Contracts and their Aftermath: A Choice of Law Analysis* (PhD Thesis, University of Nottingham, 2004).

[120] Case C-503/04 *Commission v Germany* [2007] ECR I-6153, para 25.

[121] Case C-503/04 *Commission v Germany*, ibid, Opinion of AG Trstenjak, para 71.

the supplier on termination – including the payment of lost profits on the completed portions of the contract, an approach that may be deemed inconsistent with a contract that is retrospectively terminated.

As was discussed earlier, in the World Bank context, the power to terminate contracts is reserved to the Borrower, or the agency conducting the procurement process on the Borrower's behalf. Thus, the law of the Borrower and the governing law of the contract will determine whether termination will be prospective or retrospective.

In South Africa, the provisions permitting contractual termination are not clear on whether termination will be prospective or retrospective. However, the procuring authorities that have terminated contracts on the basis of provisions similar to the PPPFA and PFMA regulations have treated termination as retrospective, although those circumstances were such that the contract had been concluded but not implemented.[122]

Whilst there is little clarity on whether termination is meant to be prospective or retrospective, it is suggested that for jurisdictions that adopt a policy of termination on disqualification, termination should only be retrospective where the contract has not been executed. In all other cases, termination should be prospective. This approach will make dealing with the restitutionary claims following termination less problematic, and may support a non-punitive rationale for disqualification where this is the case.

9.4.2 Restitution and Apportionment of Losses

Another problem accompanying termination is determining the restitutionary aftermath and apportionment of losses between the affected parties. This section is not concerned with restitution under illegal contracts, as except where otherwise stated, it is assumed that the contracts which are the subject of termination are not illegal or affected by corruption.[123]

Restitution will normally be available to a claimant where a contract has been discharged[124] and the claimant has been wronged, or the defendant has been unjustly enriched at the claimant's expense, or the claimant wishes to assert his property rights.[125] In Anglo-US law, the availability of a

[122] *Supersonic Tours*, above n 110.

[123] In the UK, see generally P Birks, 'Recovering Value Transferred under an Illegal Contract' (2000) 1 *Theoretical Inquiries in Law* 155; S Arrowsmith, 'Ineffective Transactions, Unjust Enrichment and Problems of Policy' (1989) 9 *Legal Studies* 307; Arrowsmith, *Public and Utilities Procurement*, above n 9, ch 2. For the US see H Dagan, *The Law and Ethics of Restitution* (Cambridge, Cambridge University Press, 2004).

[124] *The Evia Luck* [1992] 2 AC 152, 165; G Virgo, *The Principles of the Law of Restitution*, 2nd edn (Oxford, Oxford University Press, 2006) ch 2 at 40. Note that damages may also be available where the contract is prospectively discharged.

[125] Virgo, *Principles of Restitution*, above n 124, ch 1.

restitutionary claim may be limited by a requirement that there be a total failure of consideration and the extent of restitution may be affected in part by whether termination is retrospective or prospective. Where termination is retrospective, the contract will be unravelled in its entirety and restitution involves a return of the parties to their pre-contractual positions.[126] Where termination is prospective, restitution may include payments for benefits conferred on either party as well as the allocation of losses.[127]

Where a contract is terminated, two restitutionary issues arise for consideration: (i) has there been an unjust enrichment of either party, which requires reversal and (ii) how will the losses flowing from the termination be apportioned? An unjust enrichment will include any benefits retained by either party such as goods, services, property or money transferred, where such retention is at one party's expense and is considered to be unjust.[128] The issue of apportionment includes determining who bears losses that cannot be recovered under restitutionary principles, such as the tender costs of the contractor, the disposal of specialised goods or goods that are unusable if the contract is not fully performed because of intellectual property rights or the need for licences, and losses arising from the wasted procurement procedure and the new procurement procedure that may later be conducted.

Determining the restitutionary aftermath of termination is no easy feat and few of the jurisdictions have clear rules on how the issue is to be approached. Where the legislation is silent, then restitution in the general law may provide a model to be used in the disqualification context.

As stated, the EU procurement directives are silent on the issue of contractual termination for disqualification and the consequences of termination. There is also no indication as to whether the EU will limit Member States' discretion to terminate by imposing requirements for the consequences of termination. Thus whilst there is at present no obligation on Member States to terminate existing contracts and no requirements in relation to the restitutionary consequences of termination, draft model laws and European legislation[129] and jurisprudence in other contexts may illustrate future EU requirements in this area.

For instance, the Principles of European Contract Law (PECL)[130] deal with the consequences of termination of contracts and provide that on

[126] A Burrows, *The Law of Restitution*, 2nd edn (Oxford, Oxford University Press, 2002) 56–9. In the US see Dagan, *Law and Ethics of Restitution*, above n 123.

[127] A Burrows, 'Absence of Basis: The New Birksian Scheme' in A Burrows and A Rodger (eds), *Mapping the Law: Essays in Memory of Peter Birks* (Oxford, Oxford University Press, 2006) 41.

[128] Burrows, *Law of Restitution*, above n 126, ch 1.

[129] See Communication from the Commission to the Council and the European Parliament on European Contract Law [2001] OJ C255/1 which provides a list of Community acquis on contract law.

[130] O Lando and H Beale (eds), *Principles of European Contract Law* (The Hague, Kluwer Law International, 2000).

termination a party may recover money paid for a performance which it did not receive or which it properly rejected,[131] which is in essence restitution for a total failure of consideration. Also, a party who supplied property which can be returned and for which it has not received payment or other counter-performance may recover the property.[132] By Article 9:309 of the PECL, a party who has rendered a performance which cannot be returned and for which it has not received payment or other counter-performance may recover a reasonable amount for the value of the performance to the other party.

A similar approach is found in the European Draft Common Frame of Reference (DCR),[133] which provides extensive model rules on restitution and unjust enrichment.[134] Under the DCR, a person who has been unjustly enriched must reverse the enrichment.[135] Unjust enrichment will be deemed to have occurred unless the enriched person is entitled by contract to the enrichment, or the disadvantaged person consented freely and without error to the enrichment.[136] Where a contract becomes retrospectively avoided or ineffective, the enriched person is not permitted to retain the enrichment on this basis.[137] In addition, where a contract is terminated, a party who has received any benefit by the other's performance of obligations under the terminated contractual relationship is obliged to return it.[138] Under the DCR, enrichment may be reversed by returning the asset or its monetary value to the disadvantaged person.[139] This reversal extends also to the fruits of the enrichment.[140]

Finally, clarity on the approach to restitution may be obtained from CJEU jurisprudence. There are several cases that illustrate the principle that a public authority is permitted to restitution of money wrongly paid out,[141] and is in fact under a legal duty to recover such payments,[142] in order to prevent the unjust enrichment of the recipient, prevent the unauthorised

[131] PECL arts 9:307–9.309.

[132] PECL art 9:308.

[133] H Eidenmulller, F Faust and H Grigoleit, 'The Common Frame of Reference for European Private Law – Policy Choices and Codification Problems' (2008) *Oxford Journal of Legal Studies* 659.

[134] J Smits, 'A European Law on Unjustified Enrichment? A Critical View of the Law of Restitution in the Draft Common Frame of Reference' (2008) *Stellenbosch Law Review* 179.

[135] DCR Book VII Art 1:101.

[136] DCR Book VII Art 2:101.

[137] ibid.

[138] DCR Book III Art 3:510.

[139] DCR Book VII Art.5:101.

[140] DCR Book VII Art 5:104.

[141] Case C-54/81 *Firma Wilhelm Fromme v Bundesanstalt fur Landwirtschaftliche Marktordnung* [1982] ECR 1449; Case C-265/78 *H Ferwerda BV v Produktschap voor Vee en Vlees* [1980] ECR 617; Cases C-205–C-215/82 *Deutche Milchkontor GmbH v Germany* [1983] ECR 2633; Case C-336/00 *Huber* [2002] ECR I-7699; Case C-158/06 *ROM-projecten* [2007] ECR I-5103, para 23.

[142] Cases C-205–215/82 *Deutsche Milchkontor GmbH v Germany* [1983] ECR 2633.

use of public funds and maintain the principle of legality.[143] An individual is also entitled to recover charges made to a public authority in breach of EU law.[144] Although these cases deal with restitution where there is a breach of EU law, this approach may be instructive if in future, contractual termination for disqualification becomes a requirement under EU law. Should this ever be the case, there may be a duty on a public authority to recover payments which ought not to have been made or benefits transferred to a supplier under a contract that is subsequently terminated. Such benefits in the procurement context may include advance payments for work that has not been performed and access to services in the context of the contract, such as the use of civil servants' expertise. In addition, a supplier on a terminated contract may be permitted to recover the benefits that have been conferred on a procuring authority such as payment for goods or services supplied, or the recovery of unconsumed goods.

As discussed earlier, the UK procurement regulations are silent on the issue of termination and as discussed, there is no EU law duty on UK procuring authorities to terminate existing contracts on disqualification. As there is also no indication of how the issue of restitution and apportionment of losses will be dealt with where a contract is terminated, this issue may be dealt with under the general law of restitution.

The availability of restitution is tied to the grounds for which a contract comes to an end and as a general principle, restitution may be granted to a claimant where a contract has been discharged and it is necessary to reverse an unjust enrichment.[145] As was discussed earlier, a contract may be terminated because there is a contractual term to that effect, or because there has been a breach of statute by the supplier and money paid out by a public authority may be recovered in cases where the money is paid in breach of statute, mistakenly or *ultra vires* the public authority.[146] Should termination for disqualification become a statutory requirement in the UK, based on possible future EU law requirements, restitution may be ordered on the basis of the breach of this statutory requirement.[147]

At present, the most likely basis for termination for disqualification in the UK is a contractual term, such as a termination for convenience clause, and thus where a procuring authority includes such a clause permitting termination for disqualification in the public contract, it will be possible for the authority to claim restitution following the termination of a contract where there has been a failure of consideration.[148] As a basis of

[143] A Jones, *Restitution and European Community Law* (London, LLP, 2000) 130.

[144] A Tatham, 'Restitution of Charges and Duties Levied by the Public Administration in Breach of European Community Law' (1994) *European Law Review* 146.

[145] Virgo, *Principles of Restitution*, above n 124, ch 1; Burrows, *Law of Restitution*, above n 126, ch 1; P Birks, *An Introduction to the Law of Restitution* (Oxford, Clarendon Press, 1989) ch 1.

[146] *Auckland Harbour v R* [1924] AC 318.

[147] Jones, *Restitution and EC Law*, above n 143, 121.

[148] Virgo, *Principles of Restitution*, above n 124, ch 17.

restitution, failure of consideration will be available to a party where there is no contractual obligation to confer the relevant benefit on the defendant such as where the relevant contract has become ineffective.[149] As stated in *Fibrosa*, a failure of consideration occurs where money was paid to secure performance and this performance fails.[150] Whilst the traditional approach has been that there has to be a total failure of consideration for restitution to be possible, this appears to have been interpreted loosely by the courts and there are cases where restitution was allowed on the basis of a total failure of consideration even though some aspect of performance of the contract had been obtained.[151]

In the construction context where the contract is one for work and materials, there will be no failure of consideration once the work has commenced,[152] and the contract is not performed in apportioned stages. In such contexts, a procuring authority will be unable to obtain restitution on the basis of a failure of consideration, as the test for whether there has been a failure of consideration in such contracts was stated in *Stocznia* to be whether 'the promisor has performed any part of the contractual duties in respect of which the payment is due'.[153] There can thus be no failure of consideration where performance under such a contract has commenced, even if the claimant has not received the expected benefit under the contract.

Another possible approach to the issue of restitution may be seen in the Local Government Act 1997, which gives local authorities the power to include termination clauses in public contracts.[154] The Act gives an indication of how restitutionary issues may be approached where a contract is discharged because it is *ultra vires* and there is no agreement on the consequences of the discharge. Thus in section 7, where a contract is terminated by the courts, and there are no termination provisions in the contract, the supplier shall be entitled to be paid as he would have been paid had the contract had effect until it was determined by the courts, or as he would have been paid had the contract been discharged due to a breach of contract. Although this Act is not directly relevant to the issue of restitution on termination for disqualification, the approach in the Act may provide, by way of analogy, an indication of how procuring authorities may deal with the issue of restitution, especially where there is no failure of consideration.

From the above, it is possible to conclude that where a contract is terminated for the disqualification of the contractor, whether the termination arises from possible future EU law requirements or as a result of a

149 Burrows, *Law of Restitution*, above n 126, ch 10.

150 *Fibrosa Spolka Akcyjna v Fairbairn Lawson Combe Barbour Ltd* [1943] AC 32, 48.

151 See Virgo, *Principles of Restitution*, above n 124, ch 12; *Rowland v Divall* [1923] 2 KB 500; *DO Ferguson & Associates v Sohl* (1992) 62 BLR 95; *Goss v Chilcott* [1996] AC 788.

152 Burrows, *Law of Restitution*, above n 126, ch 10, 327.

153 *Stocznia Gdanska SA v Latvia Shipping* [1998] 1 WLR 574, 588.

154 Local Government Act 1997, s 6.

contractual term, UK procuring authorities may be entitled to restitution for sums paid out under the contract. However, for restitution to be ordered the supplier must have obtained the benefits sought to be recovered at the expense of the procuring authority and the contractor's enrichment must be deemed unjust and there must not be any reason (or defence) for denying the procuring authority a remedy.[155] Similarly, the supplier on a terminated contract ought to be able to recover the benefits or value conferred on a procuring authority where the retention of such benefits would be unjust.[156] This will be the case, even though it is the contractor's disqualification that has led to the termination, by analogy with the cases where a party in breach of contract is permitted to seek restitution where there has been a failure of consideration.

In relation to the apportionment of losses in the UK, there is no indication as to how this issue is to be addressed, where termination does not give rise to a contractual right to damages. However, one may draw an analogy with the common law approach to apportionment in frustrated contracts before the passage of the Law Reform (Frustrated Contracts) Act 1943. Thus in *Fibrosa,* the House of Lords held that where a contract is frustrated, the parties were not permitted to recover any expenditure incurred in reliance on the contract. Although this position has been rectified in relation to frustrated contracts by the above Act, it may be an appropriate approach to take in relation to contracts terminated for disqualification. The losses that are relevant here are those that do not constitute the unjustified enrichment of either party, barring the restitutionary remedies discussed above. Such losses may include the tender costs of the contractor, expenditure in preparation for the contract such as the employment of staff engaged exclusively for the contract by the procuring authority, and the costs of the procurement procedure.

The US adopts a clearer approach to the restitutionary and apportionment issues following the termination of a public contract and provides extensive rules on post-termination settlements.[157] Although US restitution law is similar to UK restitution law in several respects,[158] the FAR and the jurisprudence have provided clarity on the consequences of the termination of a public contract and as such a consideration of the general US law on restitution is not required.

In the US, convenience terminations ensure that the supplier is not unduly prejudiced by the termination, even where the termination is

[155] P Birks, *Unjust Enrichment* (Oxford, Clarendon Press, 2005) chs 9 and 10; *Banque Financiere de la Cite v Parc (Battersea Ltd)* [1999] 1 AC 221; *Portman Building Society v Hamlyn Taylor Neck* [1998] ECWA Civ 686; *Lipkin Gorman v Karpnale* [1991] 3 WLR 10.

[156] S Arrowsmith, *Civil Liability and Public Authorities* (Winteringham, Earlsgate Press, 1992) 290–91; Virgo, *Principles of Restitution*, above n 124, ch 14.

[157] FAR Part 49.

[158] Restatement (Third) of Restitution and Unjust Enrichment 2000 (United States) s 1; Dagan, *Law and Ethics of Restitution*, above n 123, ch 2.

based on the contractor's disqualification, and the approach to restitution and the apportionment of losses in the legislation is concerned with covering the losses the supplier may suffer as a result of the termination.[159] Termination for disqualification in the US is prospective and there is no issue of returning the parties to their pre-contractual positions. The FAR provides for the manner in which losses are to be apportioned between the supplier and the procuring authority.[160] Once a contract is terminated, the supplier is required to stop all work under the contract and is entitled to payment for work done prior to the termination,[161] the preparations made for the terminated portions of the contract, including a reasonable allowance for profit on the completed work,[162] but excluding the recovery of anticipated profits on the uncompleted portions of the contract.[163] The supplier may also claim any charges he may prove resulted from the termination,[164] as long as the entire settlement does not exceed the contract price.[165] Allowing the recovery of profits and losses in line with the contract price is consistent with the general law where restitution is claimed for terminated contracts and the contract price is used as a 'cap for restitutionary recovery'.[166] This is intended to avoid competition in the measures of recovery that may be available in contract and under the law of restitution.[167]

As was discussed earlier, in the World Bank context, the power to terminate contracts is reserved to the Borrower, or the agency conducting the procurement process on the Borrower's behalf. Thus, the approach to restitution and the apportionment of losses will depend on the law of the Borrower country or the governing law of contract.

The South African Corruption Act also provides limited guidance on the consequences of the termination of public contracts for disqualification. However, unlike the US and possibly owing to the punitive nature of disqualification in South Africa, the provisions are concerned with the recovery of the procuring authority's losses from the supplier. The Act provides that where the National Treasury has terminated an agreement, it may in addition to any other legal remedy, recover from the supplier any damages incurred or sustained by the state as a result of the tender

[159] R Holland, *Terminations for Convenience: A Contractor's Guide*, 2nd edn (Virginia, Management Concepts, 1998) ch 8.

[160] G Henderson, 'Terminations for Convenience and the Terminations Costs Clause' (2002) 53 *Air Force Law Review* 103.

[161] FAR 12.403(d); FAR 52.212-4.

[162] *Maxima Corp v United States* 847 F2d 1549 (Fed Cir 1988).

[163] FAR 49.201; A McConnell, 'Bad Faith as a Limitation on Terminations for Convenience: As Bad as They Say, or Not So Bad' (2003) 32 *Public Contract Law Journal* 411, 412.

[164] FAR 12.403(d); FAR 52.249(l).

[165] FAR 49.207.

[166] Dagan, *Law and Ethics of Restitution*, above n 123, ch 8, 283.

[167] A Skelton, *Restitution and Contract* (London, LLP, 1998) ch 1.

process or the conclusion of the agreement, or any losses which the state may suffer by having to make less favourable arrangements thereafter.[168]

Although it is not clear whether the state may also obtain restitution for benefits conferred on the contractor, these provisions are wide enough to include actions for unjust enrichment, since the Corruption Act provides that the state may recover losses 'in addition to any other legal remedy'. For such an action to succeed in South African law, the plaintiff must be able to show that the defendant was enriched at his expense;[169] that there is a causal link between the defendant's enrichment and the plaintiff's impoverishment;[170] and that there is the absence of cause that justifies the retention of the enrichment by the defendant.[171] It is thus possible that once a procuring authority can show that the supplier on a terminated contract has been enriched at the procuring authority's expense without cause[172] (since the underlying contract would have been terminated) the procuring authority ought to be permitted to recover any economic benefits[173] such as advance payments that were conferred on the supplier.

In the context of the South African PPPFA and PFMA regulations, it has earlier been discussed that termination under these regulations is not a consequence of disqualification, but termination is a stand-alone remedy for corruption and fraud in a public contract. Both regulations are silent as to the apportionment of losses where a contract is terminated but it is arguable that where a contract is terminated for corruption, a supplier will not be permitted to recover outstanding payments on the basis of the rule of law, which denies payment under an illegal transaction.[174] In such situations, it is also possible that the procuring authority will be able to obtain restitution for other benefits conferred on the supplier as well as compensation for the procuring authority's losses as a result of the termination. South African jurisprudence has established that illegal contracts cannot be enforced[175] and as was discussed above, the law of unjust enrichment will prevent the supplier from retaining benefits obtained under such a contract where there is no basis for the benefit to be retained.

From the above, it can be seen that not all the jurisdictions are clear on the approach to the restitutionary and apportionment issues that arise post-termination. This may cause problems in practice, as it is unlikely that a public official responsible for entering into post-termination settlements with suppliers will appreciate the technicalities of the law of restitution in

[168] Corruption Act 2004, s 28(3)(c).

[169] *Basselaar v Registrar, Durban and Coast Local Division* 2002 (1) SA 191 (D).

[170] *ABSA Bank t/a Bankfin v CB Stander t/a CAW Paneelkloppers* 1998 (1) SA 939 (C).

[171] F du Bois (ed), *Wille's Principles of South African Law* (Cape Town, Juta, 2007) ch 9.

[172] du Bois, *South African Law*, above n 171, ch 39, 1068–72.

[173] du Bois, *South African Law*, above n 171, ch 39, 1047.

[174] *Vuurman v Universal Enterprises, Ltd* 1924 TPD 488; *Chipunza v Muzangaza NO* [2004] JOL 12880 (ZH).

[175] *Chipunza*, ibid.

the jurisdiction. In the absence of clarity on these issues, it is likely that where the procuring authority and the supplier cannot come to an agreement on how to proceed in relation to these issues, the courts will determine how these issues should be addressed.

One issue that emerges in relation to restitution is determining whose interests are preferred as between the supplier and the procuring authority. The South African approach is at the end of the spectrum of possible approaches as compared with the UK and the US. The South African approach appears to favour the procuring authority by giving priority to the interests of the state, but the US appears to favour the supplier in relation to the procuring authority. In the UK, it is likely that based on the general law of restitution, the UK may adopt an approach which seeks to strike a balance between the competing interests of the supplier and the procuring authority.

Another issue that arises on which all the jurisdictions are silent is whether a supplier may challenge a termination for its disqualification on the basis that the cause for disqualification has been removed. This may not be possible where termination is based on a termination for convenience clause, as exists in the UK and US, as such clauses give the government a very wide discretion to terminate public contracts.

9.4.3 Disproportionality and the Rule Against Double Jeopardy

Terminating a contract on the basis of the disqualification of the supplier may raise issues of proportionality,[176] especially where disqualification is based on a conviction, since the conviction and the consequent disqualification will have already served to penalise the supplier for the criminal activity, and further 'punishment' in the form of the cancellation of existing contracts may be unnecessary.[177] This is especially relevant where the existing contract is not affected by corruption. The termination of existing contracts for disqualification may also be at odds with the non-punitive rationales for disqualification in relevant jurisdictions.

The termination of a contract for the disqualification of a supplier may disproportionately affect the supplier in three ways. First, past supplier performance and experience is generally an important aspect of the qualifications of a supplier bidding for public contracts, and termination may mean that in future, the supplier is unable to prove a sufficient number of projects that illustrate its experience in a particular sector. Secondly, and depending on the size of the terminated contract, the termination may

[176] Case C-213/07 *Michaniki AE v Ethniko Simvoulio Radiotileorasis* [2008] ECR I-9999, paras 46, 48, and 61.

[177] E Tomko and K Weinberg, 'After the Fall: Conviction, Debarment and Double Jeopardy' (1992) 21 *Public Contract Law Journal* 355.

adversely affect the contractor's finances, including share prices,[178] especially if the supplier operates in a specialised sector such as defence and is unable to obtain business from the private sector. Thirdly, termination may act as a further penalty for an offence for which the supplier has already been convicted and disqualified. As discussed in chapter two, where a supplier is subject to both criminal and administrative sanctions such as where disqualification is based on a conviction, the disqualification of the supplier by administrative process in addition to its criminal conviction may offend the rule against double jeopardy,[179] where the sanctions pursue the same ends.

In the EU, the rule against double jeopardy is a fundamental aspect of EU law,[180] and applies where multiple sanctions for the same offence pursue the same ends or protect the same legal interest.[181] It is possible to argue that in the context of the mandatory provisions, the termination of a contract following a disqualification and a conviction may amount to more than one sanction for the same offence, unless a procuring authority is able to show that the purpose behind termination differs from the purposes behind both the conviction and the disqualification of the supplier, which may be difficult to do. Similarly, the UK also adopts a common law[182] prohibition against being tried or punished for the same offence, and similar to the EU, multiple penalties will not offend the double jeopardy rule where the penalties do not have the same purpose.[183] However, a procuring authority may find it difficult where challenged, to argue that the purpose for terminating the contract is not met by the other measures already taken against the supplier. In the US, the rule against double jeopardy also extends to a prohibition against multiple punishments for the same offence.[184] Where a supplier has been convicted, disqualified and has had a contract terminated, it is possible to argue that in reality, the supplier is faced with multiple punishments for the same offence even if the termination is not intended to be punitive.[185] This is because

[178] *Gonzalez v Freeman* 334 F2d 570, 574 (DC Cir 1964).

[179] N Garoupa and F Gomez-Pomar, 'Punish Once or Punish Twice: A Theory of the use of Criminal Sanctions in Addition to Regulatory Penalties' (2004) 6 *American Law and Economics Review* 410; Tomko and Weinberg, 'After the Fall', above n 177.

[180] Case 18/65R *Gutmann v Commission of the European Atomic Energy Community* [1966] ECR 135; Convention for the Protection of Human Rights and Fundamental Freedoms (European Convention on Human Rights) 231 UNTS 222, protocol 7, art 4.

[181] Case T-236/01, *Tokai Carbon Co Ltd v Commission of the European Communities (Graphite Electrodes)* [2004] ECR II-1181.

[182] W Blackstone, *Commentaries on the Laws of England* (Book 4, 1800) ch 26 at 355–56; Law Commission: Double Jeopardy – A summary, Consultation Paper 156 (2001).

[183] *Borders (UK) v Commissioner of Police of the Metropolis* [2005] EWCA Civ 197, para 17.

[184] *United States v Halper* 490 US 435 (1989); G Thomas, *Double Jeopardy: The History, The Law* (New York, New York University Press, 1998) chs 1 and 2; AB Poulin, 'Double Jeopardy and Multiple Punishment: Cutting the Gordian Knot' (2006) 77 *University of Colorado Law Review* 595.

[185] *US v Halper*, ibid, 448.

the rule against double jeopardy may be offended where an additional civil sanction may not be characterised as remedial.[186] Where a contract is terminated on disqualification in the US, it is difficult to see how such a termination can be considered to be remedial, as the termination will not in itself eliminate corruption and the termination is final, in that the supplier may not resume the contract by promising to do or refrain from doing something. In addition, where the supplier has implemented rehabilitation measures, which eliminate the cause for disqualification prior to the termination of the contract, this may lend further credence to the punitive nature of the termination.[187]

Similar to the other jurisdictions, South African law also recognises a rule against double jeopardy. The judicial nature of disqualifications under the Corruption Act means that disqualifications under the Act do not offend the rule against double jeopardy because the double jeopardy rule does not 'limit legislative authority to define punishment'.[188] However, where termination follows a prior disqualification, in other contexts, it is arguable that the termination may amount to a multiple punishment for the same offence, offending the double jeopardy rule unless the aim of the termination differs from the aims of the preceding conviction and disqualification. As the main rationale for the disqualification regime in South Africa is punitive, this may suggest that termination is also punitive and may thus offend the double jeopardy rule.

Whether a jurisdiction is under an obligation to consider the disproportionate effect of termination on a supplier may be informed by the rationales for termination in that jurisdiction. However, none of the jurisdictions which provide for the possibility of termination have expressly addressed this issue. This is not surprising in the context of the EU and UK given that the legislation is silent on the issue. However, it is arguable that in line with the EU principle of proportionality,[189] a procuring authority ought to consider the impact termination will have on the supplier. In *Michaniki*, it was held that in accordance with the principle of proportionality, a disqualification regime must not go beyond what is necessary to achieve its objectives.[190] Thus, where a supplier claims that the termination of a contract following disqualification is a disproportionate penalty, the courts may be open to revoking the termination as long as this does

[186] *US v Halper*, ibid.

[187] Tomko and Weinberg, 'After the Fall', above n 177, 363.

[188] Poulin, 'Double Jeopardy and Multiple Punishment', above n 184, 597.

[189] N Emiliou, *The Principle of Proportionality in European Law* (Kluwer Law, 1996); E Ellis (ed), *The Principle of Proportionality in the Laws of Europe* (Oxford, Hart Publishing, 1999); G de Burca, 'The Principle of Proportionality and its Application in EC Law (1993) 13 *Yearbook of European Law* 105.

[190] Case C-213/07 *Michaniki* [2008] ECR I-9999, paras 47–49, opinion of AG Maduro at para 34. See also Cases C-21/03 and C-34/03 *Fabricom South Africa v Etat Belge* [2005] ECR I-1559, para 34.

not undermine the disqualification regime.[191] Arrowsmith has also suggested in the context of contracts concluded in breach of the procurement procedure that a procuring authority should consider the consequences to the supplier in coming to a decision to terminate the contract.[192]

In the US, the provisions in the FAR dealing with the apportionment of losses post-termination may limit the disproportionate impact of termination on the supplier and where a contract is terminated in circumstances where the effect of the termination is unduly disproportionate on the contractor, the courts have held that the termination was unlawful.[193]

In South Africa, whilst the National Treasury is permitted to terminate existing contracts with a disqualified contractor, the Treasury is required to take several factors into account, including the impact of the termination.[194] Although this provision does not indicate whether it is the impact of the termination on the supplier that may be considered, it is possible to interpret this provision in such a manner as to give the Treasury pause if the impact of the termination on the supplier will be unduly disproportionate.

In conclusion, it is clear that most jurisdictions convicting for corruption will aim to ensure that the penalties are tailored to fit the offence. Where further penalties in the form of disqualification and termination are permitted outside of the judicial process, these penalties increase the penalty load of the convicted person, possibly without a formal consideration of the criminal penalties the supplier has already been subject to. Thus even where termination does not offend the double jeopardy rule, the disproportionate effect of termination on a supplier should mean that termination is only utilised where it is absolutely necessary to fulfil policy objectives that were not met by the conviction, and disqualification of the supplier and termination should be limited to situations where it is necessary to protect the public interest.[195]

9.4.4 Waste and Inefficiency

Termination may be wasteful and economically inefficient and may have extreme resource and cost implications, especially in the construction context.[196] Termination could be wasteful in relation to the substance of the contract, where the nature of the contract is such that the contract must be

[191] P Craig and G de Burca, *EU Law: Text, Cases and Materials*, 4th edn (Oxford, Oxford University Press, 2007) ch 9.

[192] Arrowsmith, *Public and Utilities Procurement*, above n 9, ch 21.15.

[193] *Art-Metal USA Inc v Solomon*, 473 F Supp 1 (DDC 1978).

[194] Corruption Act 2004, s 28(3)(a)(i).

[195] Arrowsmith, *Public and Utilities Procurement*, above n 9, ch 21.13.

[196] P Henty, 'OGC Consultation on the Implementation of the New Remedies Directive' (2009) 1 *Public Procurement Law Review* NA48, 50.

fully completed before the procuring authority may derive the benefits from the contract such as the installation of a computer network system and in cases where it is not possible to engage another supplier midway through the contract.[197]

Another area in which termination may be wasteful is in relation to the losses that may follow termination. This relates to both the financial losses of the parties as well as procurement costs. Depending on the approach to the apportionment of losses in a jurisdiction, a procuring authority may be liable for the losses suffered by the supplier on the terminated contract. Where termination is not based on a contractual term and there are no deficiencies in the terminated contract, the procuring authority or the government may be liable to pay damages to the supplier.[198] Such damages may include expenditure for loss of profits and consequential losses such as the loss of future contracts as a result of the stigma of the terminated contract, or losses that that may result from the supplier being unable to meet turnover requirements for future contracts.[199] The reality of such damages is recognised and provided for by the US FAR in the provisions on convenience terminations.

In addition, unless the costs of the wasted procurement procedure are recoverable from the contractor, as is the case in South Africa, [200] the procuring authority will have to bear this loss. Further, where the contract is terminated for disqualification and is not based on the *mala fides* of the supplier in respect of the terminated contract, in the absence of regulations to the contrary, the costs of re-procurement are likely to be borne by the procuring authority, as is the case in the US.[201]

The waste that could result when a public contract is terminated is also at odds both with the value for money and efficiency goals of domestic public procurement[202] and also with the movement towards increasing efficiency and reducing waste in public procurement[203] and is another reason why termination for disqualification should be used circumspectly. The South African provisions give effect to this by requiring the National

[197] S Treumer, 'Towards an Obligation to Terminate Contracts Concluded in Breach of the EC Public Procurement Rules: The End of the Status of Concluded Contracts as Sacred Cows' (2007) 6 *Public Procurement Law Review* 371, 380.

[198] Arrowsmith, Linarelli and Wallace, *Regulating Public Procurement*, above n 1, 789.

[199] *Ronald J Rhen v US*, 17 Cl Ct 140 (1989).

[200] Corruption Act 2004, s 28(3)(c).

[201] FAR 12.402.

[202] Arrowsmith, Linarelli and Wallace, *Regulating Public Procurement*, above n 1, ch 2.

[203] For the UK see HM Treasury, *Efficiency in Civil Government Procurement* (July 1998); Gershon, *Review of Civil Procurement in central government* (April 1999) and S Norris, 'The Gershon Review: A Driver for Reform at the Heart of Central Government Procurement' (1999) 6 *Public Procurement Law Review* CS177; Arrowsmith, *Public and Utilities Procurement*, above n 9, ch 2. For the US see S Kelman, *Unleashing Change: A Study of Organizational Renewal in Government* (Washington, Brookings Institution Press, 2006) 18–21. For South Africa see Green Paper on Government Procurement (1999) and P Bolton, *The Law of Government Procurement in South Africa* (Durban, LexisNexis Butterworth, 2007) ch 5.

Treasury under the Corruption Act to consider whether extreme costs will follow from the termination.[204] It is assumed that where a contract is awarded, the award is made on the best terms possible and thus, apart from the losses that arise from the termination, where the contract is re-tendered it is likely that the government is not going to obtain best value in the re-procurement procedure, if the contract was initially awarded to the most economically advantageous supplier in the terminated contract or the supplier providing the best value to the government.

9.4.5 The Effect of Termination on the Delivery of Public Services

The decision to terminate a public contract may be accompanied by consequences that do not occur in the private sector and may compromise the delivery of public services. The adverse effect of termination on the delivery of public services is a public interest concern that ought to be taken into account when termination is considered and may also signal that termination is disproportionate in a particular circumstance.

Although there is no indication on how this issue should be addressed in the selected jurisdictions, some clarity may be obtained from the approach in other contexts. As was discussed in the context of ineffective contracts in the EU, a Member State has the discretion not to terminate a contract (or declare it ineffective) where there are overriding interests in the general interest, and this provision may be used to take public interest concerns into account. Thus, by way of analogy in the disqualification context, where termination may affect or compromise the delivery of public services, especially where those services are essential, then a public contract should not be terminated for disqualification.[205]

In *Commission v Spain*,[206] the Commission challenged a provision in Spanish procurement law which provided that where a contract is declared invalid for a breach of procurement law and implementing this decision will disrupt public services, the contract may continue until steps are taken to avoid any harm to the public. In support of Spain, the CJEU held that

> the aim of the provision is not to prevent the enforcement of the declaration of invalidity of a specific contract, but to avoid, where the public interest is at stake, excessive and potentially prejudicial consequences of the immediate enforcement of the declaration, pending the adoption of urgent measures, in order to ensure the continuity of public services,[207]

[204] Corruption Act 2004, s 28(3)(a).
[205] Treumer, 'Towards an Obligation to Terminate Contracts', above n 197, 381.
[206] Case C-444/06 *Commission v Spain* [2008] ECR I-2045.
[207] Case C-444/06 *Commission v Spain*, ibid, para 55.

and that consequently, the provision did not undermine the procurement remedies directive.

A similar approach may apply in relation to the UK. As discussed in the context of ineffective provisions, a contract may not be declared ineffective by the courts when there are overriding reasons in the general interest, including when declaring a contract ineffective would lead to disproportionate consequences.[208] Thus, it is arguable that the adverse effect of termination on the delivery of public services may be regarded as a disproportionate consequence that should preclude termination in a given case. This has been the approach in France, where effects of termination on the public interest are a key consideration in termination decisions. Arrowsmith suggests that where termination is considered, other interests that would be prejudiced apart from those of the procuring authority and the supplier should be taken into account.[209] Similarly, Treumer suggests that a decision to terminate a public contract should only be made after a consideration of the public interest.[210]

In the US, where a procuring authority wishes to terminate a contract for the disqualification of a contractor, the procuring authority is required to consider the propriety of the termination,[211] and it is arguable that termination will not be appropriate where it will adversely affect the delivery of public services.

As was discussed earlier, under the South African Corruption Act, where the National Treasury is contemplating contractual termination for the disqualification of a contractor, it must consider the urgency of the goods or services to be supplied under the contract and any other factor that may impact on the termination of the contract.[212] Thus, similar to the position in the other jurisdictions, termination may be avoided if it will adversely affect the delivery of public services.

The effect of termination on the delivery of public services necessitates a flexible and considered approach to termination and a procuring authority must seek to balance the adverse impact of termination against the desire to fulfil the rationales supporting the disqualification regime.

9.4.6 The Effect of Termination on Third Parties

Contractual termination may have severe implications for third parties. Where a contract involves subcontractors, lenders or finance providers, termination may adversely affect these persons and a contractor on a

[208] PCR reg 47L.
[209] Arrowsmith, *Public and Utilities Procurement*, above n 9, ch 21.15.
[210] Treumer, 'Towards an Obligation to Terminate Contracts', above n 197, 382.
[211] FAR 9.405-1; *Torncello v US* 231 Ct Cl 20 (1982).
[212] Corruption Act 2004, s 28(3)(a).

terminated contract may be forced to terminate subcontracts and repay unspent portions of finance, with possible penalties. Termination may also affect a subcontractor's finances and ability to tender for future work in the same way as it affects those of the primary contractor. The issue that arises in relation to third parties is determining what remedies such third parties may have either against the procuring authority or the disqualified primary contractor where a contract is terminated.

In relation to obtaining remedies against a procuring authority, in the absence of overriding statutory requirements, the doctrine of privity of contract may prevent an aggrieved subcontractor from obtaining remedies against the procuring authority. The doctrine of privity of contract operates in very similar ways in all the jurisdictions.

In the EU, although there is no European law of contract, the DCR mentioned above provides that a contract is not binding on persons who are not parties to the contract,[213] although the parties to a contract may by the contract confer a right or other benefit on a third party.[214] Thus if the contract confers a remedial right against the procuring authority on the subcontractor, the subcontractor may assert this right. However, in the absence of such a provision, the doctrine of privity will prevent the subcontractor from being able to assert remedial rights against a procuring authority.[215]

The doctrine of privity in the UK is governed by both common law and statute. The common law was adamant in providing that a person who was not a party to a contract could not sue to enforce that contract, even if the contract was entered into for his benefit.[216] The Contracts (Rights of Third Parties) Act 1999, however, gives a third party a limited right to sue to enforce a contract in cases where the contract expressly provides that he may do so,[217] and where the contract purports to confer a benefit on the third party[218] and there is no indication to the contrary.[219] Thus, if a public contract confers a right on a subcontractor to sue the procuring authority, he may do so under the 1999 Act. The remedy available to the subcontractor in such a case will be any remedy that would have been available to him had he been a party to the contract.[220]

[213] H MacQueen, E Clive and L Macgregor, 'Privity of Contract in the DCFR' (2009) *European Private Law News*. Available at: www.law.ed.ac.uk/epln/blogentry.aspx?blogentryref=7704.

[214] DCR art II: II-9-301(1).

[215] H Kotz and A Flessner, *European Contract Law* (trans T Weir), vol 1 (Oxford, Clarendon Press, 1997) ch 13; AS Hartkamp et al (eds), *Towards a European Civil Code* (Kluwer Law, 1998) ch 19.

[216] *Tweddle v Atkinson* (1861) 1 B & S 393; *Dunlop Pneumatic Tyre Co v Selfridge* [1915] AC 847.

[217] Contracts (Rights of Third Parties) Act 1999, s 1(1)(a).

[218] Contracts (Rights of Third Parties) Act 1999, s 1(1)(b); *Prudential Assurance v Ayres* [2007] EWHC 775 (Ch).

[219] Contracts (Rights of Third Parties) Act 1999, s 1(2); *Nisshin Shipping Co Ltd v Cleaves & Co* [2003] EWHC 2602 (Comm).

[220] Contracts (Rights of Third Parties) Act 1999, s 1(5).

A similar approach to the UK common law doctrine of privity obtains in the US, where only a person with whom the government has privity of contract may sue the government in relation to public contracts.[221] In relation to terminations for convenience in the US, the contract law approach is given statutory force by the FAR, which provides that a subcontractor has no contractual rights against the government on the termination of a contract and the subcontractor's rights exist against the primary contractor.[222] Once a contract is terminated, the primary contractor is bound to terminate all subcontracts that relate to the terminated contract and primary contractors are encouraged to include termination clauses in subcontracts for their protection.[223] In addition, the failure of a primary contractor to include an appropriate termination clause in a subcontract shall not affect the government's right to require the termination of the subcontract.[224] Under the FAR, the primary contractor is required to enter into a settlement with its subcontractors, which will be incorporated into the settlement between the primary contractor and the government.[225] The FAR thus regulates the relationship between the primary contractor and subcontractor on the termination of a public contract.

South African law is silent on this issue. However, under the general law and similar to the other jurisdictions, the only persons who may obtain rights or incur obligations under a contract are the parties to the contract.[226] For a third party to incur liability or acquire rights under a contract, the contract must contain a provision accepted by the third party.[227] Accordingly, if a public contract does not contain a stipulation conferring a right to sue the government directly for the subcontractor's losses on the termination of the contract, which stipulation has been accepted by the subcontractor, then the doctrine of privity will preclude the subcontractor from seeking remedies from the government.

Where the doctrine of privity of contract precludes the subcontractor from asserting remedial rights against the procuring authority as has been discussed, the subcontractor will have to seek remedies against the primary supplier. The nature of the remedies will depend on the effect that the termination of the primary contract is deemed to have on the subcontract. Although a detailed examination of this issue is beyond the scope of

[221] *Flexfab, LLC v United States*, 424 F3d 1254, 1263 (Fed Cir 2005); *Erickson Air Crane Co v United States*, 731 F2d 810, 813 (Fed Cir 1984); J Thrasher, 'Subcontractor Dispute Remedies: Asserting Subcontractor Claims against the Federal Government' (1994) 23 *Public Contract Law Journal* 39.

[222] FAR 49:108-1.

[223] FAR 49:108-2(a).

[224] FAR 49:108-2(b).

[225] FAR 49:108-2 and 108-3.

[226] R Christie, *The Law of Contract in South Africa* (Durban, LexisNexis, 2006) 260–61; *Compass Motor Industries (Pty) Ltd v Callguard (Pty) Ltd* 1990 (2) SA 520 (W).

[227] du Bois, *Wille's Principles of South African Law*, above n 171, ch 26, 815.

this book, there are three possible approaches that may be taken. First, it is possible that the primary supplier will be in breach of contract to the subcontractor owing to the termination of the primary contract. This may mean the primary supplier becomes liable in damages for the full extent of the subcontractor's losses subject to the rules on remoteness and mitigation in the jurisdiction. Secondly, the primary supplier may have included a cancellation clause in the contract, which would permit it to cancel the subcontract if the primary contract is terminated. This is the approach suggested by the US FAR to primary contractors. Thirdly, the remedial consequences may depend on whether the jurisdiction regards the subcontract as frustrated by the termination of the primary contract. For instance, under common law, it is possible that the termination of the primary contract frustrates the subcontract by making the subcontract impossible to perform, since the primary supplier and those associated with it will no longer have access to the procuring authority's premises for delivery of goods and services and of course, the underlying basis of the subcontract would have ceased to exist.[228]

The adverse effect of termination on third parties is another reason why jurisdictions should be reluctant to terminate contracts for disqualification. A policy of termination may also deter would-be subcontractors from entering into public contracts and may lead to disproportionate consequences where subcontractors are concerned.

9.5 SUMMARY AND ANALYSIS OF MAIN ISSUES

As can be seen, the termination of existing contracts for disqualification is a complex issue on which there is little clarity in many of the jurisdictions under study. The lack of a clear approach to termination and the difficulties associated with the consequences of termination may create problems for procuring authorities wishing to terminate contracts for disqualification and may result in unnecessary litigation in such jurisdictions.

9.5.1 The Existence of a Duty to Terminate

As was seen, there is no duty on procuring authorities in any of the selected jurisdictions to terminate a subsisting contract solely because the supplier has been disqualified for corruption, in cases where the existing contract is unaffected by corruption. In the EU, the limited circumstances in which contractual termination is required under the amendments to the remedies directive and the court's attitude in *Wall AG* in the context of

[228] *Davis Contractors*, above n 63; Peel and Treitel, *Law of Contract*, above n 53, ch 19.

proceedings by a supplier before national review bodies both point to the fact that Member States are currently not under a duty to terminate existing contracts for a mandatory disqualification. However, it is possible in future for the CJEU to require termination for disqualification given that the decision in *Commission v Germany*[229] left open the circumstances in which termination may be required in EU law.

In the UK, as discussed, there is no duty to terminate existing contracts for a mandatory disqualification based on EU law. There is also currently no duty to terminate such contracts under UK public law or under the common law. However, as discussed, some UK procuring authorities include termination for convenience clauses in their contracts, which may be relied on by a procuring authority to terminate an existing contract based on the disqualification of the supplier. In cases where there is corruption within the existing contract, as discussed above, public contracts often contain clauses entitling the procuring authority to terminate such contracts. The general contract law also permits the rescission of contracts induced by corruption.

In the US, there is similarly no duty to terminate existing contracts solely on the basis of the supplier's disqualification. However, all US public contracts contain a termination for convenience clause which may be used by procuring authorities to terminate subsisting contracts for disqualification. Unlike the situation in the UK/US, South African procuring entities are not permitted to terminate an existing contract for the subsequent disqualification of the supplier, and instead, the National Treasury is given the power to determine whether it will terminate a subsisting contract with a disqualified supplier. In all domestic jurisdictions, the general contract law permits termination where a contract is tainted with corruption.

In the World Bank, as discussed, Borrowers are not required to terminate existing contracts for the disqualification of a supplier, but similar to the US, the contract between the Borrower and the supplier contains a termination for convenience clause which may possibly be used by the Borrower to terminate an existing contract in this context.

9.5.2 The Nature and Consequences of Termination

Determining the nature and consequences of termination is a complex issue which may present several problems for a procuring authority. As was discussed, the first issue to be addressed will be determining whether the termination will be retrospective or prospective. In cases where the existing contract is tainted by corruption, the position is clearer as most

[229] Case C-503/04 *Commission v Germany* [2007] ECR I-6153.

jurisdictions regard corruption in the formation of a contract as a reason for the retrospective cancellation of the contract.

In the cases where the termination of an existing contract is based solely on disqualification and that contract is not tainted with corruption, most jurisdictions treat termination as being prospective. As was seen, there is no clarity on this issue in the EU and where this issue is determined under the law of Member States, this will result in an inconsistent approach among the Member States that decide to exercise their discretion to terminate existing contracts for disqualification. In the UK, where the contract is unaffected by corruption, termination is most likely to be prospective, given the approach to termination in the remedies provisions of the UK regulations and the statutory approach as illustrated by the Local Government Act 1997. Termination in the US also appears to be prospective, given the provisions on termination payments in the FAR. In South Africa, it is not clear from the law whether termination by the National Treasury under the Corruption Act is prospective or retrospective, and the limited jurisprudence available suggests that termination may be retrospective where the contract has not been executed.

The restitutionary consequence of termination is another complex issue on which there is little clarity in the selected jurisdictions. In the EU, the current position is that the EU has not circumscribed Member States' discretion to determine these issues and the restitutionary consequences of termination will thus be based on the domestic law of the Member State concerned. It was seen that there are similarities between what may be the EU law approach to restitution (based on the model laws) and the approaches in the UK, the US and South Africa, and in each jurisdiction, restitution is permitted where there is an unjust enrichment and depending on the jurisdiction, a total or partial failure of consideration.

In determining the apportionment of other losses not covered by a restitutionary claim, in the EU, this again has been left to Member States' discretion. The UK has not provided any indication on what approach it may take, but the US FAR provides for the payments of the supplier's losses, as long as those losses do not exceed the contract price. In contrast, the South African provisions permit the National Treasury to recover the government's losses from the supplier. A better approach, which lies between the South African and the US approach, may be for a jurisdiction to either seek to apportion the losses between the procuring entity and the supplier, or to let the losses lie where they have fallen, in cases where termination is sought in fulfilment of a policy objective and not because of any deficiencies in the contract.

As was discussed, the adverse and disproportionate effect of termination on the disqualified supplier, third parties and the public requires a cautious approach to termination for disqualification. It may be difficult, however, for a government to resist the calls to terminate a contract with a disqualified supplier where the disqualification involved a high-profile supplier and attracted media attention and the supplier is still seen to be performing public contracts. The upshot is that in considering termination, a government must try to balance the public interest in seeking to fulfil the policy rationale for disqualification with the interests of the parties that may be affected by the termination.

It is suggested that jurisdictions that adopt a policy of contractual termination for disqualification or that permit authorities to terminate public contracts should provide clarity in the legislation on the nature and consequences of termination, as is done by the US. This will clarify the expectations of suppliers and procuring entities and reduce the potential for litigation where such contracts are terminated.

10

Derogating From Disqualification

10.1 INTRODUCTION

A SUPPLIER MAY avoid being disqualified where a cause for disqualification exists because the legislation grants a disqualifying entity the discretion in limited circumstances to derogate from the requirement to disqualify a supplier, or because an entity such as a procuring entity is permitted where justifiable to enter into a contract with a disqualified supplier. There are two main grounds on which a supplier may avoid disqualification: exceptional situations and rehabilitation measures. Exceptional situations include public interest (including public health), national security, emergencies and the economic consequences or impact of disqualification, the presence of which make it inappropriate to disqualify the supplier even though the supplier has committed or been convicted of a relevant offence. Rehabilitation measures are those measures that a supplier may take to ensure that it is no longer regarded as corrupt, such as eliminating the cause for disqualification by terminating the employment of persons who committed offences and internal reorganisation to ensure that corrupt activity can no longer flourish within the firm.[1]

The possibility to derogate from a disqualification requirement may depend on the rationale for disqualification in a jurisdiction and the discretion the disqualifying entity possesses in deciding on the different aspects of the disqualification decision. The availability of derogation provisions in a disqualification system is important for two reasons. First, such provisions provide procuring authorities with the flexibility to refrain from disqualifying suppliers where the disqualification is not appropriate and secondly, derogations introduce an element of proportionality and fairness into the disqualification system and provide a means of relaxing what could be an otherwise harsh measure, especially where the supplier has subsequently become rehabilitated.

[1] S Arrowsmith, H-J Priess and P Friton, 'Self-Cleaning as a Defence to Exclusions for Misconduct: An Emerging Concept in EU Public Procurement Law' (2009) 6 *Public Procurement Law Review* 257, 259.

This chapter will examine the reasons for which disqualification may be avoided in the jurisdictions under study and how to prevent abuse in the implementation of derogations.

10.2 REASONS FOR DEROGATING FROM DISQUALIFICATION

10.2.1 Exceptional Situations

The exceptional situations that could be relied on to derogate from a disqualification requirement are public interest (including public health), national security and the economic costs and impact of disqualification. These are not mutually exclusive and may often overlap in practice. For instance, national security concerns and the adverse impact of disqualification may often be regarded as public interest considerations. In addition, these situations are not finite categories of situations in which derogation may be appropriate, but have been chosen as the most common and justifiable reasons for derogating from a disqualification requirement.

10.2.1.1 Public interest (including public health)

Public interest may be defined as anything which is of serious concern and benefit to the public and is in the interest or serves the interest of the public.[2] The concept of public interest assumes that there is a common good, which is in the interest of the community, even if it is against the interest of some individuals in the community.[3] Although the term 'public interest' is common in legal and political discourse, there is no universal acceptance of its meaning and many uses of 'public interest' are indistinguishable from concepts of morality,[4] public health and safety.

The EU, the UK and the US explicitly state that derogations from the disqualification requirement could be made for public interest reasons. The EU directives permit derogation from the mandatory requirement to disqualify where there are 'overriding requirements in the general interest'.[5] Although the directives do not define the circumstances in which derogations might be appropriate and have left this to the discretion of Member States, the derogations from the disqualification requirement may be interpreted in

[2] For instance, in the UK see Freedom of Information Act Awareness Guidance No 3: Public Interest Test. Available at: www.ico.gov.uk; Exemption briefing series: Public interest test: Freedom of Information Act (Scotland) 2002, s 2: www.itspublicknowledge.info/nmsruntime/saveasdialog.asp?lID=2577&sID=684.

[3] B Bozeman, *Public values and Public Interest: Counterbalancing Economic Individualism* (Washington, Georgetown University Press, 2007) 89.

[4] Bozeman, *Public Values and Public Interest*, ibid, 84.

[5] PSD art 45(1).

the same manner as existing public interest derogations[6] under the EU Treaty and the procurement directives.

Specific public interest concerns in the EU include ensuring public health and or safety,[7] and as such, public health may be relied on as a reason for derogating from the mandatory disqualification provisions. The preparatory documents to the directives indicated that derogations from the disqualifications may apply in cases of public health problems, where the only available medicines are provided by a supplier who is to be disqualified.[8] Although there is no explicit derogation from the procurement directives for public health, the recitals to the directives indicate that the directives do not affect the application of measures necessary to protect public health in so far as those measures are in conformity with the Treaty,[9] which permits derogation from the free movement provisions for public health reasons.[10]

In applying the public health derogations under the Treaty, the CJEU has considered whether such measures are the least trade-restrictive means of achieving the stated objective[11] and whether the public health claim is sustainable in light of available scientific evidence.[12] Similar reasoning may be applied to derogations from the disqualification requirement invoked on public health grounds. In addition, where such derogations are invoked, they must be interpreted in line with existing EU jurisprudence, such that any derogation would need to be appropriate, necessary and proportionate to its objective, and must not be used to discriminate against suppliers from other Member States.[13]

In implementing the EU directives, the UK procurement regulations repeat verbatim the derogation provisions of the directives without clarifying the limits of the provision.[14] As the UK must comply with the EU directives in effect,[15] the reasons for derogating in the UK may be similar to the reasons for derogating in the EU.

6 Communication from the Commission to the European Parliament of concerning the common position of the Council on the adoption of a Directive of the European Parliament and of the Council on the coordination for the procedures for the award of public works contracts, public supply contracts, and public supply contracts (25/3/2003) SEC(2003) 366 final, 8.

7 TFEU arts 9, 36, 45, 52.

8 European Parliament's Legislative resolution on the Council common position with a view to adopting a European parliament and Council directive coordinating the procurement procedures of entities operating in the water, energy, transport and postal services sectors (12634/3/2002-C5-0142/2003-2000/0117(COD)).

9 PSD recital 6.

10 TFEU arts 36, 45 and 52.

11 Case C-40/82, *Commission v United Kingdom* [1982] ECR 2793, para 41.

12 Case C-174/82 *Officier van Justitie v Sandoz BV* [1983] ECR 2445.

13 Case C-318/86, *Commission v French Republic* [1988] ECR 3559.

14 Public Contracts Regulations 2006, reg 23(2).

15 *Brent London Borough Council & Others v Risk Management Partners* [2011] UKSC 7.

The OGC Guidance document attempts to clarify the derogation provisions in the UK regulations and suggests that a national emergency, as defined by the Civil Contingencies Act 2004, would be an appropriate reason for derogating from the mandatory disqualifications.[16] The Civil Contingencies Act defines an emergency as: an event or a situation which threatens serious damage to human welfare in the UK; an event or a situation which threatens serious damage to the environment in the UK; or war or terrorism which threatens serious damage to the security of the UK. Under the Act, such an event includes one which may cause: loss of or injury to human life; homelessness; damage to property; disruption of supplies of money, food, water, energy or fuel; disruption of communication, transport or health services and contamination of land, water, air with biological, chemical or radioactive matter.[17] The Act thus includes varying public health concerns in its definition of 'emergency' and as such, public health seems a likely reason for which a UK procuring authority may derogate from the mandatory disqualification provisions.

From the above, the UK regulations may coincide with EU law in relation to appropriate reasons to derogate from the requirement to disqualify. However, as stated, procuring authorities will need to ensure that when they are invoking these reasons to derogate, the measure is exercised in line with the requirements of EU law.[18]

There are no derogation provisions in relation to the discretionary disqualification provisions in the EU and the UK. This is appropriate, given that procuring authorities have discretion to decide on all aspects of the discretionary provisions.

The US approach to derogations is to permit other procuring authorities that are bound to respect a prior disqualification to contract with a disqualified supplier where it is appropriate to do so. Thus, although there are slight differences in the approach of the EU/UK and the US, the practical effect remains the same, and a supplier who has been or who ought to be disqualified remains eligible to obtain a public contract.

The FAR permits procuring authorities to enter into a contract with a disqualified supplier where there are 'compelling reasons' for doing so.[19] Although compelling reason is not defined in the FAR, some guidance may be found in the Defence Federal Acquisition Regulations (DFARS) and other procurement regulations, which model the FAR for specific agencies. Under these regulations, 'compelling reasons' include public interest (eg where only a disqualified supplier can provide the supplies or

[16] OGC Guidance, para 9.

[17] Civil Contingencies Act 2004, s 1(2) and 1(3).

[18] Case C-31/87, *Beentjes* [1988] ECR 4635, para 37; Case C-72/83, *Campus Oil v Ministry for Industry and Energy* [1984] ECR 2727.

[19] FAR 9.406-1(c).

services;[20] the exigencies of urgency;[21] or preventing a severe disruption of the agency's operations to the detriment of the government or the general public),[22] rehabilitation measures and national security.[23]

Although these agency-specific procurement regulations provide some guidance as to what may amount to a compelling reason, the lack of explicit guidance in the FAR on what constitutes an appropriate reason for derogation has led to a situation where the term 'compelling reason' has been used loosely in some cases. For instance, derogations granted by federal agencies to MCI WorldCom in the aftermath of its temporary disqualification from government contracts by the General Services Administration (GSA)[24] were given in one instance in order not to hinder the ability of residents of an Armed Forces Retirement Home to stay in touch with family and friends.[25] In relation to WorldCom, another plausible explanation for the tenuous derogations may be because WorldCom was the US government's largest telecommunications provider[26] and switching to an alternative supplier would be expensive, time consuming and disruptive – and possibly not in the public interest. However, the WorldCom example shows that where the legislation is vague as to the kind and scope of justifiable reasons for derogating from disqualification, procuring agencies may adopt very broad concepts of derogations and there may also be a lack of uniformity in the use of derogations by procuring authorities.[27]

The World Bank and the South African legislation adopt similar approaches to the issue of derogations. In the World Bank, there is no possibility for Borrowers to derogate under any circumstances from disqualifications imposed by the Bank and Borrowers are required to examine the Bank's list of disqualified suppliers to ensure that a contract is not awarded to a disqualified supplier.[28] There are two reasons why the World Bank does not allow derogations from its disqualification measures. First, the Bank has mainstreamed its anti-corruption agenda and prioritises its anti-corruption measures over the circumstances that may make derogations for exceptional reasons appropriate to national jurisdictions. Secondly, it must be remembered that borrowing from the Bank is optional at the behest of the Borrower and should a Borrower feel that procuring from a

[20] DFARS 209.405(a)(i); Dept of Health and Human Services Acquisition Regulations (HHSAR) 309.405(a)(1)(i); *JB Kies Construction Co*, Comp Gen B-250797, 93-1 CPD ¶ 127.

[21] DFARS 209.405(a)(ii); HHSAR 309.405(a)(1)(ii).

[22] FAR 23.506(e).

[23] DFARS 209.405(a)(iv).

[24] GAO, GSA Actions leading to proposed debarment of WorldCom (GAO-04-741R, May 26, 2004).

[25] S Collins, 'What the MCI Case Teaches About the Current State of Suspension and Debarment' (2004) 5 *Public Procurement Law Review* 218.

[26] Collins, 'What the MCI Case Teaches', ibid.

[27] Collins, 'What the MCI Case Teaches', above n 25, 221.

[28] BPG appendix 1, para 8.

disqualified supplier is unavoidable, the option remains for the Borrower to utilise alternative funds for the procurement.

Although the Bank does not permit Borrowers to derogate from a disqualification for exceptional situations, as discussed below, the Bank takes rehabilitation measures into account in deciding whether to disqualify a corrupt supplier.

In South Africa, there is also no possibility for a disqualifying entity to derogate from the mandatory requirement to disqualify under the PFMA regulations or from a disqualification imposed by the courts under the Corruption Act. South Africa is the only domestic jurisdiction which denies procuring authorities the flexibility to derogate from a mandatory requirement to disqualify. This may be due to the punitive rationale for disqualification in South Africa, but this approach may be problematic for procuring authorities because public interest concerns may legitimately override the reasons for disqualification. This is especially so in relation to disqualifications imposed by the courts, as the courts may impose a disqualification where there are exceptional factors necessitating the continued business relationship between a supplier and a procuring authority, which are not apparent to the courts. However, under the Corruption Act, once the court orders a disqualification, all procuring authorities must apply the disqualification and are denied the flexibility to deal with peculiar or one-off cases that could not have been anticipated.

In imposing a disqualification under the Corruption Act, it is not clear whether the courts may take into account exceptional reasons before imposing disqualification as part of the sentence. It is possible that the courts have the discretion to take similar considerations into account, as the draft sentencing guidelines in South Africa require the courts to aim at protecting society and giving the offender the opportunity to live a crime-free life.[29] Thus it is arguable that where public interest concerns (such as protecting society from the corrupt supplier) will not be served by the supplier's disqualification, disqualification may not be necessary. It may be noted that derogations are often appropriate for specific contracts rather than for a supplier in general, but where the court takes exceptional reasons such as public interest factors into account in imposing a general disqualification, a general derogation will be made, meaning the supplier will avoid disqualification altogether.

Where the court imposes a disqualification under the Corruption Act, it should be noted that the Act does not permit procuring authorities to derogate from the disqualification decision of the court, but the Act gives the National Treasury the power to vary the period of disqualification.[30] The

[29] Draft Sentencing Framework Act 2000, available at: www.justice.gov.za/salrc/dpapers/dp91.pdf; SS Terblanche, 'Sentencing Guidelines for South Africa: Lessons from Elsewhere' (2003) 120 *South African Law Journal* 858.

[30] Corruption Act 2004, s 28(4)(a).

Act is silent as to the circumstances in which the National Treasury may take this action, but it is possible that public interest or public health may be a reason for the National Treasury to reduce the length of the disqualification, by analogy with circumstances in which South African procurement legislation permits procuring authorities to dispense with complying with procurement legislation in public contracts.[31] For instance, under the Municipal Supply Chain Management Regulations, municipal authorities are not required to apply procurement procedures in cases of emergencies where there is only one provider, or in exceptional cases where it is impractical or impossible to comply with the legislated procurement process.[32] The Green Paper on public procurement clarified the meaning of emergency and provided that an emergency includes the possibility of human injury or death, the prevalence of human suffering or deprivation of rights, the possibility of damage to property or livestock, the interruption of essential services, national security, and the possibility of damage to the environment. Thus, the reasons that may permit the derogation from procurement legislation in South Africa include public interest and public health reasons. By way of analogy therefore, it is possible that the presence of these circumstances in relation to a disqualified supplier may be relied on by the National Treasury to reduce the length of the disqualification.

10.2.1.2 National security

Another reason that may be relied on to derogate from a disqualification requirement is national security. Like public interest, national security is an ambiguous term that may not be capable of a precise definition. Buzan argues that the ambiguity surrounding the definition of national security is intentional as '[a]n undefined notion of national security offers scope for power maximising strategies to political and military elites because of the considerable leverage over domestic affairs which can be obtained by invoking it'.[33] The definitions of national security range from narrow definitions, which define national security in terms of a state being able to maintain its territorial integrity[34] or military security, to broader definitions, which define national security as the ability of a state to protect its (fundamental) values and interests.[35] In light of the broad spectrum of

[31] P Bolton, *Law of Government Procurement in South Africa* (Durban, LexisNexis Butterworth, 2007) ch 4.

[32] Municipal Supply Chain Management Regulations (Government Gazette 27636, 30 May 2005) reg 36(1).

[33] B Buzan, *People, States and Fear: The National Security Problem in International Relations* (Brighton, Wheatsheaf Books, 1983) 4, 9.

[34] J Romm, *Defining National Security: The Non-Military Aspects* (Council on Foreign Relations Press, 1993) 4.

[35] Romm, *Defining National Security*, ibid, 5–6.

definitions, Romm argues that the term has rapidly become meaningless as every problem faced by a nation is characterised as a threat to its security.[36] However, labelling a problem as 'national security' implies that it is a more severe threat than other problems and may require 'more than normal attention and sacrifice by the nation'.[37]

National security is one reason for derogating from general procurement law requirements[38] and the requirement to disqualify in most of the jurisdictions. The jurisdictions under study adopt definitions of national security that include both broad and narrow definitions, which are often limited to issues with a military bias.

In the EU, there are two kinds of national security exemptions which apply to public contracts, namely: general exemptions from the Treaty, including derogations from the free movement provisions on public security grounds;[39] and specific exemptions from the procurement directives, precluding the application of the procurement directives to public contracts declared secret, contracts which must be accompanied by special security measures and other contracts when the essential interests of the Member State so require.[40] Thus it seems likely that the derogation from the mandatory disqualification requirement could also be invoked on national security grounds. The security exemption in the procurement directives was considered in *Commission v Belgium*,[41] where the exemption was invoked to justify limiting contracts for aerial photography to firms with a special security clearance in order to protect military secrets. Here, the CJEU held the exemption to apply without examining whether measures less restrictive of the procurement directives were available to achieve the stated objective. Thus, at least where military contracts are concerned under the procurement directives, it seems that whilst the CJEU may still

[36] Romm, *Defining National Security*, above n 34, 8.

[37] Romm, *Defining National Security*, above n 34, 81.

[38] Case C-72/83 *Campus Oil Ltd*, above n 18.

[39] TFEU art 36. On the standard of scrutiny applied see Case C-72/83 *Campus Oil*, n 18, para 36.; Case C-398/98, *Commission v Greece*, [2001] ECR I-7915; N Pourbaix, 'The Future Scope of Application of Article 346 TFEU' (2011) *Public Procurement Law Review* 1; M Trybus, 'Defence Procurement: The new Public Sector Directive and Beyond' (2004) 13 *Public Procurement Law Review* 198; M Trybus, 'On the Application of the EC Treaty to Armaments' (2000) 25 *European Law Review* 663; Arrowsmith, *Public and Utilities Procurement*, ch 4; M Trybus, *European Union Law and Defence Integration* (Oxford, Hart Publishing, 2005) ch 5 and A Georgopoulos, 'Defence Procurement and EU Law (2005) 30 *European Law Review* 559.

[40] TFEU art 346; PSD art 14. The procurement directives exclude hard defence material from their ambit, which are subject to the defence procurement directive: Directive 2009/81/EC on the coordination of procedures for the award of certain works contracts, supply contracts and service contracts in the field of defence and security [2009] OJ L216/76. See B Heuninckx, 'The EU Defence and Security Directive: Trick or Treat' (2011) 1 *Public Procurement Law Review* 9.

[41] Case C-252/01 *Commission v Belgium*, [2003] ECR I-11859. See also Case C-337/05 *Commission v Italy* [2008] ECR I-2173 and Case C-157/06 *Commission v Italy* [2008] ECR I-7313.

examine whether the contract is one which falls within the derogations[42] by determining whether it relates to the security interests of a Member State, it will apply a low level of scrutiny to the application of the provision and in particular, may not consider at all the availability of alternative measures.[43]

The CJEU may apply the same approach when dealing with a derogation from the mandatory disqualification based on military security – for example, when a procuring entity claims that it is necessary to give military work to a convicted supplier on the basis that only that supplier can maintain confidentiality, or do the work to the desired standard.

It should be noted that the derogation from the mandatory disqualification does not permit a procuring authority to derogate from the other requirements of the directives, nor from the Treaty principles of transparency and non-discrimination.[44] However, the facts giving rise to the derogation from the mandatory disqualification provision – such as a need to give the work to one supplier in particular – may sometimes also justify excluding the procurement from the directives as a whole and from the Treaty.[45]

A similar approach to national security considerations may apply in the UK, since the UK regulations do not go further than the EU directives in relation to derogations. As such, it seems likely also that in the UK, national security will be considered as an appropriate reason for derogating from the mandatory requirement to disqualify. The UK procurement regulations do not apply to contracts classified as secret, or contracts that must be accompanied by special security measures, or to contracts governed by Article 346 of the TFEU.[46] Thus, the mandatory disqualification provisions should also not apply where there are national or military security concerns in relation to a contract.

Although national security is not defined in the procurement regulations, UK courts will be required to interpret a national security exemption under the regulations in a manner consistent with EU law.[47] At present, there are areas of coincidence between UK jurisprudence and EU approaches to national security. Thus in *Tinnelly & Sons v UK*,[48] the procuring authority

[42] Case C-414/97 *Commission v Spain* [1999] ECR I-5585; Case C-318/94 *Commission* v *Germany* [1996] ECR I-1949, para 13.

[43] Case T-26/01 *Fiocchi Munizioni SpA v Commission* [2003] ECR II-3951. See M Trybus, 'The EC Treaty as an Instrument of European Defence Integration: Judicial Scrutiny of Defence and Security Exemptions' (2002) 39 *Common Market Law Review* 1347.

[44] M Trybus, 'Defence Procurement: The new Public Sector Directive and Beyond' (2004) 13 *Public Procurement Law Review* 198, 221.

[45] N Pourbaix, 'The Future Scope', above n 39.

[46] PCR regs 6, 33, 36. The Defence and Security Contracts Regulations, SI 2011/1848 came into force on 21 August 2011. These regulations implement the EU defence procurement directive.

[47] *Brent London Borough Council v Risk Management Partners* [2011] UKSC 7.

[48] *Tinnelly & Sons v UK* (1999) 27 EHRR 249.

argued that national security concerns included the threat of terrorism. It should be noted, however, that where a UK procuring authority relies on derogations for reasons of national security, it must do so in good faith. Where this is not the case, the courts have indicated a willingness to declare that the procuring authority acted in bad faith.[49]

As discussed earlier, the US relies on the broad phrase 'compelling reason' for invoking derogations, and national security qualifies as a 'compelling reason' for derogating from disqualification of a supplier.[50] The DFAR indicates that a disqualified supplier may still obtain public contracts where national defence requires continued business dealings with the supplier.[51] The application of a national security derogation was also seen in the case of WorldCom discussed above, where a derogation was given in one instance to prevent the 'great harm to the national security of the United States and potential danger to its citizens and war fighters'.[52]

In South Africa, although procuring authorities are not permitted to derogate from the mandatory requirement to disqualify under the PFMA regulations or from a general disqualification imposed under the PPPFA regulations or by the court under the Corruption Act, the National Treasury may vary the length of a disqualification imposed by a court. As discussed above, national security is a reason for derogating from the requirements for competitive bidding in public contracts, and it is arguable that in the absence of guidance as to when it may be appropriate for the National Treasury to reduce the length of a disqualification, national security may be considered an appropriate reason for doing so.

10.2.1.3 The economic costs and impact of disqualification

It is possible that the cost implications of not contracting with a disqualified supplier or the adverse impact that a supplier's disqualification could have on the delivery of public services may necessitate derogating from a disqualification requirement in the public interest. The disqualification of a major supplier may also adversely affect competition, as the remaining suppliers in the market may have little incentive to maintain competitive prices, leading to higher prices for the government, especially in consolidated sectors like defence.[53]

In the EU and the UK, derogations may be necessary where either the cost of switching suppliers or the consequences of a reduction in

[49] *Tinnelly*, ibid, para 25.

[50] FAR 23.506(e).

[51] DFARS 209.405(a)(iv).

[52] See G Witte, 'Federal Ban Does not Hurt WorldCom Much', *Washington Post* (24 October 2003).

[53] J Zucker, 'The Boeing Suspension: Has Increased Consolidation Tied the United States Department if Defense's Hands?' (2004) 13 *Public Procurement Law Review* 260; E Castelli, 'EPA defends action against IBM', *Fed Times* (15 April 2008).

competition would be unduly prohibitive. However, in view of the jurisprudence prohibiting Treaty derogations for purely economic reasons,[54] the CJEU might consider that higher procedural costs in the procurement context do not merit derogation from the mandatory requirement to disqualify, unless such costs will 'seriously undermine the financial balance'[55] of the procurement system. As was seen in chapter nine in the context of the derogations from the ineffectiveness provisions, higher costs or economic detriment are not generally considered to be appropriate reasons for non-compliance with procurement rules.

In the US, the phrase 'compelling reason' is broad enough to cover derogations for economic reasons and the disruption that disqualification may cause. In 2004, Boeing's disqualification was shortly overturned due to the price increases that the Department of Defence suffered as a result.[56] In the WorldCom case discussed above, the disruption that would have been caused in switching from a disqualified supplier in large and complex contracts was relied on by procuring authorities as a reason for derogating from WorldCom's disqualification. More recently, the temporary disqualification of IBM from public contracts in 2008 was terminated after eight days, and it was suggested that the brevity of the disqualification was due to the severe disruption the government would have faced if the disqualification had remained in effect for longer.[57]

As was discussed above, in South Africa, procuring authorities are absolved from applying procurement procedures in cases of emergencies where there is only one provider, or in exceptional cases where it is impractical or impossible to comply with the legislated procurement process.[58] Similarly, the Green Paper lists the disruption of essential services as a reason for derogating from procurement legislation. Under the Corruption Act, although procuring authorities may not derogate from a disqualification imposed by the courts, as discussed above, it is possible that in the exercise of the National Treasury's power to amend or vary a disqualification imposed by the courts, the impact of disqualification or the costs to the government may be a reason for varying the length of a disqualification imposed by the courts under the Corruption Act.

[54] Case C-104/75, *Officier van Justitie v de Peijper* [1976] ECR 613; Case C-120/95, *Decker v Caisse de Maladie des Employés Prives* [1998] ECR I-1831 para 39; Case C-398/98, *Commission v Greece* [2001] 3 CMLR 62.

[55] Case C-120/95 *Decker*, above n 54, para 39.

[56] Zucker, 'The Boeing Suspension', above n 53.

[57] T Canni, 'Shoot First, Ask Questions Later: An Examination and Critique of Suspension and Debarment Practice under the FAR, Including a Discussion of the Mandatory Disclosure Rule, the IBM Suspension and other Noteworthy Developments' (2009) 38 *Public Contract Law Journal* 547, 594.

[58] Municipal Supply Chain Management Regulations reg 36(1); P Bolton, 'Grounds for Dispensing with Public Tender Procedures in Government Contracting' (2006) *Potchefstroom Electronic Law Journal* 7.

10.2.1.4 Factors to be taken into account in deciding if an exceptional situation exists

None of the jurisdictions provide information on what factors should be taken into account in determining if an exceptional situation justifying derogation exists. It would be preferable if clearer guidelines were provided, as a clearer approach would increase transparency in the disqualification process, ensure that derogations granted were not discriminatory, maintain consistency in the granting of derogations,[59] and better equip disqualifying officials to decide if an exceptional situation exists.

In jurisdictions where the disqualification decision lies within the remit of procurement officials, such officials may not always be competent to decide if there is an exceptional situation that may justify derogation, especially where the exceptional circumstance is a national security consideration. A clearer approach to derogations may also help to prevent abuse in the use of such derogations. However, as the issue of derogations is litigated in the selected jurisdictions, the courts may provide clarity on the limits of the derogations provisions in those jurisdictions. Such litigation may be instituted by suppliers who suffer a loss when a derogation is used in another supplier's favour.

As a guideline, there are a number of questions that a disqualifying official should be required to ask where derogation for an exceptional situation is considered, in order to ensure consistency and transparency in the use of these derogations. In relation to national security reasons, two questions are relevant: first, will there be a real or a potential threat to life and liberty if a particular supplier is disqualified or not awarded a contract? Secondly, will entering into a contract with another supplier compromise military security or intelligence? If any of these questions can be answered in the affirmative, then there may be a case for derogating on national security grounds.

Similar questions may be asked in relation to public interest concerns, and a disqualifying official should consider whether there would be a real or potential threat to life, liberty, public health/safety or public values/morals if a particular supplier is disqualified or not awarded a contract. A second question is whether entering into a contract with a disqualified supplier can be justified on the balance of costs and benefits. In other words, do the benefits to the public of entering into a contract with the disqualified supplier outweigh the costs to the system of transacting with a corrupt supplier? In this respect, the procuring authority will essentially be weighing public interest concerns against the losses that may be suffered by entering into business with a corrupt supplier – such as the fact that the supplier may not carry out the work to the required standard and

[59] R Kramer, 'Awarding Contracts to Suspended and Debarred Firms: Are Stricter Rules Necessary?' (2005) 34 *Public Contract Law Journal* 549.

the loss of public confidence in the procurement system where it is seen that the government engages with a corrupt supplier.

In relation to the economic costs and impact of disqualification, the questions that may be asked are: whether disqualifying a particular supplier will result in a significant increase in costs to the government; and also, whether the impact of the disqualification on the procuring authority's goals may be justified on the balance of costs and benefits. Answering these questions, however, may not be easy for a procuring authority and reinforces the need for the legislation to provide clearer guidance on the issue of derogations: either in the form of broader principles or, as is the case under the 'ineffectiveness' provisions in the EU remedies directive, a negative list of situations that will not justify derogation.

10.2.2 Rehabilitation Measures

A supplier may also avoid disqualification through the implementation of rehabilitation measures. Rehabilitation measures comprise preventive and remedial elements and include measures implemented by the supplier which show that the cause for disqualification no longer exists, has been eliminated, or that the supplier has implemented internal procedures to ensure that in future, the cause for disqualification cannot arise or corrupt activity will no longer be a problem.[60]

Rehabilitation measures are variously referred to as 'self-cleaning' or 'corporate compliance' measures depending on the jurisdiction. Corporate compliance measures have been defined as 'a formal system of policies and procedures adopted by an organisation with the purpose of preventing and detecting violations of law, regulation and organisational policy and fostering an ethical business environment'.[61] These measures may include implementing codes of ethics, corruption and fraud detection and prevention mechanisms (including whistle-blower procedures), the creation of ethics compliance departments and implementing anti-corruption policies.[62] There has been a focus on such measures as a way of avoiding

[60] These measures are not limited to avoiding disqualification, but could be used to avoid criminal penalties, defer prosecution or obtain leniency in criminal trials. See the US Federal Sentencing Guidelines (2009) Ch 8 pt B – Remedying Harm from Criminal Conduct and Effective Compliance and Ethics Program. For the EU see Arrowsmith, Priess and Friton, 'Self-Cleaning', above n 1.

[61] R Walker, 'International Corporate Compliance Programmes' (2006) 3 *International Journal of Disclosure and Governance* 70.

[62] UN Global Compact, Business against corruption: case stories and examples (2000). Available at www.unglobalcompact.org/docs/issues_doc/7.7/BACbookFINAL.pdf; B Tran, 'Corporate Ethics: An End to the Rhetorical Interpretations of an Endemic Corruption' (2008) 4 *Social Responsibility Journal* 63; S Murphy, 'Taking Multinational Corporate Codes of Conduct to the Next Level' (2005) 43 *Columbia Journal of Transnational Law* 389.

and combating corporate corruption and other corporate ills under the banner of corporate social responsibility.[63]

In the jurisdictions under study, rehabilitation measures may be a way for a supplier to limit the severity/length of its disqualification or avoid disqualification altogether. The kinds of rehabilitation measures that will be considered adequate will depend on the approach of the jurisdiction to rehabilitation and the purpose of disqualification, since rehabilitation measures may not be appropriate in a jurisdiction where the purpose of disqualification is punitive.[64]

The issues that arise with rehabilitation measures in relation to disqualification are: first, to what extent do procuring authorities have an obligation or discretion to take rehabilitation measures into account in making the disqualification decision; secondly, what kind of measures will be regarded as sufficient; and thirdly, how does a jurisdiction prevent rehabilitation measures from being abused?

10.2.2.1 Does a disqualifying entity have a discretion or obligation to take rehabilitation measures into account?

It is not always clear whether a disqualifying entity is required or has the discretion to take rehabilitation measures into account, and the US and the World Bank are the only jurisdictions which explicitly grant disqualifying entities the discretion to consider rehabilitation measures. In the EU, some Member States already took account of rehabilitation measures and have continued to do so after the passage of the current procurement directives.[65]

The EU procurement directives are silent on whether rehabilitation measures implemented by a supplier may mean it avoids disqualification. It is, however, possible that future revisions of the procurement directives may explicitly permit or require Member States to take rehabilitation measures into account, and clarify the nature of the obligation as the Green Paper of 2011 debated the issue.[66] In relation to the discretionary disqualifications, the discretionary nature of the measures and the fact

[63] See US Federal Guidelines, above n 60; T McInerney, 'Putting Regulation before Responsibility: Towards Binding Norms of Corporate Social Responsibility' (2007) 40 *Cornell International Law Journal* 171; M Almond and S Syfert, 'Beyond Compliance, Corporate Responsibility and Ethical Standards in the New Global Economy' (1997) *North Carolina Journal of International Law and Commercial Regulation* 389; R Bednar, A Styles and J McDowell, 'Self-Cleaning under non-EU Jurisdictions: United States' in H Punder, H-J Priess and S Arrowsmith (eds), *Self-Cleaning in Public Procurement Law* (Koln, Carl Heymans Verlag, 2009) 157.

[64] Arrowsmith, Priess and Friton, 'Self Cleaning', above n 1, 274.

[65] Punder, Priess and Arrowsmith, *Self-Cleaning in Public Procurement Law*, above n 63, 33–118.

[66] European Commission, Green Paper on the Modernisation of EU Public Procurement Policy: Towards a More Efficient European Procurement Market, COM(2011) 15 final, para 5.3.

that procuring authorities are not given clear guidelines on what factors may be taken into account for these disqualifications suggests that a procuring authority retains discretion not to disqualify the supplier, if the supplier is able to show that the causes for disqualification no longer exists, or that the supplier is no longer a risk to the procuring authority or public funds.[67] Relying on rehabilitation measures to defeat the discretionary disqualifications may also support some of the rationales behind the disqualifications such as ensuring the (present) reliability of suppliers[68] and protecting the government by ensuring it only transacts with responsible suppliers.

In relation to the mandatory disqualifications, the position is less clear. Although the directives are silent on this issue, rehabilitation measures are taken into account in various contexts in some Member States,[69] and in procurement by EU institutions. Thus, the EU Financial Regulations and its Implementing Regulations, which call for mandatory exclusions for a range of offences similar to those in the EU procurement directives, provide for rehabilitation measures to be taken into account when excluding suppliers from EU contracts.[70] Specifically, the Implementing Regulations provide that for the purpose of determining the length of exclusion under the Financial Regulations, an EU institution may take into account factors, including 'measures taken by the entity concerned to remedy the situation'.[71] Thus, in the context of procurement by EU institutions, rehabilitation measures may shorten the length of an exclusion, although the Financial Regulations do not contemplate that these measures will defeat exclusion altogether.

In relation to the EU procurement directives, it has been suggested that procuring authorities may retain the discretion to rely on rehabilitation

[67] See Case C-226/04 *La Cascina* [2006] ECR I-1347.

[68] Case C-226/04 *La Cascina* [2006] ECR I-1347, opinion of AG Maduro para 24.

[69] Punder, Priess and Arrowsmith, *Self-Cleaning in Public Procurement Law*, above n 63; P Davidsson, 'Legal Enforcement of Corporate Social Responsibility in the EC' (2002) 8 *Columbia Journal of European Law* 529; E Kocher, 'Codes of Conduct and Framework Agreements on Social Minimum Standards- Private Regulation?' in O Dilling, M Herberg and G Winter (eds), *Responsible Business: Self-Governance and Law in Transnational Economic Transactions* (Oxford, Hart Publishing, 2008); J Delga, 'Codes of Ethics, Corporate Ethics and Business Law in Continental Europe' (2005) *International Comparative and Commercial Law Review* 463; N Hurst, 'Corporate Ethics, Governance and Social Responsibility: Comparing European Business Practices to those in the United States' (Spring 2004). Available at: www.scu.edu/ethics/publications/submitted/hurst/comparitive_study.pdf .

[70] Council Regulation (EC, Euratom) 1605/2002/EC of 25 June 2002 on the Financial Regulation applicable to the general budget of the European Communities, [2002] OJ L248/1, as amended by Council Regulation (EC, Euratom) 1995/2006/EC [2006] OJ L390/16, art 93 [hereafter Financial Regulations]; Commission Regulation (EC, Euratom) No 2342/2002 of 23 December 2002 laying down detailed rules for the implementation of Council Regulation (EC, Euratom) No 1605/2002 on the Financial Regulation applicable to the general budget of the European Communities [2002] OJ L357/1, art 133a [hereafter Implementing Regulations].

[71] Implementing Regulations, art 133a.

measures to defeat the mandatory disqualification requirement.[72] Although the directives are silent on the issue, four factors suggest that EU procuring authorities may have an implied power to take rehabilitation measures into account. First, the draft proposals of the EU procurement directives provided for rehabilitation measures as a means of defeating the mandatory disqualification requirement.[73] This provision was, however, deleted from the final text and substituted with the provision permitting derogation from the mandatory disqualification 'for overriding requirements in the general interest'. In the absence of any evidence as to why the rehabilitation provision was deleted, it is arguable that the deleted provision has been subsumed within and given expression through the derogation provision.

Secondly, it has been argued that the EU principle of proportionality imposes an obligation (independent of the derogation provisions) on procuring authorities to take rehabilitation measures into account in deciding to disqualify a supplier.[74] Thirdly, the provisions requiring Member States to specify the 'implementing conditions' for the disqualifications may grant Member States the discretion to decide in accordance with national law whether rehabilitation measures may be used to defeat the requirement for the mandatory disqualifications. As stated, some Member States have always taken rehabilitation measures into account in disqualifying suppliers, an approach that has not been queried by the Commission.[75]

Lastly, the non-punitive purpose behind the mandatory disqualifications in the EU may require Member States to take rehabilitation measures into account.[76] As discussed earlier, the mandatory disqualifications exist for both policy and protective reasons. It is thus arguable that where sufficient rehabilitation measures have been implemented, this may eliminate the necessity to protect both the government and the EU from corruption and also fulfil the EU policy against corruption, as a reliance on rehabilitation measures by procuring authorities provides firms with an incentive to eradicate corruption.[77]

In the UK, the procurement regulations did not go further than the EU directives on this issue and are also silent as to whether a procuring authority may decline to disqualify a supplier where the supplier has implemented sufficient rehabilitation measures. As the discretion to decide on the applicability of rehabilitation measures appears to have been left to

[72] Arrowsmith, Priess and Friton, 'Self-Cleaning', above n 1, 265.

[73] Proposal for a Directive of the European Parliament and of the Council on the co-ordination of procedures for the award of public supply contracts, public service contracts and public work contracts DG C II, Brussels, 31 May 2001 SN2325/1/01 REV 1 (MAP), art 46(1).

[74] Arrowsmith, Priess and Friton, 'Self-Cleaning', above n 1, 276.

[75] Punder, Priess and Arrowsmith, *Self-Cleaning in Public Procurement Law*, above n 63, 33–118.

[76] Arrowsmith, Priess and Friton, 'Self-Cleaning', above n 1, 270.

[77] Arrowsmith, Priess and Friton, 'Self-Cleaning', above n 1, 263.

Member States, UK procuring authorities may exercise this discretion as permitted by the EU. As was discussed in the context of the EU, the principle of proportionality may also require UK procuring authorities to take rehabilitation measures into account in the disqualification context.[78] As discussed below, rehabilitation measures are already relied on in other contexts and they may possibly be taken into account in the disqualification context as well.

In relation to the discretionary disqualifications, where a supplier has implemented rehabilitation measures, the procuring authority may decide not to disqualify the supplier, since a procuring authority has the discretion to determine what factors it will take into account in deciding to disqualify. Where a procuring authority decides that rehabilitation measures can defeat a discretionary disqualification, this may also accord with the rationales behind the discretionary disqualifications in the UK.

An example of how rehabilitation measures may be relevant in the context of discretionary disqualifications may be discussed in relation to BAE Systems.[79] In the aftermath of the company's investigation by the Serious Fraud Office, in February 2010 BAE pleaded guilty to false accounting offences (in lieu of bribery and corruption charges). Since BAE was not convicted of corruption in any jurisdiction,[80] the issue of its mandatory disqualification for corruption in the UK does not arise, but it is possible that a UK procuring authority may feel that BAE's conduct amounts to 'grave professional misconduct' and it would have to decide whether to disqualify BAE, taking into account the rehabilitation measures subsequently implemented by BAE.[81]

In relation to the mandatory disqualifications, as was discussed in the context of the EU, it may be possible for a UK procuring authority to rely on the derogation provisions in the UK procurement regulations[82] to defeat the mandatory requirement for disqualification, based on the wording of the derogation provision and the EU principle of proportionality.

Apart from the above, rehabilitation measures are taken into account in relation to corporate prosecutions and in 2009, the Serious Fraud Office issued guidance on its approach to dealing with UK firms engaged in

[78] ibid.

[79] S Williams, 'The BAE/Saudi Al-Yamamah Contracts: Implications in Law and Public Procurement' (2008) 57 *International and Comparative Law Quarterly* 200.

[80] The plea bargain BAE entered into with the US Department of Justice and the UK Serious Fraud Office means that all other charges against the company have now been dropped. See 'BAE pays fines of £285m over arms deal corruption claims', *The Guardian* (5 February 2010).

[81] Woolf Committee, *Business Ethics, global companies and the defence industry: Ethical business conduct in BAE Systems plc- The Way Forward,* May 2008. Available at: 217.69.43.26/woolf/Woolf_report_2008.pdf; BAE Systems Press Release, *BAE Systems announces implementation programme for Woolf Committee recommendations,* 22 July 2008. Available at: ir.baesystems.com/investors/storage/2008-07-22.pdf.

[82] PCR reg 23(2).

overseas corruption.[83] This guidance encourages firms to self-report cases of corruption to the SFO in exchange for more lenient civil (and not criminal) sanctions where the SFO feels that a self-reporting company will impose adequate rehabilitation measures at the conclusion of the investigative process. The Crown Prosecution Service takes similar considerations into account in relation to corporate prosecutions.[84] This illustrates that rehabilitation measures by corporate entities are becoming mainstreamed in the UK criminal justice system.[85]

The US approach to rehabilitation measures differs from the approaches of the EU and the UK. The FAR provides that the existence of a cause for disqualification should not necessarily lead to disqualification, and provides a list of remedial or mitigating factors that should be taken into account.[86] Accordingly, if a cause for disqualification exists, it is up to the supplier to demonstrate that disqualification is not necessary due to the presence of rehabilitation measures.[87] Apart from the rehabilitation provisions of the FAR, since 2008, US federal suppliers have been required to establish corporate compliance programmes, self-report any wrongful conduct and exclude wrongdoers or potential wrongdoers from their organisation.[88] Compliance with such measures will also be taken into account where a supplier is facing disqualification. Thus, disqualifying entities in the US have the discretion to decide that disqualification is not necessary where the supplier has taken measures to eliminate or prevent future corrupt activity.[89] Rehabilitation measures may also be relied on to reduce the length or extent of disqualification where the reason for the disqualification has been eliminated.[90]

The approach to rehabilitation measures in the US reflects the protective rationale for disqualification in that jurisdiction. Thus, where the circumstance from which the government needs protection is no longer present, there will be no need to disqualify the supplier. The World Bank adopts a similar approach to rehabilitation measures as the US and rehabilitation measures may defeat a proposed disqualification. Rehabilitation measures affect disqualification in two ways in the Bank context. First, the under the Bank Sanctions Procedures, the Sanctions Board may consider

[83] Serious Fraud Office, Approach of the Serious Fraud Office to dealing with overseas corruption (21 July 2009). Available at: www.sfo.gov.uk .

[84] Crown Prosecution Service, Corporate Prosecutions available at www.cps.gov.uk.

[85] Note also that under the UK Bribery Act 2010, it is a defence to an offence of corruption if a firm can show that it had adequate procedures to prevent bribery in place. See s 7(2).

[86] FAR 9.406-1; *Roemer v Hoffman* 419 F Supp 130 (DDC 1976), 132.

[87] FAR 9.406-1(a); FAR 9.407-1(b).

[88] Contractor Business Ethics Compliance Program and Disclosure Requirements, 73 Federal Register 67067 (Nov 12 2008).

[89] Bednar, Styles and McDowell, 'Self-Cleaning Under Non-EU Jurisdictions: United States', above n 63.

[90] FAR 9.406-4(c).

mitigating factors in determining the appropriate sanction for a supplier,[91] and the range of possible disqualification sanctions takes into account rehabilitation measures by the supplier. Thus, a supplier may avoid disqualification and instead be sanctioned with a 'conditional non-debarment' in which the supplier will not be disqualified but will be required by the Bank to implement a compliance programme to the satisfaction of the Bank. If the supplier fails to implement the programme, this will result in the supplier's disqualification.[92] Alternatively, a supplier may be sanctioned with a 'temporary debarment with conditional release' under which the supplier will be disqualified for a period of time but will become eligible for Bank contracts once it has satisfied certain conditions set by the Bank, which could include rehabilitation measures.[93] Secondly, under the Bank's Voluntary Disclosure Program (VDP) instituted in 2006, a supplier could avoid or limit the length of its disqualification if it implemented specified rehabilitation measures.[94] The VDP aims to fight corruption through prevention and deterrence[95] and improve the Bank's investigative capabilities through private-sector cooperation. Under the VDP, suppliers engaged in corruption in Bank-financed contracts are given incentives to disclose the corrupt practices in those projects.[96] In exchange, the Bank will not disqualify the supplier and will keep the supplier's participation in the VDP confidential. However, if the supplier breaches the conditions of the VDP by continuing to engage in misconduct, withholding information relating to past misconduct, or failing to implement a compliance programme or cooperate with a compliance monitor, the Bank will impose a mandatory 10-year disqualification on that supplier.[97]

The Bank's approach to rehabilitation measures is also informed in part by the rationales underpinning the Bank's disqualification system. The Bank's disqualification system is intended to support the Bank's policy against corruption and protect Bank funds from being lost to corruption. Thus, rehabilitation measures ought to be taken into account where the measures are sufficient to eliminate the need to disqualify a supplier.

The South African approach to rehabilitation measures differs from the other jurisdictions. As discussed in the context of exceptional situations,

[91] WBSP art IX, s 9.02(e).

[92] WBSP art IX, s 9.01(b).

[93] WBSP art IX, s 9.02(d).

[94] S Williams, 'World Bank Introduces New Measures to Fight Corruption in Bank-financed Contracts and the Administration of Bank Loans' (2007) 16 *Public Procurement Law Review* NA152; S Williams 'The Debarment of Corrupt Contractors from World Bank-Financed Contracts' (2007) 36 *Public Contract Law Journal* 277, 299.

[95] Press Release, World Bank, World Bank Launches Voluntary Disclosure Program (Aug 1, 2006); P Dubois and J Matechak, 'World Bank Battles Corruption Through New Voluntary Disclosure Program' (2006) 3 *International Government Contractor* 73.

[96] World Bank, VDP Guidelines for Participants, ¶ 2 (2006).

[97] WBSP art IX, s 9.02(c)(iii).

the South African disqualification system does not permit procuring authorities to derogate from the mandatory disqualifications under the PFMA or from the disqualifications imposed by a court under the Corruption Act. However, as stated earlier, the Corruption Act gives the National Treasury the discretion to vary the length of a disqualification. Whilst the Act is silent on when this may be appropriate, it is possible that the rehabilitation of the supplier may be relied upon by the Treasury to reduce the length of the supplier's disqualification. Whilst the PPPFA regulations are silent on the issue of rehabilitation measures, the practice note from the National Treasury permits procuring authorities to amend or lift a disqualification based on 'sound reasons'. Whilst the meaning of 'sound reasons' is not clarified, it is possible that the subsequent rehabilitation of a supplier may suffice for the lifting of a disqualification order.

10.2.2.2 The kinds of measures sufficient to avoid disqualification

The range of measures that may suffice as rehabilitation measures may depend on the legal and corporate culture in each jurisdiction. However, an examination of the approaches of the jurisdictions under study gives an indication as to the kinds of measures that are considered adequate for rehabilitation.

In the EU, the lack of clarity on rehabilitation measures makes it difficult to determine what kinds of measures may be considered sufficient in the disqualification context. However, some guidance may be obtained from procurement by EU institutions. Thus the Implementing Regulations[98] provide that in determining the period of exclusion, the Community should take into account 'measures taken by the entity concerned to remedy the situation'. Although there is no further description of such measures, this may include measures taken to undo the damage caused by the corrupt activity, such as restitution, cooperation with law enforcement and possibly the termination of the employment of culpable persons.

Arrowsmith et al, in examining the use of rehabilitation measures in the EU, have created a four-fold classification of rehabilitation measures: clarifications of facts through cooperating in audits and investigations; repairing the damage through payment of damages and other restitution; personnel measures such as terminating the employment of the relevant staff; and structural and organisational measures which will prevent a recurrence of the corrupt activity in the future, such as corporate compliance measures.[99] This classification takes into account the remedial and preventive aspects of rehabilitation measures and may usefully be

[98] Implementing Regulations, art 133a.
[99] Arrowsmith, Priess and Friton, 'Self-Cleaning', above n 1, 259–61.

adopted by a Member State seeking to determine what should suffice as acceptable rehabilitation measures.

Since the UK in adopting the EU directives did not go further than the EU in relation to the issue of derogations and possible rehabilitation measures, it is possible that the classification suggested by Arrowsmith et al may be adopted by the UK. The SFO Guidance mentioned above may also give an indication as to what may be appropriate in the UK context.[100]

The US approach to rehabilitation measures differs from that of the EU and UK and the FAR clearly specifies the kinds of rehabilitation measures that a disqualifying entity may take into account. These measures are listed as: effective standards of conduct and internal control systems; timely and full cooperation with the authorities during the investigation into corrupt activity and any court action; independent investigation by the supplier and submission of the investigative report to the procuring authority; payment of all criminal, civil, and administrative liability for the improper activity, including costs incurred by the government; the taking of appropriate disciplinary action against the individuals responsible for the corrupt activity; the implementation of remedial measures, including any identified by the government; the institution of new or revised review and control procedures and ethics training programmes; and a recognition and understanding of the seriousness of the misconduct and the implementation of programmes to prevent recurrence.[101]

Further, US procuring authorities may utilise suppliers that have committed acts that could lead to their disqualification by requiring such 'flawed but competent' suppliers to conform to integrity standards by hiring an Independent Private Sector Inspector General (IPSIG).[102] In the US, the role of the IPSIG is to promote corporate integrity, prevent corruption and fraud in public procurement, ensure that a supplier complies with relevant laws and also to uncover, detect and report unethical conduct within the supplier and supervise the reform of corporations.[103] The IPSIG reports both to the supplier and the procuring authority, and where a

[100] Serious Fraud Office, Approach of the Serious Fraud Office to Dealing with Overseas Corruption, para 14, lists measures such as restitution, monitoring by an independent individual acceptable to the SFO, a programme of culture change and training acceptable to the SFO and measures against individuals where appropriate as being relevant in determining whether a corporate body will face criminal or civil sanctions for overseas corruption. Available at www.sfo.gov.uk.

[101] FAR 9.406-1.

[102] J Jacobs and R Goldstock, 'Monitors & IPSIGS: Emergence of a new Criminal Justice Role' (2007) 43 *Criminal Law Bulletin* 217, 223; S Lupkin and E Lewandowski, 'Independent Private Sector Inspectors General: Privately Funded Overseers of Public Integrity' (2005) 10 *New York Litigator* 6; F Anechiarico and R Goldstock, 'Monitoring Integrity and Performance: An Assessment of the Independent Private Sector Inspector General' (2007) 9 *Public Integrity* 117.

[103] Anechiarico and Goldstock, 'Monitoring Integrity and Performance', ibid; Jacobs and Goldstock, 'Monitors and IPSIGS', ibid.

supplier hires an IPSIG, its prior disqualification may be waived by a procuring authority.[104]

Where a supplier relies on the presence of rehabilitation factors to avoid disqualification, it bears the burden of proving that its disqualification is not necessary[105] and the courts may annul a disqualification where a procuring authority has not taken mitigating or rehabilitation factors into account.[106]

The World Bank adopts a similar approach to the US and provides a list of the kinds of measures that would be sufficient for the supplier to avoid or limit its disqualification. The Bank suggests that a supplier's disqualification would be withheld and the supplier sanctioned instead with a conditional non-debarment during which the supplier must comply with remedial, preventative or other conditions such as: actions taken to improve business governance, the implementation of corporate compliance or ethics programmes, restitution, disciplinary action or reassignment of employees.[107] If the supplier meets the expectations of the Bank, it may avoid disqualification altogether. Alternatively, a supplier could be temporarily disqualified from Bank contracts until it meets the Bank's requirements in relation to specified internal measures.[108]

Further, under the Bank's VDP, firms that are not under active investigation by the Bank may also avoid a subsequent disqualification by the Bank where they voluntarily admit to and disclose past corruption and adopt a 'robust best practice corporate governance compliance program' acceptable to the Bank.[109] The Bank is not prescriptive as to the contents of the compliance programme and the supplier determines what the elements of the programme will be.[110] The programme must however be acceptable to the Bank.

As has been mentioned previously, the South African legislation is silent on the issue of rehabilitation measures and as has been suggested, rehabilitation measures in South Africa may be relevant in relation to the power of the National Treasury to vary the length of a disqualification imposed by the court under the Corruption Act. In South Africa, there is no information on the content of rehabilitation measures, and the use of corporate compliance measures in other contexts is of little probative value in the rehabilitation context, since corporate compliance in the South African procurement context is directed towards ensuring that firms promote the participation of

[104] Lupkin and Lewandowski, 'Independent Private Sector Inspectors General', above n 102, 6.

[105] FAR 9.406-1.

[106] *Roemer v Hoffman* 419 F Supp 130 (DDC 1976); *Silverman v Defense Logistics Agency*, 817 F Supp 846 (DSD Cal 1993).

[107] WBSP art IX, s 9.01(b).

[108] WBSP art IX, s 9.01(d).

[109] World Bank, Voluntary Disclosure Program: Guidelines for Participants, para 3.

[110] ibid, para 5.6.

historically disadvantaged individuals in business and also that suppliers applying for public contracts on the basis that they are 'black empowerment' companies, meet those requirements.[111]

From the above approaches of the jurisdictions, one may extrapolate a general view of the kinds of rehabilitation measures that ought to be sufficient to limit the length of a disqualification or prevent it altogether. These measures will either be preventive or remedial. Preventive rehabilitation measures will generally include corporate compliance, organisational measures or internal controls that are aimed at preventing the occurrence of corrupt activity. Such measures may include the adoption of written codes of business ethics or conduct; ethics training or awareness programmes as well as the employment of compliance monitors. Remedial measures may include: investigation-related measures, such as cooperation with government agencies in investigations as well as making the results of independent investigations available to relevant government agencies; restitutionary measures such as the payment of damages to the government, including costs incurred in investigations; and disciplinary measures against individuals responsible for the corrupt activity, including the termination of employment and voluntary self-reporting measures.

10.3 PREVENTING ABUSE IN THE USE OF DEROGATIONS

One issue that arises where derogations are permitted is how to prevent abuse in the use of derogations. Abuse is likely where there are unclear or non-existent guidelines as to the factors that may be taken into account in deciding to derogate from a disqualification requirement or there is a lack of transparency and accountability in the use of derogations. Abuse may take the form of using derogations in a manner that may be discriminatory to favour certain suppliers or granting derogations for reasons that may not be justifiable. Where derogations are abused this is inequitable to suppliers who have not committed any offences and may give an unfair advantage to suppliers who have neglected their statutory or ethical obligations and are more competitive as a result, such as where the offence relates to the non-payment of taxes or social security contributions.[112]

In relation to the discriminatory granting of derogations, empirical evidence from the US suggests that large businesses appear to benefit more from derogations than small businesses.[113] Evidence for this may be

[111] Bolton, *Law of Government Procurement*, above n 31, 293–6.

[112] Arrowsmith, Priess and Friton, 'Self-Cleaning', above n 1, 273; Case C-226/04 *La Cascina* [2006] ECR I-1347, opinion of AG Maduro; C-213/07 *Michaniki AE v Ethniko Simvoulio Radiotileorasis* [2008] ECR I-9999, opinion of AG Maduro.

[113] D Brian, 'Contractor Debarment and Suspension: A Broken System' (2004) 5 *Public Procurement Law Review* 235, 236; J Karpoff, S Lee and V Vendrzyk, 'Defense Procurement Fraud, Penalties and Contractor Influence' (1999) 107 *Journal of Political Economy* 809; Canni,

obtained from the high-profile disqualifications in 2004 of WorldCom and Boeing, which were both granted derogations by some federal procuring authorities.[114] However, derogations in favour of large firms may be attributable to the fact that it may be impractical to use disqualification against large firms, especially in consolidated sectors or where there are few firms operating in the sector.[115] This is because disqualification may have adverse effects on competition,[116] and where a major supplier exits the market as a result of its disqualification[117] the suppliers that remain are not under pressure to keep their bids low as they are aware that they may not face much or any competition.[118] An example can be seen from Boeing's disqualification, which was shortly overturned due to the price increases that the US Department of Defense suffered as a result.[119]

Kramer also suggests that large firms appear to benefit more from derogations than small firms as larger firms have the resources to fix the problems for which they were disqualified, such as implementing corporate compliance measures or recruiting an IPSIG. As a result, larger disqualified firms may eventually pose less of a business risk to the government than smaller firms. She also suggests that more compelling reasons may be available to derogate from disqualification against a larger firm that may have a large market share in a specialised sector, whilst smaller firms may often supply goods or services that may easily be procured elsewhere.[120] Evidence for this view may also be seen in the 2008 disqualification of IBM, which lasted for just eight days due to IBM's large share of government contracts – it was the 16th largest federal supplier in 2008 and used its resources and leverage based on the government's need for IBM products to negotiate its way out of the disqualification.[121]

In relation to the granting of unjustifiable derogations, again the US provides practical evidence for this. It was seen that in relation to the disqualifications against WorldCom in 2004, several procuring authorities

'Shoot First, Ask Questions Later', above n 57; Schooner, 'Suspensions are Just a Side Show' (May 1 2002). Available at: www.govexec.com/features/0502/0502view1.htm .

[114] Brian, 'Contractor Debarment and Suspension', above n 113; Schooner, 'Suspensions are Just a Side Show', above n 113.

[115] Zucker, 'The Boeing Suspension', above n 53, 260.

[116] R Berrios, 'Government Contracts and Contractor Behaviour' (2006) 63 *Journal of Business Ethics* 119, 122.

[117] A Schutz, 'Too Little Too Late: An Analysis of the General Service Administration's Proposed Debarment of WorldCom' (2004) 65 *Administrative Law Review* 1263, 1273.

[118] J Cosentino, 'New York City's Procurement System: Reversing the Cycle of Corruption and Reactionary Reform' (1998) *New York Law School Law Review* 1183, 1186; F Anechiarico and J Jacobs, 'Purging Corruption from Public Contracting: The Solutions are Now Part of the Problem' (1995) *New York Law School Law Review* 165–8.

[119] Zucker, 'The Boeing Suspension', above n 53.

[120] Kramer, 'Awarding Contracts to Suspended and Debarred Firms', above n 59, 548–9, Bednar, Styles and McDowell, 'Self-Cleaning under non-EU Jurisdictions: United States', above n 63, 170.

[121] Canni, 'Shoot First, Ask Questions Later', above n 57, 593–4.

granted derogations for reasons that may not have been justifiable if those derogations had been subject to critical scrutiny. In the US, one reason why it is possible for unjustified derogations to be granted is because procuring authority heads wield absolute discretion in granting derogations,[122] there are no guidelines or reviewable standards for the decision, which remains that of the procuring authority head and is rarely overturned by the GSA.[123]

Although the derogation provisions in the EU and the UK have not been tested by the courts, the discretion available to procuring authorities and the lack of guidance in the legislation may also lead to the abuse of derogations in these jurisdictions.

There are several factors that may limit the potential for abuses in derogations. First, in all jurisdictions, the enabling instrument ought to provide more guidance as to when the use of derogations is appropriate. Such guidance need not be prescriptive to retain the flexibility that may be required in unexpected situations, but should be clear enough to ensure that procuring authorities know what is not an appropriate exceptional reason or rehabilitation measure. If such an approach is regarded as being too restrictive, given the range of circumstances that may warrant derogation, then an analogous approach to derogations in the amendments to the EU remedies directive discussed in chapter nine may be considered. The remedies directive provides that EU procuring authorities must declare a contract 'ineffective' in given situations,[124] and also provides that procuring authorities may derogate from this requirement to declare contracts ineffective. Instead of giving a list of circumstances when derogation is appropriate, the remedies directive adopts a negative approach by enumerating the instances when derogation would not be appropriate.[125] Similarly, disqualifying entities in the jurisdictions may be given guidance as to when derogation is not appropriate in order to guide their coming to a decision to derogate from a disqualification requirement. Secondly, as is the case in the US, the power to grant derogations may be reserved to the head of a procuring authority, or where one exists, a central authority that has supervisory functions over procuring authorities. Although reserving the power to grant derogations to senior personnel may not have been able to prevent abuse in the use of derogations in some cases, it is preferable to giving this power to the procurement officials who may be desirous of procuring with a particular supplier.

Thirdly, another approach could be that where derogations are granted, the decision may need to be *confirmed* by an independent entity. For instance, in the UK, the OGC Guidance suggests that the '[a]ccounting

[122] FAR 23.506(e).
[123] Collins, 'What the MCI Case Teaches', above n 25, 222.
[124] Remedies directive, art 2d.
[125] Remedies directive art 2d(3).

Officer or Minister, as appropriate, should be satisfied that the circumstances are such that they will justify the exception'.[126] Although this may lead to delays in the procurement process whilst the procuring authority awaits confirmation, procuring authorities may be more careful in granting derogations as they know their decision will be subject to scrutiny. This will also increase transparency and accountability in the derogation process and may facilitate the collation and dissemination of data on derogations.[127]

Whichever approach is adopted in a jurisdiction, the emphasis should be on ensuring that procuring authorities have the flexibility to derogate but that derogations are applied in a manner that is transparent and non-discriminatory.

10.4 SUMMARY AND ANALYSIS OF MAIN ISSUES

As was seen from the above, the selected jurisdictions approach the issue of derogations by providing broad statements permitting derogation from a mandatory requirement to disqualify as in the case in the EU/UK or permitting derogation from a general disqualification imposed by another entity as is the case in the US and in South Africa under the Corruption Act.

The problem with this broad approach, however, is that procuring entities are left to define both the contents of a justifiable derogation and the circumstances in which derogation is appropriate. This may be an undue burden on procuring authorities who may not have the competence or resources to determine what amounts to a sufficient reason for derogation, especially where rehabilitation measures are concerned. As was discussed in chapter six, a procuring authority required to decide whether a supplier's rehabilitation is sufficient to warrant a derogation in favour of the supplier may not understand the nuances of company law and ownership presented by the supplier's rehabilitation. It was seen in the context of derogations in the US that procuring entities may apply derogations that may not stand up to critical scrutiny and this will ultimately weaken the disqualification regime.

As was suggested, what may be required is for the legislation to provide clearer guidelines, either in terms of clearer general principles, or perhaps an indication of the kinds of appropriate measures or the circumstances in which derogation is not justifiable. The provision of clearer guidelines will strengthen and improve the effectiveness of the disqualification system and limit the potential for abuses in the use of derogations.

126 OGC Guidance, para 8.

127 GAO, Additional data reporting could improve suspension and debarment process (GAO 05-479, July 2005).

11

Remedies for Affected Suppliers

11.1 INTRODUCTION

THE PROCUREMENT SYSTEM of most jurisdictions provides suppliers with some form of remedies where the procurement legislation is not complied with or there are other breaches of the procurement process.[1] The availability of remedies for procurement violations may be necessary to ensure the proper functioning of the procurement system by securing compliance with, and deterring and correcting violations of, the procurement rules.[2] The nature and availability of remedies for procurement violations may depend on the nature of the forum reviewing the procurement decision and the kind of breach that has occurred. There are various approaches that may be adopted in implementing a procurement remedial system which have been detailed elsewhere, which include a review of procurement decisions by the procuring authority or review by an external authority, which could be judicial or administrative.[3] The jurisdictions generally adopt a multiple forum approach in providing for a system of review of procurement decisions, the appropriate forum being determined by the nature of the breach complained of, the kind of relief sought and the supplier's standing to obtain this relief.[4]

[1] S Arrowsmith, *Remedies for Enforcing the Public Procurement Rules* (Winteringham, Earlsgate, 1993); Arrowsmith, *The Law of Public and Utilities Procurement*, 2nd edn (London, Sweet & Maxwell, 2005) ch 21; A Tyrell and B Bedford, *Public Procurement in Europe: Enforcement & Remedies* (London, Butterworths, 1997); S Arrowsmith, J Linarelli and D Wallace, *Regulating Public Procurement: National and International Perspectives* (The Hague, Kluwer Law, 2000) ch 12; X Zhang, 'Supplier Review as a Mechanism for Securing Compliance with Government Public Procurement Rules: A Critical Perspective' (2007) 5 *Public Procurement Law Review* 325; D Gordon, 'Constructing a Bid Protest Process; The Choices that Every Procurement Challenge System Must Make' (2006) 35 *Public Contract Law Journal* 427; GAO, *Bid Protests at GAO: A Descriptive Guide* (2009); M Shaengold & R Brams, 'Choice of Forum for Government Contract Claims: Court of Federal Claims vs. Board of Contract Appeals' (2008) 17 *Federal Circuit Bar Journal* 279; M Shaengold, T Michael Guiffre and E Gill, 'Choice of Forum for Federal Government Contract Bid Protests' (2009) 18 *Federal Circuit Bar Journal* 243.

[2] Arrowsmith, Linarelli, Wallace, *Regulating Public Procurement*, above n 1, ch 12; Zhang, 'Supplier Review', above n 1, 326–8.

[3] Arrowsmith, Linarelli and Wallace, *Regulating Public Procurement*, above n 1, ch 12.

[4] X Zhang, 'Forum for Review by Suppliers in Public Procurement: An Analysis and Assessment of the Models in International Instruments' (2009) 5 *Public Procurement Law Review* 201.

Whilst providing suppliers with remedies for procurement violations may enhance the efficiency and transparency of the procurement system, a remedial system may also be accompanied by certain drawbacks, such as: costs and delays to the procurement process; the difficulty of proving that a violation has occurred and determining appropriate damages; as well as the possibility of 'over-compliance' by procuring authorities, to avoid procurement disputes, which may make procurement more bureaucratic.[5]

As is the case in other areas of procurement decision-making,[6] remedies may be available to a supplier in respect of actions taken during the disqualification process. In relation to disqualification decisions, an aggrieved supplier will generally be seeking redress where it claims that it ought not to have been disqualified, either because the disqualifying entity did not take relevant factors into account and as such the decision to disqualify is not justified, or because the disqualification decision was taken in breach of due process. A supplier may also challenge specific aspects of the disqualification decision such as the length of the disqualification as being disproportionate or excessive or may claim that another supplier who ought to have been disqualified was not disqualified, in breach of mandatory rules on disqualification.

This chapter will examine the availability of remedies to a supplier who challenges a disqualification made in respect of that supplier or another person. The chapter will consider whether a supplier has a right to challenge a disqualification decision, the forum in which this challenge may be brought and the basis on which a supplier may challenge a disqualification decision (ie whether the supplier possesses the required standing to bring a challenge) and the kind of remedies available to a supplier in a successful challenge procedure.

11.2 THE AVAILABILITY OF A RIGHT OF REVIEW

A supplier aggrieved by actions taken within the procurement process may be entitled to a review of the disputed actions. Rights of review are an aspect of developed procurement systems and a supplier challenging a disqualification decision ought to have the same rights, subject to the issue of standing, as suppliers challenging other aspects of procurement decision-making. In granting a right of review, a jurisdiction ought to specify the forum in which this right may be expressed and the basis on which a supplier may approach the forum.

[5] Zhang, 'Supplier Review', above n 1.
[6] Arrowsmith, *Public and Utilities Procurement*, above n 1, ch 21.

11.2.1 The EU

In the EU, the discretionary and the mandatory disqualification provisions do not indicate what rights of review are available where a supplier contests the decision to disqualify him or the decision in respect of another supplier. However, all contracts covered by the procurement directives are subject to the EU public sector remedies directive[7] or the utilities remedies directive[8] which specify the redress that should be available in domestic courts to affected persons where the procurement directives are infringed. The public sector remedies directive imposes an obligation on Member States to provide aggrieved suppliers with effective and rapid rights of review where there have been breaches of procurement legislation.[9] The utilities remedies directive also imposes a similar obligation on Member States.[10] The EU requires domestic courts to enforce these remedies in accordance with Treaty principles requiring that remedies available to persons affected by violations of EU law should be effective and comparable to those available for similar violations of domestic law.[11]

The EU remedies directive gives standing to challenge procurement decisions to a supplier where he has or had an interest in obtaining a particular contract and has been or risks being harmed by a legal infringement.[12] Thus, a supplier challenging his disqualification in respect of past or present offences, or a supplier who did not obtain a public contract which was given to a supplier who ought to have been disqualified, ought to have access to review procedures, since he is a person who has suffered or is likely to suffer harm where there are irregularities in the disqualification decision. It is up to Member States to determine, within the requirements of EU law, the forum that will carry out review in the first instance, which could be the procuring authority or an independent entity.[13] The CJEU has also interpreted the remedies directive as imposing an obligation on

[7] Directive 89/665/EEC on the laws, regulations and administrative provisions relating to the application of review procedures to the award of public supply and public works contracts [1989] OJ L395/33 as amended by Directive 2007/66/EC amending Council Directives 89/665/EEC and 92/13/EEC with regard to improving the effectiveness of review procedures concerning the award of public contracts [2007] OJ L335/31 [remedies directive].

[8] Directive 92/13/EEC coordinating the laws, regulations and administrative provisions relating to the application of Community rules on the procurement procedures of entities operating in the water, energy, transport and telecommunications sectors [1992] OJ L76/14 [utilities remedies directive]

[9] Remedies directive, art 1.

[10] Utilities remedies directive, art 1(1). This chapter will not deal with remedies in relation to the special complexities of utilities.

[11] P Craig and G de Burca, *EU Law: Text, Cases and Materials*, 4th edn (Oxford, Oxford University Press, 2007) ch 9; Arrowsmith, *Public and Utilities Procurement*, above n 1, ch 21.

[12] Remedies directive, art 1(3); Case C-145/08 *Club Hotel Loutraki AE v Ethniko Simvoulio Radiotileorasis* [2010] ECR I-4165.

[13] Remedies directive, art 2.

Member States to provide judicial review of procurement review decisions taken by non-judicial bodies.[14]

11.2.2 The UK

As a Member State, the UK is bound to provide an effective remedial system against breaches of EU procurement law. The UK has done this by including provisions on remedies in the procurement regulations.[15] Under these provisions, a procuring authority owes a duty to suppliers to comply with the procurement regulations, and a breach of this duty is actionable in the High Court.[16] A supplier may institute proceedings in the High Court where he suffers or risks suffering loss or damage as a result of a breach of the procurement regulations.[17] Therefore, in challenging a wrongful disqualification, a supplier who asserts that he was wrongly disqualified,[18] either in respect of past offences or offences committed within the specific award procedure, or who asserts that a supplier who ought to have been disqualified was allowed to participate in the procurement,[19] ought to be able to apply to the High Court for redress, since he is likely to suffer loss or damage from the decision taken by the procuring authority.[20]

The UK regulations provide for the High Court as the forum for review in the first instance. However, there is scope in the regulations for an aggrieved supplier to obtain information from the procuring authority on both disqualification and procurement decisions. A procuring authority is required to notify a disqualified supplier of its disqualification and a supplier may possibly challenge the disqualification decision with the procuring authority at this time,[21] ensuring that a procuring authority serves as the first line of review of disqualification decisions. This notification of disqualification may give the aggrieved supplier the opportunity to challenge the disqualification before the procuring authority before a contract is concluded.[22] A procuring authority is further required to give bidders notice of its award decision and the reasons why they were unsuccessful.[23] Where a supplier challenges its disqualification before the courts, the regulations

[14] Case C-570/08 *Simvoulio Apochetefseos Lefkosias* (unreported 21.10.10).

[15] Public Contracts Regulations 2006, reg 47.

[16] PCR regs 47A and 47C.

[17] PCR reg 47C; *Letting International Ltd v Newham* LBC [2008] EWHC 1583 (QB), paras 136–48.

[18] *R v London Borough of Enfield ex parte Unwin* [1989] COD 466.

[19] *R v National Lottery Commission ex parte Camelot Group* [2000] All ER (D) 1205.

[20] Arrowsmith, *Public and Utilities Procurement*, above n 1, ch 21.6 et seq.

[21] PCR reg 29A; Case T-465/04 *Evropaiki Dynamiki v Commission* [2008] ECR II-154.

[22] PCR reg 32A; Case C-455/08 *Commission v Ireland* [2009] ECR I-225; *DR Plumbing & Heating Services Ltd v Aberdeen City Council* (3 February 2009, unreported).

[23] PCR reg 32; Case C-455/08 *Commission v Ireland*, above n 22.

provide a time limit for instituting proceedings in the High Court and proceedings must be started within 30 days from when the supplier knew or ought to have known that the grounds for starting the proceedings arose, but the court may extend this period to three months where there is a good reason for doing so.[24]

As stated, the UK regulations give an aggrieved supplier a right to institute proceedings against a procuring authority, where there has been a breach of the procurement regulations. Whilst this approach may be appropriate in cases where the rules are clear and the breach can be clearly identified, it may be difficult for a disqualified supplier to claim that there has been a breach of the rules regarding the disqualification process, as the procedural rules and standards for disqualification are not identified in the UK procurement regulations. This lack of clarity may mean that an aggrieved supplier may be unwilling to claim that an infringement has occurred.

An aggrieved supplier may also seek remedies in an action for judicial review of the procuring authority's decision.[25] Judicial review is available to a supplier for public law breaches, such as a failure of due process unconnected with specific provisions of the Regulations.[26] Public bodies are under a duty to exercise their functions in accordance with common law principles of natural justice and procedural fairness,[27] and their decisions must not be unreasonable,[28] arbitrary or reached without sufficient evidence.[29] In the disqualification context, an action for judicial review[30] may be available in circumstances where the disqualification decision is in breach of these public law principles.[31]

[24] PCR reg 47D(2) as amended by Public Procurement (Miscellaneous Amendments) Regulations 2011, SI 2011/2053, reg 12. See Case C-406/08 *Uniplex (UK) Ltd v NHS Business Services Authority* [2010] ECR I-817; *Sita UK v Greater Manchester Waste Disposal Authority* [2011] EWCA Civ 156.

[25] *R (on the application of Cookson & Clegg) v Ministry of Defence* [2005] EWCA Civ 811.

[26] S Bailey, 'Judicial Review and the Public Procurement Regulations' (2005) 6 *Public Procurement Law Review* 291, 307; Arrowsmith, *Public and Utilities Procurement*, above n 1, ch 21.1 et seq.

[27] *Council of Civil Service Unions v Minister for the Civil Service* [1985] AC 374; *R v Secretary of State for the Home Department Ex parte Pierson* [1998] AC 539 at 591F *per* Lord Steyn; C Lewis, *Judicial Remedies in Public Law*, 4th edn (London, Sweet & Maxwell, 2008) ch 1.

[28] *Associated Provincial Picture Houses v Wednesbury Corp* [1948] KB 223.

[29] *Gavaghan v Secretary of State for the Environment* (1989) 60 P & CR 515.

[30] S Bailey, 'Judicial Review and Contracting Decisions' (2007) 3 *Public Law* 444–63; Bailey, 'Judicial Review and Public Procurement', above n 26; *Cookson & Clegg*, above n 25; Lewis, *Judicial Remedies*, above n 27, chs 2 and 4.

[31] Including where there has been fraud, corruption, or bad faith in decision-making – *R (on the application of Menai Collect Ltd & North West Commercial Services Ltd) v Dept of Constitutional Affairs* [2006] EWHC Admin 724; *Mercury Energy Ltd v Electricity Corporation of New Zealand* [1994] 1 WLR 521; *R v Lord Chancellors Department ex p. Hibbit & Saunders* [1993] COD 326, *R v Legal Aid Board ex parte Donn & Co* [1994] 3 All ER 1; Bailey, 'Judicial Review and Contracting Decisions', above n 30, 446.

11.2.3 The US

In the US, procedural differences exist between the longer and shorter disqualifications and there are also slight differences in the area of access to remedial rights. As will be discussed, both kinds of disqualifications may be challenged before the procuring authority and the courts. Procuring authorities are required by Executive Order to establish inexpensive and informal protest procedures at a level above that of the procuring (disqualifying) official[32] and a supplier is permitted, although not required, to submit protests to the procuring authority[33] in the first instance.[34] The cheapest and quickest forum for an aggrieved supplier to apply to is the procuring authority, although it has been argued that such protests are often tainted with the perception that the procuring authority may not be impartial in reviewing its own decision to disqualify the supplier.[35]

In relation to the longer disqualifications, a supplier is given the opportunity to make representations and challenge a proposed disqualification before the procuring authority.[36] However, in relation to the shorter disqualifications, a supplier is granted more limited remedial rights and is only given the opportunity to oppose the disqualification with the procuring authority after the decision to disqualify has been made.[37] Once he has been given this opportunity, a supplier is not permitted to bring a challenge against the shorter disqualification in any other forum apart from the courts. The limits on the remedial rights in relation to the shorter disqualifications may be due to the need to balance the tension between the government's right to quickly temporarily disqualify persons with which it does not wish to deal,[38] and the supplier's rights to be able to challenge its disqualification.[39] This balance is found in permitting a procuring authority to impose the shorter disqualification without extensive procedural or challenge rights, with the supplier being able to challenge a

[32] Exec Order No 12979, 60 Fed Reg 55171 (1995).

[33] FAR 33.102–33.103.

[34] E Troff, 'The United States Agency-Level Bid Protest Mechanism: A Model for Bid Challenge Procedures in Developing Nations' (2005) *Air Force Law Review* 113.

[35] W Wittig, 'A Framework for Balancing Business and Accountability within a Public Procurement System: Approaches and Practices of the United States' (2001) 3 *Public Procurement Law Review* 139, 152; Zhang, Forum for Review by Suppliers in Public Procurement', above n 4, 210; Shaengold, Michael Guiffre and Gill, 'Choice of Forum', above n 1, 274.

[36] FAR 9.406-3.

[37] FAR 9.407-3(b).

[38] Castelli, 'EPA defends action against IBM', *Fed Times* (15 April 2008).

[39] T Canni, 'Shoot First, Ask Questions Later: An Examination and Critique of Suspension and Debarment under the FAR, including a Discussion of the Mandatory Disclosure Rule, the IBM Suspension and other Noteworthy Developments' (2009) 38 *Public Contract Law Journal*, 547, 550–51; *Shinwha Electronics* Comp Gen B-291064, (Sept 3 2002).

shorter disqualification before the procuring authority within 30 days of the disqualification being imposed. [40]

For a supplier to have standing to bring an action at the level of the procuring authority, his challenge must meet two criteria: the challenge must be regarded as valid;[41] and only a person who is an actual or prospective bidder may submit a challenge.[42] It should be noted that a supplier in the US may not challenge a procuring authority's decision not to disqualify another supplier,[43] but may only challenge the determination that a supplier is responsible, which is required prior to contract award.[44]

Although the Government Accountability Office (GAO) is vested with statutory authority to adjudicate bid protests by the Competition in Contracting Act 1984,[45] both the shorter and the longer disqualification disputes are excluded from the GAO's jurisdiction.[46] The GAO has held that a disqualified supplier has no standing to appear before the GAO to challenge an adverse disqualification decision and such a disqualified supplier is not an 'interested party' for the purposes of maintaining a challenge.[47] Similarly, where a supplier is challenging the application of a disqualification decision in one agency, where the initial disqualification was imposed by another agency, a supplier may not be able to bring such a challenge before the GAO, but an exception occurs in cases where the supplier is alleging that the other federal agency is mistaken in excluding it, perhaps because its disqualification has expired.[48] In such cases, the procedures for submitting a dispute to the GAO are stated in the GAO Bid Protest Regulations[49] and the FAR.[50]

At the court level, an aggrieved supplier may seek judicial review of a shorter or longer disqualification decision in the Court of Federal Claims (COFC),[51] which has exclusive jurisdiction over federal procurement claims. The courts have upheld the right of a disqualified supplier to have

[40] FAR 9.407-3(c); Canni, 'Shoot First, Ask Questions Later', ibid, 550.

[41] FAR 33.101; 31 USC § 3551–3556.

[42] 31 USC § 3551.

[43] *Heckler v Chaney* 470 US 821, 831–2 (1985)

[44] *Impresa Construzioni Geom Domenico Garufi v United States* 238 F3d 1324, 1334–9 (Fed Cir 2001); FAR 9.103(b).

[45] Pub L No 98-369; S Patoir, 'An Overview for Agency Counsel' (2002) *Army Lawyer* 29.

[46] 4 CFR 21.5(i).

[47] *Waste Conversion Inc* B-234761 (April 11, 1989). 89-1 CPD ¶ 371; *K & K Engineered Prods Inc* Comp Gen B-239838.2 (July 9, 1990), 90-2 CPD ¶ 22; *Triton Electronic Enterprises Inc* B-294249, (July 9 2004).

[48] *RJ Crowley Inc*, Comp Gen B-253783, (Oct 22, 1993), where the GAO sustained a protest of a disqualified supplier, when a contracting official improperly relied on an outdated eligibility list in excluding the supplier from a procurement.

[49] 4 CFR part 21.

[50] FAR 33.104.

[51] 28 USC § 1491 (2006); J Schwatz, 'Public Contracts Specialisation as a Rationale for the Court of Federal Claims' (2003) 71 *George Washington Law Review* 863, cf S Schooner, 'The Future: Scrutinizing the Empirical Case for the Court of Federal Claims' (2003) 71 *George Washington Law Review* 714.

the disqualification procedure conform to the tenets of due process,[52] and be accompanied by 'exacting procedural safeguards', thus giving judicial recognition to bidders' rights in relation to disqualification.[53] A supplier may base its action on the lack of due process in the disqualification decision or on the grounds of review under the Administrative Procedure Act, 1946[54] and the court will overturn a disqualification where it is 'arbitrary or capricious',[55] an abuse of discretion or otherwise not in accordance with the law.[56] However, it is usual for a claimant to first exhaust all administrative remedies before seeking judicial redress.[57]

Standing in the COFC is extended to an 'interested party', defined as an actual or prospective bidder whose direct economic interest would be affected by the award or failure to award the contract.[58] A bidder would thus have access to the courts where it can be shown that it was 'denied a reasonable opportunity to compete'.[59] In adjudicating on disqualification issues, the COFC makes its decision on the evidence found in the record and gives a lot of deference to agency disqualification decisions[60] and will not substitute its decision with that of the agency or overturn a decision unless the decision cannot be 'substantiated by the record'.[61]

11.2.4 The World Bank

As discussed earlier, the World Bank utilises two kinds of measures against corrupt suppliers, the one-off disqualification and the longer disqualifications. The Bank's approach to the review of disqualification decisions differs considerably from that of domestic jurisdictions and the availability of rights of review are very limited.

In relation to the rejection measures, a bidder who has his bid rejected by the Borrower at the instance of the Bank is entitled to an explanation

[52] *Gonzalez v Freeman* 334 F2d 570, 574 (DC Cir 1964); *Related Indus Inc v United States* 2 Cl Ct 517, 526 (1983).

[53] W Kovacic, 'Procurement Reform and the Choice of Forum in Bid Protest Disputes' (1995) 9 *Administrative Law Journal of American University* 461, 472; *Scanwell Labs Inc v Shaffer* 424 F2d 859 (DC Cir 1970), *Transco Security Inc of Ohio v Freeman*, 639 F2d 318 (6th Cir 1981).

[54] Pub L 79-404, s 10(e); 5 USC §500.

[55] *Lion Raisins Inc v United States* 51 Fed Cl 238 (2001).

[56] *Banknote Corp of Am Inc v United States* 365 F3d 1345, 1350 (Fed Cir 2004); *Axiom Resource Management v United States* 564 F3d 1374 (Fed Cir 2009).

[57] *Facchiano v United States Dep't of Labor* 859 F2d 1163 (3d Cir 1988).

[58] 31 USC § 3551 (2000); 28 USC § 1491(b)(1) 2006; FW Claybrook, 'Standing, Prejudice and prejudging bid protest cases' (2004) 33 *Public Contract Law Journal* 535.

[59] C Peckinpaugh, *Government Contracts for Services: The Handbook for Acquisition Professionals* (American Bar Association, 1997) 238.

[60] *Impresa Construzioni*, above n 44, 1334–5.

[61] *OSG Product Transfers LLC v United States* 82 Fed Cl 570 (2008); *Axiom Resource Management*, above n 56.

from the Borrower in writing or at a debriefing meeting.[62] The outcome of this meeting should be submitted to the Bank and bidders may write to the Bank directly if the bidder has a complaint against the Borrower.[63] Where a bidder is not satisfied with the explanation offered by the Borrower, the bidder may request a meeting from the Bank's Regional Procurement Adviser (RPA) of the borrowing country.[64] The meeting between the bidder and the RPA is not a hearing and a bidder is not entitled to submit representations on the Bank's decision to reject its bid. The purpose of this meeting is for the supplier to obtain further information on why it was disqualified from the particular procurement process; the meeting is limited to a discussion of the complainant's bid and not those of competitors;[65] and there is no provision for the taking of remedial action by the Bank.

The absence of remedial rights in this context stems from the fact that suppliers do not have any rights of recourse against the Bank, as there is no legal relationship created between suppliers or potential suppliers and the Bank for the purpose of instituting a challenge procedure.[66] The relationship between a supplier and a Borrower is governed by the bidding documents and any contracts which arise exist between the supplier and the Borrower.[67] Suppliers do not have rights or claims arising from the existence of the loan between the Borrower and the Bank.[68]

However, where a Borrower improperly rejects the bid of a supplier without the authority of the Bank, it may be possible for the supplier to seek remedies against the Borrower under its domestic law.[69] This would, however, depend on the extent to which the actions of the Borrower are subject to judicial scrutiny in the procurement context. Further, in relation to obtaining remedies against the Bank, although as has been discussed, there is no possibility for a supplier to directly obtain a remedy from the Bank, it is possible that where a supplier appraises the Bank of the improper actions of the Borrower, such actions may constitute a breach of the Loan Agreement between the Borrower and the Bank under which the Bank may compel the Borrower to fulfil its obligations under the Agreement, which usually incorporate the Bank's procurement guidelines.

[62] BPG, para 2.65.

[63] BPG, appendix 3, para 15.

[64] ibid.

[65] ibid.

[66] Arrowsmith, Linarelli and Wallace, *Regulating Public Procurement*, above n 1, 110.

[67] BPG, para 1.1.

[68] ibid. See also M de Castro Meireles, *A Critical Analysis of Remedies and Secondary Policies under the World Bank Procurement System* (PhD. Thesis, University of Nottingham, 2006) 95–7.

[69] B Malmendier, 'The Liability of International Development Banks in Procurement Proceedings: The Example of the International Bank for Reconstruction and Development, the European Bank for Reconstruction and Development and the Inter-American Development Bank' (2010) 4 *Public Procurement Law Review* 135, 137.

It has also been argued that the Bank is under an obligation to provide effective remedies to a supplier where a Borrower has failed to properly conduct the procurement process, as this failure stems from the Bank's failure to properly supervise the Borrower.[70] According to Malmendier, the Bank has a responsibility borne out of its authority over the Borrower to efficiently use the monitoring and review instruments available to it[71] and even though there is no direct contractual relationship between the Bank and suppliers, an extra-contractual relationship exists, which obliges the Bank to ensure that a 'bidder will not be discriminated against in breach of the procedural principles issued by the bank'.[72]

In relation to the Bank's disqualification measures, whilst a supplier may challenge a proposed disqualification at the Sanctions Board, there is no indication whether a supplier may obtain relief either against the Bank or a Borrower where a Borrower mistakenly or improperly excludes from a Bank-funded contract, a supplier that was not previously disqualified by the Bank.

In Sanctions Board proceedings, once the Board has affirmed a disqualification proposed by the Evaluations Officer,[73] the supplier may not challenge its disqualification in a domestic court or in any other forum. Further, the Bank does not provide remedies for suppliers with complaints against the manner in which the disqualification process was conducted. Thus where the Bank did not comply with its own disqualification procedures, a disqualified supplier would have no recourse against the Bank, as the procedures do not confer any rights or privileges on a supplier.[74] In addition, where a supplier feels he was unfairly treated or the length of a disqualification is too harsh or that a supplier who engaged in fraud or corruption was not disqualified, such a person has no legal or administrative remedies against the Bank or its staff.

There are several reasons for this. First, the Bank and its staff have immunity from domestic jurisdiction for anything done in connection with their employment.[75] This also applies to actions taken in the disqualification context. This immunity frees the World Bank from the peculiarities of national politics by immunising the Bank from legal process.[76] Secondly, the procurement guidelines and anything arising out of them, once incorporated by reference into the Loan Agreement, become

[70] Malmendier, 'The Liability of International Development Banks', above n 69, 139.

[71] Malmendier, 'The Liability of International Development Banks', ibid.

[72] Malmendier, 'The Liability of International Development Banks', above n 69, 145.

[73] WBSP, art VIII.

[74] WBSP, art XIII s 3.03.

[75] P Sands and P Klein, *Bowett: The Law of International Institutions*, 5th edn (London, Sweet & Mawell, 2001); C Jenks, *International Immunities* (London, Stevens, 1961); IBRD Articles of Agreement, art VII. Cf K Wellens, *Remedies against International Organisations* (Cambridge, Cambridge University Press 2002) 118.

[76] *Mendaro v World Bank* 717 F2d 610 (DC Cir 1983).

international law and cannot be overridden by domestic law.[77] Thus a supplier may not allege that the Bank's actions are not in conformity with due process as determined by national law, as the Bank is 'insulated from accountability within domestic legal systems'.[78] Thirdly, as mentioned, bidding for a Bank contract does not create any legal relationship between the Bank and potential suppliers for the purpose of instituting a review procedure. The Bank's refusal to create a remedial system for suppliers has, however, been criticised,[79] and as argued by Malmendier, suppliers ought to be able to rely on an extra-contractual relationship created between the Bank and bidders on a Bank contract.

Where a Borrower improperly disqualifies a supplier, there is no indication whether a supplier may obtain remedies against the Bank or the Borrower. Although the Bank does not conduct the procurement process, and despite the absence of a formal relationship with the supplier, the Bank influences the outcome of the procurement process and should thus 'take responsibility for the fate of procurements', since it is in fact substantially involved in decision-making.[80] Thus, where a Borrower has wrongly excluded a supplier from a Bank-funded procurement, mistakenly or out of malice, the supplier ought to be able to request an investigation into the circumstances from the Bank and the Bank should not tolerate or acquiesce in breaches of its procurement principles or procedures by Borrowers.[81]

Providing suppliers with an opportunity to challenge improper decisions by the Borrower in the disqualification context may improve the effectiveness of the disqualification policy. It has been argued that a review system could significantly increase the ability of the Bank to uncover corruption and impropriety in procurements,[82] as these challenges will serve as an avenue for such acts to be revealed,[83] as well as a deterrent to improper conduct.[84]

As discussed in the context of the Bank's one-off disqualification measures, whether a supplier may obtain remedies against the Borrower under domestic law for improper disqualification will of course depend on the law of the jurisdiction in question, but it has been suggested that in some developing countries, judicial enforcement in relation to public procure-

[77] J Head, 'Evolution of the Governing Law for Loan Agreements of the World Bank and other Multilateral Development Banks' (1996) 90 *American Journal of International Law* 214, 229.

[78] Arrowsmith, Linarelli and Wallace, *Regulating Public Procurement*, above n 1, 149.

[79] Meireles, *A Critical Analysis*, above n 68, ch V; S Williams, 'The Debarment of Corrupt Contractors from World Bank-Financed Contracts' (2007) 36 *Public Contract Law Journal* 277; Malmendier, 'The Liability of International Development Banks', above n 69.

[80] Malmendier, 'The Liability of International Development Banks', above n 69, 150.

[81] Malmendier, 'The Liability of International Development Banks', above n 69, 136.

[82] Arrowsmith, Linarelli and Wallace, *Regulating Public Procurement*, above n 1, 129.

[83] D Gordon, 'Constructing a Bid Protest Process; The Choices that Every Procurement Challenge System Must Make' (2006) 35 *Public Contract Law Journal* 427.

[84] Gordon, 'Constructing a Bid Protest Process', ibid.

ment leaves a lot to be desired[85] and in some cases, remedies in respect of Bank contracts may be wholly unavailable under the domestic law of the borrowing country.[86]

11.2.5 South Africa

South African law grants aggrieved suppliers rights to review of procurement decisions before the procuring authority and the courts.[87] Similar to the US, there is a statutory obligation for procuring authorities and an independent entity to review procurement decisions. In relation to procuring authorities, the Municipal Supply Chain Management Regulations, applicable to local authorities, provides that the authority must appoint an independent and impartial person to assist in the resolution of disputes arising from a procurement procedure or contract award decision.[88] In addition, the PFMA regulations provide that the National Treasury and each provincial treasury must establish a mechanism to consider complaints regarding alleged non-compliance with the prescribed minimum norms and standards and make recommendations for remedial action if non-compliance is established.[89] Finally, the Local Government Municipal Systems Act also gives aggrieved persons the right to challenge or appeal political or administrative decisions made under a delegated power or duty.[90] Thus, if a supplier makes a complaint about the procedural standards used to disqualify him, he is entitled to have his complaint investigated by either the procuring authority or the relevant Treasury and to be provided with adequate remedies if his complaint is justified.

On the judicial plane, because all aspects of the procurement process amount to administrative action within the meaning of section 1 of PAJA, the decision to disqualify a supplier must accord with PAJA, and afford the supplier remedies in judicial review proceedings where procedural standards have not been met. Under PAJA, the courts are not required to review administrative action until internal administrative remedies have been exhausted.[91] Access to judicial review is also available in terms of a general power under the common law, and judicial review would be available where there has been an abuse of discretion, where power has

[85] Malmendier, 'The Liabilty of International Development Banks', above n 69, 136.

[86] Arrowsmith, Linarelli and Wallace, *Regulating Public Procurement*, above n 1, 143.

[87] See G Quinot, 'Enforcement of Procurement Law from a South African Perspective' (2011) 6 *Public Procurement Law Review* 193; P Bolton, *The Law of Government Procurement, in South Africa* (Durban, LexisNexis Butterworth, 2007) chs 11–13.

[88] Municipal Supply Chain Management Regulations, reg 50(1).

[89] PFMA reg 16A9.3.

[90] Local Government Municipal Systems Act, 2000 (Government Gazette 21776, 20 November 2000) s 62(1).

[91] PAJA, s 7.

been exercised unlawfully, without authority or where there has been an error of law.[92] However, as PAJA has incorporated many of the common law reasons for judicial review, most actions for judicial review are brought under PAJA.

Standing in South African courts is granted to a person who has a 'sufficient, direct and personal' interest in the matter in the sense that the person's rights must have been infringed or his financial interests prejudiced.[93] Thus a supplier who is claiming that he ought not to have been disqualified or that another person ought to have been disqualified should meet the requirements for standing.

Apart from judicial and agency-level review, an aggrieved supplier may be able to seek redress from the Office of the Public Protector (OPP), established under the Constitution,[94] which is empowered to investigate improper conduct in the public administration or conduct that will result in impropriety or prejudice and take appropriate remedial action.[95] Thus, in the disqualification context, an aggrieved supplier may approach the OPP where there was impropriety in the disqualification process.

To summarise, a supplier disqualified by a procuring authority under the PPPFA or PFMA regulations may approach the agency, the relevant Treasury, the courts or the OPP for a review of the disqualification decision. However, where the courts have disqualified a supplier as part of a criminal sentence for corruption under the Corruption Act, the supplier has limited avenues for redress. With the exception discussed below, judicial disqualification under the Corruption Act cannot be subject to review by a procuring authority, since disqualification is a part of a criminal sentence for corruption. The disqualification cannot also be subject to judicial review since redress under PAJA does not apply to judicial decisions.[96] The only option available to a supplier is to seek for the disqualification to be overturned in an appeal against the conviction, which includes the disqualification order.[97]

Although a supplier disqualified by the courts may not ordinarily challenge its disqualification before a procuring entity, where a supplier claims that the procuring entity is mistaken as to the identity of a listed supplier, it may ask the procuring authority to review the decision to exclude it or apply for judicial review of the procuring authority's decision. Also, in relation to disqualification imposed by the court, if the complaint relates to other aspects of the disqualification that are considered to be 'adminis-

[92] C van de Merwe and J du Plessis, *Introduction to the Law of South Africa* (The Hague, Kluwer Law International, 2004) ch 3.

[93] ibid.

[94] Constitution of South Africa, s 182.

[95] Constitution of South Africa, s 182(1); Preamble to the Public Protector Act 23 of 1994 (Government Gazette 16107, 24 November 1994).

[96] PAJA s 1(ee)

[97] Corruption Act 2004, s 28(3)(b).

trative action', a supplier may be entitled to seek judicial review of that aspect of the decision. For instance, as discussed in chapter six, it is the National Treasury that determines the period of disqualification and maintains the Register for Tender Defaulters containing information on disqualified suppliers. It is thus possible for a disqualified supplier to seek judicial review of the decision determining the period of the disqualification where there are irregularities in this determination or where incorrect information on the supplier is entered into the Register.

11.3 THE KINDS OF REMEDIES AVAILABLE

The kinds of remedies available to a disqualified supplier who mounts a successful challenge in the disqualification context will depend on the nature of the forum in which the challenge is brought. Thus, whilst review at the level of the procuring authority or an independent administrative entity may lead to interim remedies, a reversal of the disqualification decision, or a cancellation of the procurement procedure in which the disqualification decision was taken, a procuring authority or independent entity may not have the power to award damages. However, where the review is heard in a court or other judicial forum, the court would generally have the power to award damages in addition to other remedies, as long as the supplier is able to prove his loss.

In the EU, as discussed, Treaty principles require that remedies provided by national courts in relation to breaches of EU law should be effective and comparable to the remedies available for similar violations of domestic law.[98] Aside from this obligation and because of the importance of national remedies in ensuring the effective enforcement of EU procurement rules,[99] the public sector remedies directive specifies the types of redress that should be available in national courts for a breach of award procedures covered by the procurement directives. The directive provides for several types of remedies: interim relief,[100] the setting aside of unlawful decisions – a remedy which must be effectively available against any

[98] P Craig and G de Burca, *EU Law: Text, Cases and Materials*, 4th edn (Oxford, Oxford University Press, 2007) ch 9; Arrowsmith, *Public and Utilities Procurement*, above n 1, ch 21.

[99] D Pachnou, 'Enforcement of the EC Procurement Rules: The Standards required of National Review Systems under EC Law in the Context of the Principle of Effectiveness' (2000) 2 *Public Procurement Law Review* 55; Arrowsmith, *Public and Utilities Procurement*, above n 1, ch 21; A Tyrell and B Bedford, *Public Procurement in Europe: Enforcement & Remedies* (London, Butterworths, 1997); A Brown, 'Effectiveness of Remedies at National Level in the Field of Public Procurement' (1998) 8 *Public Procurement Law Review* 9; R Williams, 'A New Remedies Directive for the European Community' (2008) 2 *Public Procurement Law Review* NA19; S Arrowsmith, 'Public Procurement: Example of a Developed Field of National Remedies Established by Community Law' in H Micklitz and N Reich (eds), *Public Interest Litigation before European Courts* (Baden-Baden, Nomos, 1996) 125–56.

[100] Remedies directive, art 2(1)(a).

reviewable decision in the award procedure,[101] ineffectiveness,[102] damages[103] and penalties that may be imposed on the procuring authority such as fines or the shortening of the duration of the contract.[104] The utilities remedies directive is similar, although with some additional and alternative provisions.

Where a successful challenge is brought for a wrongful disqualification, the remedies will comprise those specified in the remedies directive. An effective remedy (from the supplier's point of view) will be to suspend or set aside the decision taken,[105] which clearly may cause disruption to the procurement process. Where it is claimed that a supplier who ought to have been disqualified was not disqualified, the complainant may, if successful, be entitled to interim relief or a set-aside of the decision to include that supplier in the process, which again may cause disruption. Where a supplier requests interim measures in the disqualification context, it is likely that the CJEU will apply the same approach that is used in determining whether interim measures are warranted in other contexts. Here the standard is quite high and interim measures will be granted on the balance of interests and must be necessary to prevent 'serious and irreparable' damage to the applicant.[106]

Generally, where a dispute arises during the procurement process, prior to the contract award, most jurisdictions have procedures to stay the procurement process. In the EU, the remedies directive provides that where a supplier seeks review of a procurement decision before a procuring authority, the application for review shall result in the immediate suspension of the procurement process.[107] This suspension may give the procuring authority enough time to review the decision complained of, and also grant the supplier sufficient time to request interim relief in court. Further, where an authority independent of the procuring authority reviews a procurement decision in the first instance, this must also have a suspensory effect on the procurement process until a decision has been made.[108] Beyond these provisions, review measures are not required to have a suspensory effect on a procurement procedure.[109]

[101] Remedies directive, art 2(1)(b); Case C-81/98 *Alcatel Austria v Bundeministerium fur Wissenschaft und Verkehr* [1999] ECR I-7671, para.43.

[102] Remedies directive, arts 2d and 2e.

[103] Remedies directive, art 2(1)(c). Proof of fault is not required: Case C-314/09 *Stadt Graz v Strabag AG* [2011] 1 CMLR 26; H Leffler, 'Damages Liability for Breach of EC Procurement Law: Governing Principles and Practical Solutions' (2003) 4 *Public Procurement Law Review* 151.

[104] Remedies directive, art 2e.

[105] Case C-81/98 *Alcatel*, above n 101.

[106] Case C-87/94R *Commission v Belgium* [1994] ECR I-1395; Case T-511/08R *Unity OSG FZE v Council of the European Union* [2009] ECR II-0010, para 22.

[107] Remedies directive, art 1(5).

[108] Remedies directive, art 2(3).

[109] Remedies directive, art 2(4).

Finally, damages are also available in principle, although this may be difficult to claim in practice because of the problems of proving loss.[110] It should be noted that the EU does not give any indication as to the conditions for or extent of damages,[111] but it seems to be settled that damages must compensate for the loss suffered.[112] However, in the disqualification context, proving loss would be difficult where a supplier has been disqualified before it has had a chance to submit a tender, as it would be extremely difficult to determine whether its tender would have stood any chance. This may make damages unlikely in this context, and suppliers may focus instead on obtaining interim relief whilst they attempt to have a disqualification decision set-aside.

As discussed in chapter nine, the amendments to the remedies directive introduced some changes to the EU remedial scheme.[113] One important change is the introduction of a 10-day mandatory standstill period prior to the conclusion of contracts to grant aggrieved bidders a chance to lodge complaints.[114] This provision gave legislative force to the CJEU decision in *Alcatel*.[115] Also, procuring authorities are now under a duty to declare a contract 'ineffective' where there are certain breaches of the directives.[116] As discussed earlier, the list of circumstances under which a contract may be declared ineffective appear to be exhaustive and a breach of a duty in relation to disqualification may not render a concluded contract ineffective.

The problem of providing effective protection for participants and an effective system for enforcing EU rules, whilst avoiding undue disruption to the procurement process, is a difficult one: suffice it to say that Member States will no doubt apply in the disqualification context, the same system of remedies they have implemented for other procurement violations, the disqualifications merely adding another possible violation that may form the basis of legal proceedings.

In addition to the rights of suppliers and tender participants to challenge a procurement procedure under the remedies directives, the Commission may initiate proceedings against a procuring authority under Article 258 TFEU for non-compliance with EU law.[117]

[110] Remedies directive, art 2(1)(c); Leffler, 'Damages Liability for Breach of EC Procurement Law', above n 103; S Treumer, 'Damages for the Breach of the EC Public Procurement Rules – Changes in European Regulation and Practice' (2006) 4 *Public Procurement Law Review* 159.

[111] D Pachnou, *The Effectiveness of Bidder Remedies for Enforcing the EC Public Procurement Rules: A Case Study of the Public Works Sector in the United Kingdom and Greece* (PhD Thesis, University of Nottingham, 2003) ch 3.

[112] Joined Cases C-46-48/93 *Brasserie du Pêcheur SA v Germany and R v Secretary of State for Transport, ex parte Factortame Ltd (No 3)* [1996] ECR I-1029.

[113] Williams, 'A New Remedies Directive', above n 99.

[114] Remedies directive, art 2a.

[115] Case C-81/98 *Alcatel*, above n 101.

[116] Remedies directive, arts 2d and 2e. J Golding and P Henty, 'The New Remedies Directive of the EC: Standstill and Effectiveness' (2008) 3 *Public Procurement Law Review* 146.

[117] F Martín, 'The European Commission's Centralised Enforcement of Public Procurement Rules: A Critical View' (1993) 2 *Public Procurement Law Review* 40; F Martín, *The EC Public*

The UK procurement regulations provide for several kinds of relief, as required by the EU remedies directive.[118] These are interim relief,[119] setting aside of the contract,[120] awarding damages,[121] a declaration of ineffectiveness,[122] which is the prospective termination of the contract and the mandatory standstill period.[123] However, once a contract has been concluded, and the grounds for a declaration of ineffectiveness do not apply, the only remedy available to an aggrieved supplier is an award of damages.[124]

A supplier who challenges a wrongful disqualification[125] or who asserts that a supplier who ought to have been disqualified was allowed to participate in the contract ought to be able to apply to the High Court for interim relief or a setting aside of either the decision to disqualify him from participating in the contract, or a setting aside of the decision to include a supplier in the procurement process.[126] As mentioned, damages may also be available in each case, as long as the supplier can show that the procuring authority's breach was the cause of his loss,[127] although as discussed above, this may be unlikely where the supplier has been excluded from the tendering process.[128]

In implementing the amendments to the EU remedies directive, the UK also provided for the suspension of the decision to enter into a contract, where proceedings are instituted and the contract has not been entered into.[129] This suspension continues in effect until the court determines the proceedings or makes an interim order.[130] In determining whether to suspend a procurement procedure, UK courts also adopt the balance of convenience test, which is used in deciding whether an interim injunction

Procurement Rules: A Critical Analysis (Oxford, Clarendon Press, 1996); A Delsaux, 'The Role of the Commission in Enforcing EC Public Procurement Rules' (2004) 13 *Public Procurement Law Review* 130; D Pachnou, 'Bidders Use of Remedies to Enforce European Community Procurement Law' (2005) 2 *Public Procurement Law Review* 256.

118 Remedies directive, art 2.

119 PCR reg 47H.

120 PCR reg 47I.

121 PCR regs 47I and 47J; *Harmon CFEM Facades (UK) Ltd v Corporate Officer of the House of Commons* [2000] 2 LGLR 372 (QBD).

122 PCR regs 47J, 47K and 47M.

123 PCR regs 32 and 32A.

124 PCR reg 47J(2)(d); *Ealing Community Transport v London Borough of Ealing* [1999] COD 492

125 *R v London Borough of Enfield ex parte Unwin* [1989] COD 466.

126 *Lion Apparel Systems v Firebuy Ltd* [2007] EWHC 2179 (Ch.).

127 M Bowsher and P Moser, 'Damages for breach of the EC Public Procurement rules in the United Kingdom' (2006) 15 *Public Procurement Law Review* 195, 198; *Aquatron Marine v Strathclyde Fire Board* [2007] CSOH 185.

128 *R v Portsmouth City Council ex parte Bonaco Builders* (1997) 95 LGR 494; S Arrowsmith, 'Interpretation of the Procurement Directives and Regulations: A Note on R v Portsmouth City Council, ex parte Bonaco Builders' (1996) 5 *Public Procurement Law Review* CS90.

129 PCR reg 47G(1) as amended by Public Procurement (Miscellaneous Amendments) Regulations 2011, SI 2011/2053, reg 21.

130 PCR reg 47G(2).

ought to be granted in other contexts.[131] The courts consider whether there is a serious issue to be tried and the harm to the parties and the public were the procurement suspended. The governing principle here is whether an award of damages would adequately compensate the supplier for the losses it would suffer should the procurement procedure continue. Whilst this question will be answered in the affirmative in other contexts,[132] in the disqualification context it may be hard for a supplier to prove its losses and this may mean that in practice, interim relief may often be granted in disqualification challenges.

As discussed earlier, if a supplier seeks judicial review of the disqualification decision, then his remedies will be the specialised remedies granted in a successful action for judicial review. The remedies available in an action for judicial review are: the prerogative remedies which are quashing orders, mandatory orders and prohibiting orders; declarations, injunctions as well as damages and recovery of money. These remedies may be granted in combination where it is appropriate to do so. These remedies are similar in some respects to the remedies provided for in the regulations, with the exception of the specific rules relating to ineffectiveness and the standstill period and with a more limited right to damages.

Damages are available in an action for judicial review where the action complained of constituted a tort or a breach of contract. In the disqualification context, a claimant will clearly be unable to make a claim for damages for breach of contract, but may be able to claim damages for either the tort of misfeasance in public office or the tort of breach of statutory duty.[133] Where damages are granted in tort, they will include lost profits, but will generally not include bid costs.[134] The payment of lost profits and the exclusion of bid costs from damages in the UK differs from the US approach, as will be seen, where bid and procurement related costs are recoverable whilst lost profits are not generally recoverable where there have been anomalies in the procurement process.[135]

In the US, there are different remedies available to a supplier depending on the forum in which the challenge is brought. The powers granted to procuring authorities in the US to resolve disputes are quite wide and they have the power to take any action to ensure disputes are resolved, such as overturning a disqualification decision and the payment of costs,

[131] *Exel Europe v University Hospitals Coventry and Warwickshire NHS Trust* [2010] EWHC 3332; *American Cyanamid Co v Ethicon Ltd (No 1)* [1975] AC 396.

[132] *B2Net Ltd v HM Treasury* [2010] EWHC 51 (QB); *McLaughlin & Harvey v Department of Finance and Personnel* [2008] NIQB 25; *Burroughs Machines Ltd v Oxford Area Health Authority* [1983] ECC 434; *European Dynamics v HM Treasury* [2009] EWHC 3419. Cf *Letting International v Newham* [2007] EWCA Civ 1522.

[133] *Harmon CFEM Facades v The Corporate Officer of the House of Commons* [2002] 2 LGLR 372; *X v Bedfordshire County Council* [1995] AC 633, 739B. See generally, S Arrowsmith, *Civil Liability and Public Authorities* (Winteringham, Earlsgate Press, 1992) ch 7.

[134] *Harmon*, ibid; Arrowsmith, *Public and Utilities Procurement*, above n 1, ch 21.19.

[135] *Heyer Products Co v US* 135 Ct Cl 63 (1956).

and in general may take any action that could have been recommended by the GAO.[136] Also, similar to the EU/UK, where a challenge is filed before a procuring authority before the contract award decision is made, the award will not be made, but where the challenge is made after the award decision, the procuring authority is not required to suspend the contract unless the challenge is filed within 10 days of the contract award decision.[137] Although there is no automatic standstill period, the filing of a protest results in the suspension of the procurement process where a protest is received within 10 days of a contract being awarded, and procuring authorities are required to immediately suspend the award of the contract pending resolution of the dispute unless the performance of the contract is necessary for urgent and compelling reasons or is in the best interests of the government.[138] The FAR also gives procuring authorities the discretion to implement a voluntary suspension of contract award and contract performance where a protest does not succeed at the agency level and the supplier files a protest at the GAO.[139] Suspension in the US will take effect until the dispute is resolved.[140] As will be seen, South African legislation does not provide for a similar suspension mechanism.

However in the US, where a procuring authority decides to continue with the performance of the contract, a supplier may challenge this decision in the COFC,[141] and the courts will review the procuring authority's decision on the standards in the Administrative Procedure Act and will override the decision where it is arbitrary, capricious, irrational, an abuse of discretion, or otherwise not in accordance with law.[142] Although the courts give substantial deference to agency determinations[143] that continuing with a procurement or contract is in the best interests of the government,[144] in examining the decision to override the suspension provisions, the courts will among other factors, consider whether an authority had reasonable alternatives open to it and will overturn the decision to override the suspension where this is the case.[145] The courts, however, may give more deference to agency decisions where the override is made in the interests of national security.[146]

[136] FAR 33.102(b).

[137] FAR 33.103(f).

[138] FAR 33.103(f); 31 USC § 3553.

[139] FAR 33.103(f)(4).

[140] FAR 33.103(f)(3); FAR 33.104(c).

[141] 31 USC § 3553(c)(2); *RAMCOR Servs Group Inc v United States* 185 F3d 1286 (Fed Cir 1999).

[142] Y Cho, 'Judicial Review of the Best Interests of the United States Justification for CICA Overrides: Overstepping Boundaries or Giving the Bite Back' (2005) 34 *Public Contract Law Journal* 337; *DTH Management Group v Kelso*, 844 F Supp 251 (1993); *PGBA LLC v United States* 57 Fed Cl 655 (2003).

[143] *Honeywell Inc. v United States* 870 F2d 644 (Fed Cir 1989).

[144] *Universal Shipping v United States* 652 Fed Supp 668 (DDC 1987).

[145] *Reilley's Wholesale v United States* 73 Fed Cl 705 (2006); *Superior Helicopter LLC v United States* 78 Fed Cl 181 (2007).

[146] *Maden Tech Consulting v United States* 74 Fed Cl 786 (2006).

In the limited circumstances in which the GAO may review a disqualification decision, the remedies that the GAO may provide include the payment of costs to the aggrieved supplier (excluding lost profits) as well as tender preparation costs.[147] The GAO may also recommend that the procurement is repeated, or a contract terminated, or that the procuring authority reimburses the applicant's costs of the suit.[148] GAO determinations have the status of recommendations, which may be disregarded by the procuring agency provided it informs the GAO of its intentions not to comply.[149] In addition, a dispute decided by the GAO may still be the subject of a lawsuit.[150]

As is the case where a challenge is brought before a procuring authority, challenges brought before the GAO may also result in the suspension of the procurement process once the procuring officer has notice that a challenge has been filed with the GAO, unless urgent and compelling reasons justify the award of the contract.[151] Where a contract has been awarded and the challenge is filed within 10 days of the contract award, a stay of performance may be imposed pending the outcome of the protest.[152]

Where a bidder seeks judicial relief from the courts, he is entitled to equitable relief in the form of an injunction or a declaratory judgment if his action is filed prior to contract award.[153] Other than obtaining injunctive relief or reimbursement for bid and procurement costs, a supplier is not entitled to damages against a procuring authority for irregularities in the procurement process.[154]

In South Africa, there are similar as well as further remedies for alleged breaches in the disqualification context. The PAJA lists six remedies that may be available where 'administrative action' is challenged before the courts. First, a court may order the procuring authority to furnish the supplier with written reasons for its decision.[155] Secondly, a procuring authority may be ordered to do[156] or refrain from doing a particular action.[157] Thirdly, a decision may be set aside and remitted for re-consideration by

[147] FAR 33.104(h).
[148] 31 USC § 3554.
[149] 31 USC § 3554(b).
[150] M Shaengold, T Michael Guiffre and E Gill, 'Choice of Forum for Federal Government Contract Bid Protests' (2009) 18 *Federal Circuit Bar Journal* 243; Peckinpaugh, *Government Contracts for Services*, above n 59, 230; *Ace-Federal Reporters v Inc v FERC*, 734 F Supp 20 (DDC 1990).
[151] 31 USC § 3553(c)(1). *Dairy Maid Dairy Inc v United States* 837 F Supp 1370 (ED Va 1993).
[152] 31 USC § 3553(d)(1).
[153] *United States v John C Grimberg Co Inc* 702 F2d 1362 (Fed Cir 1983)
[154] *Hadaller v Port of Chehalis* 97 Wash App 750, 986 P2d 836 (Div 2 1999). For remedies in the contractual context see SE Hutmacher, 'Government Contracting Disputes: Its Not All About the Money' (2009) 8 *Army Lawyer* 31.
[155] PAJA, s 8(1)(a)(i)
[156] PAJA, s 8(1)(a)(ii). Bolton, *Law of Government Procurement*, above n 87, ch 11.
[157] PAJA, s 8(1)(b).

the procuring authority.[158] A set-aside will be ordered where the decision to set aside will not be 'unduly disruptive or practically impossible to implement'.[159] A similar remedy to setting aside and remitting for reconsideration is the order to set aside the decision and correct it.[160] In such situations, the court sets aside the decision of the procuring authority and substitutes its own decision.[161]

Fourthly, PAJA permits in exceptional circumstances that the public official pays compensation to the affected parties,[162] where the administrative action is wrongful, invalid and a loss has occurred for which there is no appropriate remedy.[163] Further, the court may issue an order declaring the rights of the parties in relation to the decision, which was taken.[164] Finally, a court is permitted to grant any other temporary relief.[165]

Where a successful challenge is brought for a wrongful disqualification, an effective remedy (from the supplier's point of view) will be to set aside the decision taken, which may cause disruption to the procurement process. Where a supplier claims that a supplier who ought to have been excluded from the procurement process was not excluded, the complainant may, if successful, be entitled to temporary or interim relief or a set-aside of the decision to include that supplier in the process, which again may cause disruption. However, PAJA allows the courts to refuse interim measures when this is warranted by their adverse effects,[166] and the courts may also refuse to order a set-aside where it would not be 'just and equitable' in the circumstances.[167]

South Africa differs from the other jurisdictions in that there is no provision for a procurement process to be stayed pending the resolution of a dispute. The Municipal Supply Chain Regulations provide that aggrieved persons may lodge a written objection or complaint within 14 days of becoming aware of the decision complained about,[168] but do not indicate whether the procurement process will be stayed pending the resolution of

[158] PAJA, s 8(1)(c)(i); *Claude Neon Ltd v Germiston City Council and Another* 1995 (3) SA 710 (W).

[159] N Seddon, *Government Contracts: Federal, State and Local*, 4th edn (Annandale, Federation Press, 2009) ch 8.3; *Sebenza Kahle Trade CC v Emalahleni Local Municipal Council and another* [2003] 2 All SA 340 (T), where the court refused to grant an order of set-aside because the contract had been completed.

[160] PAJA, s 8(1)(c)(ii)(aa).

[161] *Grinaker LTA Ltd v Tender Board (Mpumalanga)* [2002] 3 All SA 336.

[162] PAJA, s 8(1)(c)(ii)(bb).

[163] J de Ville, *Judicial Review of Administrative Action in South Africa* (Durban, LexisNexis Butterworths, 2003) ch 7, 353–62; *Olitzki Property Holdings v State Tender Board and Another* (2001) 3 SA 1247 (SCA).

[164] PAJA, s 8(1)(b) and (d).

[165] PAJA, s 8(1)(e).

[166] *GNH Office Automation CC and Another v Provincial Tender Board and Others* (1996) 9 BCLR 1144 (TK).

[167] PAJA, s 8(1).

[168] PCR reg 49.

this dispute. Although there is no formal standstill period, some procuring authorities have interpreted the requirements of section 62 the Local Government Municipal Systems Act – which gives aggrieved persons the right to appeal against political and administrative decisions within 21 days after the decision was taken – as providing for a 21-day standstill period in which contracts will not be concluded.[169] Also, in cases where a supplier seeks judicial review, the courts are able to grant temporary relief,[170] as discussed above, which may include the stay of the procurement process where it has not been concluded. In South Africa, similar to the standard in the UK, interim relief will be granted where it is required by the urgency of the situation, where the claimant has a clear right, where he will suffer injury and no other remedy will suffice.[171]

Damages are also available in principle, although as was discussed in other contexts, these may be difficult to claim in practice because of the problems of proving loss,[172] and a supplier may not claim for lost profits.[173] However, recent jurisprudence has suggested that damages may only be available where there has been fraud,[174] or where a decision is made 'in bad faith or under corrupt circumstances or completely outside the legitimate scope of the empowering provision'.[175]

11.4 SUMMARY AND ANALYSIS OF MAIN ISSUES

The disqualification of suppliers from public contracts is a serious sanction against a supplier and has been described as a 'corporate death penalty'. This is certainly true where a supplier's main or only business is derived from the public sector. To ensure that the disqualification mechanism is effective and is not abused, it is necessary that remedies are available to a supplier aggrieved by the disqualification process. Whilst the availability of a review system is a necessary component of any procurement system, it is important that reviewing decisions in the disqualification context is done as effectively and as quickly as possible.

[169] *CC Groenewald v M5 Developments* [2010] ZASCA 47, para 21.

[170] PAJA, s 8(1)(e). *Digital Horizons (Pty) Ltd v SA Broadcasting Corporation* [2008] ZAGPHC 272.

[171] *Transnet Ltd v Proud Heritage Properties Pty Ltd* [2008] ZAECHC 42, *Digital Horizons (Pty) Ltd v SA Broadcasting Corporation* [2008] ZAGPHC 272

[172] Arrowsmith, Linarelli and Wallace, *Regulating Public Procurement*, above n 1, 795–803; de Ville, *Judicial Review of Administrative Action*, above n 163, 359.

[173] *Olitzki Property Holdings v State Tender Board and Another*, above n 163.

[174] *Minister of Finance v Gore NO* 2007 (1) SA 111 (SCA).

[175] *Steenkamp NO v Provincial Tender Board, Eastern Cape* 2007 (3) SA 121 (CC), para 55.

11.4.1 Balancing the Tension between Effective Remedies and Delays to the Procurement Process

In the jurisdictions, there are similarities in the nature of the administrative and judicial options for the review of the disqualification decision as well as in the kinds of remedies available to suppliers in the disqualification context. However, one issue that merits further consideration in relation to the provision of remedies is the approach in the selected jurisdictions to balancing the rights of the supplier with the need for the procurement process to be conducted with speed and efficiency. The tension here is how to prevent delay to the procurement process, whilst providing suppliers with effective rights when a breach has occurred.[176] This tension is met by the provision of interim relief remedies or remedies that suspend the procurement process, the conclusion of an awarded contract or the performance of a concluded contract, pending or as a result of the adjudicative process.

As discussed, where a dispute arises after the conclusion of the procurement process but prior to the conclusion of the contract, the supplier's rights are usually preserved through the use of a standstill period in which the contract will not be signed. For instance as discussed above, the EU and the UK provide a mandatory minimum 10-day period between the decision to award a contract and the conclusion of the contract.[177] In the UK, where a contract award decision is challenged during the standstill period, and the procuring authority becomes aware that a claim form has been issued in respect of that decision, a contract will not be entered into.[178] Although there is no automatic standstill period in the US, similar to the UK, where a protest is received within 10 days of a contract being awarded, procuring authorities are required to immediately suspend the conclusion or performance of the contract pending resolution of the dispute.

It should be noted that where a dispute arises after the conclusion of a contract, most jurisdictions do not provide for the suspension of contract execution pending the resolution of a dispute. This is due in part to the adverse effect that suspending contract performance may have on the delivery of public services and the potential for litigation that a procuring authority may be exposed to, where it fails to deliver public services. However, the US differs from the other jurisdictions and provides for the suspension of contract execution where a dispute is filed with a procuring agency or the GAO within 10 days of the conclusion of a contract.[179] Where

[176] Gordon, 'Constructing a Bid Protest Process, above n 83, 430. See *Jobsin v Dept of Health* [2001] ECWA 1241 *per* Lord Justice Dyson.

[177] Remedies directive, art 2a(2); PCR reg 32A.

[178] PCR reg 47G (1) as amended by Public Procurement (Miscellaneous Amendments) Regulations 2011, SI 2011/2053. See also PCR reg 47H(1)(a) and *Indigo Services v Colchester Institute Corp* [2010] EWHC 3237 (QB).

[179] FAR 33.103(f)(3); FAR 33.104(b); *BDM Management Servs Co* Comp Gen Dec B-228287, 88-1 CPD ¶ 93

contract performance is suspended, the period of suspension will not last longer than 35 days where the dispute is filed with a procuring authority, as all disputes should be resolved within this time.[180] By these provisions, the US goes further than the suspension provisions of the EU and UK, although the fact that suspension only takes effect if the dispute is filed within 10 days of contract award means that in most cases, actual performance may not have commenced or the incumbent may continue performance of the contract.[181]

Another area in which the US differs from the EU/UK is that where a procuring authority is required to suspend the procurement process where a challenge is instituted, the procuring authority has the power to override the requirement to suspend where this is justified. This override may be done for reasons similar to the reasons for derogating from the disqualification provision discussed in Chapter ten. As the suspension provisions are tested in the EU context, it may become necessary for a similar approach to be adopted by the EU.

In conclusion, it can be seen that although interim measures are generally available in all the jurisdictions, the standard for obtaining interim relief is quite high, where the measures are not automatic on the commencement of a challenge procedure, and this is one way the jurisdictions balance the tension between providing effective relief for suppliers and not causing undue delay to the procurement system.

11.4.2 The Availability of a Right of Review

In relation to the availability of a right of review, it was seen that the domestic jurisdictions generally provide more than one forum for adjudicating procurement disputes. The UK, however, goes against this approach and establishes the High Court as the sole forum for procurement disputes. This may limit the effectiveness of the procurement remedial system, as suppliers who do not wish to undertake an adversarial process are left without a less formal, more conciliatory avenue for dispute resolution unless the procuring authority exercises its discretion to resolve disputes informally. It should also be mentioned that research has shown that UK suppliers are often reluctant to institute judicial proceedings due to prohibitive legal costs.[182] This has the effect of limiting suppliers' access to justice and it would have been preferable if suppliers were formally permitted to approach the procuring authority, as is the case in the US.[183]

180 FAR 33.103(g).
181 *Superior Servs Inc v Dalton* 851 F Supp 381 (1994).
182 Pachnou, *The Effectiveness of Bidder Remedies*, above n 111, ch 5.
183 FAR 33.103(b).

The US approach, which provides multiple forums for procurement dispute resolution, ensures that suppliers have comprehensive access to remedies. Suppliers may either submit a formal/informal complaint to the procuring authority, or submit a formal complaint to the GAO in limited circumstances or the courts. One drawback of the US system is the fact that disqualification is excluded from the GAO's jurisdiction in spite of the fact that the GAO has the jurisdiction to examine determinations of non-responsibility which have the effect of excluding a supplier from a particular procurement process. This is anomalous and the GAO should be able to examine disqualification determinations, given the advantages the GAO possesses over the procuring authority and the courts, such as independence, experience and cheaper, less formal and faster resolution of disputes.[184] A second drawback is that in the limited cases in which a supplier can approach the GAO in the disqualification context, GAO determinations are not binding on procuring authorities, which may disregard them if they so wish.[185] It would be preferable if there could be mandatory enforcement of GAO decisions, given the wealth of experience possessed by the GAO in procurement dispute adjudication.[186]

[184] R Metzger and D Lyons, 'A Critical Assessment of the GAO Bid-Protest Mechanism' (2007) *Wisconsin Law Review* 1225.

[185] However, agencies routinely follow GAO decisions as they are regarded as being legitimate. See R Saunders and P Butler, 'Timely Reform: Impose Timeliness Rules for Filing Bid Protests at the Court of Federal Claims (2010) 39 *Public Contract Law Journal* 539, 555.

[186] Saunders and Butler, 'Timely Reform', ibid. See also J Nagle and A Lasky, 'A Practitioner's Roadmap to GAO Bid Protests' (2010) 30 *Construction Lawyer* 5.

Index